INITIATE

ABOUT THE AUTHOR

Thuri Calafia (Portland, Oregon) is an ordained Wiccan minister and High Priestess who has been teaching the Wiccan path for over thirty years. The founder of the Circles system and the Circles School of Witchcraft and Wicca, she is actively involved in her local community and teaches workshops, presents public rituals, and provides intuitive readings. She lives with her beloved partner, Robert, and their four-legged "child," Miss Alyssa Ramone.

THURI CALAFIA

INITIATE

A WITCH'S CIRCLE OF WATER

A COURSE OF STUDY IN THE OLD RELIGION

Llewellyn Publications
Woodbury, Minnesota

Based on a book design by Steffani Sawyer
Cover art: Blue background © iStockphoto.com/Tania Oloy
        Water texture: © Eyewire
        Background texture: © PhotoDisc
Cover design by Ellen Lawson

ISBN 978-0-7387-2064-7

Llewellyn Publications
A Division of Llewellyn Worldwide, Ltd.
2143 Wooddale Drive
Woodbury, MN 55125-2989

Printed in the United States of America

PREVIOUS BOOKS BY THURI CALAFIA

Dedicant: A Witch's Circle of Fire

FORTHCOMING BOOKS BY THURI CALAFIA

Adept: A Witch's Circle of Earth

Master: A Witch's Circle of Spirit

Acknowledgments

An author's work is more than just putting words on paper, so the support she receives is about far more than just the direct help she receives with ideas and concepts, wording and flow, computer glitches, or any other "nuts and bolts" issues. To that end, I wish to offer special thanks to:

Helios, Aradia, and Brighid, my ever-present Muses, for illuminating my gifts and inspiring me daily.

Elysia Gallo, my esteemed editor, for your unwavering support, both professionally and personally. Your shoulder has been a true gift through many dark times, and I appreciate you more than you know. Thank you for your encouragement, compassion, humor, and unwavering insistence on excellence. This book's success is very much to your credit. But then, you know that.

Brett Fechheimer, my new-titles editor, for your humor and consistency, and for your patience with me on those long mornings when I was one cup short of coherent. Your unfailing wisdom and savvy-ness saved my butt (and this book) from many a bleary-eyed mistake. Thanks for helping it shine.

Crow Woman, for faithfully walking this Initiate's Path that others may find their footing, and for having the courage to dare with each and every challenge!

Willow, for your courage also. Going into our own darkness is never easy, but you have bravely dared the first steps, which is an inspiration to all who will follow you.

Dreywolf, for the exemplary adorations, and for the purity of faith they inspire.

All of my star students, for reminding me, at crucial times, just why I walk the Path of Insanity that is being a Witchcraft teacher and occult writer. Thank you, again, for teaching me how to teach.

My fellow authors and new friends: Christopher, for the great career advice, inclusion, and care; Raven, for filling my heart with the light of your prayers, for your endless support and love, and for being the best hugger on the planet; and John Michael, for inviting this nervous, starry-eyed newbie to sit at the "cool kids" table with such a great author as yourself. Gentlemen, you have inspired and uplifted me in more ways than you know through your work, your kindness, and your wisdom, and I am forever in your debt.

And last but certainly not least, I wish to thank Ellen, Jenne, KaTerra, L'aura, Sienna, and all of the wild and beautiful sistahs (whose names are too numerous to mention) I found here in the paradise that is the Pacific Northwest, for calling me home.

You've been walking in circles, searching.
Don't drink by the water's edge.
Throw yourself in.
Become the water.
Only then will your thirst end.
—Jeanette Berson

Dedication

For my Eagles, and my sister, for teaching me
the true meaning of the word *Family*:
Jerica, spirit-daughter, with your exemplary kindness and grace,
you are a true priestess,
regardless of the manner in which you walk your path.
My beloved Robert, for the lessons of spirit, even after all these years,
and for being the Way-Shower, still.
And for Michelle, who never *once* made me invisible,
and who gave me the keys to the realm.

Contents

Introduction   *1*

PART ONE
Tempering the Vessel: Initiate Foundation Work

1. The Earth Tides and the Circles System   11

2. The Power of Language   15

3. Personal Responsibility   21

4. Initiate Basics   25

PART TWO
Priming the Vessel: The Thirteen Moons

5. The First Moon—Core/Ground   55

6. The Second Moon—Pride   69

7. The Third Moon—Power   85

8. The Fourth Moon—Compassion   105

9. The Fifth Moon—Connection   121

10. The Sixth Moon—Understanding   135

11. The Seventh Moon—Devotion   149

12. The Eighth Moon—Purpose   161

13. The Ninth Moon—The Path   171

14. The Tenth Moon—Expansion   187

15. The Eleventh Moon—Fruition   201

16. The Twelfth Moon—Overcoming   213

17. The Thirteenth Moon—Wholeness   225

PART THREE
Attuning the Vessel: The Solar Wheel

18. The December Lesson   247

19. The January Lesson   259

20. The February Lesson   269

21. The March Lesson   287

22. The April Lesson   295

23. The May Lesson   305

24. The June Lesson   315

25. The July Lesson   327

26. The August Lesson   351

27. The September Lesson   361

28. The October Lesson   371

29. The November Lesson   383

PART FOUR
Flooding the Vessel: Adept Initiation

30. Benevolence: The Call to Service   393

31. The Wisdom of Silence   405

Appendix   417
Glossary   423
Bibliography   431
Index   437

Introduction

*On a rainy autumn evening in the city, a man steps out onto the sidewalk. He's just finished his Witchcraft 101 at the local metaphysical shop and bought himself his first chalice, as a gift for all he's accomplished. The class was good; he learned many things about the Old Gods, the Sabbats, and the basics of his newfound religion. His teacher's last words to the class ring in his head as he walks along the glistening street: "Now you have all come to the place where you can say you are ready to **begin** to learn. Blessed be, and good luck."*

*He feels he's way past being ready to **begin** learning the Craft, and to put into practice all the things he learned in class. Like a racehorse pushing against the starting gate, he feels excited, compelled, driven to his Path, but, also like a racehorse pushing against the starting gate, he feels frustrated, thwarted, held back. He wants to soar! But how to get airborne? He ignores his frustration and focuses instead on his joy. He looks around himself, then up at the sky, letting the rain wash over his face, and laughs out loud. He can't help it; all the people passing by are huddled in their coats and jackets, hoods pulled about their unhappy faces, umbrellas straining against the wind that accompanies the rain. He feels so connected to nature, even here in the city, that the coldness of the day can't touch him, at least not in a negative way. He wants to embrace the cold wetness of the Mother's waters, and so he opens himself up to her, to the tides of the earth, spreading* his arms so his jacket opens up too, to symbolize his feelings, and he grins and whoops loudly, laughing, as the chilly rain soaks his shirt. He inhales deeply of the freshly washed air, and splashes through puddle after puddle of clean, cold water as he makes his way home, joyously reveling in his soaked, cold feet.

A short while later, he turns the key in the lock and opens his door. He is exhilarated, spirit soaring, filled with hope and faith, and soaked to the skin.

"And that is as it should be," he chuckles to himself, for he knows he's ready to "test the waters" of this wonderful new spiritual Path he's found, but he's not ... quite ... sure ... just how to go about it.

After changing into some dry clothes, he lights a charcoal briquette in his censer, and as he watches it crackle and pop, he begins to feel a little trancy. He looks at the books on his shelf, ponders which one to read next, and pulls out a text. He scans the table of contents, finding it nearly identical to the book he just read for his Wicca 101, which was just like the one before that, and the one before that. He places a measure of incense on the charcoal and lights the special study candle he's had since his dedication, which he keeps near his favorite place on the sofa. He lights more candles as he moves around the room. He cleanses and charges his new chalice, fills it with cool water, and sips from it reverently, appreciatively. He fishes in his backpack for the new book, the one his Wicca teacher recommended as the next step in his learning, and sits down to read it, but finds it's much the same as the others. He sets it next to the candle beside him, along with the chalice, takes a few deep breaths, and settles back into the sofa. The frustration and depression he's tried to ignore ever since his teacher said goodbye to the class begin to surface. He longs to go deeper, but none of his books reveal how.

"You can't get 'deeper' from a book," he says to the air, quoting a man he admires greatly in the Pagan community, words the man said to him just a month or so ago at a summer festival when they were discussing his great desire to deepen his power and faith. He relaxes into the cushions.

"Please, Lord and Lady, show me the way," he asks in earnest, and lets his mind open to Spirit as he closes his eyes and breathes deeply, evenly ...

In his inner landscape, he sees many mountains, which he understands to be symbols of the goals he has chosen for himself and his life. More details reveal themselves as he looks around: a deep, smooth river; thick forests of both evergreen and deciduous trees; bushes he recognizes as sagebrush, rosemary, roses, and many others he doesn't recognize, filling the *space between him and the mountains. His mountains; his goals. The snowcaps gleam pink in a bright, rosy sunset, looking both inviting and challenging. A slender crescent moon rises over the highest peak, and he finds himself feeling anxious, frustrated. He wants to reach his goals **now**, today, but he has no idea how. His longing is almost desperate, as he's waited for so long, but there is no road, not even a narrow track, and the landscape, though beautiful, reveals a lushness that would make walking cross country tricky at best, and he senses hazards and delays in the thick vegetation before him. He knows this landscape has revealed itself in this way because this is exactly what he's been feeling, what he's been hiding from himself, just under the surface, as the time came closer and closer to the end of his classes. Now, however, there is no escaping his feelings.*

*He paces the river's shoreline, caught between his exuberance, his longing to move forward, to act, to ... **become**, and his increasing frustration over what seems to be a huge obstacle before him, when suddenly he laughs out loud for the third time that evening. A small boat is tethered to a tree nearby, and upon further inspection he sees that the river points directly toward the highest, most beautiful mountain peak—the peak that is crowned by the crescent moon, which now also glows pink with the Sun God's fiery touch.*

He steps into the small boat gently, purposefully, looks for the oars, and smiles. No oars are needed, of course, as the river knows exactly where he wants to go. With merely a thought, he moves his boat away from the shore, and his journey begins ...

Many people, like the man in the scene above, feel a little lost after finishing a basic Wicca class, and are left to their own devices just when they've reached the momentum required to compel them forward to deepen their power and their faith. However, unlike the man in the story above, many folks never find that boat on the shore, and so they have no clear idea how to reach their goals, or where to go next in their spiritual journey.

For the solitary student, finding the way can be exceptionally frustrating. Like the man in the story above, when I was ready to deepen and grow in my Path, I just kept finding books that were the same as the ones I'd already read. They were all good books, but I needed a way to go deeper. Over the years, the deepening happened, but looking back I can see that I took a lot of detours I needn't have taken in my search for my personal spiritual Path.

And, also over a period of years, I learned that what is most needed at Initiate level is a deep focus on energy work. Many folks, especially the coven trained, fall into this training quite naturally, as they are practicing with other experienced Witches. Ideally, their seniors in the coven teach them how to evoke, aspect, and invoke elements as well as deity; how to effectively sense and raise energy in circle and when to release it; how to ground deeply; how to help ground others. They learn how to run energy through their own bodies, chakra by chakra, how to open their psychic centers, and how to sense energy patterns in others. They learn how important it is for folks who follow an earth-based spiritual Path to get out in nature as often as possible in order to recharge and replenish their energy, and they learn ways to recharge when getting out in nature isn't an option that particular day. They learn how much easier their energy work can be if they are healthy and strong, and they learn ways to enhance their own vibrance, which leads to becoming powerful.

They see, in their seniors, the paths both of discipline and of excess, and often experience both of these energy patterns themselves. They are encouraged to keep growing spiritually by compassionate, and often strict, High Priests and High Priestesses. Most of all, they learn to know themselves in the deepest, most intimate way possible because they are challenged and pushed and molded by their leaders into being who they most aspire to be. Finally, they are guided to explore and bring forth their gifts— their own truest spiritual callings, that they may grow into priests and priestesses who give the best of who they are to their gods through serving their covens and communities in the ways that bring them their deepest joy.

This course of study will teach the motivated Initiate student all of this and more. *Dedicant: A Witch's Circle of Fire, A Course of Study in the Old Religion* taught the basics, the foundation work required to get the student to this place of bright beginnings that she may go further into her spirituality, expanding and deepening her connection to her patron gods and matron goddesses, tempering the vessel she forged as a Dedicant. If the Dedicant course was the foundation, then this Initiate course is the actual *house*, so now, we must temper the vessel we forged as Dedicants, prime those spiritual vessels by filling ourselves up with the clear water that is the energy work, and then attune our vessels, like the clear ringing one makes with a crystal goblet by running a finger along the rim, through revisiting the Wheel of the Year and finding and honing our spiritual gifts to a shine. Thus we prepare ourselves for service.

The Adept level, the traditional second degree, is the level of *service*. Without this crucial foundation of energy work and self-knowledge, many who begin to serve get burned out rapidly, and often either quietly withdraw from service work, sometimes for years, in order to recharge their batteries, or become petty tyrants and prima donnas who sit on their proverbial thrones, arrogantly ordering their coveners and students about in order to hold on to the remains of their flagging energy. This course will help the motivated student to avoid both extremes by encouraging a personal practice that will teach him not only what his limitations are but also how to tap into universal energies so he doesn't deplete his own. The energy work offered here is fundamental to a solid structure, which will support the traveler on his spiritual Path for many years to come.

In *Dedicant: A Witch's Circle of Fire,* I stated that I wrote that course of study to help others, who, like myself, are self-taught and self-motivated. This is true of the whole series, of course, but this Initiate course in particular is close to my heart as I never had the energy work, being self-taught, or at least not in any kind of cohesive structure or course; it was all pretty much the "hit-and-miss" school of Wicca for me. Because of that, even after all these years as a Wiccan, after all my years of running covens and teaching, after all these years of keeping a solitary practice, I *still* don't feel like I've done enough energy work. Therefore, I have endeavored to take this course with you, my student, to the best of my ability, while also working at my "day job," doing my regular community service work, teaching Circles classes, and writing this book.

It hasn't been an easy journey. However, my matron goddess Artemis saw fit, whenever I felt unable to pursue the Pathwork, to give me life lessons that somehow *miraculously* followed the energy pattern I was writing about at the time (to heck with "mysterious"—the gods sometimes work in ridiculously *obvious* ways!). So even when I didn't consciously intend to follow the Path with you, I found myself doing so anyway. What made it so difficult to finish was the cycle of crippling depression and chronic ill health I was in for nearly a decade, energy patterns that, looking back, I can see exacerbated each other and reached their peak in late 2010.

Since then, I've studied and learned as much as possible about three conditions I've been battling: osteoarthritis, pre-diabetes, and hypothyroidism. I saw various healers about these conditions over the years; some of them wanted to put me on hormones for the thyroid as well as for my menopausal symptoms, and I ran screaming in the other direction (metaphorically, of course!). I weighed the advantages and disadvantages of herbal blends, simples, and allopathic meds, and developed a system for tracking my healing and health through dietary and movement (exercise) changes in my life, as well as any supplements I took. Healing finally began to slowly take place.

Today, I continue to learn as much as I can about my particular conditions, and to try new things that sound and feel right for me, and I am now a huge advocate of people becoming our own healers.

I feel it's very important that we take charge of our personal health. There is much information in the July lesson regarding this topic, as well as tips for you to begin your own path to healing. I've come to believe very strongly that we need to become our own healers for many reasons, not the least of which is because you will need bright vibrant energy, dear Initiate, for this Path and all that it brings. Yes, your spirituality can and will feed you. But I won't kid you—this is a tough course. There is a lot to be done at this Initiate level, in order to hone your power and skill as a Witch, in order to prime that pump that is your spiritual vessel. If you don't at once have the energy for the outpouring that is the Adept level, you will crash and burn. Becoming your own healer can make all the difference in the world, for if your vessel is filled with vibrance, it will overflow with joy and abundant energy for the work ahead. From there, you can only prosper, and this work will reward you a thousandfold in ways you can't begin to imagine.

And so, we begin another circle of Circles, spiraling upward even as we sink our roots deeper, ascending to the heights of our gods and guardians, becoming one with our own true Paths…

PART
ONE

Tempering the Vessel:
Initiate Foundation Work

HOW TO KNOW IF THIS BOOK IS FOR YOU

In the Circles system, the Initiate student is fully grounded in the basic beliefs of this religion, has been around the Wheel of the Year at least once, and has written at least a half-set of Sabbats (all the lesser ones), a few to several Esbats, and spellwork whenever needed. She knows what the Witch's tools are and how to use them; has a personal relationship with her chosen deities, her matron goddess(es) and patron god(s) (or is pursuing this relationship *in earnest*); and is of course fully committed to her spiritual Path. She is acquiring skill with two chosen divination methods (I recommend two, as one can give clarity and depth to another), and she understands how important it is to pay attention to her dreams, so she tracks them regularly, knowing they can and do give much guidance and wisdom to her waking life.

She has developed the *courage to dare* to perform *all* aspects of circle work for her solitary rites, and, *if applicable,* has performed all beginning-level duties (grounding and centering, cleansing, purifying, charging, calling quarters) in any group rites she's been asked to help with. She has a working table of correspondence (TOC) in her grimoire for dream symbols, colors, genders, elements, community, sexuality, deity, gratitude, moon phases, astrological associations, death and the Mysteries, and probably more. She is also familiar with the basics of *energy work*, such as shielding, filtering, projecting, and blasting (as covered in the discussion of the Tree of Life in *Dedicant*.[1] The exercise itself is on page 28 in the "Initiate Basics" chapter of this book), and has tried evoking at least once.

In this course, you will continue all of the above practices learned at Dedicant level, in addition to learning and practicing a lot more with energy; in fact, this is where many self-taught Wiccans have holes in their training. I know I did. The emphasis on energy work here is designed to help you grow, expand, and deepen your skills and power as a Witch.

JUMPING ON THE WHEEL: HOW TO NAVIGATE THE TWO WHEELS

Once you're finished with the foundation work of this first unit, you will be ready to begin the heart of the book: the *Part Two—Priming the Vessel: The Thirteen Moons*

---

1. Thuri Calafia, *Dedicant: A Witch's Circle of Fire* (Llewellyn, 2008), 37–39.

lessons and *Part Three—Attuning the Vessel: The Solar Wheel* lessons. To do this, you will be clicking both wheels at the same time. Complicated? Uuuhh-yep. But so is *living life* as a Wiccan priest or priestess. This course of study will help to prepare you for all the juggling required on the Path of Insanity (oops, um… the Path of *Service!*) that is being clergy in this religion.

On each new moon, dear Initiate, you will begin with a *Thirteen Moons* lesson to read and follow through on, and at the beginning of each calendar month, you will also have a *Solar Wheel* lesson to read and follow through on. Balancing and keeping track of these, as well as following through on the reading, homework, energy work, and grimoire work, will give you a pretty good idea of what it is to be clergy—as life often pulls experienced Witches in seventeen different directions, and one must be ready and able to switch focus at a moment's notice in order to keep up.

For folks whose lives are just too busy to click both wheels at the same time, it's best to do the *Thirteen Moons* first, as this part of the book gives you the solid foundation of energy work that will help keep you vibrant and energetic for the more service-oriented, outward reaching focus of the Solar Wheel lessons. However, I do recommend trying to complete the course in a year and a day, as it gives a very realistic view of what life will be like for you as a spiritual leader.

For the *Thirteen Moons* lessons, simply start with lesson one on or just before the next new moon, and proceed through lesson thirteen, beginning a new lesson with each new moon. It's a good idea to get a calendar that shows you the moons, and preferably the signs the moon is in as well, as this will help you plan your Esbats. The *Old Farmer's Almanac* is a good choice, as are most Witchy almanacs on the market, and so are astrological ephemerises. My favorite tool for tracking moons and other energy patterns is Llewellyn's little *Astrological Pocket Planner*—it's concise, accurate, easy to read, and *small!* Mine fits in the front pocket of my daytimer, as well as the back pocket of my jeans, so mine is always with me, which is really convenient. I've used them for years and years. There are also many other planner-style calendars that will show you when the moons occur, what sign they're in, as well as void-of-course moons and Mercury retrogrades. You have only to choose one that works for you.

For the Solar Wheel lessons, simply start with the current or upcoming month. My recommendation is to start with the *current month* if today's date is on or before the 10th of the month, or to start with the *upcoming month* if it's past the 10th, as this gives you time to prepare for whatever Sabbat is coming up. Then, just follow the wheel around the year with your lessons, taking each month in turn, until you've completed them all, and then you'll be ready to move to *Part Four—Flooding the Vessel: Adept Initiation*. This is how my classes are set up, so that students don't have to wait to start, but can just join the rest of the class with the monthly lessons once the foundation work is completed, branching off when it's time to proceed with the *Adept Initiation* section and the Rite of Passage (ROP) that is the Adept Gate.

1: The Earth Tides and the Circles System

You've heard the siren song of nature on the wind in the spring; in the crackle of energy as summer's heat waxes; in the crisp crunch of autumn leaves under your feet; in the silence of winter's deep nights when all is shrouded in snow. In fact, the longer you live in your particular region, the more you feel in tune with its seasonal rhythms and changes, to the point that you can actually feel the energies of a season or two ahead of you, pulling you, calling to you, across the Wheel of the Year.

*You've likely also felt the pull of the moon tides in your dreams, your waking consciousness, your very blood as she waxes and wanes, and at times you feel you could pinpoint her position in the sky with your eyes closed. You know the Old Gods live in you, surround you and protect you, guide you to your highest ideal. That's why you're here: this subtle energy that allows you to **feel** the approach of each holiday, each moon, regardless of weather or time of day. The feeling grows stronger with even the most subtle change of temperature, shadow length, scent, and sound. It's an awareness that runs like blood through your veins, connecting you with the All.*

These "earth tides" are what the Circles system is all about. The Circles system is the same as other Wiccan learning systems in many ways, the most fundamental of which is that it *is* a system of levels. These levels are based on what I have found to be effective in teaching my students over the years, as well as what I have learned from more traditional systems. By studying within this system, when and if you decide to join a coven or other magical group, you will be on roughly the same degree level as your peers. Circles is *different* from other Wiccan systems of learning in many ways, one of which is that study is orchestrated to harmonize with the cycles of the earth, in order to instill, early on in the student, an awareness of these earth tides.

You undoubtedly feel these tides, dear Initiate, for whether or not you've followed the Circles Dedicant program, by the time you initiated and became a priest or priestess, the earth tides have taken hold of your awareness, for they are the heart and soul of Wicca. No matter what your tradition—Dianic, Celtic, Egyptian, some other tradition, or an eclectic mix of many—these tides run through your rites, your life, your very blood, just as they did in the minds and bodies of the Ancients. As you grow in your religion, so these tides, too, will grow stronger, and you will feel them pulling you, urging you forward to the next point on the Wheel, for these tides are the basis for our beliefs—the earth turns in a circle, an endless cycle of seasons. Death precedes life just as life precedes death. Planting, sprouting, growth, harvesting, and gleaning of the fields are the same as the planting, quickening, birth, maturation, and inevitable death of all living beings. Once death takes place, our souls are born again to new bodies, new lessons, new enlightenment. The cycle continually renews itself, just as it does in the fields.

Your patron gods and matron goddesses oversee some of these cycles, and by now they have taught you much about them. Whether young or old in nature, of the earth, moon, or sea, the Old Gods all have much wisdom and energy to share with us. As we connect with them, so we connect with those energy patterns. In this Initiate course, you will be connecting with as many gods and goddesses as you choose, dear Initiate, so keep in mind that not only the gods of light and love are your allies. There is much shadow work ahead, and the darker deities can help a great deal with such work. Remember always to tune in to the energies of the season and the region, for there is power in using the natural flows. Allow yourself to feel the call of the tides; open to them, rejoice in them! For us, the earth tides are a feeling of certainty and connection, a *knowingness* that harmonizes with the basic, primal, and compelling call to also honor the gods and the cycles that are on their way to us. Pay close attention when you're caught off guard with visions of breezy warmth and flowers as you crunch dry leaves under your heels; these energies are telling and can herald both joy and pain. How does the energy around you feel at this very moment? The earth calls out as the world rolls by, and the earth tides run in us *all*.

You pause a moment on your walk to your doorway and breathe in the scents deeply. Though it's only the beginning of winter, you're seeing the flowers in bloom in your mind's eye, and you swear you can smell the flowers and hear the sounds becoming rounder even as winter makes them more crisp. You wonder what such energies herald as you enter your home, prepared to study and learn what nature's message means.

2: The Power of Language

Words are, of course, the most powerful drug used by mankind.
—Rudyard Kipling

A WAR OVER WORDS

"Dianic Wicca is a contradiction in terms."

"…So I told her, you're no Witch; a Witch would never do that!"

"Oh, you can't possibly be Wiccan; you're a lesbian."

"Witches heal. If you're not a healer, you're not a Witch."

"The word *Wicca* was coined by Gardner, so Gardnerians are the only 'real' Wiccans."

"My teacher told me that since I'm not a lesbian, I'll never be a true Witch, because having sex with a woman is the only way I'll truly understand the Goddess."

"Only a circle that has the same number of men as women, alternating placement by gender around the circle, is a 'real' Wiccan circle."

"I don't refer to someone as a Witch or priest/priestess until they have been initiated as such."

There are a lot of folks in the Wiccan and Pagan community who will try to tell you that Wicca (or Witchcraft) is what they are/do, and "not Wicca/Witchcraft" is what they aren't/don't do, and they are adamantly, passionately certain that their interpretation is the *only* "correct" one. This is where we can get into trouble, as no one can lay claim to this word and apply it to their truth only—to the exclusion of everyone else's. As we know, the word *Wicca* is the root of the word *Witch*, and it means to "bend or twist" (some say "to bend or to shape").

For several decades now, many of us thought the word also meant "wise" or "wise one," but John Michael Greer, in *The New Encyclopedia of the Occult*, clears up the misconception, as illustrated by Raven Digitalis, in his excellent *Shadow Magick Compendium*: "Linguistically," Digitalis states, "the Old English term for 'wise one' is actually the root of the modern word *wizard*. *Wicca* and *wicce*, however, come from a verb meaning 'to bend or to twist.' This meaning has also been interpreted in a positive light by many practitioners of modern Witchcraft, who view it as implying a magick-worker's ability to bend, twist, and shape reality to their will. However, if we examine the Old English usage of the term, we find that 'twist' was the antithesis of 'straight' (meaning 'proper'), revealing that the term was used to refer to someone who was twisted, crooked, or otherwise morally unacceptable."[2]

So, taken in the light of the times in which the word's definition was originally established, the word *Witch* (and therefore *Wicca*, by its very nature of being the *root* of the word) means "someone who is twisted; a morally unacceptable person." Hmmm. Not exactly a title to be proud of, is it? What I would like to offer here is that words also have a way of bending and shaping *themselves* over the years, so words can *come to mean* something in addition to, but not instead of, what they once meant. I offer the words *virgin* and *gay* as classic examples.

The unfortunate thing is that there are boatloads of people out there in the magical community who are awfully fond of defining *other* folks' spiritual Paths for them, in an "us vs. them" prejudice. The whole reason I went on a quest for the origin of the word *Wicca* was because of this highly charged and, in my opinion, completely pointless war over words that can never be won. Even in all my digging, I never found the information Greer found, which illustrates how easy it is for us to think we have a piece of information correct, when in fact we haven't. It takes diligence, care, and more than a little humility to understand and accept that we goofed or that we were incorrect in our beliefs or that we didn't quite find the piece we were looking for.

---

2. Raven Digitalis, *Shadow Magick Compendium* (Llewellyn, 2008), 181.

We in the magical community owe Greer a great debt of gratitude for digging a little deeper and finding this information for us, and Digitalis as well, for both men were brave enough to dare to bring us the truth about this word. Now, what are we going to do with that?

Should we just abandon the words *Wicca* and *Witch* then, and find something more clear or less loaded, to define ourselves? Should we change the spelling, in hopes it'll keep others from using "our" word, such as what's happened with the word *magic*, which lots of folks now spell "Crowley-style" as "magick"? Many have made such changes. Many others have abandoned them in favor of the less loaded and more generic "Pagan," because of the judgments and condescending remarks made to them or about them, by others who think they can lay claim to words exclusively. I would ask, however, how long it will be now before someone starts up a campaign to exclude "those others out there" from using "their" word *Pagan* (or perhaps start spelling it "Pagyn")? This is highly reminiscent of the Star-Bellied Sneetches![3] Can we possibly be more judgmental? I contend that the more we fight this ridiculous war, the more we give away our power! After all, who is the authority and the expert of our personal spiritual Paths? We are! And by the gods, we can use whatever word or words sing to us personally, and no one can tell us we can't! Yes, we must be cognizant of the word's origins (and therefore its susceptibility to misinterpretation), as well as its evolved meaning. We cannot say that because one tradition practices Wicca/Witchcraft differently than another, that one is "real," and the other is not. Unfortunately, this judgmentalism and elitism is rampant in the Pagan community.

I have long held that no one can define another's path for them, and when I finally had my fill of the comments I quoted at the beginning of this chapter, which by the way were all said by real people, I launched my quest for the "real" meaning of the word. The last quote listed at the beginning of this chapter was actually a misquote from my own work in a review of *Dedicant*. Well, sort of. The sentence in the text of *Dedicant* (page 10) doesn't actually include the word *been*. The reviewer inserted that word, completely changing the meaning of the sentence, and then used the misquote to give her reasons for writing a rather scathing review. The review upset me at first, then amused me when I realized the above, but then I found, to my horror

---

3. Theodor Seuss Geisel, *Sneetches and Other Stories* (Random House, 1961).

and utter embarrassment, that I myself had mistakenly worded the defining sentence in my glossary *exactly as she had*!

So let me just clear this up here and now: I feel that an initiatory Rite of Passage is *essential* in making the life change and energetic commitment that makes one a Witch. Whether a person initiates himself, or is initiated by others in a group setting, I believe both are equally valid, though totally different experiences. In fact, in my "real life" classes, I usually encourage my students to do a self-initiation prior to the more formal group one. What's most important, in my opinion, is the *intention* and *acknowledgment of this level* by the Initiate himself, and the *heartfelt commitment* to his spiritual Path. I've heard many folks and have had several students over the years just pop out with "Oh, I'm a Witch," or "I'm a 'natural' Witch," when they have no idea what that really means. Some of these were students who thought they could simply start at the "top rung of the ladder," so to speak—they wanted to be Witches but didn't want to do any of the actions or practices (in other words, the *work*) or study involved in becoming a "shaper of energy."

So in keeping with the truth that language is indeed powerful, I personally don't believe it's appropriate or kind to call someone a Witch unless she has gone through that vital initiation rite, either surrounded by peers and loved ones, or alone, under the watchful eyes of her patron gods and matron goddesses. Otherwise, how could the word possibly have any power or meaning?

Yes, language is indeed powerful—we can use it to apply labels to ourselves and our experience, creating a beautiful and colorful web of meaning that connects and resonates at any number of shimmering points with our fellows, or we can use it to tear others down, pass judgment, misinterpret and invalidate their Paths and their experiences. When the time comes for you, dear Initiate, which will you choose?

THE POWER OF LANGUAGE IN CIRCLE

From all the trappings of ritual, the incense, the candles, the garb and the tools, the bells and whistles, as it were, nothing, *no **thing*** is as important as our language. With it, we conjure spirits, evoke emotions, raise energy, enhance sensations, and call our gods. When we participate in a really moving ritual, we remember many things about it, but the words are what resonate through us, especially if the timing flows well. Now, this is not to say that if someone flubs a line that all is lost. Intent is also key. But the signals, the ideas, and concepts that are communicated are what will propel the magic into action, so the language of our rituals needs to be clear, strong, and preferably smooth in order to send that magic home.

The important thing to remember is that language is indeed *powerful*—beyond measure. If we take care to practice ethics and personal responsibility, thinking always how our words will affect the fabric of our lives, then language can be a dear and awe-inspiring ally to both our magical practices and our spiritual expressions.

3: Personal Responsibility

I am free, no matter what rules surround me.
If I find them tolerable, I tolerate them;
if I find them too obnoxious, I break them.
I am free because I know that I alone
am morally responsible for everything I do.
—Robert Heinlein

The more we walk our spiritual Path, the more we see of the world around us and our role in it, the more we must realize, dear Initiate, that everything we do comes back to us, sometimes in gentle ways, and sometimes in not-so-gentle ways. This, we must know by now, is the nature of karma (cause and effect) as well as the basis of the Law of Three-fold Return (what we send out comes back, times three). So to live as a Wiccan priest or priestess means we accept the responsibility to live ethically and consciously, promoting harmony within the world and within ourselves.

We all have many circles around us, and as you go through this course, you will see them outlined clearly, not in so many words, but as the energy patterns that surround you. We will be working with all kinds of relationship energies: connections with our selves; with other people; with the Divine; with our communities; with our planet. The moon work ahead will help you to hone and build your personal power, and the shadow work can absolutely be daunting. However, in order to heal and grow, we must accept that the only person who can dance with our shadows is *us*.

As we go along, there will also be many things to look at in terms of how we relate to others—whether close personal relationships such as lovers, family, and true friends (you know who these special people are: they are the people you need and rely upon, whom you share an intimate bond with, who both want you and need you in their life); extended family bonds such as covenmates and more casual friendships; or acquaintances, our spiritual communities, and the world. Each of these levels of closeness can be looked upon as a circle that radiates out from our core, growing more casual in many ways as the circles expand further out. These things include our survival energies, our desires, our power, our compassion, our communications, our intuition, our devotion, our purpose, our paths, and much more.

To say that you have a responsibility to all those you hold dear is an extreme understatement, and as a priest/ess, you are now in a position of service. Serving your personal gods, then, means you also are here to serve those in your personal circles, from yourself to your community, and of course, our Mother Earth. However, you must remember to put yourself first in terms of health in all of the five sacred directions, or you will end up depleted.

What this means is that we take care that our needs are met on many levels: that we understand the basics of self-care, that we deserve abundance, good nutrition, exercise, relaxation, fulfilling relationships, satisfying sex, and deep sleep.

On my corkboard I have a diagram, with the word *foundation* written at the center, surrounded by the words *mental*, *passionate*, *emotional*, *physical*, and *spiritual* written in a circle around it. Then, beginning about two inches out, there is a circle, inside of which I have listed the same things as I described above, such as my mate (of course, it's his name, Robert, rather than the word *mate*), then my beloved four-legged daughter, Alyssa. The next circle holds the names of my close friends and family, and the next, the words *students* and *coveners*; the next circle has the word *community* and all the various services I'm currently involved in, and finally, the Great Mother. Peppered throughout are words describing actions I take to help or serve. This circle diagram reminds me always of the priorities in my life, and that I am only number one in terms of keeping my personal energies balanced. This reminds me quite clearly and immediately that unless all these energies are working properly, I have nothing to give anyone, so if I'm ill, or off, I will indeed put "me first" until such time as I feel whole again and am able to serve my gods with my best efforts and energies.

As you go along, you will find, dear Initiate, that as people of power (which you will become more and more as you go through this course), we, as Heinlein states in the quote that begins this chapter, are free to make our own choices regarding the rules surrounding us. However, we must be ever mindful that if our choices run counter to cultural mores or laws, we must be prepared to deal with the consequences should we find ourselves "caught."

For example, many years ago, when I worked as a professional cake decorator in a grocery store bakery, I would usually keep a cup of ice water underneath the counter where I worked. The other decorators and bakery clerks kept cups of water hidden in similar fashion. Knowing that if the health department should come in to inspect we could be severely fined and possibly even shut down (if there were repeat violations), the bakery manager, we'll call him Dave, would walk through on occasion and throw all the cups of water away. One day after he did so, one of the bakery clerks, we'll call her Julie, got very angry.

"Well Julie, you can hardly blame Dave; he's just doing his job."

Julie turned to me, indignant, and said, "You're one to talk! You do it, too!"

I said, "Yes, I do, but I don't get mad at him for it. I'm the one breaking the rules. It's not his fault he caught me," and as soon as he was out of the area, I got myself another cup of water. And so it is with life. As powerful, magical, ethical people who know how to use energy, we certainly can and do make our own rules. We just need to always remember whose responsibility it is for every action we take.

4: Initiate Basics

*If you are aware that no one else can make you happy, and that
happiness is the result of love coming out of you, this becomes
the greatest mastery of the Toltecs, the Mastery of Love.*
—don Miguel Ruiz

The Initiate level is the first serious step toward becoming
clergy. Yes, as an Initiate, you already are clergy; however,
there is more to being a member of the Wiccan clergy than
just initiating, and you know this, dear Initiate, or you
wouldn't be taking this course. The operative word here is
serious.

As you work through this course, you will become
more tuned in to the energies, weather patterns, and psychic currents in your area. You will find yourself connecting more deeply to the earth and moon tides, develop
stronger psychic skills, and your abilities and creative skills
will also increase. All of these things will deepen your connection to your guardians, your power animals, and the
elemental energies and allies around you. You will become
aware of your own spiritual gifts. As this deepening occurs,
of course you will also find yourself becoming closer and

closer to your chosen deities; your matron goddess(es) and patron god(s), and you will want to express that love and devotion.

You should already be doing daily devotionals at this point (a devotional, you may remember from *Dedicant*,[4] is an act of speaking our gratitude and love to our chosen deities, but not asking for anything—as with a prayer), but during this course, your devotionals will deepen and expand into that of the adoration. An adoration is similar to a devotional in that you are giving praise and gratitude to your chosen deities, but as the energy runs through your body, as you become more and more familiar with your gods through study, evocation, and aspecting, you will find your devotionals aren't just heartfelt *words* any longer, but are often heart-pounding, teary-eyed, full-body-vibrating, passionate *expressions*. Following are two excellent examples of devotionals, written by a bright and beautiful young student of mine, whose heart for the gods is a true inspiration. These devotionals are so immediate and so powerful they could absolutely be used as adorations. The first time I read them, they brought tears to my eyes.

DAILY DEVOTIONAL TO ARTEMIS[5]
By DreyWolf

Artemis,

Beautiful Huntress,

You guide me when I no longer know where to turn.

You help me to see myself and everything connected together.

You teach me the ways of the Hunt: How to live, How to love, How to respect.

You teach me how to honor myself and others, how to respect all things as equal.

By Your waxing crescent, You teach me to walk, to see and to feel.

You calm my fears, dispel my insecurities, and reassure my abilities.

In the night, I hear Your Pack calling, singing Your praise, and I feel myself respond.

Your night Song sings in my life, my heart beats Your tune.

I am forever grateful to You for all You have done and continue to do for me.

---

4. Thuri Calafia, *Dedicant: A Witch's Circle of Fire* (Llewellyn, 2008), 29.

5. DreyWolf (Cassandra Roepke), *Daily Devotional to Artemis* and *Daily Devotional to Cernunnos*. Used with permission.

DAILY DEVOTIONAL TO CERNUNNOS

Cernunnos,
King of the Dark, Keeper of the Dark Times.
Full of pure masculinity,
Gentle, yet full of passion.
You lead me through the woods, Your sure steps guiding me to our destination.
You rule the night, Gentle king of love and sex, power and control.
Your gentle hands steady me as I fall, taking care of my bruises.
You are always with me, Holly Lord, always ready to help me should I stumble.
Your passion drives me and Your love steadies me.

DAILY PRACTICE AND PATHWORK

I wish to emphasize here that the Initiate level is very much about solitary practice even if one is in a coven, as it is the connection to our gods, the energy work we do, and the exploration of our spiritual gifts that will ultimately *prime* our spiritual vessels and make us ready for the outpouring that is the Adept level, which is the level of service to our gods and communities.

Solitude, then, will become your ally. You will need to create a space in your home somewhere (and another space outdoors as well, if at all possible), where you can be alone and undisturbed during your "prime" time of day (the time of day when you have the most energy, when you are most alert), for doing your daily work.

Touchstones can help with the transition from mundane to sacred space and time, and can take many forms: going directly to your altar upon arriving home (or upon awakening) and saying words of welcome and transition to yourself and your gods; lighting a special candle to symbolize the end (or the beginning) of the day; leaving your shoes outside your doorstep as a symbol of leaving your mundane, psychological "dirt" outside the home; washing your face and hands immediately upon arrival home; actually touching a special stone to help ground and center; or keeping a water vessel of some sort just outside—or just inside—the front door of your home (my personal favorite) so you can ground, center, and wash your third eye, hands, and feet before entering your home. These actions can also be done in conjunction with your daily devotionals.

If you are not sure what you should do to show your devotion to a particular deity, just ask them. For example, when I wasn't sure what to do to show my love to one of my darker patron gods, he told me to meditate on the shadows in the foliage I see, and to go into the shadows in the woods whenever possible, to feel and acknowledge his presence. My matron goddess Artemis asks me to walk in the woods with her, and of course, there is her constant and repeated command, "Bring them to Me!"

THE TREE OF LIFE AND EARTH TIDES WORK

The Tree of Life has become a beloved and widely used exercise for grounding and centering throughout Pagandom. Just go to nearly any public ritual, and you will be guided through it. If you're not familiar with this exercise, just read through the following until you feel comfortable with the process. Then, do the exercise as often as you like, changing whatever you need to in order to take ownership of it and make it smoothly memorized, deeply connecting, and gratifying—yours!

First breathe deeply, in through the nose and out through the mouth, and as you exhale, visualize roots stretching down from the soles of your feet, your legs, your buttocks, anywhere your body touches the earth (or, if indoors, the floor or chair underneath you)… keep visualizing these roots stretching down and, as you do, visualize a large taproot extending down from the base of your spine, down and down to the center of the earth. Continue extending those roots out and down and see them becoming smaller and smaller, no more than a hair's breadth, just like the tiniest roots of a tree or plant in the earth… and breathe…

Now, with each exhaled breath, start pulling energy up by visualizing tiny points of golden light coming into those "capillary" roots, filling those roots up and up as you inhale, filling them with light as they begin merging with each other… and as you reach center, see and feel a huge column of silvery light coming up from the heart of Mother Earth… and pull that light and energy up and up until it reaches and fills your body, the column connecting with your taproot, filling, clearing and healing your chakras as they spin, one by one, root… base… solar plexus… heart… and as you reach your heart chakra, now with each exhaled breath, push that light up and up through the rest of your chakras: throat… brow/third eye… crown… and now see and feel branches sprouting from the top of your head, the tops of your shoulders, growing up and up into the sky (or out through the ceiling and rooftop if indoors) extending out and up, out and up... sweeping the sky, gathering golden light from the Sky Father, the sun and a thousand stars, overflowing and dripping off the ends of your branches, falling to the Earth Mother to be absorbed deep within her, only to be brought in again by your thirsty, seeking root tips... and breathe... feel the circuit.

As you breathe and tune in to the earth in this exercise, you will begin to feel a deep connection to the energies around you as well. Your consciousness will stretch forward and back, and usually you will tune in to a particular seasonal or Sabbat energy... this is the Wheel of the Year calling you to attention, connecting you to the energies that most need your attention. After a while of following the Wheel of the Year, you will sometimes be caught unaware as you're crossing the street, or opening a window, and you'll feel the approach of that holiday or season. This is what I call the *earth tides*, that deep inner knowingness of our place on the Wheel.

GUARDIANSHIP OF THE HOME—SETTING WARDS

To set up wards, you simply need to acknowledge the directions and ask them to stay and watch over your space permanently. What I do, in every home I live in, is to first do a house clearing and blessing, to eliminate any negative energies that were there before I moved in, then I cast a permanent, permeable circle, set up like a huge filter, which keeps negative energies out. I then invite the guardians of the directions to come and stay and watch over my space. I "refresh" this every few seasons, at the very least annually, with plenty of gratitude and offerings for the work they've done (offerings usually take the form of special candles, incense, or other herbals I feel the elemental energies would appreciate, including smoking to the four directions, as the Native Americans do).

A FEW WORDS ON USING ENERGY

As a Dedicant, you learned the basics of how to use energy, as well as something of an overview of how energy works. Something to keep most assuredly in mind as you go through this Initiate course is that *energy is REAL!* I cannot emphasize this enough.

The whole reason I am discussing this here is that, as I've gone to public events and interacted with folks in many magical communities, from the wide-eyed newbie who hasn't yet begun magical training, to priests and priestesses with a bazillion years' experience, this simple fact is something I think gets forgotten, time and time again, often to our detriment. I sometimes wonder if it's because a lot of Witchy beliefs and practices are hitting the mainstream, either through a somewhat misguided New Age guru of sorts, or because of movies like the *Harry Potter* series or *The Craft*. I actually heard an NPR reporter the other day refer to President Obama as "channeling" Teddy Roosevelt. Hmmm... really? I don't think so. Yet, we hear these erroneous references made, in both the mundane and magical communities, fairly often.

One example is a humorous story a friend of mine, we'll call her Jessie, told me about her daughter Belinda, who wanted nothing more than to connect with the faerie realm on her eighteenth birthday. Belinda was so blissed out after having made this connection, despite Jessie's warning that the fey world is not a force to take lightly, that she just went along her merry way. Soon, Belinda began having trouble with things... *disappearing*. Jessie tried to convince her daughter that maybe playing with faeries wasn't such a good idea, but Belinda assured Jessie she could handle them. After a week or so of losing countless items, Belinda *herself* seemed to have become lost one afternoon, and when Jessie tried calling her on her cell phone that evening, there was no answer. Jessie tried texting, and when there was still no answer, which was very unlike Belinda, Jessie started getting worried (though she suspected it was the faerie energy her daughter had been bent on conjuring). Finally, Jessie went to Belinda's best friend's apartment, and Belinda, clad only in her underwear, cracked open the door and peeked out. Jessie laughed out loud. Belinda couldn't leave the apartment, you see, because not only could she not find her cell phone, her car keys, or her shoes, but she was also missing her *pants*!

Another classic example was when I attended one of my first festivals here in the Pacific Northwest. It was fall, and that's the time when the rains begin in earnest; however, the prediction for that weekend was sunshine, so I was delighted to go. At the opening ritual for this festival with the theme of the Inner Child, as the quarters were released, they were invited to "stay and play!" Needless to say, the wind and rain began soon after, and continued through the entire festival, rendering any outdoor activities impossible from that point on.

These examples are humorous, but very real. Other examples aren't always so humorous, such as when we see people casting a circle *through* the participants (please, go *outside* the circle of people to cast!), or an occurrence I observed at a merchanting event I attended recently, when three women wanted to bring sales into their area. Together, they *pushed* the energy out *through* a fourth woman who was set up in front of them. When asked what they were doing, as the woman felt very "pushed out" herself, she was told that they were "sweeping the energy out and then pulling it in from the street to bring in customers." Needless to say, the woman they pushed that energy *through* felt a bit sickly all day, certainly felt unwelcome, and didn't have a single sale, while the other women made money hand over fist. This type of behavior is very inconsiderate and irresponsible! The energetically correct (not to mention *polite*) thing to do would have been to explain their intentions to the fourth woman, giving her the opportunity either to participate (best) or to leave the area while they did their energy work.

Finally, I have heard people mention things about "carrying" energies, usually of a deity, for extremely long periods of time, anywhere from a few days to an entire year. When questioned, these individuals often express that they are *invoked* with that deity. While I won't try to define what another person's reality is, in my experience, invocation is an *intense* experience, and the energy one holds is *huge*! When the Lady leaves my body after I've invoked her, I am nothing but shivers from head to toe, and I'm quite depleted. Granted, there are different levels of invocation, but I can't imagine holding that intensely large energy for more than a few hours.

As an Initiate, you will be doing *actual* invocations of the elements, not just inviting them into your ritual circles as you did as a Dedicant. (Many call this "invocation." Remember—to *invoke* an energy is to *draw it into your body*!) As you grow as a Witch, I encourage you to take your training to a higher level, and when you invite the elements into your circle, you will be sensing, feeling, experiencing, and interacting with them on a much more profoundly connected level. Then, in your magical circles, as you become more and more familiar with the elemental energies, your actions will involve *holding* those energies much more than simply *thinking about* them.

Yes indeed, dear Initiate, working with energy is real, more real than we sometimes care to notice. And although the energies we conjure can sometimes be playful, they are not *play toys*; the energies we conjure can be darkly destructive, too, and the sooner we accept the fact that our actions do indeed have consequences, the better. To be cognizant of that fact whenever we conjure something is to make sure that we, and not it, are in control.

So, let's be responsible as we work with energy, my darlings, and take time and thought to consider *all* of its implications! Please remember that the energy we work with is, indeed, real, and can manifest in a myriad of ways, and use caution and care when we do our bending and shaping—its effects are more far-reaching than we sometimes realize.

REQUIRED READING

In many Witchcraft teaching systems, good scholarship is emphasized, and Circles is no exception. I believe there are a lot of good books filled with important and valuable information out there, not just mine. This, as you know, dear Initiate, is not just a Witchy "how-to" book; it is a course of study. To that end, I offer your required reading list:

Initiate reading list

FICTION AND MYTHOLOGY:
- ❏ *The Sea Priestess* by Dion Fortune
- ❏ *Lammas Night* by Katherine Kurtz

NONFICTION:
- ❏ *The Soul's Code: In Search of Character and Calling* by James Hillman
- ❏ *The Four Agreements* by don Miguel Ruiz
- ❏ *A Witches' Bible* by Janet and Stewart Farrar
- ❏ *Wheels of Life* by Anodea Judith
- ❏ *The Dark God* by Nicholas Mann
- ❏ *Drawing Down the Moon* by Margot Adler
- ❏ *The Inner Guide Meditation* by Edwin Steinbrecher
- ❏ *Dreaming the Divine* by Scott Cunningham
- ❏ *Myth and Sexuality* by Jamake Highwater
- ❏ *The God of the Witches* by Margaret Murray
- ❏* *The White Goddess* by Robert Graves

ELECTIVE:
- ❏ *Ancient Mirrors of Womanhood* by Merlin Stone
- ❏ *Wheel of the Year* by Pauline Campanelli
- ❏ *Shadow Magick Compendium* by Raven Digitalis

*NOTE:

The White Goddess, by Robert Graves, is required to be finished by Master (the traditional third-degree) initiation. If this step is foreseen, I suggest beginning this valuable book soon. Remember, however, that Graves was a poet, not an historian, so take his work as the beautiful and inspiring devotional work to the Goddess that it is, and re-check any perceived "facts" before repeating them as such.

Out-of-print books

From time to time, books on my recommended reading list have gone out of print. Sometimes you can find out-of-print books through Amazon.com or online rare-book searches, at used bookstores, at library archives, even at garage sales. If you're one of my "real life" students, you don't get off the hook that easily; I have a loan library with all the Initiate-level books available. If you are not a real-life student of mine, my best advice to you is to make a solid effort to find these wonderful volumes, for, as I've said to many a student before, these books are the cream of the crop of what I've read, and I've read a *lot* of books! If you are unable to find them, of course that doesn't mean you can't "graduate" from this program, but you will have missed an important chunk, however small. So keep your eyes out for them; you may be surprised at what you find. And you can always read them later if need be.

SHADOW WORK

In our solitary work, we will learn to go deep within ourselves and dispel our shadows—not the Mysteries we treasure and hold dear, for we will explore and hold fast to those, but the shadows of fear and pain we all bear from past experiences and trials. Dispelling these shadows can only lead us to greater mental and emotional health, which in turn will lead us into better physical health and vibrancy, which will naturally add to our power as Witches.

With each lesson in the *Thirteen Moons* section, there will be opportunity to look at the shadows that touch that particular aspect of our lives, and to heal the ones that haunt us and keep us from realizing our full potential. Esbat assignments, then, can and should be used to create ritual that will heal any negative energy patterns in that category in our lives and beings, bringing us to greater power through achieving balance of both our light and our darkness. Raven Digitalis says, "Shadow magick is all about navigating darkness, both internal and cosmic, assimilating its strengths and transforming it into something positive. Therefore, the apparently negative in your life may be used as fuel for advancement."[6] *Fuel for advancement.* Yes, absolutely. Much power lies in the ability to both recognize these patterns and attempt to work healthy changes, as all of life's challenges can be seen as lessons and opportunities to become stronger through Right Action and a warrior's attitude. My friend Marcella laughingly calls her life's challenges "FOGs" (F-ing Opportunities for Growth). And indeed, if we can laugh at the discomfort, work to heal it, and relentlessly pursue the shadows, we can only succeed.

SERVICE WORK

There will also be an emphasis on beginning, or at least contemplating ways in which we can serve our communities. These *Pathwork Focus* discussions emphasize our spiritual gifts, or callings. As we progress along our spiritual paths, especially at this Initiate level, we often find ourselves in a place of deep gratitude for all our gods have given us, and we start wanting to serve them by serving our communities. We all have a spiritual gift or two (or several!), and as we go through the *Solar Wheel* unit, we'll explore one spiritual gift at a time as that particular gift relates to the place we are on the Wheel, and by the time of your Adept initiation, you will have a pretty good idea of some things you can do to serve your community. Please do not let these suggestions limit you in any way; these are just some of the many, many things one can do to serve one's gods through one's community, though they're probably the more common ones. You can choose to serve your community in as many ways as you wish, but I suggest that you focus on one or two areas at a time. The *Pathwork Focus* suggestions are all various ways that you can eventually serve your community, and some are things you could possibly make a living at if you choose to. So the choice should be considered carefully.

A fun option to consider is how to mark your spiritual calling physically on your ritual garb. In my own covens, we've wrapped colored thread crosswise around our cords near the ends, to symbolize various spiritual gifts. Other ways you could use color are perhaps with symbols embroidered at the cuffs or hems of your garb, or even special pieces of ribbon or cording woven into your Sacred Cord somehow, using trim

---

6. Raven Digitalis, *Shadow Magick Compendium* (Llewellyn, 2008), 35.

or ribbon. Another option I've seen used is a beaded necklace the whole coven wore. For each talent or spiritual gift a person had, there would be a colored bead on their necklace symbolizing that calling. Any way you would like to symbolize these gifts is appropriate so long as it's meaningful for you. Although there are undoubtedly dozens of ways one can serve one's gods and community, I can only present so many, so do not let these ideas limit you in any way. Emerson said, "Every calling is great when greatly pursued." I agree; for however we choose to serve our gods, if we give our passion and our love to their service, we become much greater than we once were.

YOUR SPIRITUAL CALLING—THE PATHWORK FOCUS OPTIONS

A calling to the Magical Crafter's Path

This person is skilled in one or many magical craftwork techniques, and sometimes sells his goods. He may have a single skill or a myriad of them, and knows much of the magical use of color as well as the design and creation of other ritual tools and toys. Coupled with this Pathwork focus is a focus on the Sacred Clothier's Path— those folks who feel a call to make ritual gowns, tabards, cloaks, robes, and other items we Pagans love to dress up in, to show our truest colors to our gods. Good symbolic colors for these gifts would be orange, for the physical (red) manifestation of an idea (yellow).

A calling to the Smith's Path

The smith is skilled in blade and sometimes jewelry making, anything that involves metal. He may or may not also make ritual headpieces and torques. A person who feels a strong calling to smith work may wish to symbolize this calling with silver, or perhaps gray, the color of metal.

A calling to the Bard's Path

The bard is skilled in communication of one or several types, such as writing, songwriting, storytelling, and mythology. This person should have a good grasp of history if she wishes to have mythology as part of her repertoire. The symbolic color could be yellow, for mental clarity and creativity. In the Druidic tradition, however, the color for a bard is blue, so this presents another choice you can make about symbolizing your calling.

A calling to the Guardian's Path

There is a relatively new movement in the American Wiccan community of folks who feel that they are here to protect and watch over magical rites rather than lead them. This service is becoming necessary not only due to the sheer volume of people this religion is attracting, but also because we as a community are becoming more involved in the deeper Mysteries. It's a nice feeling to know that a "physical" someone is out there watching over the circle along with the gods for some kinds of magical work. In addition, many people consider themselves guardians of the earth in a more concrete way, through political activism and consciousness raising. These folks I would call "Earth's Guardians," or even "Earth's Warriors." Since these callings are often intertwined, I present them together. The color could be gold (or, more appropriately, black laced with gold)—for the God in his role as guardian, but this Pathwork focus is not limited to men in any way.

A calling to the Healer's Path

This person knows a lot about how to move energy through her own body, as well as her client's. She will also undoubtedly be skilled in herb lore, energy healing, and intuitive work, as well as, perhaps, some sort of non-magical form of healing. The symbolic color choice might be red, the color of healthy blood and tissues. If you are one of those wonderful folks who specialize in healing animals, an alternate color choice for this could be brown laced with red.

A calling to the Herbalist's Path

This person is skilled in either medicinal or magical herb usage, or both. He is knowledgeable about toxic and poisonous herbs, and possesses the skills required to make various compounds, capsules, infusions, decoctions, salves, tinctures, and the like. You may choose to use green to mark this calling.

A calling to the Astrologer's Path

This person is skilled in producing natal charts with a high degree of accuracy, as well as being able to produce comparison charts, progressions, and other charts as needed. The symbolic color could be deep blue, for the night sky.

A calling to the Dreamweaver's Path

This person is skilled in dream interpretation, dream control, and lucid dreaming techniques, such as astral projection. She is skilled in various meditative techniques, which include but are not limited to power animal work, guided meditations, transcendental meditation, and deep trance. The color might be silver, for the Lady, the Ruler of night, and our inner Mysteries.

A calling to the Intuitive Reader's Path

This person is skilled in many divination methods, and is highly accurate in readings performed, for no matter which method is used, the person with a strong calling to Intuitive Reading is going to be reading *psychic currents* much more than they're reading any tool or symbol. The color to symbolize this calling would likely be black, for the Deep Dark of the Mystery.

A calling to the Spiritual Counselor's Path

Spiritual or pastoral counseling is something that is sorely needed in our community. Often, our own friends and High Priest/esses are too busy or just too unfocused to counsel those who need a little help with a spiritual problem or dilemma. For solitary practitioners, often there is no one to talk to, especially about our spiritual and psychic experiences, so our spiritual counselors are worth their weight in gold. This person has good listening skills, compassion, and a nonjudgmental attitude to begin with, as well as a great deal of diplomacy. He has had experience or training in both Wicca and counseling to be qualified. The symbolic color could be bright blue, for healthy emotions.

A calling to the Sexual Healer's Path

More and more these days, we are finding Pagans who help heal people's sexuality through sexual teachings and counseling, sexual surrogate work, and teaching sex magic and Tantra, as well as those who practice the art of sacred prostitution. These are all not only valid spiritual gifts, but much-needed services in an unhealthy culture like ours. A good color to symbolize this calling could be purple, for passion, which is the physical (red) manifestation of an emotion (blue).

A calling to the Historian's Path

This person has a good deal of study under her belt. She has read many books on the history of the world, not just the history of Wicca, and likely knows a great deal about several world religions. She has a pretty solid opinion of the world's timeline, and bases her perception of events on facts, probably with a good bit of personal opinion to pepper the pot (as all historians do, not just Wiccan ones). But she is fully aware, and will promptly admit, where her opinion leaves off and the facts begin. A nice color for this one would be white, that the Historian may shed bright light on our past.

A calling to the Stone Whisperer's Path

This person has a passion for rocks and stones, from precious and semi-precious to the seemingly ordinary rock. He is well versed in all aspects of the spiritual properties of stones, and many of the geological properties as well. He has an eye for finding the sacred in the mundane, and has probably accumulated vast treasure in his own back yard. The symbolic color could be deep brown, for all things earthy.

A calling to the Witchcraft Teacher's Path

This person, first and foremost, loves to teach. She has to know a good deal about all of the above Pathwork Focus options, and is diplomatic and generous in her manner toward others. She is certain of her facts, and she looks things up when she doesn't know the answer. I think this calling would best be symbolized by rainbow colors, for a little of everything.

TRACKING OUR PROGRESS—THE TRANSCRIPT

I once did some volunteer work for a Wiccan school. At that school, one of the requirements for teachers was to regularly review the student's Book of Shadows. While I personally found this extremely uncomfortable (it felt like I was going through the student's underwear drawer), I do respect and understand the need for a teacher to track the student's progress. In the Circles system, that is the function the *transcript* serves, and so teachers can leave a student's grimoire alone, unless the student *requests* to have it looked at. I came to the idea of creating a transcript when I wanted to know what degree level I was on in my early years on this path. The friend who had agreed to help me fill in the holes in my training was a very busy person, so I just wrote everything down for her—books read, energy work done, community service (the public and private rituals and workshops I'd led), my aspirations and anything else I could think of pertaining to my Path. I realized then that this little document could show a teacher all she needed to know about her student's progress, without ever having to examine his grimoire. In my classes, the transcript is always assigned at the end of the Basics lesson for that level, so you might wish to start yours now. My suggestion for layout is this:

Begin by titling it *My Path* or *My Transcript* or *A Brief Summary on the Journey of* ___, whatever feels right to you. Somewhere near the top it is best to write "Updated:___," so you will know each time you take it out or pull it up on your computer how up-to-date it is. First, write a paragraph describing your beginnings—what brought you to these ways. Next, write short paragraphs describing the following topics: *personal exploration; schools and spiritual callings; energy work; spellwork and rituals; divination/dreamwork; Mystery experience* (at Initiate level, you likely won't have had this yet). Leave all sections blank that you haven't experienced yet. They'll get filled up soon enough.

Next, list your *gifts*, then your *community service activities*. Finally, list *all books* read that relate to the topic of Wicca, religious history (yes, the Christian Bible counts—immensely!), magic, spirituality, or anything that serves to expand the mind and spark the imagination. Last, it is good to title one section *Currently*, for what you're doing now, and another section *Upcoming*, for keeping track of your spiritual and magical goals.

THE REGIONAL WHEEL OF THE YEAR

In some regions, Wiccans view the solstice and equinox points on the Wheel as being the middle of each season, and in other regions, Wiccans find the standard calendar's "first day of the season" resonates more closely with the earth tides in their particular region. In the Circles system, since there is such a strong focus on tuning in to the earth and moon, it only makes sense to follow the seasonal changes you experience personally, and that means *locally*. Therefore, someone in Georgia is going to look at the autumnal equinox differently than someone in Montana, Canada, or Celtic Europe. If you tune in to the earth tides, you will know with certainty how your own regional Wheel turns.

AN EARTH TIDES EXERCISE

Every day, take a few moments and go outside, ground and center, and tune in to the earth and sky. Yes, even if it's pouring or windy or whatever. Now, stretch your awareness out, feel the circuit and the connection to the earth and sky. Tune in to the energies of the upcoming Sabbat... then stretch further out to the next season, and the next... open yourself and touch the energy there. Now stretch forward to the next one, and feel that energy. Focus on the Earth Mother, the Sky Father, and the interconnectedness of all... Now, return slowly back along the same seasonal pattern, back to where you're standing, hear and see and feel the energy of life all around you. If it's fall or winter, feel the energies of death and decay... and know that this is compost for new life, know that all will be renewed, reborn. If it's spring or summer, tune in to the vitality of life energies bursting forth, flowering and growing all around you. Stretch your consciousness toward it. Try to sense the energies ahead of you as well as behind you in time. And just breathe... hear and smell and taste and feel the energies of the season. Hold these energies in your awareness.

Only a few minutes each day will help you focus on and tune in to these earth tides. Remember, too, to tune in to the moon tides in much the same way. What is her phase right now? Where is she in the sky? Remember the traditional saying: The new moon rises at sunrise; the first quarter at noon; the full moon rises at sunset; the last quarter rises at midnight. Let the earth and moon pull you to them, and your awareness of the life all around you will increase.

THE INVESTMENT OF ENERGY AND TIME

As you know, dear Initiate, you get out of life what you put into it, and nowhere is that more true than with magic. The time you spend on your daily practices is going to increase exponentially now that you're a priest or priestess. You should plan on spending about a half hour each day meditating, doing the energy exercises and daily devotionals, and fifteen minutes to a half hour doing your ritual planning or reading. Homework assignments shouldn't take that long—maybe two or three hours total per month, depending completely on how deep you wish to go and how much time you're willing to invest.

Remember that the level of time and commitment increases with each Gate—each Rite of Passage to a higher level, but this is as it should be, as this training will prepare you for the higher levels (Adept and Master) when you will be an active leader in your spiritual community. Always remember you needn't be in a hurry. Enjoy your learning. If you are called, time will go by quickly enough.

Also in this course, just as in the Dedicant-level course, there will be homework and reading assignments, suggested grimoire work, and much more. For your convenience, there is a worksheet in the appendix that can be copied and filled in for each *moon lesson* to help you keep track of your practices. Journaling your coincidences, intuitions, and psychic experiences is still important, and if you're not logging these things, the time to begin is *now*.

Unlike the Dedicant-level course, the Initiate course will have two Wheels to follow and keep track of: a lunar one (the *Thirteen Moons* section) and a solar one (the *Solar Wheel* unit). Because of the two Wheels and all the options for more intensive study, it can be easy for your daily practices to become overwhelming in this course, but that's true of most Initiate programs. The Initiate level, whether coven taught, self-taught, or learned through this course, is, by its very nature, deep and intense, and it can be rather all-consuming, especially for the more motivated and enthusiastic student. Please remember you have other aspects of your life to live, too, and that taking longer to complete this course if need be does not mean you're not taking it seriously. Your study, your homework, and your daily practices should be uplifting, positive, and special, but never addictive or adhered to so rigidly they become dull and obligatory. It is absolutely okay, then, for those of you with busy lives, to take the two Wheels in this course one at a time and take two years (or longer!) rather than one to complete the course. However, I will caution you, just as most active spiritual leaders in the Wiccan community will: The amount of time spent doing this coursework—following both wheels for a year and a day—is comparable to the average, active Wiccan priest's or priestess's *"normal" life*. We're a busy lot, we are! This course will have you well prepared for the lifestyle of a Wiccan spiritual leader by the time you approach the Adept Gate.

It becomes vitally important, then, at this stage in your training, to know yourself deeply, and any tool you can use in order to facilitate that end is a good idea. For this reason, in my real-life classes, I require that students either do their own natal charts or have them done during the year and a day they take to complete this course. We can see many things in the chart: our strengths and weaknesses, our potentials, our karma, and to some degree, our spiritual gifts. In addition, there is a spread in Ralph Blum's *The Book of Runes* called "the Destiny Profile,"[7] which I strongly recommend doing, or, if you're not drawn to the runes, you can try using another divination method to explore these types of energies. I would also recommend having your palms read if you can find a reputable reader in your area. All of these types of explorations can and will give you deep insights into character and calling, and will greatly benefit you as you deepen your self-knowledge.

Through this self-knowledge, at this Initiate level, you will learn and develop a healthy self-love. The Goddess in *The Charge* says "And you who seek to know Me, know that your seeking and yearning will avail you not, unless you know the Mystery: For if that which you seek you find not within yourself, you will never find it without."[8] Your relationship to your chosen deity, then, is the same as/intrinsic to/ connected with your relationship to your*self*. We must love ourselves *passionately*! Now, I'm not talking about ego or conceit here, as those energies are just backward forms of insecurity; I'm talking about a healthy and deep caring about our mental, passionate, emotional, physical, and spiritual well *be*-ing. In light of this, of course, the idea of putting our gods first in our lives is essential, and, I submit, *the same as* putting ourselves first, as our gods are the ones who guide us to our own highest good. Surrendering our will, then, doing devotionals and adorations, following where our chosen deities lead us on our individual Paths are all saying the same thing: that we love, honor, and respect ourselves and are committed to acting in our own best interest. If you do not love yourself; are in a place of ego; think your ways are the only ways that are valid; find yourself judging others to the point of (gods forbid!) being compelled to "correct" them, especially in public; are rigid in your beliefs to the point that you find yourself judging and abusing yourself or others—you will not succeed. Conversely, if you are so insecure that you constantly question everything you do, from the color candles you choose for a Sabbat ritual or whether or not you should take the job or commit to the relationship(s) of your dreams, you will never see the opportunities the Divine will send your way. Humility and honor are about knowing our worth as it truly is—neither magnified nor diminished.

_____

7. Ralph Blum, *The Book of Runes* (St. Martin's Press, 1982), 70.

8. See this book's appendix for *The Charge of the Goddess* in its entirety.

It is through this deep self-love and energy work that we can begin to *attune our spiritual vessels,* to become *prepared* to prepare ourselves for service.

HOMEWORK FOR THIS SECTION

1. **Begin (or update) your transcript** with all pertinent and current information. For guidelines, see page 39.

2. **Start thinking about (and saving up for) having your natal chart done.** You can also do it yourself, but unless you're pretty experienced in this art, I recommend having it done professionally. It can be expensive, but some astrologers will do exchanges, and truthfully, you're *worth* it! It's vital information for the deep inner knowledge of the Self.

3. **Read** *The Four Agreements* by don Miguel Ruiz, and Part I in *Drawing Down the Moon* by Margot Adler.

PART
TWO

PRIMING THE VESSEL:
THE THIRTEEN MOONS

THE MOON

The moon is the earth's natural satellite, and she was formed about the time the earth herself was, some 4.6 billion years ago. She was formed of dust and earth particles when a wayward planet even bigger than Mars struck the earth. The dust and particles that flew into the atmosphere began conglomerating and eventually formed one mass that is the moon as we know her now. Contrary to popular opinion, it is when the moon is between the earth and the sun that we see her as the dark, or new, moon, and just when one would think the earth would be casting the shadow over the entire surface to create that new moon—when the earth is between the moon and the sun—that we see her as full. Interestingly, she rotates on her axis at the same rate in which she orbits us, so she shows us the same face constantly.[9]

She rises approximately fifty-one minutes later each day, and so is rather predictable in her rising times. We can count on the full moon every cycle to rise at sunset, and the new moon at dawn, with the quarters in between. There is an old saying regarding this, but I remember more easily with a poem I made up, based on the old Tuscan legend[10] about Diana, the moon, falling in love with her brother, Lucifer, the sun, and chasing him around the sky:

> The quarter moon rises
> When the sun rides high
> Chasing her brother
> Through afternoon's sky
>
> At sunset, the full moon
> Shows her bright face
> Flushing pink with vain effort
> To quicken her pace!

---

9. "Moon Facts," *National Geographic News* (2004). Online at http://news.nationalgeographic.com/news/2004/07/0714_040714_moonfacts.html.

10. Charles G. Leland, *Aradia, or, the Gospel of the Witches* (Phoenix Publishing, 1998), 18.

The last quarter stealthily
Climbs midnight's dark stair
Disappointed again
That her brother's not there

But the new moon, invisible,
So cleverly waits
To catch him at sunrise,
And so, wins the chase!

An interesting fact to note is one that farmers of old went by: if the crescent moon looks like it would hold water poured into it from above, it's not yet time to plant, but if it looks as though the water would spill out, then planting time has arrived. Also of interest, if you have trouble remembering whether the moon is waxing or waning when you look at her, just mentally draw a line from the bottom point of the crescent, up through the top point, extending up for about the same distance. Is the "letter" you just made a *b* or a *d*? If it's a *b*, the moon is waxing, or being "born." If it's a *d*, the moon is waning, or "dying."

No matter her phase, the moon, which represents our beloved Goddess in so many ways, speaks to us of harmony and blending, as her silvery light softens and diffuses the landscape. Her many phases, running in twenty-eight-day cycles, reminds us of all things female, for human women typically follow that same cycle with their bloods. The moon shows us our sameness, for under her bright countenance, we see a landscape of ever-harmonizing shadows of softened edges and dappled light.

The moon orbits the earth in a little over twelve and a third moons per solar cycle (because a lunar cycle actually is just a bit *over* twenty-eight days), with an extra, thirteenth moon showing up as a "blue moon"—the second full moon in a calendar month, about every three years.

And so the *Thirteen Moons* will show you, dear Initiate, in a little over a year and a day, how very much you are like the Goddess, with many faces and phases, a harmonized blend of dark and light, waxing and waning energies, and we will work with the energies of receptivity, harmony, self-exploration, and more throughout this course, one moon at a time.

NAVIGATING THE THIRTEEN MOONS

As stated in the *Jumping on the Wheel* segment (page 8) at the beginning of this book, this *Thirteen Moons* section is designed to be followed one moon at a time, from one through thirteen. Each lesson will have an exploration of the energy for that moon; chakra lore and Thirteen Harmonies work discussions; a tool for that moon; an exploration of one or two of the eight virtues described in *The Charge of the Goddess*; a suggested posture of power for that chapter's energy pattern; and of course, homework. Homework will include daily chakra energy work and recommended reading from Anodea Judith's *Wheels of Life*, a suggested *Thirteen Harmonies work* exercise, and an elemental evocation that later evolves into elemental invocation, deity aspecting, and finally, invocation. There will also be Esbat ritual assignments, suggestions for moon tides and daily devotional work, other applicable required reading, and astral temple work.

Thirteen Harmonies work includes and expands upon *The Eightfold Paths*, a vital part of traditional Wicca. These ways of making magic are listed in *A Witches' Bible* as being from Gardner's own Book of Shadows.[11] In *The Magician's Companion*, Whitcomb clarifies and simplifies the definitions of these eight different actions that lead "to the center," or eight ways of making magic, of achieving altered states of consciousness.[12] These are: meditation or concentration, trance, rituals, opening the gates, dance, control, discipline, and the Great Rite. I find that there are other, additional things that help us to achieve altered states. These are: chanting (or singing), projecting energy, embracing (actively receiving) energy, visualization, and invoking. Although invocation is discussed in the thirteenth moon (chapter 17, "Wholeness"), I've saved the *requirement* to try invocation for the Adept Initiation section (Part Four), as much of the Thirteen Harmonies work is designed to both help prepare the student and lead up to facilitating that end. Each *Thirteen Moons* chapter will include one of the above energy patterns to be explored in depth.

The *Postures of Power* are simply different ways in which we can use gesture or a pose to further express ourselves within the energy pattern we're exploring. Each one

---

11. Janet Farrar and Stewart Farrar, *A Witches' Bible* (Phoenix Publishing, 1981), part II, 52.

12. Bill Whitcomb, *The Magician's Companion* (Llewellyn, 2004), 146.

begins with the words "If it works for you to do so," because I recognize we all have different physical abilities and preferences, and some of the positions may not be comfortable for all people. I believe these exercises will work best only if you *feel powerful within that posture*. Therefore, if something feels uncomfortable, or if you're physically unable to do the posture, please feel free to adapt the posture to something that does work, invent your own way to express the energy, or simply skip the exercise.

Astral temple work will take you step by step from building the foundation—connected to the Core/Ground energies in the first-moon chapter all the way through to the fully constructed temple, ready for you to "move in," in the thirteenth moon chapter (Wholeness). The reasons we might wish to have an astral temple are manifold. First, it can serve as a springboard, if you will: a place of power to begin our meditations and spiritual journeying from. It can also serve as an inner sanctuary—a place of beauty and repose that we can go to in our minds when life is overwhelming and we need a mental and spiritual retreat. It can also serve as a place to meet with our chosen deities, for guidance as well as for working more closely with their energies, such as beginning our invocations. It can also be a place of safety in mind and heart to do our shadow work, or to use when we need to examine traumas or abuses that occurred in our past (or, gods forbid, our present). Finally, as we look at how our astral temple is being constructed, we can meditate on those constructs and pathways to learn a great deal about ourselves. Do we *have* to have an astral temple to do all that? Certainly not, but it can be a valuable tool. For myself, once the power place I'd found and established at my initiation was violated, I found a need for a secret, secure, and more powerful place, a place that did not exist on the material plane, so that it could not be breached. My astral temple is mine alone, and the only entities that come there with me are the ones I invite. So yours will be for you; from the moment you lay the foundation, you can begin working with it and in it, for all of the above reasons, and more.

Finally, in this *Thirteen Moons* section, there will be a deep focus on *shadow work*. Chasing our shadows becomes vitally important as we work toward becoming healthier and stronger mentally, emotionally, and physically, which makes us much more powerful! There will be suggested shadow work contemplations and/or exercises with every moon in the *Thirteen Moons* section also.

Moon work, including Esbats and the planning of them, is very much of the Goddess; it is of the inner planes, and so by its very nature it is reflective, personal, deep, intuitive, meditative. As in most traditional systems, Esbats emphasize spell and energy work, so this section of course emphasizes the same, and is designed to strengthen the Witch's skills and power. This section emphasizes *working*; learning and experiencing what energy is all about, how to feel it pulling and coursing through our bodies, enhanced by our clear intention and focus, and releasing that energy toward a specific goal. At this point, the student has deepened into the beginnings of his power, and must now work more directly with deity in order to prime his vessel.

The *Thirteen Moons* chapters, therefore, are all about *energy work*. In each lesson, you will be presented with many different ways that a particular energy can be observed, changed, and manifested for the energy pattern we're exploring. You will be writing an Esbat for each moon, and making decisions as to when in the moon cycle you will do your working. A good guideline to go by is as follows:

FIRST WEEK: The waxing moon is for constructing, building energy. Begin brainstorming for the upcoming full and dark moons, decide what needs to leave or come into your life, and begin planning an Esbat ritual, either full or dark, Diana's Bow or Crone's Sickle,[13] based on when it's most appropriate to do the work. Do the rite, if it's a Diana's Bow ritual.

SECOND WEEK: Begin planning and writing a personal Esbat, or do the rite, if it's simply for waxing moon energies.

FULL MOON: Do the ritual, if a full moon rite, or do divinations, basic energy work, or a meditation on something you wish to bring to light if no rite is planned for the full moon.

THIRD WEEK: The waning moon is for contemplation and deconstructing. Consider the energies that are fading from your life, or from this cycle, and continue working on your Esbat if it's for a dark moon, or Crone's Sickle, and do the working if it's simply for waning moon energies.

---

13. In many traditions, 'Diana's Bow" is the term used for the slender crescent just a few days out from the new moon, as it looks a bit like a bow. This is very good energy for engaging in new projects. Upon pondering these types of energies one evening, I came up with the idea and term "Crone's Sickle" to describe the last slender crescent of the waning moon, also a few days out (only on the other side, of course) from the new moon. The Crone's Sickle phase is very good for endings, cutting threads, for seeing the seeds of light in a Mystery or shadow pattern, etc.

FOURTH WEEK: Continue thinking about deconstructing—breaking old patterns, letting go of that which no longer works. Do the rite you've been planning, if it's for the Crone's Sickle.

NEW MOON: Do the dark moon working or meditation. When finished, begin a new cycle, a new moon lesson.

As you go through your *Thirteen Moons* work, there will be a point when your daily devotionals will take on a new depth—that of the *adoration*. Our adorations help us to attune to our matron goddesses and patron gods, and the archetypal energies they embody. Through the course of this unit, we will move from evoking into aspecting and then invoking the elements, from evoking to aspecting and finally invoking deity, facilitating a deeper connection both to our chosen gods and goddesses and to ourselves. The adoration is a tool to help you get your vessel to the point that it can contain that invoked deity. A strong self-love, then, is also a fundamental tool to success in the *Thirteen Moons* work, so identifying and healing our shadows is emphasized in this section as well. We've all had personal trials in our lives, often leaving us with baggage; energy patterns we need to heal. Many of us have baggage left over from past lives as well. These energy patterns can create huge holes in our spirits. In order to become powerful, and to *own that power*, it is essential that we heal those holes through whatever means are useful and available. Now, exploring and identifying the energy patterns that created our shadows is not the same as having a "victim mentality." A victim mentality is the belief that because _____ happened to me as a kid, I now have an excuse to sit on my butt and not deal with life. Chasing our shadows is following the thread of the energy pattern down to its beginning in order to find the cause. Once we know the cause, we can often find that we have the key to heal it. This can be emotionally difficult work, but ultimately, it will give us great coping tools for dealing with those energy patterns. This section will offer several ideas and opportunities to bring about that healing action as we go along.

The Initiate level is, by its very nature, deeply personal; a solitary Path. Whether or not one works with a partner or magical group, an Initiate's success is going to be *determined by,* and *a direct reflection of* how much time and effort the individual puts into his solitary workings, his devotionals and adorations, chasing his shadows, and honing his focus and intent. This very personal work is important to do alone, under the watchful eyes of one's personal gods. This is also not to say that working with a group isn't important, too—in fact, if at all possible it's best to do both. So if you have friends who are also on the Path, you might think about doing the energy work together once a week or twice a month, and do your daily work alone.

To help you keep track of all this, you will find a worksheet in the appendix that you can copy and use for your moon work. This worksheet has blanks for all the suggested work, as well as spaces you can use to add your own plans and goals for that cycle.

PRIMING YOUR SPIRITUAL VESSEL

To prime something is to fill it up and make it ready for outpouring. In order to transfer the contents of one water bucket to another, for example, we can create a basic pump by simply filling a hose with water, and placing one end in the bucket that's full, and the other end in an empty bucket. This creates a vacuum pressure that allows the water to flow to where it's needed. So it is with the magical path. As you become more and more full, dear Initiate, with love and joy, with power and purpose, with devotion to your gods, so you become ready to share your knowledge, experience, and skill with others, to begin the outpouring that is the Adept's Path; the Path of *Service*.

Now there will be those of you who come to this path with *broken vessels*, and if this is the case for you, you will want to spend some time clearing the negative energies of your past from your spirit through the shadow work we'll be exploring as we go along. You may also want to do a thorough deprogramming ritual prior to beginning the unit, or along the way, or both. In *The Four Agreements*, don Miguel Ruiz speaks extensively about deprogramming ourselves and suggests a couple of techniques for destroying "the parasite"[14]—the fear-based energy pattern that keeps us from experiencing true self-love and personal freedom. Like a many-headed monster, sometimes the parasite must be destroyed head by head. Throughout this unit, you will find shadow work suggestions in each moon lesson designed to help you tackle that parasite, issue by issue. You will also find, in the moon that completes each "triplet" of moons, a discussion of the shadow that affects those three: the shadow of shame, the shadow of blame, the shadow of fame (the dark side of

---

14. Don Miguel Ruiz, *The Four Agreements* (Amber-Allen Publishing, 1997), 104–5.

community service), the shadow of the Path, and finally, with the thirteenth moon, the Shadow of the Shadow.

This unit, then, is designed to build power within the Witch through much personal hands-on experience, something that is typically taught at Initiate level in covens. This is where so many self-taught Witches have holes in their training. To be self-motivated to do the work is core and key to the successful completion of this unit. That being said, let's get started!

5: The First Moon—Core/Ground

*What we do and what we are prepares us for what we are
to be. I am becoming, continuously becoming.*
—Bill Bond

MOON ONE—THE STORY

*The moon is dark tonight, emphasizing your inner Mysteries.
You sit rooted to your spot on the floor, contemplating the energies that have brought you to this place. You breathe deeply, ground and center, focusing on the roots of your Tree of Life as they stretch deep, down and down, deeper and deeper into the Mother.*

You follow their course as they twist and turn, growing smaller and smaller until they're barely the size of the hairs on your head. You push the root tips down, deeper and deeper, letting them run where they will, entwining the rocks and soil far, far under the surface.

In this meditative state, you can see your past: your youth, your childhood and babyhood, possibly even past-life energies, and you wonder at the causal effects various events and lessons are having on the life you live now. Tiny lights fill those capillary roots, and you draw them in. You can see how all of the energy patterns of your past have combined to make you who you are today, and you can feel your root chakra spinning, brilliant red,

THE FIRST MOON CORRESPONDENCES

Keywords: source energies, self-care, center, steadfastness, stability, prosperity

Energy: survival

Chakra: root

Chakra color: red

Element: earth

Elemental color: green, brown, black

Herbs and flowers: white sage, patchouli

Incense: Druid's Grove, Forest Blend

Stones and metals: gypsum, obsidian, iron

13 Harmonies: dance

Tool: drums

8 virtues: strength

Astral temple work: foundation

Shadow group: the Shadow of Shame

Energy keyword: self

Energy group: source—self-awareness and care

as you examine the ones that directly affect your survival as a human being on this planet. Like bubbles of energy, these little lights draw your attention, and you find you can move closer if you choose to, in order to view the scenes portrayed there. Some you examine closely, others you simply let go their own way for now. Some of those scenes are nightmarish in nature, for these are the things that have created holes in your spirit; the things that affect your ability to survive in a world that, for all of its comforts and choices, is really no less brutal than the world of our ancestors. You can see that humankind has simply traded one set of problems for a **better** set of problems.

For now, you choose one or two issues to examine, to understand, and ultimately, to heal. Keeping your breathing steady and even, you will yourself to remain detached in order to more effectively explore the energies, acknowledge that your own spirit created the situation *in order to learn and evolve. Your root chakra spins and spins, bright red and luminous, as you contemplate how to embrace the lesson, forgive the spirits involved, and let go, turning pain into promise, confusion into hard-won wisdom. You store this information in your chakra and in your mind, pulling strength and power from the lesson, knowing that often it is our scars that form the foundation of our personal strength and power. You open your eyes when you are ready, and emerge wiser and more powerful, knowing you can explore these energies whenever you need to.*

THE ENERGY OF SURVIVAL

In this lesson, we take a look at our spiritual core. What is at the center of you? What are your long or deeply held beliefs about yourself, your fatal flaws and shining strengths? What do you live for? What would you die for? What sparks you to action, and what drives you to your bed in despair? If all were stripped away, what would you be left with; what would you find at your spiritual core? Building and fortifying that core is what the Initiate level is all about, and that's why in so many ways, the deepest part of the Initiate's Path is and must be a solitary journey. On this, the first of the thirteen moons, dear Initiate, whether you're working with a group or not, it is time to come to terms with that simple fact, and to make a decision to spend some considerable time alone during this year-and-a-day cycle of your journey.

Survival is all about that which sustains us, our very foundation, our ground. In exploring these energies, we must consider our current life situation. Are we able to provide for ourselves in all the essential ways? Do we have enough food, shelter, warmth? If not, why not? And what can we do to heal the situation?

This is pretty basic stuff—our survival in life depends on us having a firm foundation, both within and without. And so again, we must look to our own inner truths. In ancient times, survival energies would have had us contemplating the hunt, the harvest, our physical health in terms of how to get enough to eat, our shelter and the needs that go along with keeping it strong and warm against the elements. In addition, there would be issues of confidence in our strength and intelligence—if we didn't believe in ourselves and our abilities, our survival would be much less assured than if we stood strong in our core belief in ourselves.

In these modern times, a great many of our survival needs are met through that lusted-after and ever-present medium: money. And again, our healthy ground hinges upon not only our means of making money, but also our confidence in our ability to earn and keep it. What are our attitudes about money? Why does it seem that so many Pagans are poor, or struggling? Do we think we don't deserve abundance? Dig deep and examine your own feelings about money and the flow of it in your life. How do we feel about our ability to earn, save, and wisely spend money? How do we feel about our place of employment and the resulting demands on our time? How about the daily commute to our workplace, how can we make it easier? Safer?

How do we spend our money? Do we hold it tightly, desperately afraid that if our savings account dips below a certain figure, all is lost? Conversely, does money slip through our fingers, so that no matter how much or how little we make, we seem to always be living from paycheck to paycheck, terrified of possible emergencies that would spell certain disaster? It's time to contemplate our money attitudes now, and take steps to ensure financial peace and confidence to help this energy stay on track.

How do we feel about others who have more? Are we happy for them or angry that they have more than we do? Feelings of envy and deprivation will only serve to deplete our spiritual energy, and won't help us a bit. If we are happy for others' financial well-being, it can add to our energy and keep the universe mindful of the fact that we believe money is a positive thing, which will help open channels for money to flow into our lives more freely.

Survival energies also encompass our physical health, which involves much more now than in those distant times, for now, rather than worrying about having enough to eat, many of us now worry about eating too much, or eating the "wrong" foods, and whether those things we eat will cause ill health. Getting proper exercise is an issue the Ancients most assuredly never had to worry about, as they were in motion almost constantly. Imagine how they would laugh to see our efforts as we huff and puff, power walking and jogging in parks and along city streets, straining and pushing against resistance machines in gyms! Our shelter needs are equally complex now, involving money again: the ability to pay rent or house payments, utility bills, maintenance bills, water and sewer bills, and costs for fences and screens to keep pests out and privacy in.

The "fight or flight" response is still alive and well in our consciousness, but it's often triggered by much different reasons than in those distant times. The response can kick in over the fear of walking to our cars in a dark parking garage or from having a stranger approach us on an empty street for whatever reason; it can kick in when we feel our jobs are threatened in some way; if our children or pets wander too far from our sight. In some of these situations, we may feel our bodies have betrayed us, especially if the situation doesn't warrant a rush to action, but our bodies don't know that; they simply respond to a threat with racing heart, hypervigilance, and tensed muscles. We can feel pretty silly when this happens because a homeless person was simply asking for some spare change, but it is wise to honor these feelings, as there could be energy currents sparking an intuitive response to real danger. Once we've determined we are, indeed, safe, it's a good idea to earth that fight-or-flight energy by grounding and centering and doing some deep breathing until the adrenalin rush has subsided.

What does survival mean to us on a planetary level? Most Pagans are staunch environmentalists. As humans are (presumably) one of the more intelligent species on the planet, as well as the ones who do the most damage, it is clearly our responsibility to make sure we do whatever we can to ensure the earth's good health and survival. What this means is that we study and learn how to decrease our individual energy "footprint" by using only the energy resources we need, and not wasting them. Several things factor into our energy footprint, including, but not at all limited to: where we live; how we eat; what kinds of and how many appliances we use (even whether those appliances remain plugged in when not in use); whether or not we recycle; and of course, probably the biggest determining factor is how we get to and from work or school. It's not an easy thing to change; we've been raised in an age (and, if American, in a country) focused on convenience and hedonism. However, it is vital that we make an effort to conserve and reduce the amount of carbon we produce as individuals.

Our close connections can affect our survival energies as well, sometimes profoundly. An old friend of mine, Moonstar, in discussing life's hardships once said to me, "You have to *make* your friends before you *need* them," and this philosophy was made crystal clear to me during a time when I lived alone in an area of the country that was completely counter to my energy pattern. In this place, I found it very difficult to make connections of any kind, as I was reminded often enough that I was "different," so it was an unhappy and lonely place to be.

Community—a chosen family of reliable and compassionate friends—was (and is) extremely important to most folks' personal survival. Yes, we are all quite strong, quite capable of managing on our own. However, certain situations in life are so much more difficult (and costly!) without that vital support system, and so Moonstar's words continue to ring true for me: We must *make* our friends before we *need* them! If we are living in a place that is counter to our own energy patterns, where people are unfriendly or even hostile to people of "our kind" (whatever that means to the individual), where compassionate connections are difficult or impossible to make, we *must* extricate ourselves from that situation and get to a place where such relationships are possible.

What about our spiritual survival? Our deepest core energies? There are religions that put forth the idea that if we don't behave in certain ways, we won't ascend to their "heaven." What do our life patterns and actions mean to the average Pagan? We believe in karma—not reward and punishment, but cause and effect. What actions have we taken in this life that have been less than positive? Has that energy "boomeranged" back yet? What energy patterns still haunt us? Are there lessons that continually repeat themselves in our lives? We can see these energy patterns as they become bigger and more intense. Perhaps we were abused as a child. Then, growing up, we end up in abusive romantic relationships that are even more intense. Perhaps we leave an abusive lover for another lover who, lo and behold, ends up abusing us even worse. We must have *the courage to dare* to look at that, figure out what we are doing to draw that energy to us, amend the energy pattern spiritually, and then follow up with real-life action in order to heal it. These are our own shadows, and no one is going to rescue us from their grip but *us*! So it's important that we examine these shadows to find the keys required to heal them.

Other things that affect our core can be connected to experiences we had before we ever came into our current lives. Through the years as I've come in contact with more and more Pagans, I have heard many stories of past lives and the belief that incidents in those lives are affecting the energy patterns of people's current lives. This makes a lot of sense. Some astrologers believe we can see our karma in the natal chart, in the form of retrograde planets. We can learn profound truths about our pasts by studying our natal chart, and with this knowledge, we can move forward to healing much that ails us in this one. Remember that these explorations are recommended as things to discover and heal *in order to make you stronger*, dear Initiate, not to make you feel sad or victimized, or to excuse our own hostile behaviors. No good can come from wallowing in the discovery that you were crushed by a clumsy dinosaur in a past life and now so deeply fear anyone who's bigger than you to the point that you feel you must pick fights all the time (just kidding, I know dinosaurs and humans didn't exist at the same time). When we make these discoveries, our job then is to work to heal them, in order to move on with our lives in a productive and healthy manner.

Survival is about still more. It's about loving ourselves enough to understand and find ways to meet our most basic needs on a fundamental level. If something is lacking, we need to explore those energy patterns, find out what is needed to bring ourselves to balance, and take the actions required for the betterment of our lives and spirits. This isn't always easy. Sometimes, taking care of ourselves is about having an attitude of loving discipline toward ourselves. If we are ill or if our health is suffering in some way because of an energy pattern surrounding us, such as living in a place that is counter to our truest self, or because of actions we are making the choice to take (getting involved in relationships too quickly for example, when they may not be good for us, or ignoring our body's basic needs), it is absolutely okay to tell ourselves "No," even when, and perhaps *especially* when, our habit or inclination is to do the opposite. Likewise, it's okay to tell ourselves "No" if we are burnt out from being *too disciplined* and want to relax or cut loose a little. An old acquaintance of mine used to say, "Everything in moderation, *including moderation!*"

It is always okay to tell others "No" when demands on our time and energy are too much, and we need more rest, or exercise, or need to incorporate more time for spiritual activities and study into our day or our lives. A good exercise for this, as silly as it may seem, is to simply practice saying "No." Say it several times at a stretch, then visualize situations in which you perhaps need to say "No," or haven't said "No" in the past, and then practice saying the word *loudly*, and with much feeling. Then you can begin practicing your "No" in real-life situations as they come up.

THE ROOT CHAKRA

The root chakra is located near the perineum (between the genitals and the anus). Its color is red. The Hindus call it *muladhara*. When our root chakra is not in balance, we may find ourselves feeling a need to sit "rooted" on the earth, to ground ourselves, to eat more hearty foods, or to hold stones such as hematite, a naturally grounding stone. We may feel a need for stability, especially if things in our lives are constantly up in the air, or we may feel a strong need for the touch of another human being. The need for human touch is very real, as has been evidenced by studies on babies who are deprived of touch. When I was living in the place I referred to earlier, I learned to give myself reassuring touches—I'd hug myself, and rub my shoulder or pat my leg in the same way I'd use touch to reassure a friend. This action is very self-affirming, and can help a lot in expressing self-love. Anodea Judith, in *Wheels of Life*, talks about the energy pattern of the root chakra as feeling we have a "right to be here," and that's extremely important in building our ground.

For folks who were unwanted as children, feeling we have the right to exist can be a difficult belief to hold, especially if we find ourselves in relationships that continue the pattern of rejection and isolation as adults (which is not only very easy to do, but darn well inevitable if we haven't worked on those shadows). Until we can heal this pattern within ourselves, find a way to truly believe we belong, we will spend our lives feeling like we're standing on shale, as the energy patterns of our thoughtforms will manifest in creating constant change, leaving us "uprooted" from the places where we've tried to put down a solid foundation for ourselves. Indeed, our spirits will hear our inner dialogue that tells them we have no right to be here, and will do everything they can to create the energy patterns inspired by that belief, which will keep us in a state of constantly trying, but not succeeding, in building a life for ourselves. Anodea Judith states, "If we are involved with constant change, we are like a rolling stone that gathers no moss. We're kept at a survival level because we are constantly building new foundations."[15] So, clearly, healing our core requires chasing the shadows that gave us this erroneous belief to begin with.

It can also be helpful to acknowledge ourselves with the affirmation "I belong to *me*," or simply "I belong." This can help us get to a place in our hearts that don Miguel Ruiz describes as the "Magical Kitchen,"[16] a personally fulfilling accomplishment to be sure, though we must work at it every day. And so it is also with our shadows.

THIRTEEN HARMONIES WORK—DANCE

Dance is associated with our core energies because it speaks to our deeper, more primal natures on a fundamental level. It resonates with our core energies because

---

15. Anodea Judith, *Wheels of Life* (Llewellyn, 1999), 72.

16. Don Miguel Ruiz, *The Mastery of Love* (Amber-Allen Publishing, 1999), 91.

the way we move to music, whether on a dance floor in a nightclub or in our own living rooms, is a direct expression of who we are as individuals, if our spirits are free enough to allow that action.

According to Bill Whitcomb, dance is one of the eight paths believed to lead "to the center," to help one make magic.[17] There are many different ways one can use dance to achieve a slightly altered state. From the wild, free-form type of dance typically done in bars and living rooms to the beat of rock music, to the more focused and concentrated trance-state dances that take place in a ritual circle, many forms of dance produce a feeling of well-being, which, when heightened, can lead to euphoria, ecstasy, and bliss.

Trance dancing is a common and more personal type of dancing done by the individual. At any Pagan drum circle or ritual gathering, one can find people swaying and twirling, bobbing and weaving, to the beat of the drums. As the drumbeat becomes more frenzied and energy rises on the air, it seems to feed the dancer's energy, bringing her to a trance state. She moves to the rhythms, and in her bliss, her energy rises also, and so feeds the drummers. Dancers and drummers alike build and build the energy—and as each "set" comes to its own peak, the energy is fired into the air like a rocket, drumming becomes more frenzied, people start whooping and whistling, and the dancers spin faster until the cone is released. Then, silence falls for a few seconds, and soon someone starts a simple beat, pulling the revelers into the rhythm again, and the pattern repeats until everyone is exhausted or until the venue closes for the evening.

One can do trance dancing alone at home, as well, and the music or drumbeat used can be anything the dancer enjoys. I recommend using music without lyrics for the best effect, as the words tend to pull one's focus into the songwriter's world instead of allowing the mind and spirit to open to their own wanderings and intentions. Just turn off the phones and lock the door so you won't be disturbed, put a tape or CD on the player, and let your body find its own way. You can also sing or chant while dancing, letting the words of the chant unravel into primal sounds, if you choose to. The object is to let your mind go blank, and to open yourself to the energy of the Divine. Sometimes, you will achieve a heightened state of bliss, ecstasy, and sometimes within

---

17. Bill Whitcomb, *The Magician's Companion: A Practical and Encyclopedic Guide to Magical and Religious Symbolism* (Llewellyn, 1993), 146.

that bliss, you will receive important messages. It's best to try to remember these messages, and taking a moment after dancing to write them down can be quite beneficial.

Group dances can produce a similar trance state. There are many types of dance used in group rituals, from spiral dances to grapevines, to simple "treading the circle" dances, which are more like lively walking. Spiral dances are most successful when led by an experienced leader, but prior practice can help immensely. The trick is to not let the spiral get too tight before turning and spiraling out again. Grapevine dances are easy, too, and are also lots of fun. For these, you want half of the circle's participants going deosil, and half of the participants going widdershins. Then, simply weave in and out, alternating paths. The Maypole dance is a classic example of a grapevine dance step.

TOOLS—DRUMS AND DRUMMING

Drumming also speaks to core energies, and to the root chakra. I've long thought of drums as the heartbeat of the Mother, and I think many others do as well. There's just something so earthy and vital in the sound, and the deep thrumming vibrates the air. When we hear the strong, steady beat of a drum, our bodies can't help but respond. We bob our heads, drum our fingertips, tap our feet. In shamanic practices, drumming is what takes the practitioner on his spiritual journeys, whether to long-forgotten or faraway places, or to commune with his power animal on another plane. Many folks would rather drum than dance at drum circles, as this is the energy that speaks to them, and trance states can be reached through drumming as well. For myself, I would always rather drum than dance, and I tend to become really spacey when I trance dance—I've fallen into more than one drummer sitting on the ground nearby. They don't appreciate that too much!

In working with our *power animals*, having a pre-recorded drumbeat CD is great; there are some really good ones on the market, but having a partner to drum the journey to your specifications (for example, more slowly or more softly) is ideal. With either mode, you can then go into your inner landscape, find your power animal, and receive much wise counsel on your life and your spiritual Path.

THE EIGHT VIRTUES OF THE GODDESS—STRENGTH

In *The Charge of the Goddess*, the Lady gives us eight virtues, and the second one listed is strength. This of course relates to our core, our survival, for without strength, we can't do much on this plane. For some folks, strength has to do with physicality: the strength to move, to walk, to maneuver a wheelchair, or to lift and carry things.

On a deeper level, the energy of strength speaks to the ability to stand up for oneself, to weather life's storms, and to rise to the challenges presented to us. In what ways are you strong? In which ways do you feel you need to become stronger? How does this affect your survival, your core? Take some time and contemplate the energy of strength in your own body, emotions, and spirit. Note any changes you would like to make, and take some time this moon discovering ways in which you can build your personal strength.

POSTURE OF POWER

If it works for you to do so, try sitting with your legs crossed and extend your energy down to the ground, sending your roots deep into bedrock. Hold this posture, pulling energy up from the earth and out in your Tree of Life, focusing intently on the connection your root chakra makes with the earth. Visualize the Mother filling you with strength at your core. Be blessed.

HOMEWORK

Make sure you do daily energy work of chakra spinning. From a grounded and centered state of consciousness, focus your attention on your root chakra as it spins, brilliant red, deep in your lower torso, near your perineum (between the anus and genitals). Breathe deeply and steadily, feel the power flowing through you, see your Tree of Life keeping you grounded, centered, and filled with energy… now look closely at your chakra as it spins. Is it spinning in a way that seems "normal" to you? That is to say, is it spinning smoothly, unencumbered, glowing brilliant red? Or is it "sticking" a bit, spinning slower than you think it should? Does it have "mud" or some other substance clinging to it? For myself, whenever a chakra is a little off, it always looks muddy—the colors aren't bright, and the spin is affected. If this happens, in your mind and spirit's eye visualize a smaller version of yourself standing next to it, cleaning the mud off, polishing the chakra to a shine. After your meditation, think about what may have caused your chakra to malfunction, and work to amend those energies.

As the moon cycles continue, you'll be reminded to do chakra spinning, focusing on one chakra at a time, and by the time you come to the twelfth moon, you will be able to tune in to all of them at once, along with the entire kundalini. Moving forward (in this course, and in your life thereafter), this will enable you to clear and heal your entire chakra system as needed. For now, however, just continue the practice with each chakra in turn as they occur throughout the lessons, noting especially the way the energy flows and pools, and whether there is "mud" clinging, what needs smoothing, and what needs healing.

In your daily practices during this moon cycle, take a few moments to do some earth evocations. In your mind and spirit's "eye," feel the cool, solid earth under your bare feet; feel the tender grasses with your hands (if you can actually go outside and do this physically, all the better!). Breathe in the scent of freshly turned earth, and deepen into the blackness of the Mysteries under the soil. Surround yourself with these energies, let them into your circle and into your consciousness; let them touch you. Breathe deeply and fully, focusing on your muscle and bones, as well as your root chakra and ability to feel grounded and centered with awareness.

Sometime this month, consider trying some sacred dance movements. Let your imagination guide you, and dance to the heartbeat of the earth. Use whatever music you like and let yourself fall into trance.

Examine your shadows around survival. Take some time to contemplate what still needs healing in terms of your core survival issues. Do you need to heal your money attitudes? Your physical health? Your issues around *your right to be here*? If you find there is something to heal, consider writing your Esbat this month for that healing. Is it more appropriate to do this work on the full moon? The dark moon? Perhaps the Crone's Sickle moon would be the best time—only you can decide. Remember that if you choose to do shadow work this moon cycle, you need to give yourself light to hold on to when you come out of the working. Corny as it may sound, counting your blessings is a good exercise after shadow work, as are positive affirmations relating to your core. Good ones to use are: I know who I am; I am strong; I am capable of taking care of myself; I am beloved of the gods, and am therefore sacred; I am healing.

Write a personal Esbat. Begin brainstorming for the upcoming full and dark moons, decide what needs to leave or come into your life, and begin planning an Esbat ritual, including when it's most appropriate to do the work. Consider moon energies: What sign is she in, if any? What phase? Consider solar energies: Where are you on the Wheel of the Year? What time of day or night will you do the work? What day of the week? Consider other energies as well, such as whether Mercury or other relevant planets are in retrograde, your personal schedule, as well as your personal vibrance level (how good do you feel?) and the energies of your household (will you be able to be alone and undisturbed?).

Moon-tides work and devotionals: Don't forget to take some time each evening (or day, depending on her phase) to get outside and look at (or contemplate the position of) the moon. Tune in to her energies; feel her power; let her love fill you. Remember to say your daily devotionals to your matron goddess(es) and patron god(s). Let their energies fill you; let them show you their love and truth as you express your love and truth to them.

Read the first 99 pages of Anodea Judith's Wheels of Life (up through chapter 2—"Chakra One: Earth"). Do some of the exercises presented if you like.

Take some time this moon to begin building an astral temple. In your meditations, focus this first moon cycle on finding the perfect power place and begin *laying the foundation.* Will it be wood, concrete, marble, or some other material? How big will it be? In what shape? Use the strength and the energy patterns you've been working with to help you create this space.

6: The Second Moon—Pride

Confidence that one is of value and significance
as a unique individual is one of the most precious
possessions which anyone can have.
—Anthony Storr

MOON TWO—THE STORY

You breathe deeply of the cool air of dawn's twilight. The world
is freshly washed; the rain only just ended an hour or so ago
after pouring all night, and the little glass bowl you set out is
nearly overflowing with rainwater. You will bottle and label
it later, to use for projects that need the blessing of newness,
and the bright push of waxing moon energy. You look up at the
starry sky, and try to sense the presence of the moon. She hasn't
risen quite yet, but you know she's on her way, as the new moon
rose with the sun a few days ago, so you know this slender cres-
cent will rise in another hour or two. Diana's Bow. You con-
template the energy. A drawn bow speaks to that still moment
of intense focus right before releasing energy toward a desired
goal. You, too, are ready to move toward an important goal,
and you, too, are in that place of central stillness, honing your
focus and taking a final breath just before acting. Just a few
small details to work out yet, and then you'll be ready to fire
the energy. Tonight will be the perfect time for your ritual. The

THE SECOND MOON CORRESPONDENCES

Keywords: confidence, individuation, personal growth, discernment, self-love, faith, trust

Energy: true pride; individuality

Chakra: base

Chakra color: orange

Element: water

Elemental color: blue or teal

Herbs and flowers: rose, damiana, tulip

Incense: Damascus rose, amber

Stones and metals: tiger-eye, copper

13 Harmonies: Great Rite

Tool: cauldron and staff

8 virtues: beauty

Astral temple work: walls

Shadow group: the Shadow of Shame

Energy keyword: sexuality

Energy group: source—self-love

moon is in the right sign for your purposes, and there is so much promise in the air you can feel it singing in your spirit, your heart, your entire body.

You think about how strong you've become in your walk on the Path of the Wise, and you realize you're much more confident now in many aspects of your life because of your spiritual work. You realize that true pride is the opposite of ego, and includes humility. Pride is about knowing your strengths **and** your weaknesses, honoring the strengths for what they are, and working diligently on the weaknesses. Everything feels so right, yet so new in this fresh and growing day. You open your arms in blessing and welcome to the Sun God, now fully visible in the sky, and to the Moon Goddess, whom you cannot yet see, but sense strongly as she moves upward toward the horizon, bringing the bright energy of change and will to the day, and to *your life. You raise your little bowl of water in salute, pour a small libation, and open your heart to the bright new day.*

THE ENERGY OF PRIDE

With this second moon, we move from our core—our deep, innermost self—to the face we show the world. What's the first thing we become aware of as babies? Mother, certainly, but we also begin to notice that we are separate from mother, so we begin developing our ego—our individual personality. We begin to differentiate where we leave off and "the world" begins. Pride, then, reflects that energy—that awareness of the self, the very basic energy of this second moon. Now, we're not talking about false pride, conceit, or arrogance here, but more about *healthy* pride: confidence in our individuality, our abilities, personal expressions, and sense of self. In this discussion of pride, we must consider several factors: self-love and self-esteem; individuality; self-reliance; growth; confidence; faith and trust in ourselves; and so of course, this is where we start thinking about and setting goals as well.

Remember the saying "Give thy word sparingly and adhere to it like iron." We do this because these actions program the mind to a deep level of self-trust. Do we keep our word just because it makes us look good? Just because it's the "right" thing to do? While keeping our word is certainly a Right Action, the most important reason we keep our word is that when we are performing spellwork and say the words "So mote it be," our spirit hears those words and responds based on what we know, on a deep level, of how reliable we are. It's as if our spirit says (if we are unreliable), "So mote it be? Well, okay… *maybe*." We need to know deep within our spirits that our word *means something*! If not, it's no surprise when our spells don't work.

As we start thinking about and understanding the energy patterns around who we are, we must also look at our desires. What do we want from life? What are our fondest hopes and wishes? This moon is also about sexuality, as connecting with and relating to others is part of this emergence from our core. Even if connection is not sought at this time, we are thinking about what kinds of connections we would like to have, what kinds of people we are drawn to, whether sexually or platonically. What are the spiritual energies surrounding these connections? Where do we want the relationship to go?

Most typically, in woman, nature's prominent energetic programming in terms of desire manifests as *receiving*, pulling that which we desire toward us. In man, the energy of desire manifests most often as *projecting*, and if it's a woman he wants, he projects his desire toward her. If she is untrained, she will often feel it acutely, as if it's her own desire. If she is trained in energy work, she can easily shield from his projections, if the projections are unwelcome. If they are welcome, that can be a wonderful thing if both parties are truly desirous of, and free to pursue, the attraction. However, this isn't always the case. Men who are untrained may not even be aware of the fact they are projecting.

As we become more proficient at using energy, it's often rather easy to create an energy pattern that pulls in (if you're a woman) or projects desire toward (if you're a man) the object of our desire, without ever doing spellwork to initiate that action, sometimes without even *thinking* about it! So shielding can become even more important for us to learn and become proficient at, not to *keep another's energy out* of our personal sphere this time, but more importantly, to *hold our own energy in*.

Our sexuality becomes important to explore with this second moon, as part of finding and expressing who we are has a great deal to do with how we relate to others we wish to be close to. And of course, our self-esteem is wrapped up in that energy pattern. How do we truly feel about ourselves? Our ability to attract? In Western culture, our self-esteem is often bound up with false images of youthful, airbrushed perfection we see in magazines and on TV. Any negative body image issues or other outer appearance issues must be healed before we can truly come into our power as Witches, and quite often, this must be done again and again. For this moon's Esbat, you may want to consider doing shadow work to begin that healing process.

We must love ourselves *passionately*! This is not about conceit, as that is just a backward manifestation of insecurity and nothing more, but about *honoring* ourselves, *respecting* ourselves enough to take good care of ourselves, and to know in our hearts that we have *real* choices, not just the cardboard-cutout choices our culture presents us with, which really aren't choices at all.

How effectively has our culture programmed us in terms of our relationship connections, both sexual and otherwise? Many folks don't really walk the "beaten path" of loving relationships (whatever *that* is!), but our schools and our childhood upbringing don't always teach us that we have options, such as loving someone of the same gender, or being involved romantically with more than one person concurrently (polyamory).[18] So when folks find themselves falling in love (or lust!) with "good friends," rather than questioning their programming, often they just think they're inherently bad and wrong for having those feelings. It can take time and real effort to heal from that "domestication," as don Miguel Ruiz[19] puts it. So I encourage you, dear Initiate, to examine very closely *all* the choices you've made in your life thus far. How many decisions were made based on what *someone else* defined your reality as? What would you like to change? What would you like to keep in place, based on personal preferences and choices?

This moon is the time when we start to look at all of our choices, our past relationships (and the shadows therein that need to be healed), and our outer projections, how we present ourselves to the world, as well as what we wish to find in terms of connection, relationship. What kinds of people would you choose to connect with, if you could have whatever you desired, and moreover, what would those connections look like? Feel like? How would these relationships feed you? You can have whatever you desire, you know; it's simply a matter of making the choice to spend the energy required to get there.

In this moon cycle, in terms of relationship, it's a good time to discuss the ethics around doing love and lust spells. This was covered at length in *Dedicant*,[20] but if you didn't read that book, you still should have some idea of those ethics by now, dear Initiate, as love spells and the subsequent cost to our karma is pretty basic Witchy knowledge. Remember it's never a good idea to do a love or lust spell on an actual person (better to pull someone to you based on qualities you desire in a mate, rather than affecting another's karma, as it will affect yours as well), unless that person is already a lover and *has given you permission* to do so. If you desire an intimate connection at this time in your life, or wish to spice up the relationship you currently have, you might consider doing love or lust magic for this cycle's Esbat work. If your partner is Pagan and willing, you might wish to try a Great Rite. Great Rites are excellent

---

18. *Polyamory* is a term coined by priestess Morning Glory Zell, and it means "many loves." Folks who identify as polyamorous choose to love romantically more than one person concurrently. For more information on polyamory, see Raven Kaldera's *Pagan Polyamory: Becoming a Tribe of Hearts* (Llewellyn, 2005), or Dr. Deborah Anopol's *Polyamory: The New Love Without Limits; Secrets of Sustainable Intimate Relationships* (IntiNet Resource Center, 1997).

19. Don Miguel Ruiz, *The Four Agreements* (Amber-Allen Publishing, 1997).

20. *Dedicant: A Witch's Circle of Fire* (Llewellyn Publications, 2008), April lesson.

for many types of spellwork, especially for enhancing and deepening a relationship, encouraging a deep and solid bond that cannot be broken through ordinary means.

THE BASE CHAKRA

The base chakra is located in the lower abdomen, between the navel and the genitals. Its color is orange. The Sanskrit name for this chakra is *svadhisthana*, and its element is water. Those who have a lack of base chakra energy may feel they have trouble flowing with the changes of life, may feel they don't have a right to express themselves, especially sexually. Those with a "different" sexual style from the social norms may feel a bit outcast, and may need to spend time making peace with their sexuality in order to stand strong, to take pride in their differences, and to move forward in a healthy manner. Judith puts forth the idea that, while the first chakra is about stillness, holding on, and belonging, the second chakra is about pushing forth, letting go, and finding our individuality. In a culture that advocates a mindset of "honor diversity, but not *too much* diversity," this can be sometimes be rather difficult. However, we can remember that the Pagan community is much more accepting and capable of honoring others' differences than the vast majority of Western culture, so even those with very different life/love styles can find love and acceptance here.

THE PRICE OF OUR TABOOS—THE ENERGY OF PLEASURE

The energy of pride and individuality is also about the energy of pleasure of all kinds. In Western culture, allowing ourselves to experience pleasure without guilt can be a real challenge. Anodea Judith puts it well: "Unfortunately," she states, "we are taught to beware of pleasure, that it's a dangerous temptress waiting to lure us away from our true path."[21] This brings about and perpetuates the split between mind and spirit.

The mind/spirit schism is illustrated clearly in many New Age and even Pagan and Wiccan texts. In the extremely hetero-biased *Twin Souls,* Patricia Joudry and Maurie Pressman write of the bliss one achieves when one meets and unites with one's spiritual twin, when sex is no longer "necessary," and the relationship seems to somehow "transcend" the "lower" forms of connection (i.e., sexuality), thereby becoming "higher" and "better" than a relationship where all aspects of loving are allowed:

---

21. Anodea Judith, *Wheels of Life* (Llewellyn, 1999), 119.

"… [I]n their meetings they refrained from sexual relations, intuitively sensing that the body would be an encumbrance. The truth was they had progressed beyond the physical in their expressions of love. They now knew that what people yearn for in the joining of the flesh is the complete reunion that is possible only to spirit bodies."[22] *Progressed beyond the physical? Complete reunion is only possible to spirit bodies?* Excuse me?

We hear this quite often in New Age thought, that the pleasures of sex are somehow "beneath us" (some even say "no better than animals" but we are, indeed, animals!); that if we are to pursue our Path as spiritual beings, we must "transcend" our sexuality. This is neither correct nor healthy. Just as Judith cautions against folks staying focused on only the upper chakras, we must be mindful that sexuality is completely healthy and neither "below" nor "less than" spirituality. Indeed, a great majority of Wiccans agree that healthy sexuality is *a part of*, and not *apart from*, spirit. However, one often still finds Pagan and Wiccan authors and leaders patently dismissing any form of sexuality they personally don't resonate with, assuming all Pagans are carbon cutouts of themselves.

Lira Silbury, in her book *The Sacred Marriage*, talks about language and how certain words for body parts or sexual acts "make us feel ugly and ashamed" and serve to "cheapen" the act of love, suggesting we replace these words with ones she personally finds more palatable, such as "lance and grail,"[23] inferring that those who use different or more common words are not as "enlightened" or as healthy as those who use her suggested words. The popular "High Sex" author Margo Anand makes these same assumptions regarding the language we use for sex, implying that we've been using the *wrong* words if we're not using her preferred words and terms "Vajra," "thunderbolt," "scepter of power," and the like for the penis, and "Yoni," "Valley of Joy," "Enchanted Garden,"[24] and the like for the vulva. The "crude" and "derogatory" names that are common to our culture, she states, "diminish the possibility that anyone could find spiritual expansion and ecstasy through [them]." This assumption that "everyone" is offended and unhappy with any particular words for genitals (specifically, the ones *she* doesn't like), coupled with the suggestion that we create names

---

22. Patricia Joudry and Maurie Pressman, *Twin Souls* (Hazelden, 2000).

23. Lira Silbury, *The Sacred Marriage: Honoring the God and Goddess within Each Other* (Llewellyn, 1995).

24. Margo Anand, *The Art of Sexual Ecstasy: The Path of Sacred Sexuality for Western Lovers.* (Tarcher, 1989), 215.

for them that carry a "happy, positive meaning," negates and invalidates those who do like and use certain words and phrases, and excludes even more folks from her extremely narrow audience of rich, young, athletic people who are deeply unhappy with their sex lives. "High Sex," indeed. This may be very satisfying for some folks, but what about Dark Sex? What about the folks who simply wish to learn about Tantra without all the judgments and reprimands attached?

Jamake Highwater, in *Myth and Sexuality*, rails against Augustine's belief that humankind has sacrificed immortality and spiritual bliss for the pleasures of sex, stating that this belief implies human lust was born with Adam and Eve's expulsion from the Garden of Eden. "If sex existed before the expulsion," Highwater writes in reference to Augustine, "it had existed innocently and without appetite."[25] Well, that certainly sounds appealing, now doesn't it? We must remember, dear Initiate, that human sexuality runs a vast, deep, and wide spectrum, and that there are folks who would be uncomfortable at best, with referring to their lover's genitals as a "valley of joy" or "scepter of power." I submit many of us would find such words and phrases utterly laughable, if not a downright turnoff. In addition, there are many, many Pagans who walk the BDSM road who may very well find such words and concepts diminishing and offensive, so it's important that we honor diversity by accepting *all* avenues in human sexuality (including those who choose celibacy, by the way), and take care not to judge others, nor to let the judgments of others inhibit *our* choices. Otherwise, how will we ever accept the more unusual aspects of our own sexuality, much less ever truly find them? The Goddess in *The Charge* says, "All acts of love and pleasure are my rituals." The important thing to remember, then, is to base our practices on *true choice*, for the highest pleasure and dignity of all concerned.

On the flip side, we have Pagan and Wiccan community leaders and authors who insist that the only way to true enlightenment (or the only way one can be initiated to the upper degrees of their Witchy school) is to have sex with the High Priest or High Priestess. This is absolutely unacceptable, manipulative, and a blatant abuse of power. I would caution anyone against getting involved with such a group, as they clearly are not there to teach you; they are there to exploit you. In many traditional systems, a Great Rite is required for the attainment of Master (in traditional systems, the third degree), but any ethical and responsible Craft teacher will tell you that a symbolic

---

25. Jamake Highwater, *Myth and Sexuality* (Plume, 1990), 23.

Great Rite is just as acceptable and powerful for one's third-degree ROP as an actual one.

The truth is that sex and sexuality, sensuality, and pleasure are gifts given to us by our gods, which we in turn give as gifts to the partner(s) of our choosing. Sexuality is an extremely strong drive, second only to hunger in our survival mechanisms. Relating to and connecting with other human beings is something most humans crave, and often our desire for such connections forms a great deal of our individuality: how we dress, how we communicate, the choices we make regarding personal habits, hobbies, where and how we socialize, and again, even, and perhaps most importantly, our spirituality is connected to this energy pattern as well. Many of us seek those of like mind to form romantic, as well as deeper platonic, relationships with, and a great number of Pagans and Wiccans hold sexuality sacred. To deny what we truly are in this regard is what diminishes and cheapens the sacredness of our sexuality, not whether or not we have sexual relations (or "transcend" the urge), what words we use, or whether we have "appetite." Certainly some of these things come into play in assessing *compatibility* with a potential partner(s), but these things do not make us "bad" or "wrong"; they make us *individuals*. So finding and pursuing partners with similar tastes and drives is essential to our well-being and personal power. If we have chosen a partner with tastes and needs extremely counter to our own, it can (and often will) only serve to keep us in the shadow of our individuation, never coming to balance or peace.

THIRTEEN HARMONIES WORK—THE GREAT RITE

The Great Rite is a wonderful way to build a deep bond with another human being (or human beings, if you're polyamorous). And of course, you can also choose to use the energy for other ends. To prepare for this incredibly sacred work, first you may wish to choose to build the energy through increased arousal over a specified period of time. To do this, you will want to allow yourself to get to the threshold point just prior to orgasm, and then stop or slow stimulation until the urge toward orgasm decreases slightly, then begin stimulation again, until orgasm is imminent, and back off again, effectively holding the energy at the edge of the fire. Teasing, in other words, but with a clear intent and deep focus. Key words or phrases to let your partner(s) know when to back off stimulation help considerably. For my most ardent Great Rite partner and me, the phrases "Oh, my Lord!" and "Oh, my Lady!" given as warning, worked very well. You may wish to use these phrases or find your own—whatever's most comfortable and natural for you and your partner(s) is best.

If you wish to build the sexual energy in this way, I recommend a span of no more than a few days at first, working your way up to longer periods of time as you become more experienced with this work. Men, especially, should take care not to build the energy for prolonged periods of time until they're more experienced; my partner and I decided to build the energy for ten days for what was only our second Great Rite, and for hours after the ritual, he had painful spasms in his penis. So take care: building up stamina for these rites by gradually increasing the energy-building time period will help prevent such things from happening.

Some schools of thought dictate that a Great Rite is only possible when one is invoked. I think these types of Great Rites are wonderful, but do not agree that invocation is the single determining factor in what makes a Great Rite genuine. For those who have never practiced invocation, a Great Rite can still be extremely powerful and successful act in and of itself. I have done many of them, only a small handful while invoked.

To set up for this sacred work, you will want to prepare the space first by cleaning it thoroughly, then decorating it with those things you find romantic and sexy. Tulips are sacred to Aphrodite, as are roses. Check Cunningham for other herbs and flowers you can use to honor your personal deities with. Good incenses are rose, patchouli, and you can even add a sprinkle of mugwort (increases intuition, which will help you to really rev up your partner!). A favorite of mine is to mix equal parts of the resin incenses Ebony Nights and Damascus Rose. I call the scent "Ebony Rose," and I feel it sings to the darkness of the Mystery on the wings of romantic love, which is perfect for setting the mood for the intense and passionate work of a Great Rite. Candles around the room are a nice touch, in all the colors you personally associate with love, romance, and lust.

One powerful addition to this work is the use of symbols around the room that speak to your purpose for the rite. For one very special Great Rite a partner and I did years ago that was designed to deepen our bond with each other, I used certain runes, drawn in a series that had the runes gradually changing shape and blending together to form other runes and bindrunes. I taped them to the walls around the bed where we'd both be able to see them while we made love.

Another powerful action you can add to the rite is a pointed and specific chant. You can even practice the chant during the energy-building phase in the days prior, so that when it's time for the ritual, you'll have it memorized, which greatly helps your concentration in the moment. The following is a simple yet powerful and effective Great Rite chant, designed to build and deepen the bond between two partners. Looking deeply into each other's eyes while making love, each partner says one set of words:

A: Two minds

B: One truth

A: Two passions

B: One will

A: Two hearts

B: One love

A: Two bodies

B: One goal

Repeat this first part until high sexual energy is reached. As you ride the wave to and through the threshold before orgasm, the chant then changes, and both partners say the words together:

Two spirits

One light

One source

One dream

We open

We deepen

We bond

This part is repeated until orgasm is imminent, and then, as you ride the waves of orgasm:
We are one, we are one, we are one!

Of course, if the energy raised is to be used for a specified magical end, you would choose different words at the end ("I am/You are healed!" "We prosper!" "Our garden thrives!" for example).

TOOLS—THE CAULDRON AND STAFF

Just like the chalice and athame together, the cauldron and staff (or sword) can be used together for a symbolic Great Rite, though items that big would be more likely to be used in a larger public rite, or at least an outdoor setting. However, the symbolism is the same. One action you could take with these in your Great Rite would be to place them near each other prior to the rite, and then place the staff into the cauldron as the ritual begins, or at another specified time in the rite.

THE EIGHT VIRTUES OF THE GODDESS—BEAUTY

As we look at the energy of pride, beauty, or our perception of our own beauty, comes to the forefront. In a culture obsessed with youth, where near-anorexia is seen as an ideal, and beauty magazines abound with pictures of airbrushed-perfect models interspersed with ads that alternate between rich desserts and diet products, it's no wonder so many women are both unable to view themselves as beautiful and are completely confused about what is and is not right for them personally. I remember reading a man's comments on a lifestyle discussion board a few years back, where he stated that he liked women of all shapes and sizes, but that he wouldn't consider dating any woman who was not comfortable in her own skin. The women on that discussion thread wasted no time in letting him know that he would have to choose his dates from a very, very small pool. It's sad but true that the vast majority of women in our culture are never satisfied with their appearance. And it's no wonder; we are told practically from birth that we are not good enough as we are. We must have the right clothes; we must wear makeup so thick that it hides our real skin (real skin, is, well, real, and therefore flawed); we mustn't be too thin or too thick; we must always smile; and ohmyGods, what's up with that hair? The hair must be perfect too, of course. We must have the right-sized breasts, and if they're too big or too small, they must be surgically altered along with our noses, eyes, and lips. Finally, we have the lie that some put forth, like the gentleman referred to above, that "confidence is the sexiest thing a woman can wear." Some of the most confident, beautiful, and voluptuous larger women I've ever seen are rejected repeatedly by men (and women!) in favor of the waifs, and some of the most equally confident, willowy, model-perfect women I've seen are lonely as can be, because so many folks think they're "not good enough" to approach them.

Men don't have it a whole lot better. Although you don't really see six-year-old boys on extreme diets like you do six-year-old girls these days, plenty of men are now obsessed with perceived imperfections with their bodies, hair (or lack thereof), and clothing too.

But what is true beauty? Are there people you know who are beautiful by Western society's standards who simply repulse you? Conversely, are there people you consider quite beautiful though they don't necessarily follow our culture's model? What about yourself? When you look in the mirror, what do you see?

The bottom line is that appreciation of one's true beauty can only come from within. An expression we're hearing a lot these days is "Change the way you see, not the way you look." What do *you* consider beautiful? Sexy? Try to ignore your culture's narrow parameters for a few moments and think about the folks *you're* attracted to. What do they look like? How do they act? What is their personality like? How does their energy feel to you? Now, using that same measuring stick, take a look at yourself. I'll bet you'll be surprised at how much more attractive you'll look and feel to yourself. One thing that helped me a lot was to look at some good pictures of myself while remembering consciously that same measuring stick. Don Miguel Ruiz, in his book *The Mastery of Love*, states, "If others see you and judge you beautiful or not, if you are aware of your own beauty and accept your own beauty, their opinion doesn't affect you at all." Later, he also states, "The only difference between the beauty of one person and the beauty of another is the concept of beauty that people have."[26] This is the healthy place we need to get to. Then, if there are things you genuinely don't love about your looks, based on *your* standards and no one else's, perhaps you can work on ways to change or improve those things. Take some time this moon cycle and think about beauty, and if spiritual work is needed to heal your perception, your looks, or your attitudes, plan that for your next Esbat.

---

26. Don Miguel Ruiz, *The Mastery of Love* (Amber-Allen Publishing, 1999), 150–51.

POSTURE OF POWER

If it works for you to do so, begin by standing up, grounding and centering yourself, and then straighten your posture, and allow yourself to relax into the stance. Pull your shoulders back, tilt your chin up, let your smile spread slowly across your face. Allow yourself a few minutes to focus on all of your good qualities, and notice how your posture straightens and relaxes as you do so. Remember that whenever you lack confidence you can adopt this posture, wherever you are or whatever you're doing, and the energy will fill you with confidence. If it's tough to muster, try saying these words, either out loud or in your head: "I was made by the gods, and am therefore perfect as I am. I can change or remain the same, and still be beautiful and wonderful, for I am still myself, and I shine."

HOMEWORK

Make sure you do daily energy work of chakra spinning as outlined in the homework section in the first-moon chapter of this unit. The base chakra is a bright orange, and is located just above the genitals.

In your daily practices during this moon cycle, take a few moments to do some water evocations. In your mind and spirit's "eye," feel the ebb and flow of water all around you, and focus on flowing with the tides of your life, your individuality, your sexuality (if you can actually go into a lake or other body of natural water and do this physically, all the better—even a pool or bathtub can work well with this one!). Surround yourself with these energies, let them into your circle and into your consciousness; let them touch you. Breathe deeply and fully, focusing on flowing with the desires of your life without judgment, and know that you are cleansing and healing your sexuality and attitudes about yourself, as well as your bodily fluids with the water, as well as your base chakra and ability to feel desire and confidence.

Consider performing a Great Rite. You can do this symbolically, too, either simply, with a chalice and blade, staff and cauldron, or a bit more complex, such as planting a tree or other earth-enhancing action, or do an actual Great Rite either with yourself or with a partner or partners. You can also write a Great Rite ritual to be performed later.

Shadow work: Examine your shadows around pride. Take some time to contemplate what still needs healing in terms of your self-esteem pride, honor, and sexuality.

Do you need to heal your attitude about attractiveness and attraction? Your individuality? Your issues around your desires in connecting with others? If you find there is something to heal, consider writing your Esbat this month for that healing. Which moon would be most appropriate for this work? Remember that if you choose to do shadow work this moon cycle, you need to give yourself light to hold on to when you come out of the working; count your blessings and use positive affirmations to keep yourself uplifted. Good ones to use are: I honor myself; It's okay to be who I am; I am beautiful/handsome; I am wise and strong; I am beloved of the gods, and am therefore sacred; I am healing.

Write a personal Esbat. Begin brainstorming for the upcoming full and dark moons, decide what needs to leave or come into your life, and begin planning an Esbat ritual, including when it's most appropriate to do the work. Consider moon energies: What sign is she in, if any? What phase? Consider solar energies: Where are you on the Wheel of the Year? What time of day or night will you do the work? What day of the week? Consider other energies as well, such as whether Mercury or other relevant planets are in retrograde, your personal schedule, as well as your personal vibrance level (how good do you feel?) and the energies of your household (will you be able to be alone and undisturbed?).

Moon-tides work and devotionals: Don't forget to take some time each evening to get outside and look at (or contemplate the position of) the moon. Tune in to her energies; feel her power fill you. Remember to say your daily devotionals to your matron goddess(es) and patron god(s). Let their love fill you, let them show you your personal truth.

Read Anodea Judith's *Wheels of Life*, chapter 3—"Chakra Two: Water." Do some of the exercises presented if you like.

Take some time this moon to continue work on your astral temple. In your meditations, focus now on building the walls, from your foundation up, for your temple. What are your boundaries? What kinds of energy will you strive to hold in? To keep out? Make some decisions about where the rooms will be, the windows and doors, as well as what the walls will be made of. Will they be wood, or stone, or some other material? Use the energy patterns you've been working with to help you create this space.

7: The Third Moon—Power

*If Nature behaved like man behaves, gangs of elephants
would have trampled every other ground-dwelling species on
three continents (probably starting with us), and prides
of lions would have eaten their way through every living thing
in Africa... and then promptly starved to death. Clearly, the
ability to kill shit just because you can does not define
"strength" under Nature's way.*[27]
—Phil Brucato

MOON THREE—THE STORY

*As you make your way home in the dusk of a weekday evening,
she calls to you. High up in the sky, she shines down, her slender
figure filled out considerably from a week ago, when she was
new, and you can feel her insistent pull, compelling you to your
altar. You had other, yet tentative plans for the evening, but as
you reach your door and turn to face her, you know: everything
must now take a back seat to this work.*

*Your space prepared, you cast your circle slowly, meticu-
lously, for you're not sure exactly why you're here, you just
know that she insists upon your presence, demands that
you... stand. You're not sure yet what that means, but you
know it is required; as the words keep running through your*

---

27. Phil Brucato, "Essay: Thoughts About Being a Man." Portland, OR: April 2010.

THE THIRD MOON CORRESPONDENCES

Keywords: personal responsibility, self-mastery

Energy: power

Chakra: solar plexus

Chakra color: yellow

Element: fire

Elemental color: red, orange

Herbs and flowers: cinnamon, ginger, yarrow

Incense: frankincense, dragon's blood

Stones and metals: diamond, gold

13 Harmonies: rituals

Tool: sword

8 virtues: power

Astral temple work: fortifications and protections

Shadow group: the Shadow of Shame

Energy keyword: strength

Energy group: source—self-power

head, you can **feel** them, strong and insistent it in your gut. "I must stand," you whisper, and then, "Yes, my Lady," acknowledging the wishes of both your matron goddess and yourself. As you connect the end to the beginning of your circle, it hits you: she desires this connection as much as you do, desires you to understand fully your own power. You sweep your blade to encompass that which is above, that which is below, and the sphere that is your magical space is complete. You call the quarters and prepare to call your deities, to ask them to protect, to deepen, to loan energies for . . . you know not what, when you realize your most cherished deities are already there. You light the candles you prepared for them, whispering words of welcome, and open yourself to the energy.

Power. Crackling, vital, perpetually in motion, the energy fills you as you breathe deeply, grounding and centering yourself. You whisper words of love and devotion, thanking your god for his protection and guidance, thanking your goddess for all the gifts she's brought into your life: the joys and challenges, the pleasure and the pain, for you know that even the most difficult lessons are just that—**lessons**. And learning is always positive no matter how difficult it may have been. To "stand," then, as the Goddess puts it, is to take responsibility for all of your actions, to step up to the task of acting as clergy for those who need you, to humbly, yet honorably, acknowledge how very important and vital you really are. With this knowledge you also realize you can never again simply wallow in self-pity, totally avoiding your problems, but that, once you've dusted yourself off, as it were, you must face life's challenges head on, with the courage and power within which you most certainly possess; for to **be** an Initiate, a priest/ess of the Old Gods, **is** to stand, to take responsibility, to truly own your power.

You are guided to pick up the water vessel from your altar, which is filled with salt water from your purifications... you begin sprinkling the sacred water over yourself, cleansing your hands and feet, and then dip your fingers into the vessel again, spreading drops over your chakras. Finally, you sip from the chalice, letting the salt water's energies permeate your being from within.

You then take up the censer and waft the sweet smoke over the same places on your body, charging yourself with this new knowledge and the personal responsibility it brings. You sniff the smoke in small sips, filling yourself with the energy of fire and air. Finally, you dot each place with anointing oil and open yourself to What Will Be.

You can feel your chosen deity so acutely that your whole body buzzes with the energy. You hear your sacred name whispered in your ear, followed by the words, "We are one." You try not to think, but just to feel the words and the electric touch of this deity. Your skin tingles with the energy and power, and your heart races in anticipation. You will yourself to stay calm.

"We are one," you repeat, and at that moment, you know it to be true. You and this deity have chosen each other for a reason. You review in your mind all the things you admire about him (or her), all the ways in which you have aspired to be the same, and realize that the work you've been doing has paid off: the two of you are more alike than you ever thought you would be: more, even, than you dared hope you could be. You begin saying a devotional prayer, and find your emotions have escalated, your words fervent, impassioned; you are so filled with love that it makes you weep. Suddenly, you feel the energy of powerful loving arms around you, and you realize many of the things you have said to this deity in devotion and *love tonight you are also saying to yourself. You say it again, as you realize how very much alike you really are: "We are one, we are ONE!"*

There's not a hair's breadth of difference between you. Your will is totally in accord with your deity, who whispers words of love and devotion to you, and you are amazed! Then, you are given a charge—a sacred duty, a task. You know you will fulfill this request, for it will heal you and add to your power just as much as it will please and serve your chosen deity to do so.

With that acknowledgment, the energy begins to smooth out and dissipate. You reach out a hand, touching the beloved memory of his or her fingers as the energy gently departs. You find you feel energized, exhilarated, and filled with purpose. You pause a moment, lingering in the warm glow of the energy, and then begin the sacred work you now know you must do…

THE ENERGY OF POWER

As a Dedicant, you began to learn to use your will, which of course is all about power. As an Initiate, you are learning and developing the *courage to dare*, which of course is all about power, too, but with a different focus. You already have the skills required to work your will, so now you're honing those skills, and using them to brave the darkness, both without and within. This is why shadow work as an Initiate is so important; healing our shadows will not only stop our energy from draining away, but will help to turn the energy around so it feeds us instead.

Raven Digitalis, an expert on working with the shadow, says, "To recognize and actively work with the deepest and most imbalanced aspects of our consciousness is to constructively dance with the shadow. It lets us truly act on the ancient edict: 'Know thyself.'"[28] If any keywords could be given for this entire book, those would be the ones, for to truly know oneself is extremely powerful; and that power is, to a great degree, what gives us that vital *courage to dare*, dear Initiate, so work this course as you will, but be ever mindful that the more you put into it, the more power you will build!

I'm sure you well remember Ruiz writing, in *The Four Agreements,* of personal importance as a way we diminish our personal power. "Personal importance," he states, "or taking things personally, is the maximum expression of selfishness because

---

28. Raven Digitalis, *Shadow Magick Compendium* (Llewellyn, 2008), 34.

we make the assumption that everything is about 'me.'"[29] These two concepts are not as contradictory as they sound. Self-importance is all about insecurity; not believing in ourselves and our own worth, we constantly need validation from the outside, and our self-esteem becomes flotsam in a river, always buffeted around by the opinions and actions of others, which robs us of true personal power. Looking again at the ancient edict "Know thyself," we must acknowledge that this is the path to true personal power. Once we chase down and come to understand our darkest shadows, we become equipped with keys to heal them, which pulls us out of the mire of insecurity and into a healthy self-esteem. And, as Ruiz teaches throughout his work, once the cultural spell of this need for validation is broken, we can heal that shadow and stand strong in who we truly are. This takes time and buckets of patience; don't kick yourself if you can't make this happen overnight.

For myself, the path to true self-love and acceptance wasn't easy; I was fully domesticated by my culture and even, to some extent, my chosen subcultures (the queer and Pagan communities), and of course I've still got issues I'm working on, as all humans do. But as I look back, I can laugh at myself; in those early years, it was almost as though I was broadcasting the message "I am committed to being 100 percent myself, and if people don't like it, they are just going to have to deal with it! Is that okay?" It took me a long time to lose the qualifying question at the end.

The New Age movement has given us an interesting little buzzword in recent years, and I've written and spoken many times about what I call "the myth of 'empowerment.'" This word, from the first time I ever heard it, has always made me a bit twitchy. I never knew why, however, until I looked a little more closely at the breakdown of the word. This word, obviously created by a culture that fears true power, is often referred to as "female" power, which at once disrespects women in a "separate yet equal" excuse, and dilutes her power in a big way. If we take the word apart, the prefix *em-* means "to place into or upon," and the suffix *-ment* means "the means of or state of being." In creative writing courses, we are taught that both prefixes and suffixes "weaken" words. So *empowerment*, in my perception, means "to place (weakened) power upon," which in itself is a power-stripping procedure, because it implies that we become powerful (but not seriously powerful) *only through and by the permission or actions of another*! When used in the context of "female power," it is most assuredly another way our culture

---

29. Don Miguel Ruiz, *The Four Agreements* (Amber Allen Publishing, 1997), 48.

both condescends to women and keeps them "in their place." That is *not* power! So the only time we are truly "empowered" is when we have *given ourselves permission* to own our power, which makes us *more powerful*, and not in need of "being empowered" by another.

In America certainly, but even in our little Pagan subculture, it is still looked at as being somewhat unsavory for people (and women especially) to admit a desire for power of any kind, and if we don't use qualifiers, we usually get the fish-eye. How many of us have said, "Sure, I want power," and then quickly qualified our statement by adding, "But not *anyone else's* power." To get a real picture of that kind of statement, imagine its equivalent said at a banquet (because food is a form of energy, and energy, power, is abundant in the universe, so life is a banquet, right?). Okay. The table is laden with food, there are bowls and dishes of every kind, and there are eight people sitting at the table with you. You've had, say, a salad. Your first course. Now, you want to really sink your teeth into something, some lovely grainy bread, perhaps. You're good and hungry, and your mouth is watering. You say, "I want some more food, but not anyone else's food." Chances are, the people at your table will look at you like your porch light just went out.

Women qualify their power statements, almost every time. We don't generally hear men doing this, but we do it constantly, and it limits us. We need to give ourselves permission to want power. (As you read this, are you saying, "Yes, but"? It's pretty uncomfortable to say it, at first. Our culture has done a great job of domesticating us.) A good exercise to do is to say the statement "I intend to become more powerful" without qualifying it. Keep practicing until you can say it without cringing. Then try something scarier: Say, "I am becoming more powerful." Not so easy? All the more reason to say it. Finally, I challenge you to strip all the power-robbing modifiers out of your discourse, come into the present moment with your words, and simply say, "I am *powerful!*" And now, say it again. Loudly. And again, even louder! Good.

There is nothing whatsoever wrong with wanting to become more powerful. In the last two moon chapters, we talked about self-care, honoring and respecting ourselves enough to make sure our survival needs are met. We expanded and built upon that energy by then examining and doing work to understand our need for connection with others, how we present ourselves, and what our deepest desires were made of. Now, we can pull that energy up into our solar plexus, our power center, and begin to work our will for the betterment of our lives and the lives of those we love. This builds power.

However, we must first take care to examine how power is blocked from us, as well as how we block our own power from manifesting itself. Again, I ask you, dear Initiate, to take a look within. Ruiz speaks of domestication, the ways in which we are trained by our culture, the agreements we've made without even thinking about them. It's so easy to just go along, oblivious to the "choices" we are (or are not) presented with: Should I, a woman, go on the carbohydrate-restricting diet that allows me to eat roots but no beans, or the one that allows me to eat beans but no roots? To break my domestication, I might ask myself why I have to accept my culture's insistence that I conform to an impossible ideal of thinness in the first place. A man is presented with the "choice" of marrying the woman he loves or continuing with the other woman he loves. To break his domestication, he might ask himself why he can't continue his relationship with both of them, even forming a bond, such as a hand-fasting, with both of them, effectively marrying them both. In order to break your domesticated patterns, I challenge you, dear Initiate, to question *everything*. Ever hear the baked ham story?

A woman is preparing a whole ham for a holiday meal. Her husband is in the kitchen with her, and he notices she's sliced both of the rounded ends off the ham before placing it in the baking dish. He asks her why she did this, and she replies, "I don't know. My mother always did it this way." They go back to their tasks, not giving the issue any more thought. Later, after the guests are all gone and the dishes are done, her curiosity gets the better of her, so she calls her mother and asks.

"I don't know," her mother replies, "My mother always did it that way." Unable to stifle her curiosity, she then calls her grandmother.

"Grandma," she asks, "I was wondering why you always slice the rounded ends off the ham before you bake it. "

Grandma's reply was classic: "Well, honey, that's the only way it will fit in my baking dish."

This illustrates clearly that we humans do so many things in life simply because we are taught that this is the way it's "supposed to" be done. Why? Again, dear Initiate, I encourage you to question *everything*! Take a look at all of your attitudes and habits, your judgments of others as well as (and most especially!) your attitudes and judgments of yourself. Take a long, hard look at why you think and do the things you do, and make a choice to *live consciously*.

THE SHADOW OF SHAME

The first three moons cover *source* energies—the energies that affect us at the deepest level. We've covered the energy of survival and symbiosis, of individuation and desire, and with this moon, of power and all its inherent possibilities and blocks. Now is the time to really examine where our energy has leaked out, been given away or stripped away by relationship, domestication, our own fears, or something else entirely. There are many techniques one can use, such as the exercises that have been given thus far in this book.

Shame is taught to us all from a very early age. When we did things as children that could possibly have been harmful to us, such as running out into the street, our parents disciplined us, typically with an energy of fear and alarm, as they know how easily a car could have come around the corner and snuffed out our little lives. Shame-based discipline energy, however, has a much different flavor. Usually, it has to do with a parent's (or school teacher's, or other authority figure's) *embarrassment*. We are caught masturbating, or we put on clothes that don't match, or we pick our little noses in public. Perhaps we're singing too loudly, eating too much or too enthusiastically, or in some other way are caught acting "too much like a kid." As we grow older, our peers jump on the bandwagon to help shame us, and we learn to participate in shaming others as well. Most of it is about appearances. What would people think? How would it look? So and so has pimples, or has gained weight, or is wearing the "wrong" clothes. As we grow into adulthood, with all of this social programming, we become experts at shaming ourselves. We berate ourselves constantly over such trifles! This zaps our power and energy in a big way. In order to clear and heal these shadows, we must first examine them fully, question everything, and ask ourselves *why*. Why do we feel a need to conform to agreements and energy patterns we never subscribed to in the first place? Now is the time to look at those shadows and cast them to the outer darkness! Through this action, we can begin to come into our true power.

Sandra Ingerman, in her book *Soul Retrieval*,[30] gives the technique of having a shaman go in search of the pieces of soul that have been lost to us through trauma or pain. She cautions that only a shaman who has been trained in soul retrieval techniques do this for you. This is certainly valid, as this is not a process to be taken lightly, but I personally think a Wiccan who is trained in energy work can successfully use these techniques, as I have personally chased my own soul fragments in this way with great success. It's not an easy thing to do, but with courage and determination, I believe it can be done by a highly trained priest or priestess, which you, dear Initiate, most certainly are becoming. If you do decide to chase your shame shadows in this way, I highly recommend reading her book first, to get a good idea of the technique involved, and then create your own process, using some or all of her methods.

Ruiz, in *The Four Agreements*, talks about stalking and waging war against the parasite of fear and doubt by either refusing to feed it anymore, or by creating *the dream of the second attention* by taking an inventory—writing down all your agreements and replacing them with new, healthier agreements.[31] This can be done as affirmations. I have also used this technique with a great deal of success, starting decades ago when I first read Louise Hay's *You Can Heal Your Life*,[32] and again when I read Ruiz's work. As I've said many times, his book changed my life.

Raven Digitalis, in his book *Shadow Magick Compendium*, gives yet another technique, that of a ritual designed to purge negative shadows within by first focusing on what they are, then allowing your consciousness to summon or draw a spirit energy (the Grim Reaper) toward you to shatter those shadows, leaving you free and unencumbered.[33]

All of these authors have great ideas for chasing inner shadows and healing our spirits. The thing to remember is that, number one—chasing shadows is not work that can be done once and then simply forgotten. As you heal from your shadows, they will reach up out of the abyss, grab your ankles, and try to pull you down into the mire again. Especially if those shame energies are thoroughly ingrained, which, in our sadly unhealthy Western culture, they most certainly are. Like killing bindweed

30. Sandra Ingerman, *Soul Retrieval: Mending the Fragmented Self* (HarperSanFrancisco, 1991).

31. Don Miguel Ruiz, *The Four Agreements* (Amber-Allen Publishing, 1997), 106.

32. Louise Hay, *You Can Heal Your Life* (Hay House, 1985).

33. Raven Digitalis, *Shadow Magick Compendium* (Llewellyn, 2008), 35.

in a garden, it will take several attempts, vigilantly clearing those weeds from the soil in your inner landscape, before the nasty little rascals are sufficiently kept at bay. I honestly believe they can never *really* be completely eradicated. As soon as you think they are, that's when they'll make their grab for your ankles! Secondly, to keep things manageable, you may want to work on one group of shadows at a time, rather than try to conquer them all at once. Last, I give here a technique that was given to me by my matron goddess Artemis, as a way to help me deprogram myself after a long dark passage:

I did this *deprogramming work* on myself using four clear quartz crystals and one amethyst crystal in a dark-moon working. First, I spent a great deal of time finding and studying the keys to my issues and making sure I was good and tired of dragging the weight of these old issues around with me. Then, in a deep ritual on a dark moon, under the supervision of my Lady Artemis, in a circle protected by my beloved Cernunnos, I lay down on the floor with a good-sized crystal at each hand and foot, and said prayers asking her to drain me of the negative, unhealthy energy patterns that were causing problems in my life. As each issue's energy pattern flowed out of me, I saw pictures in my mind of how these old, angry patterns had both begun and manifested. I allowed myself all the time I needed to let the shadows drain away. Once that part of the rite was completed, I was guided to cleanse the crystals thoroughly in salt water while I drank a "fortifying" tea[34] and deeply re-grounded myself. Then, I dried and charged the crystals, reprogramming each one with the patterns I desired to *create* in my life. At this point, I added the amethyst crystal, which I programmed to be a "lens." I drank more of the tea, ended the rite, and then ate a hearty grounding meal.

As follow-up, I then placed one of these programmed crystals in each corner of my bedroom, pointing in toward the bed, as I'd been directed to do. I was told to lie in bed (in the center of the crystals' energy field), holding the amethyst crystal "lens" to my solar plexus chakra, my power center, every night for the last few minutes before falling asleep. Then, focusing on my Tree of Life, I pulled the energy *through* the crystals in the four corners of the room and into my power center, letting the energy flow from there, distributing the power of my intentions throughout my entire being. This, I came to understand, was her way of "programming" my energy patterns so that I would

---

34. I chose oatstraw infusion, which is highly nutritious and is listed as a "fortifying" infusion in Susun Weed's *New Menopausal Years: The Wise Woman Way* (Ash Tree Publishing, 2002), page 239 and throughout the text.

awaken ready to do the actions required to heal my life and work toward my dreams. Please understand—just as I stated above, this was not a one-time ritual, nor is it seen as a quick fix or cure-all. In fact, it's important that we, as trained priests and priestesses, understand there is no such thing as the "quick fix" we often hear about and are sometimes tempted to believe will work. We can't just take a pill and be more psychic. (I once actually heard that ingesting "one frankincense tear per day" will make one more psychic, and I actually tried it! I noticed no difference, either, by the way.) Nor can we simply go to an energy worker of some stripe and have them "access" our consciousness in order to "fix" us (for the low, low discount rate of a bazillion dollars per hour), thereby eliminating years of therapy, moons of shadow work, or any real effort on our part to heal ourselves or to change self-destructive behavior. Yes, kids, I'm here to tell you that there is no "Instant Witch" kit; to learn to use energy requires effort. Work. Sometimes very hard work. And that is as it should be.

So, using these crystals, I believe, not only absolutely works on an energetic level, but it's also a way of *programming the mind* to work toward the goals intended, as well as having a very real element of "placebo effect." And none of the work would be fruitful, of course, if our follow-through in waking life didn't also occur. Repetition is extremely helpful in this type of work. As of this writing, I've done the deprogramming and reprogramming rite four times, and can foresee doing it again and again, whenever I start feeling those shadows trying to grab me around the ankles, as it were.

Our culture is deeply invested in people following the "dream of the planet," as Ruiz puts it, and that we must be ever vigilant in "hunting the parasite," changing our energy patterns, as the old patterns are so entrenched that they can slip in on us when we're not paying attention. Vigilance and gentleness, merciless discipline and total compassion for the self are key in this work. Think of the archetype of the Dark Mother as you chase your shadows. She loves us deeply and unconditionally, which is why she cuts the threads when it's time. She does this action without mercy, yes, but with total compassion. This is the attitude you must take with yourself when doing these types of actions; it took us a long, long time to become programmed with unhealthy or undesirable patterns; it will take time to deprogram them as well.

THE SOLAR PLEXUS CHAKRA

Sometimes called the "power" chakra, the solar plexus chakra is located in the abdomen, near and just above the navel. Its color is yellow. The Sanskrit name for this chakra is *manipura*, and its element is fire. The solar plexus is often the point where, when doing our Tree of Life exercise, we go from pulling energy in and up on the inhale and pushing it up and out on the exhale. When we project energy, typically we use our solar plexus chakra, our power center, to push it out. It is also the area of our bodies where we feel power, especially shared power, most profoundly. When we are excited by something, it stimulates our power centers, alerting us that power is present, and we feel "butterflies" in our "stomach." The sensation isn't really in our stomach, but in the same general area, as our power chakra is activating in order to send us a message. Perhaps we share power with a person or place, or the situation is going to add to our power in some way. Likewise, when we feel nauseated or have "the jitters" in our solar plexus, the sensation can serve as a warning. Years ago, a woman whose marriage was in trouble said to me, "It just makes me *sick to my stomach* to think I might lose my husband." I have, on numerous occasions, asked my students, "How does that feel in your gut?" These sensations are all about the solar plexus chakra activating.

THIRTEEN HARMONIES WORK—RITUALS

When does ritual begin? For some folks, it begins the minute they cast the circle. For others, it's when they are in the ritual shower, cleansing away the psychological "dirt" of their day. For still others, ritual begins the moment they begin to put their ideas on paper.

As we examine the role power plays in our lives as priests and priestesses, ritual comes to the forefront. How powerful are our rituals, and what can we do to make them more so? One of the things I look at whenever I am ready to do a ritual, especially for my more potent and powerful spellwork, is my physical energy. After all the preparations, the reading or meditation that tells me whether or not to do the working and what the focus should be, as well as any elements to the work I may not have thought of, after the date and time are chosen and the altar dressing decided upon, the most important thing I consider is how to maximize my energy for the work at hand. The night before the rite, I try to make sure I get plenty of good sleep, and the day of the ritual I try to make sure I eat lightly and healthfully, and get some exercise in the fresh air if at all possible, because exercise, as most folks will tell you, actually *gives* energy to the physical body, rather than taking it away.

Then, I shower before the rite, making sure to concentrate on any frustrations I've had throughout the day being washed away with the water, and the meal before the rite is always fairly simple and light, usually the volume of a healthy snack. The trick is to eat enough that your stomach won't start growling and cause you to be distracted, which zaps power from your rite, or to get in a hurry to finish so that you can go eat, which can actually diminish the power of a spell, but to also not eat so much that you're sluggish and sleepy. You will want to make sure more healthy food will be available afterward, as you will likely be hungry. This will also help you to ground yourself. All of these things serve to keep the physical body in a state of high energy, which greatly enhances the magic.

The ritual writing process is important, too. For the most powerful spellwork, it's best to incorporate all the senses: we have candlelight and symbols that serve both to draw spirits and to enhance and stimulate us visually; the incense and sage stimulate our sense of smell (and sage changes the ions in the air from positive to negative, which sounds like the opposite of what we want, but it's actually the negative ions that put folks into a positive mood); the cakes and wine or other edibles in the rite of course stimulate our sense of taste; the bells, the words, the chanting or drumming stimulate and enhance our sense of hearing, but also our emotions, as the words in a ritual are often the thing we hold fast to, and which resonate within us long after the ritual is over. Our sense of touch is stimulated by our ritual garb, the smooth cool crystals, the weight of our blades, and the physical sensations of touching other objects on the altar with the actions we take. All of these enhance and build the energy of that wonderful and satisfying place between the worlds we Wiccans so love to visit.

Doreen Valiente, in *An ABC of Witchcraft*, talks about the four powers of the Magus.[35] These are *to know, to will, to dare, to keep silent,* and when all four are in balance, they create a fifth power: the power *to go.* These powers are all connected to the elements, and of course, the various components of ritual relate to these powers as well: the smell of the incense is carried on the air; the taste of the cakes and wine

---

35. Doreen Valiente, *An ABC of Witchcraft Past and Present* (Phoenix Publishing, 1973), 150.

relate to water in the digestive process from the moment they touch our tongues; our sense of touch is connected to the energy of earth; and the candles and symbols on the altar need to be used in a ritual action, so they stimulate our power center and therefore speak to the element of fire. The words and bells or chimes go into our ears (air), driving deep into our emotions (water), stimulating our power centers (fire), convincing our Thinking Self (air), and our bodies (earth) that our magic will manifest, so these things speak to the element of spirit, which ties all of them together, creating that vital fifth power of the Magus: the power to *go*!

Following is a chant I use for building personal power. I wrote the majority of it many years ago, and had a problem with the diction in one part of it, so I tossed it into the massive pile of papers and scraps of notes that is my current grimoire. One day, as I was trying to come up with a powerful chant for a public Esbat I was going to do, I remembered this one, dug it out, and to my surprise, found it easy to fix the troublesome line. I repeated it a few times, and found myself becoming quite energized. Over the next few days, I used it more and more, and found it to be extremely powerful for me—whenever I'd chant it seven times or more, I found myself absolutely *filled* with energy and power! I even made the mistake of chanting it while lying in bed that first night, practicing for the ritual ahead, and became so energized and power-filled I couldn't sleep for hours! Since then, I've taught it to many people who report similar reactions to its use. Some folks have made it a part of their morning spiritual routine, and some folks have told me they "save it" for when they really need it, so it'll have more impact. It can be used whenever you feel you need to strengthen your own resolve about a particular issue, to fill you up when you feel depleted, or simply as a reminder that you are, indeed, a powerful being because you *choose* to be one. The diction is a little tricky to get used to; just read each line in its entirety, keeping a simple beat.

A caveat: the strength of the energy you can build with this chant will absolutely be *in direct proportion* to how strong your convictions are that the following words are true *of* you, and *for* you. All the more reason to always stay good to your word. Additionally, I believe this chant has even more power if written in your own handwriting, so when I teach it in public venues, rather than give a handout, I recite it and have folks copy it down. Try it, and see if there's a difference!

THE CHANT OF THE MAGUS

I have the intent to know;
To see with truth and light,
I have the power to will;
To exert my passion's might,
I have the courage to dare;
To transform all with love,
I have the wisdom to keep my silence;
And honor the gods above.
East and south and west and north
Create the sacred road.
To know, to will, to dare, to keep silent
Bring forth the power to go.

Note: When the power peaks, I usually chant the last two lines an additional two times (to total three times through) to "seal the spell."

TOOL—THE SWORD

The sword itself, as a ritual tool, will have the same energies and purposes of the athame; it's just bigger. Like the athame, the ritual sword is traditionally double-edged and black handled, but of course this is the *traditional* sword. For eclectic Wiccans, the sword's appearance may vary widely from this description. Also like the athame, the sword is a very personal tool. Sometimes, a coven will have a group sword, but that is still highly personal—personal to the coven. The sword is used more typically in outdoor workings, where there's more room and less likelihood of someone accidentally getting nicked with it.

As with the athame, there has been a lot of speculation and difference of opinion as to whether this sacred blade belongs in the east or the south. The blade is forged in fire, projects the energies of passion and will, and is shaped like a spiking flame, which speaks very much to the energy of the south, but it's also a tool of discernment that we use in drawing our lines in the sand (and in the magical circle!), slicing through the hubris of our lives, clearing away the old that the new may thrive, which speaks of the energies of intellect, the mind, and therefore, the east. So again, the elemental associations are up to you to decide. No matter how you slice it, it is a tool of the God. Some folks even keep their blades in the southeast, or have a blade for each of the "male" directions.

THE EIGHT VIRTUES OF THE GODDESS—POWER

Power is a double-edged sword in its own right. As we learn and grow in our spiritual practices, as we become more powerful, we can see many occasions in our lives where possessing power can have two sides. It feels good to help people, and to help ourselves, but sometimes we can project energy without even trying, just from having such a strong desire, and that energy can (and often does) manipulate others, especially the uninitiated. Unfortunately, it's really easy for men to do this, as it's a natural flow—male energy projects. I have experienced, more than once, the quite powerful, pointed, and on one occasion, completely overwhelming sensation of desire when a man was interested in me romantically and I didn't share the feeling. In most cases, the man didn't even know he was projecting his energy, but in one case he did, as he was a trained priest who knew how to use energy. Luckily, I was a trained priestess when this happened, and was able to figure out that I was being manipulated.

The thing to remember, dear Initiate, is that the person receiving these projections will feel this energy *as if it's her own*, which is why it's so important for women especially, but for all students of magic in general, to learn to shield, as well as to project—if the energy is sustained and coercive, you will want to be able to use your energy, not only to protect yourself, but also to *push the sender away*! Once your protective circle is up, you will be able to tell where the energy came from. If it's still just as strong, you may want to examine your true feelings for the sender, or check how skilled you are at shielding. If the feeling is gone, however, it's a clear indication that the sender was indeed projecting toward you, whether cognizant of it or not.

Women, on the other hand, naturally receive. As a general rule, what does a man do when he's interested in someone? He moves toward him or her. What does a woman do? She *beckons*. This beckoning energy can also be manipulative, pulling someone toward her when the inclination may not be there naturally, which is why it's also important for men to learn to shield, and of course the same checks and balances above would apply once the man's shield is up.

I feel it's also important for men to learn to receive energy, not only for their own Witchy education, but also because receiving energy is connected to prosperity and gifts. Now, again, this is *typically* the pattern our gender's energy takes—it doesn't mean that there aren't women out there who are good at projecting or men who don't receive—it's just that the above are the most common forms human energy takes, through both nature and our domestication.

POSTURE OF POWER

If it works for you to do so, stand tall, with your legs apart. Ground and center, and focus on your solar plexus and its ability to project. Breathe deeply and let the energy come up through your root and base chakras, and let it pool for a moment in your solar plexus chakra. Raise your arms up and out, lowering your chin in concentration, then pull energy in by pulling your arms toward you, crossing your arms and cupping your hands over your shoulders. Raise your head and look the world straight in the eye while holding this energy. Say out loud, "I am powerful!"

HOMEWORK

Make sure you do daily energy work of chakra spinning as outlined in the homework section in the first-moon chapter of this unit. The solar plexus, or power chakra, is bright yellow, and is located just above and behind the navel.

In your daily practices during this moon cycle, take a few moments to do some fire evocations. In your mind and spirit's "eye," feel the crackle and flow of fire all around you, and focus on the physical manifestation of emotions in your life, your personal power, the power of passion. Surround yourself with these energies (sitting near an actual fire, such as a campfire or fireplace, can help this visualization immensely!), let them into your circle and into your consciousness; let them touch you, noting that although you can feel the intensity of the heat, it does not burn you. Breathe deeply and fully, focusing on feeling, then manifesting, your passions there in your circle, and know that you are warming and healing your desire and will with the fire, as well as your solar plexus chakra and ability to work your will.

Consider performing an act of power. What would make you feel stronger? We all have things that we are hesitant to do, even a little afraid to do. Perhaps you could plan to push your boundaries in some way, take a stand, make a change, chase a shadow. You may want to incorporate such energies into your next Esbat. Take some time and think about what an act of power would be for you, and then plan to do that action.

Shadow work: As we finish this first triplet of moons, we have moved through the basics of self-care and self-acknowledgment. We've examined and learned about our *source energies:* our core, our pride, and our power. Now it's time to put together what we've learned about the shadows surrounding these aspects of Self, in order to keep our spiritual vessel clear and strong. What needs healing? We must take a hard look at the obstacles in these realms, and determine what may have created these blocks. Remember that a great many of our challenges in life come from outer sources, but a great many more come from within—in our own attitudes and actions. Again, this is not a time to judge ourselves, but to find the keys to causes, which are ultimately the keys to healing.

Our physical body is one of the most basic, core issues. Take a moment and focus on your body—how have you judged it? How have you abused it? Has it been abused by lack of information regarding nutrition and exercise? What can be done to help your physical body in order to restore it to vibrant health? Along with our body, we must also consider the core issues of finance and our ability to provide for ourselves. Take a long, nonjudgmental look at your finances, as well as your attitude about money and survival, and then consider how you can heal this aspect of your life. Sometimes it's a matter of taking baby steps until we're well enough to take bigger strides. Remember that the ways in which we have been domesticated to think and act in terms of survival issues are not necessarily healthy ways or ways that work best for us. Now, as we consider our shadows, I'll say it again: we must *question everything*!

Are you safe? Do you feel strong enough to stand up for yourself? Consider also your ability to attract. How do you feel about yourself as a sexual and lovable being? Most folks have issues in this realm, as we are bombarded daily with pictures of culturally perceived perfection in magazines, movies, and TV, and it's sometimes difficult *not* to compare ourselves (unfavorably) to these images. Remember that the models we see in these pictures make up a mere fraction of the population, that those pictures are all airbrushed to hide any imperfections, and that most folks look much like you and me. Many of us would do well to change the way we *see*, rather than the way we *look*. I suspect that an awful lot of us have been rather unkind to ourselves—both when we look in the mirror, and when we make less than healthy choices. We can heal these shadows by making a commitment to be kinder to ourselves, and to make healthier choices.

Go deeper now, and examine the shadows you have around your sexuality. Are you living the life you wish to in this realm? If not, why not? What needs to heal? Attitude or action? Take some time this moon to go deep within and find your way to clarity. If you have been or are being abused in any way, seek help. Invite your patron god(s) and matron goddess(es) into your home to help watch over you and help you dispel these shadows, as well as to guide you to safety.

Are you someone who has no trouble keeping commitments to others, but has a hard time keeping commitments to yourself? This would be a shadow around the strength of your will. Anytime we do not honor our commitments, we are telling our spirits that we cannot be trusted to our word. Then, when we say the words "So mote it be," our spirit doesn't take it too seriously. It's time now to examine our shadows around the strength of our will. If it's hard to keep our commitments or work our will in other ways, we need to amend that, in order to take full control of our power as Witches. Finally, we must look at whether we can "stand." Do you act in accord with your highest good, or do you put off your own needs for the wants and whims of others? To ignore our own needs is to rob ourselves of power. If we do not pursue good health, if we do not believe in ourselves, if we choose not to work our will in order to achieve that which we desire, we will not be able to come into true power or to clear the lower three chakras, which relate to these things.

Take some time this moon to consider all of the above issues and to begin to clear and heal the shadows around them. Remember that this will be ongoing work, as we never heal instantly or with one action. Baby steps, remember. Once our foundation is clear and solid, we begin to thrive, not just live, and this readies us to reach out and connect with others.

Write a personal Esbat. Begin brainstorming for the upcoming full and dark moons, decide what needs to leave or come into your life, and begin planning an Esbat ritual, including when it's most appropriate to do the work. Consider moon energies: What sign is she in, if any? What phase? Consider solar energies: Where are you on the Wheel of the Year? What time of day or night will you do the work? What day of the week? Consider other energies as well, such as whether Mercury or other relevant planets are in retrograde, your personal schedule, as well as your personal vibrance level (how good do you feel?) and the energies of your household (will you be able to be alone and undisturbed?).

Moon-tides work and devotionals: Don't forget to take some time each evening to get outside and look at (or contemplate the position of) the moon. Tune in to her energies; feel her power fill you. Remember to say your daily devotionals to your matron goddess(es) and patron god(s). Let their love fill you, let them show you how to become more powerful.

Read Anodea Judith's *Wheels of Life,* chapter 4—"Chakra Three: Fire." Do some of the exercises presented if you like.

Astral temple work: Take some time this moon to continue work on your astral temple. In your meditations, focus now on how you will fortify and secure your temple. Will you install locks, invite your guardians to watch over it, set psychic wards, or leave it wide open with an intent and belief of total trust? It's your decision how you will hold this space on the astral plane. I advise setting wards at the very least, but this decision is of course yours to make.

8: The Fourth Moon—Compassion

If someone comes to you entreating aid, do not say in refusal:
"Trust in God; He will help," but act as if there were no God,
and none to help but you.
—The Sassover[36]

MOON FOUR—THE STORY

You stand on the edge of the clearing, watching as the first
glimmer of her silvery light crests the horizon. Soft pink clouds
reflect the sunset behind you, adding a surreal quality to the
scene. Everything is so perfect tonight; it's neither cold nor hot,
the city noises are too far away to be discernible, the air is per-
fumed with the earthy scents of forest and wild herbs, and you
are filled with the energies of love and tenderness. As her full,
round form clears the edge where earth meets sky, you raise
your arms and open your heart. Spiritually naked, you are so
wide open that you are a blank slate in this moment, both preg-
nant and empty, receptive to any messages she has for you in
the deepening twilight. Behind, in the shadows, you know he
watches; the Dark God, the protector of both the Goddess and
of yourself.

You breathe deeply, pulling energy up from the earth, down
from the sky, creating a circuit, and the power of your intention

36. Louis I. Newman, comp., *The Hasidic Anthology*, 186.1, 1934.

THE FOURTH MOON CORRESPONDENCES

Keywords: love, care, stillness, serenity, empathy, unconditional love

Energy: love

Chakra: heart

Chakra color: green

Element: air

Elemental color: yellow, sunrise pink, and lavender

Herbs and flowers: rose, lily, forget-me-not

Incense: lavender, myrrh

Stones and metals: rose quartz, ruby

13 Harmonies: discipline

Tool: scourge

8 virtues: compassion

Astral temple work: windows

Shadow group: the Shadow of Blame

Energy keyword: relating

Energy group: relationship energies—caring for others

---

flows through your mind, your emotions, your body. You cast your circle. Tonight, you have a single purpose: to help a friend in need. You invite the elements and both your friend's and your own personal deities. You can't imagine yourself ever being in the situation your friend is in, yet you feel so much tenderness and love for her that you can empathize with her pain.

You state your purpose and intention for your magic. As you recite the litany of your friend's problems and causes, you find yourself speaking with much more urgency than you felt even moments ago. Your friend has long been fighting this battle, and you feel your heart well up with such love and compassion for her that you find you desire her healing nearly as much as she does. Your impassioned pleas reach a crescendo that leads you into a prayerful chant, which leads you into yet another chant, this time of power and praise, ris-

ing up to such a peak that it leaves you breathless. You will the power to rise just a smidge more ... then release it as your body reels with the pent-up emotion. Finally, you earth the power, breathing deeply of the earthy scents around you, pulling more energy from earth and sky to balance your flagging strength. With each breath, you feel better, more energized, stronger.

As you put away your tools after opening your circle, you feel confident your work will help your friend. You're a bit surprised at how strong the passion of your will was during the rite; you had no idea you felt this strongly about the situation, but at the same time, it makes sense. You've long felt your friend was one of your Sacred Charges, so her spiritual well-being is a responsibility you gladly take on. There's no question you love her deeply, and that she gives you much to be grateful for. As a symbol of your gratitude for both your friend and your gods, you raise the bottle of blessed wine from your ritual to the sky in offering, then pour half of it on the ground, in thanks.

THE ENERGY OF COMPASSION

The first thing we must address in any discussion of compassion is the difference between compassion and pity. With pity, we feel sympathy, we feel sorry; we may be moved by someone's loss or lack in some area. Perhaps they don't have proper resources, or motivation, or skills, to succeed in pulling themselves out of a bad situation. Folks in poverty-stricken countries, for example, children or animals who are mistreated, mentally ill people, all deserve and often inspire our pity, so we take actions *for them*, sending aid or getting them to a shelter, etc., because we know they can't make it on their own; they need our help. This is part of serving our gods and communities, but we must take care not to cross the line with our peers—many spiritual masters say that among equals, to pity someone is an insult.

With compassion, we feel *empathy* for someone; we can *relate* to their experience and often can well imagine what they must be feeling. This is not the same as being an *empath*—when one is an *empath* or is experiencing *empathic feelings*, one actually *feels* what the other is feeling. We can become more empathic as time goes on, by becoming more connected to nature, more tuned in to spiritual energies, by our work in our communities, by helping people, and by doing our energy work and psychic exercises. Many healers are *empaths*, and although this can make them better healers, it can also make them extremely vulnerable to illness and pain. We can have situations in life where we are more or less empathic, too, and certainly our companion animals (especially dogs, who seem to run on primarily emotional intuition) can be *empaths*. This is one of the reasons that it's so important for all of us to practice shielding pretty regularly as we walk our spiritual paths.

Compassion, however, is about feeling *empathy*; it's about *relating*—being able to understand to some degree how someone must be feeling, and in many cases, this is easy. As with so many human experiences, we've likely been in their shoes ourselves. In compassion, while we still feel love and caring for someone, we recognize their ability to help themselves, so the energy is about *respect*, about believing in them, having faith that they will be all right. The energy is about shared power; we tell them we know they are strong, that they can do it, so we take actions and share power *with them*, loaning them our helping hand. A good healer exhibits compassion every day; she advises and recommends nutrition, exercise, and supplements designed to help the patient get well. She doesn't do it *for* them; she knows they can care for themselves, but she *listens* and provides empathy and tools in an attitude of loving discipline. Another classic example of compassion is when we stand up *with* folks who may be having trouble standing up for—or by—themselves because of the power-over actions of another, such as taking a stand against racist or otherwise prejudicial comments. This doesn't always go over so well.

Just recently, a woman on a website I often visit called another woman to task on a racist comment she'd made, and the offending party then called her "an overly sensitive politically correct type." To accuse someone of being "overly sensitive" because they clearly have enough respect for others to *not* throw out blanket stereotypes is just throwing out another stereotype, which is equally disrespectful. Standing up for others, especially in a public forum, takes a great deal of courage and compassion, which is admirable. In American culture the term "political correctness" seems to have become a term folks use to disparage and disrespect those who stand in defense of folks being bashed, seemingly so they can feel justified in spewing their hatred and prejudices. That's incredibly uncool.

In *The Mastery of Love*, Ruiz says that pity is fear-based, and compassion is based on love and respect. He says that loving someone means supporting them in their efforts to "make it," knowing that they are, indeed, capable of making their own choices, stating: "I don't have to make your choices for you. You can make it. If you fall, I can give you my hand, I can help you to stand up."[37] So when we use our compassion to do spellwork to help people (always with their permission, of course), that is exactly what we are doing: we are helping them to *stand*.

Compassion, coupled with gratitude, is possibly the strongest driving force behind what motivates the earnest priest or priestess to service. I have long believed that one of the best ways we can serve our gods is by serving our communities. Whether we provide counseling, ritual, teaching, healing, or other services that help to nourish the body, mind, and spirit, we are driven to these actions largely through compassion. I recognize that there are a few scattered individuals whose motivations lie in the realm of the unethical: who teach Witchy 101s to troll for new lovers, who use public ritual to glorify themselves, who hold classes or workshops for personal promotion or money alone, but I believe these people are few and far between. For the vast majority of us, our public service work, though rewarding indeed, tends to wear us out to some degree (which is why, dear Initiate, I emphasize a strong personal practice and self-care; to strengthen you, to charge you up and prepare you for that outpouring), but our duty to our chosen deities and our love and compassion for our communities keeps us coming back again and again.

HAVING A SACRED CHARGE

As you grow and learn on your spiritual Path, there will come a time when you have a "special needs" student, friend, or covenmate. This person is one you would obviously feel compassion toward, who is struggling to gain control over some aspect of their life, and as their senior on the Path, you will be called upon to take them under your wing, so to speak; to loan them that helping hand, sometimes for an extended period of time, until they've learned to stand on their own. This bond between you and your charge is sacred, therefore; it speaks of a special relationship and energy, as you are in a position to be held responsible, to some degree, for their spiritual well-being (and sometimes their emotional and physical well-being also). I, like many spiritual teachers, consider all of my students, both past and present, my Sacred Charges, and I am 100 percent present and available to them should they need me for any reason, but in most cases my students can hold their own. Still, there are always exceptions.

---

37. Don Miguel Ruiz, *The Mastery of Love* (Amber-Allen Publishing, 1999), 61.

Years and years ago, I met a man who I came to believe was my twin soul. I read a few books on the subject and was deeply disappointed; the authors didn't seem to understand what was happening to us. They were all very hetero-biased and made it clear that only gender opposites could ever be twin souls, and it was automatically assumed that these relationships would be sexually intimate. That wasn't the case with us: although we were strongly attracted to each other's presence and energy, it wasn't a sexual attraction; it was a platonic one. That may sound strange, but the energy was much the same as a being in love; it just manifested itself differently, like what the Greeks called "agape"—a spiritual love. Though we were both bisexual, we were both in long-term, monogamous relationships with same-gender partners, but even if we hadn't been, it wouldn't have mattered, because, again, the connection wasn't about sex; it was about spirit. In many ways, he felt like a deeply cherished and long-lost brother. A twin brother. We were so connected that this man and I even finished each other's sentences! Over time, we did a series of mutual meditations together that revealed much to us about our relationship, why we met in this lifetime, and how our last life together ended. I felt responsible for much of what went wrong, and wanted to make sure that I did everything "right" in this lifetime. He was in every way my Sacred Charge, and my experiences with him taught me a great deal about what service to the gods, as well as having someone so spiritually dependent on me, was all about.

During the time we were together, through my meditations and experiences, I developed a list of things to keep in mind about how to help someone in such a "special needs" role. This list became important to me, not just because of my role with him, but also because I have had (and continue to have) so many students with broken vessels, so many dear and Sacred Charges, so the list evolves continuously. Some of these suggestions came directly to me in meditations with my most authoritative matron goddess and patron god, and are marked as such.

To have a Sacred Charge ... (a partial* list)

Sacred—Consecrated by love or reverence, dedicated to a person or purpose. Entitled to reverence or respect; not to be profaned; inviolable. **Charge**—To have the responsibility or control of.

1. *From the Lord:* Put their needs before yours.** Always. Without fail.

2. Swallow your pride. This isn't about you.

3. Think of their spiritual well-being first and foremost.

4. If they are going through rough times, check up on them, and reach out in love and compassion, but give them space if they need it (ask!).

5. Never assume anything! Ask always and often, "What do you need?" And then act on that.

6. Listen to what they **don't** say—read their body language, their face, their eyes!

7. *From the Lady:* **Tune in!** Listen to the psychic currents and then *give a damn.*

8. Listen to your intuition—if something "feels" wrong, contact them! Act on your intuition where they're concerned. Always.

9. Make sure their needs are being met. If not by others, then by **you**.

10. Be available for whatever they need, but don't push them too hard.

11. Never assume they are okay if they've been through rough times recently—especially if they are a "rock." Remind them that there is strength in leaning on someone who loves and looks out for them.

12. If they need to cry, but cannot, or don't want to, remind them of the healing power of tears.

13. Listen, listen, listen!

14. Never expect them to be anything they are not.

15. Remember that you are here to serve them and not the other way around.

16. Never "keep score"! Do everything you possibly can for them.

17. Always give them 100 percent of the very best of yourself.

18. *From the Lord:* Be generous with your body—hug them, touch them, but let them take the lead in this.

19. *From the Lady:* Be generous in spirit. Believe in them. Trust them.

20. Support their ideas and dreams, but also help them to be realistic. Be gentle with this realism.

21. Never let them leave your presence if they are upset and acting crazy. Try to calm them, try to get them to talk to you. Do not take **no** for an answer.

22. *From the Lady:* Meditate on how best to help them, and act on the answers you receive.

23. *From the Lord:* Be subtle. Be discreet. Keep their secrets close.

24. *From the Lady and the Lord:* Always be truthful and forthcoming about your feelings for them—even if it makes you feel vulnerable and afraid. Chances are, they are even more so, and it's up to you to keep the relationship strong by expressing your love.

25. Don't say "No" without good reason. Remember, their needs are more important. If you feel your needs are more important, see #1.

26. Go out of your way to assure them that they are both **wanted** and **welcome** in your life.

27. Spend quality time with them—and do what they want to do more often than not. *From the Lord:* Let them take the lead in terms of how much time you spend together.

28. Get to know them. Ask questions. Learn who they are.

29. Remember always that you are responsible for their spiritual (and to a large degree, their mundane) well-being. It is up to you to make sure they are traveling the Path in the way they choose.

30. *From the Lady:* If they are hurting and needful, make sure that they are the first thing on your mind upon awakening and the last thing on your mind before sleep.

31. *From the Lord:* Strive to eliminate boundaries. Open yourself to their love and trust. Nurture their spirit. Honor their wishes.

32. Know when it is time to let go. They need to go where they need to go and when.

This list is "partial" because the gods always have the final say in these matters.

** *Who's number one? We all are…*

Putting the Sacred Charge's needs before yours applies to every aspect of life save personal health. The structure of a coven (or a group of Sacred Charges and their guide) is very much like that of a tree; the HP/S or guide is the center structure, the foundation, and acts as God/dess to those she serves. She is the lifetree, if you will, and her branches sweep down and enfold her charges, protecting and nurturing them with all she has to give. They are number one, in terms of everything but her personal health in the five sacred realms: her mental health, her passion, her emotions, and her physical and spiritual health. If one of her charges needs something she can give, she will give it gladly and willingly, without hesitation, above and beyond any personal wish or whim.

But her health is first, and if any aspect of it is out of balance, she has nothing to give anyone. So she takes care of her personal circle first and foremost, always. And whatever safeguarding of her health she needs to do should be accepted, understood, and supported by coveners and charges alike. The stronger and more vital she is, the more she has to give to those she serves. And so the Wheel goes on, the guide spinning us into our highest energy patterns, teaching and providing service through truth and love, spiraling us upward to our gods, our Paths, our destinies…

PRIEST/ESS OR CONGREGANT?

For many on this Path, it is enough to go to the occasional public Esbat and Sabbat celebrations as a congregant—a Wiccan or Pagan who simply follows the religion; to have a personal practice that doesn't include any deep commitments. There is nothing whatsoever wrong with this. For others such as yourself, dear Initiate, there is a strong calling to be closer to one's deities, to honor the cycles of the earth and moon by facilitating one's own rituals and spells, to stand at the hub of the Great Wheel; to be a *priest/ess and Witch*—a mover and shaper of energy. Eventually many of you will wish to provide ritual for your communities or covens. Compassion, then, takes a central role again when we talk about service.

For many folks, service is a sacred duty. Duty is different from obligation. Etymologically, duty is defined as a responsibility to some person or persons; one's duty may be to others or to himself. Obligation is that to or by which one is *bound*; obligations are responsibilities to others. Duty arises from the nature of things; obligation may be created by circumstances, as by one's own promise or by acceptance of a trust.[38] Our culture has its own spin on these two words, neither of which is seen as very positive. With obligation, one does a task because it's the "right" thing to do, because perhaps one has made a promise of some kind, or because one feels "guilty." With obligation,

---

38. *Funk & Wagnalls Standard Dictionary* (J. G. Ferguson Publishing, 1978), 394.

the boyfriend sets up a camping date because the girlfriend says she feels like he never wants to go camping with her. So he does this to appease her, to avoid conflict, because he feels he *has* to, but not because he truly wants to.

With duty, and the same camping trip example, the boyfriend knows his girlfriend needs to be in nature regularly in order to feed her spirit. He gets to be in nature quite often himself, but he knows she hasn't been out in a while. Since he genuinely cares about her well-being, even though he may feel he would rather spend the weekend at home, he knows it's his duty to go on the trip, so she can recharge her spiritual batteries.

In the light of service, duty can manifest as a priestess performing a public ritual she may not really have time and energy for, but perhaps no one else volunteered, or perhaps the organizer of an event really likes her work or needs some special skill she possesses. In this case, she feels it's her duty to step up and serve when and where she's needed. She genuinely *desires* to do the work because she wants to help and she likes to serve, but she would rather get some much-needed rest. Obligation would be more of the flavor of she doesn't really want to do the ritual, but feels she has no choice. It's a fine line, but one that can feel considerably different depending which side of it you're on.

THE UNION OF OPPOSITES

Anodea Judith, in *Wheels of Life*, discusses the six-pointed star in the center of the twelve lotus petals as the symbol of the heart chakra. She mentions that this symbol represents the Sacred Marriage, the balance of male and female.[39] This symbol, also known as the Star of David, is a beautiful reminder of the sacred balance of these energies, both within ourselves and in our relationships.

In every healthy relationship, whether it's between opposite or same genders, there is a constant, dynamic balance of "male" and "female" energies, of action and reception, give and take. As we look at this fourth moon and the energies of compassion, we can see that even in the bright passion of the Great Rite, there is an underlying depth of love and respect, an opening of the heart and spirit that allows for and creates a sacred bond. This bond, this depth, this sublime and abiding grace induces

---

39. Anodea Judith, *Wheels of Life* (Llewellyn, 1999), 193.

and invokes *compassion*. So although the Great Rite is a sexual act, it is also very much a spiritual and loving one.

THE HEART CHAKRA

The heart chakra is located in the middle of the chest, at the level of the heart. Its color is green. The Sanskrit name for this chakra is *anahata*, which means "unstruck." Its element is air. Judith states, "When the chakra is free of grief from old hurts, its opening is innocent, fresh, and radiant," and that "if the third chakra has done its job, our circumstances are easier to accept."[40] How many times have we had to "get something off our chest," and upon doing so, find our "heart" is eased? I believe these feelings do not come from the organ itself, but from the chakra. Because it is the fourth of seven chakras, it is the "middle" one, and so it brings balance to the other six, which makes sense when we consider that the lower chakras are all about self-awareness and manifestation, and the upper chakras are about awareness of others and liberation, or sending out of energy. In the heart, there is stillness, peace, a moment of calm before taking action. It is our filling up that enables us to do the outpouring that manifests in loving our world. So it is with the heart chakra.

THIRTEEN HARMONIES WORK—DISCIPLINE

Discipline may seem like an odd subject in a chapter on compassion, but when you think about how much we must truly care about and respect ourselves in order to put the kind of energy required into important life goals and changes, it makes a lot of sense. It's not an easy truth to face, but in order to help anyone, love is not enough— we must have that essential compassion in order to bring about the effort required to do the action that will help. In other words, we must have a respectful regard for ourselves. This is especially true when it comes to helping ourselves. One could even say that without self-respect, discipline would be difficult, if not impossible, to achieve. This was illustrated quite clearly to me one summer day a few years ago, when I was out on one of my morning walks.

I was ranting and raving to the Lady about some of my frustrations—I'd been having difficulty making the kinds of changes I needed in my life, and I was feeling

---

40 Anodea Judith, *Wheels of Life* (Llewellyn, 1999), 196.

lonely, scared, and unimportant in my personal relationships. Finally, spent, I opened myself to her, let my mind go blank, and I sort of fell into this walking meditation... a few seconds later (after I'd finally shut up), I heard her voice in my head, crystal clear:

She said, "You don't respect yourself."

I stopped in my tracks and said, "Whuuuuut? That's not true—I *love* myself! I spent three long years doing nothing but healing my self-loathing patterns, coming to terms with my flaws, and I busted my butt to get to this place. You're wrong, Lady. I *love* myself!"

Her voice came again. "You love yourself, but you don't respect yourself. If you did, you'd follow through on your commitments to yourself."

And right then and right there, I finally got it. My beloved Artemis loved me enough to teach me about both discipline *and* compassion—that in order to change my situation, I would have to start *respecting* myself enough to make good on my intentions with myself, to stop making excuses and start being more consistent in the actions that would lead to my goals. That's called *discipline*! I wish I could say that my attitude changed so much that very day that I never failed in my promises to myself again, but old habits die hard, as they say, and it took a little more practice and a lot more life changes and deep healing before I got to a place where I could truly follow through on my commitments to myself with any kind of regularity. There were many shadows around the reasons why, and as we know, shadow work is by its very nature a constant in the life of a person who seeks truth. But I can say that things are a lot better now.

So we must accept the fact that our lives are the way they are because we have made them that way. No matter what our circumstances, we have made a series of choices that have landed us here. In order to change these energy patterns, we must hold enough compassion for ourselves to do the actions required, which call for self-respect—discipline.

TOOL—THE SCOURGE

The *scourge* typically has a short handle from which many long, soft strings or strips of leather hang, and it can be used in a variety of ways, such as the historic (and current) use as a tool of flagellation or self-flagellation, punishment and/or pain of a either a spiritual or sexual nature, or both. In many Wiccan traditions, it's more symbolic than anything else, used in a mock-punishment way. Finally, my favorite way the scourge can be used is as a gentle tool that helps induce trance.

To use the scourge this way, simply brush the strands lightly over bare skin for several moments. This will cause the blood to flow to that area and away from the brain, which renders the subject slightly lightheaded and deeply relaxed, primed for trancework. It's easier to have someone do this for you, on your back, but you can do it yourself in different areas. Just use as large an area on your skin as possible (such as a thigh), get very comfortable, and relax into the experience.

You can make your own scourge pretty easily by attaching strips of leather, silk cording, or embroidery floss to a handle (wood works well). You can wrap the handle with cloth or leather, or carve it, making it personal and magical. Some folks knot or bead the ends of the cords, especially if they're using something very small and light like embroidery floss to help give the cords weight and drag.

THE EIGHT VIRTUES OF THE GODDESS—COMPASSION

The Lady teaches us that compassion is one of the most important virtues a person can have. Love is the greatest force in the universe, love and truth in accord. Compassion is an acknowledgment of that truth, coupled with love and a respectful regard. To have compassion for another's situation (or even our own) is to understand that helping is not *doing for*, but a *sharing of* power. When you see someone hurting, does it pull at your heartstrings? Do you ask, "How can I help?" Or do you simply walk away, unconcerned? Compassion is the ability to get out of yourself and to care about others. And again, compassion is a big part of what motivates the true Witch and priest/ess to service.

POSTURE OF POWER

If it works for you to do so, sit or stand, focusing your energy on what nature is saying to you on the wind, the rustle of leaves, the sound of the rain or ocean. Open your heart and mind and hear what the spirit whispers in the silences. Make a circle with your thumbs and forefingers together, palms facing outward, over your heart, letting the energy flow in and fill you. Ground and center, and focus on your heart chakra and its ability to feel love and compassion. Send out your deepest respect and empathy through this gesture as well. Breathe deeply and let the energy flow. Let yourself feel the unconditional love of the gods and the universe.

HOMEWORK

Make sure you do daily energy work of chakra spinning as outlined in the homework section in the first-moon chapter of this unit. The heart chakra is a bright green, and is located just to the right of the heart, in the center of the chest.

In your daily practices during this moon cycle, take a few moments to do some air evocations. In your mind and spirit's "eye," feel the cool, clean breeze on your skin, inhale it into your lungs. Surround yourself with these energies, let them into your circle and into your consciousness; let them touch you (if you can go outside and actually feel the breezes, all the better!). Breathe deeply and fully, focusing on cleansing your lungs, and know that you are cleansing and healing your blood and body with the oxygen, as well as your heart chakra and ability to feel compassion and care.

Consider performing an act of compassion. For some of us, exhibiting compassion is easier than for others. If you find yourself in a situation where someone you care about is in pain, try to get out of yourself enough to reach out to that person in a way you know *they need* you to. And if you don't know what they need, if you aren't 100 percent sure, for the love of the gods, ask! Too many times, we make the mistake of treating others as we would want to be treated, but that's often not what they need. Consider the person who needs closeness when she's in pain, with a friend or HP who needs "space" when he's in pain. If that HP or friend follows his own energy pattern, he'll end up with a friend or covener who is convinced he doesn't care.

As priests and priestesses of the Old Gods, we *must* be able to get out of ourselves enough to understand and feel compassion for other human beings. This often means we must abandon our own comfort zones enough to learn *who they are* and *what they need*, and not project our own preferences onto the them or make assumptions. So your assignment this moon is to pay attention! Get to know someone you love by asking them, "What do you need?" and then listen to them and act upon the information. This is compassion.

Shadow work: Examine your shadows around compassion, especially your compassion toward *yourself*, which is reflected in your *self-respect*. Take some time to contemplate what still needs healing in terms of your ability to reach your personal goals. How much do you sabotage yourself? How much do you drive yourself? Are you too hard on yourself? Do you give yourself negative messages? Take a look at how you feel about and treat others in terms of compassion, too. If you find there is something to heal, consider writing your Esbat this month for that healing. Which moon would be most appropriate for this work? Always remember that when we do shadow work, we need to give ourselves light to hold on to when we come out of the working. Affirmations help greatly, as does grounding with a good meal or hot cup of tea and some grainy cookies or bread.

Write a personal Esbat. Begin brainstorming for the upcoming full and dark moons, decide what needs to leave or come into your life, and begin planning an Esbat ritual, including when it's most appropriate to do the work. Consider moon energies: What sign is she in, if any? What phase? Consider solar energies: Where are you on the Wheel of the Year? What time of day or night will you do the work? What day of the week? Consider other energies as well, such as whether Mercury or other relevant planets are in retrograde, your personal schedule, as well as your personal vibrance level (how good do you feel?) and the energies of your household (will you be able to be alone and undisturbed?).

Moon-tides work and devotionals: Don't forget to take some time each evening to get outside and look at (or contemplate the position of) the moon. Tune in to her energies; feel her power fill you. Remember to say your daily devotionals to your matron goddess(es) and patron god(s). Let their love fill you; let them show you your personal truth.

Read Anodea Judith's *Wheels of Life,* chapter 5—"Chakra Four: Love." Do some of the exercises presented if you like.

Astral temple work: Take some time this moon to continue work on your astral temple. In your meditations, focus now on putting in the windows. Many people say the eyes are the windows to the soul; in your astral temple, the windows are both the windows to your soul and the "eyes" of your temple. What kind of glass, if any? Will they be square, round, oval, or a combination, depending on where and what purpose they will serve? What about embellishments or stained-glass patterns? How many will there be? It will probably directly relate to how open you are in your life today. Try pushing the envelope, and put in a few more windows than you would normally be comfortable with. Conversely, if you're a "wide open" person who wears your heart on your sleeve, try putting in a few *fewer* windows than your natural inclination dictates. Use the energy patterns you've been working with to help you create this space.

9: The Fifth Moon—Connection

… it's always going to begin with you. You need to have the courage to use the truth, to talk to yourself with the truth, to be completely honest with yourself.
—don Miguel Ruiz

MOON FIVE—THE STORY

As you cast your circle, you can feel the power flowing through you, for you are filled with your purpose tonight. Just a week ago, when the moon was full, you had a sticky miscommunication that led to a terrible fight with your best friend. It's a huge temptation to blame the stars—Mercury was in retrograde when you tried to discuss a delicate matter—but still, you know that much of the argument was your fault, and you want clarity and truth to come to light so your apology can be complete and honest. More than anything, you want this fight behind you. The waning moon's last quarter just rose a couple of hours ago, and although the hour is quite late, you know that this is the best time to do this work, for Mercury has finally just gone direct again, the moon is finally in the right sign and phase, so the energy feels right for getting communications back on track. Besides, you miss your friend terribly and feel certain all will be well once the two of you start talking again.

THE FIFTH MOON CORRESPONDENCES

Keywords: communication, truth, candor, relationship ethics

Energy: truth

Chakra: throat

Chakra color: bright blue

Element: fire

Elemental color: red, orange

Herbs and flowers: lemon, lavender, sweet pea

Incense: lavender, magic temple

Stones and metals: malachite, silver

13 Harmonies: chanting and singing

Tool: prayer candles and holders

8 virtues: honor

Astral temple work: doors and open passageways

Shadow group: the Shadow of Blame

Energy keyword: connecting

Energy group: relationship energies—love for others

You call the darker gods to come to you tonight; for protection, and for help and strength to understand your part in the problem—both what you did and why—for you feel the key is hidden deep inside somewhere, and once found, can be used to heal and improve your communications with everyone in your life. You ask for guidance, for truth and clarity to come to you, before relaxing your body into a meditative posture. You breathe deeply and open yourself to the journey.

At once, you see Mighty Hecate, standing at a crossroads. You approach reverently, and ask her to show you the way. She points to the middle road, by far the smoothest path, and tells you that walking away from the friendship is the easiest route to take. You tell her you cherish your friend and would never just walk away. She smiles and nods knowingly. She points then to a path leading up a gentle slope that becomes steeper and rockier as it travels onward. The path looks tough, but you know you can do it. She tells you this is the "high ground," the path one takes when one wants to move beyond a problem, but isn't really interested in examining one's part in it. You take a deep breath, knowing that's not the way for you, for you want to look yourself in the face honestly, take responsibility for what you did wrong in the argument, truly apologize for your errors so you can feel whole within the relationship again, with no muck or baggage between you and your friend.

Hesitantly, you look toward the third path, the one Great Hecate has been shielding you from with her body. As she draws back, you see your worst expectations revealed: a shadowed path full of deep ruts, large sharp rocks, and, starting just a few yards in, thick thorny vines twisted across the path as far as your eyes can see. The hungry howl of a wolf in the distance brings a chilling answer: the rising call of what sounds like dozens more wolves. At that exact moment, the waning quarter moon slips behind a heavy cloud, obliterating all light from the path. Your eyes are round with surprise and trepidation as you look toward the powerful Goddess again. She tells you this is the path only the bravest of souls dare to tread, for this is the path of shadows, the path that leads to your own inner darkness and fear, your own judgments and mistakes. You tell her that you have no choice; this is the path you must take.

"Child, you **always** have choices," she says, then sweeps her hand to indicate the smoother path in the middle. "You can still choose to ignore your responsibilities"—she turns to indicate the second path—"or to acknowledge them without a care." As she points to the second path, you hear your own voice in your head, standing on the pedestal of your own making, blathering out the lamest of apologies to your friend: "If I've hurt you in any way, I am so sorry . . ."and you bow your head, afraid to look Wise Hecate in the eyes, for this is the path you're most inclined to take, stupid and irresponsible as you feel it is. You take a deep breath and set your foot on the darker path. She places her hand beneath your chin, lifting your eyes to hers. They are blacker than black, infinitely deep, timeless.

"You choose the path of power, then, Witch," she says, nodding her approval. "I am proud of you."

A lump fills your throat as tears fill your eyes. Knowing she approves of your choice gives you courage and infinite patience.

"I'm . . . I'm just not sure how to cut the brambles," you whisper hoarsely.

*"Take heart, child. If this is truly your will, you'll find a way," she says, her eyes never leaving yours as she steps aside to allow you through, "for that is the challenge, **and** the lesson. Go well."*

You set your jaw, mustering your fiercest will, determined that your love for your friend will give you the courage to brave the thorns, even if you have to cut the damn vines with your teeth. With this very thought, a silver sickle appears in your hands, and the waning moon slips back out from behind the clouds, shedding a modicum of light. Nodding your thanks to the powerful Goddess, you square your shoulders and walk warily, yet deliberately, down the path of thorns.

THE PATH OF THORNS—THE ENERGY OF TRUTH

The Path of Truth is not always an easy one. In our connections with others, however, trying to evade the truth can indeed be a slippery slope. From avoiding gossip to speaking out about that which we feel most strongly about, expressing our truth can be a real exercise in courage. The thing to remember as we walk the Path of the Wise is that our spirits know how honest we are, and this will therefore affect our magical work, for good or for ill. Remember the discussion of the Wiccan saying "Give thy word sparingly and adhere to it like iron."

Truth is *fundamental* to connecting with other human beings if one wants to have clear and honest, rewarding and satisfying relationships. From close friendships to deeply romantic love, if we do not present ourselves truly, the connections will be based on pretty shaky ground, and that ground can shift and fall away, leaving us wounded by our own devices. This may seem simplistic, but it is surprising how many folks will present themselves as something they are not, just to make a connection (especially romantic ones). I know; I spent several years as a young adult trying to live up to everyone else's expectations, to the point that I never pursued the life I desired. Then, once my spiritual Path began to unfold before me, I started finding the courage to truly be myself, and many of my relationships fell apart because the people I was involved with thought I was *someone else*! That has of course changed now, but it took some serious relearning and real work to rebuild my spiritual foundation.

It's still difficult sometimes; being a spiritual leader in my community puts me in touch with all kinds of people, from prima donnas and posers to kind and humble servants and shining stars. Keeping my mouth shut about things that are none of my business, not taking things personally or making assumptions, and stating my truth without judgment or anger at the appropriate times can be a delicate balance. And believe me, I don't always hit it. None of us are perfect, and lest it ever be assumed I think I am always "spot on," in terms of any of the advice given in this chapter (or in this *course* for that matter), let me just say here and now that I have f'd up *grandly* so many times in my life, and I'm relatively certain that I will do so many times again, and thank the gods too, for that gives me a great deal of fodder for personal change and growth work, in addition to a wealth of information to advise you, dear Initiate, on how *not* to mess up *your* life! I am as far from perfect as any other human on the planet, and I have no delusions to the contrary, and truly, it's been said many times that we learn best from our mistakes, right? One of my favorite quotes, by a man named Jared Spool, hangs on the wall above my desk, and reminds me of this daily. It reads: "Good judgment comes from experience. Experience comes from bad judgment." So in my little blond-by-bottle brain, it follows then, that good judgment comes from ... *bad* judgment! See?

Don Miguel Ruiz states that being impeccable with your word is the first, most important agreement, though it is often the hardest to honor: "The word is not just a sound or a written symbol," he states. "The word is a force; it is the power you have to express and communicate, to think, and thereby *to create the events in your life.*"[41] As Witches, we must know on a deep, inner level that we create our lives with every thought, word, and action we make. In Alcoholics Anonymous, they say, "What you *think* about, you *talk* about, you *bring* about." This is also very true—for the flow of energy runs quite naturally in this pattern. So in our connections with others, if we are true to who we are, if we are impeccable with our word, we avoid a lot of excess baggage that could otherwise undermine the relationship. But as in the story at the beginning of this chapter, sometimes the Path of Truth is the hardest and scariest one to take.

We take the Path of Truth, braving those thorns, because as Witches we understand the importance of personal responsibility. The circles around us are filled with the people who are woven into our lives, in increasingly closer and deeper levels, and every action we take where they're concerned will affect our connections with them.

---

41. Don Miguel Ruiz, *The Four Agreements* (Amber-Allen Publishing, 1997), 26. Italics are mine.

THE ENERGY OF CONNECTION

In chapter 3, the Personal Responsibility chapter, we talked about the circles around us, radiating out from the center, which is self, to the larger community, the world community, and finally the earth herself. Certainly, our connections with our patron gods and matron goddesses are highlighted on this Initiate's Path, as we learn the solitary work and deep personal connection to our deities that feeds and nurtures our spirit. How will you express the energy of that connection? By now, you likely have a solid routine with your daily devotionals, whether they're short, simple words acknowledging your gratitude for another day of life, or deeply felt and pre-written poems expressing your love and appreciation of all you have been given, or something in between. These simple words of acknowledgment and love not only speak volumes to your chosen deities of your love and desire to connect with them, but they also serve to deepen and expand your connection to deity on a very personal level that can and should uplift you to a state of joy and spiritual contentment.

Many of us who identify as Pagan are ardent environmentalists, as we feel we have a duty to see that the earth is cared for, and so we do our best to reduce our own carbon footprints and to clean up the trash in our paths, so to speak. Moreover, our connection to the earth is expressed through our interactions with all of nature, and spending time in the wild places, then, becomes imperative for us to experience on a regular basis, to feel the energies of the elemental and animal spirits, as this recharges our spiritual batteries in a big way. Keeping our karma clean in terms of our impact on the planet helps a great deal in keeping our connection to Mother Earth clear and strong as well; it's not going to do your spirit much good if you claim to honor the earth in one moment, and in the next, you're flicking cigarette butts or throwing trash on the ground.

In the larger community, of course we must make sure we're presenting ourselves truly, but there are also concerns about how "out" we are as Witches. Certainly the Western world is open to the idea of religious freedom now, but that hasn't always been the case, and no one knows what the future holds. At any given time, the current administration could decide to revoke those rights under a false label of caring concern (remember George Bush Jr.'s faith-based initiatives?), so it's always good to be mindful of those around you whose beliefs could possibly be in conflict with yours.

Additionally, although we have a sacred duty as priests and priestesses to help people, we must also understand that they do not always desire or appreciate our help. What if someone's religious beliefs prohibit them from taking our help? We can't take that personally. You see someone hurting—a co-worker, perhaps, has an illness you feel you could send energy to help heal, but when you ask permission to do so (because, of course, you *always* ask permission before performing any kind of energy work on someone!), the person says no, and maybe not in a very kind way. We must remember that not everyone has the ability to be open-minded, and that the refusal is not about you. Sometimes, all we can do is light a candle for *ourselves*, with a simple prayer or spellwork to help us deal with not being allowed to help.

As we attend events and festivals, open full moon and Sabbat rituals, we'll have the opportunity to get to know folks in our larger magical communities, and our connections with them are also important to be mindful of. Sometimes, when people first meet in the Pagan community, the conversation can seem like a pissing contest—who knows what and whom, which person has the "proper" magical technique or knowledge or spin on the Way Things Are, and so on. There are even folks who seem to have assigned themselves the role of "magical police," who will make the rounds at community events, whispering poison into people's ears about so-and-so and such-and-such not doing "it" in a way that is considered "right," sometimes even remarking quite loudly and disapprovingly when someone does a ritual action or practice differently than the way they do it. Sometimes such individuals actually have the nerve to go around "correcting" people's pronunciations, because of course, the pronunciation of a word is much more important than the intent behind it (just kidding—we all know that's not true), embarrassing folks and putting them on the spot for no reason other than to stroke their own massive egos. Indeed, there are so many prima donnas and egomaniacs in some Pagan communities it can be overwhelming to even think about attending a festival or public ritual or event. But there are many, many more genuinely open-hearted individuals out there, too, who will welcome you with a smile and who will truly listen without judgment to what you have to say. Likewise, it is your duty to remain open-minded and to listen to what others have to say.

We all come to this Sacred Road from different backgrounds, experience, and intelligence levels, and no one has the One Right Way. It's human nature, I think, and awfully easy when learning anything new, to fall into the trap of thinking there actually is such a thing, and that one possesses such knowledge exclusively. It is unfortunately all too common for folks who are relatively new to a certain path or lifestyle in particular to fall prey to this delusional type of thinking. Just remember no matter how sure you are that you've got the "correct" handle on things, there are going to be dozens of people who have a different spin, who are just as "right" as you are. It is Western culture's "us vs. them" attitude that keeps us from understanding the simple truth that two people can see things differently and both still be "right."

In terms of helping someone magically, sometimes our friends will seek out our help, and sometimes the things they ask for may test our ethics to the extreme. Like the friend who's been jilted by a boyfriend and now she wants revenge? Do you help her? I should think not, unless perhaps the boyfriend was abusive or has wronged her in a very tangible way—and even then, we must take a great deal of care and thought as to how we can help without damaging our or our friend's karma. Sometimes the best thing we can do is work to heal the friend and let the boyfriend's karma take care of itself.

Finally, and most importantly, the energy of connection is about communicating with *ourselves*. Going deep within, we can determine what it is that we really are wanting in life, what our truest desires are. For many of us in Western culture, there is a tendency to follow along, to desire what we've been *programmed* to desire, which Ruiz refers to as society's dream, or the Dream of the Planet. But we are Witches, which means we are on our *own* Paths, and it is up to *us* to decide how we will walk it. At this time on your personal Path, dear Initiate, as I've said before, I encourage you to question *everything*, even, and perhaps most especially, those things you are strongly attached to. All of them. What have you been domesticated to believe? More importantly, what have you been domesticated to *desire*?

A classic example is what I call the Cinderella Dream. When it comes to romance and intimacy, our culture has programmed men and women with separate and distinctly different dreams. In Western culture, you'll quite often find that women want marriage and commitment, and men want personal and sexual freedom. Why? This puts us at odds with each other from the get-go, especially if we're heterosexual. Many gays and lesbians experience this imbalance as well; the dynamic can of course be a bit different in those relationships, though not necessarily.

Our culture has set us up so well. No matter what we do or how we conduct our relationships, there is always this underlying feeling that we're not… quite… getting it, isn't there? So many false beliefs… if your man truly loved you, he'd automatically know exactly what you wanted and would just give it to you… if your woman truly loved you, she'd drop everything to give nurturance… if the relationship is worth anything, it's worth cementing it spiritually or otherwise, with a ritual or license.

It's a good idea at this time to take a long hard look at all of our connections. What could we do to make them stronger, healthier? How can we heal our connections with ourselves? What old attitudes and ideas are better left by the wayside, and how can we express our personal truth? We also need to examine and possibly change the messages we give ourselves.

The shadows around connection

Finally, we must take some time and examine our shadows around connection—the way we interact with others, but more importantly, our relationships with ourselves. How many of us could take home the grand prize at a boxing match for the horrible things we use to beat up on *ourselves* with? We do it so well, as this is what we've been domesticated to do. We carry on the messages we were given in childhood, either from dysfunctional families or oblivious teachers who don't know us or have any idea how we think or feel. Then, in adulthood, suddenly we realize the things we've been saying about ourselves are not true, and are, in fact, creating dis-ease and inhibiting joy and healing. In my own path to healing, I realized that I'd perpetuated the belief (and said it a thousand times to myself and others), carried over from childhood, that I was "lazy." When I made this discovery, I started trying to train myself not to say that to myself, and in doing so, realized how very often I actually said it! These types of negative affirmations are very self-perpetuating. Stop them now! The best way I know to do this is to replace the negative statement (e.g., "I'm lazy") with a positive statement that expresses its opposite (e.g., "I'm sharp/lively/energetic/vibrant"), or, depending on the situation, making statements of *truth*, rather than passing judgment, about our experience ("I'm tired" or "I've worked hard!" vs. "I'm lazy").

So this moon cycle, it's a good idea to not only stop saying the things we use to beat ourselves up, but to examine, deeply, the reasons we say them. Chances are pretty good there's no valid reason to be so unkind to ourselves.

THE THROAT CHAKRA

The throat chakra is located at the base of the throat. Its element is sound, and its Sanskrit name is *visuddha*, which means "purification." Its color is bright, cerulean blue. This is the chakra that becomes activated whenever we need to speak up about something. Judith calls the throat chakra the "gateway to consciousness," as it's communication through sound, rhythm, and words that makes consciousness possible. The throat chakra is also responsible for creativity and self-expression, not only through the communications mediums, but through communication with the self as well as the Higher Self, through the signals and sounds of nature and spirit.

THIRTEEN HARMONIES WORK—CHANTS AND SONGS

The harmonic resonance of chanting and singing are highlighted with this moon, which makes sense; these are ways of connecting to both our gods and our guardians, as well as our communities. Living in several different Pagan communities has been an interesting experience for me; in some areas of the country, the entire community seems to be singing old and creating new wonderful Pagan songs and chants, and in still others, it seems that no one has ever even heard the idea that there might be Pagan songs. I love learning and collecting Pagan songs and chants and teach them to anyone who'll listen.

For this work, you only need look as far as your local or online Pagan bookstore or metaphysical shop to find songbooks and CDs with lots of great Pagan songs. I recommend asking to listen before buying a CD, as there are lots of good (and bad!) ones out there, and it's best to know what you're buying beforehand. Then, once you find some you like, take some time to learn them, and *sing your heart out*! They can be great used as devotionals, and are very uplifting. Of course, there is your local festival as well; in most areas of the country, you can learn a song or two at fest. Chanting has its place, too, and, as you likely remember from chapter 7, the Power chapter, can lift you up and help you build energy as well.

You can use chants and songs to achieve trance pretty easily. Once you have some favorites and a purpose for using them, you can "chant into trance" by repeating, softly, your chosen chant or song, over and over until it fades away (you won't want to use the Chant of the Magus for this work, as it builds energy up, rather than mellowing it down).

TOOL—PRAYER CANDLES

One of the best ways to connect with others on a spiritual plane is to light a candle for them, sending energy in prayer to those who need our help. These little prayer candles you light for others (or yourself) for specific purposes can be powerful allies as you walk this sacred road. Remembering the layers of magic, you can simply buy candles and light them, or you can add carved symbols or oils or both, to make the magic more powerful.

I sometimes use the little colored fifty-cent candles you can find at most any occult shop, which I anoint with oil and place in small holders or a dish of sand. I also have several colored glass holders I like to use. After choosing the appropriate color, I then hold and pray over a tealight, anoint it, and then drop it into the holder and let it burn all the way down. A really fun variation I made for myself and my real-life students one Yule were little sets of prayer candle holders, using terra cotta plates that I painted with acrylic paints. Each set had one plate in each of the rainbow colors, plus one each of black and white, which I then embellished with little symbols painted on with glitter and glue. It was an easy and rewarding craft project, which brought many smiles and lots of good use.

A simpler idea I've also done, which can be even more specific to the individual, would be to draw mandalas on small pieces of nice paper for each person, complete with runes, words and symbols, even prayers, then slip them, placemat-style, under a tealight, reading the words and symbols out loud to help one focus, while anointing and lighting the candle. I like this technique so much, as it's simple and easy to remember, and for busy Witches, these little notes can be really helpful.

Sometimes, the prayer being said is for an ongoing project, such as a major healing or prosperity work. For those purposes, I of course use a bigger candle, such as the pillar candles I use whenever I write. These are in jars that I keep on either side of my computer's keyboard, to honor and invite the energies of my personal muses. The prayers and anointing actions are of course the same, though the prayers or affirmations are said each time the candle is lit.

THE EIGHT VIRTUES OF THE GODDESS—HONOR

"Give thy word sparingly and adhere to it like iron" is all about honor. The diction-ary defines *honor* as "respectful regard,"[42] "a nice sense of what is right," to "treat with courtesy or respect," "to worship." To be honorable, then, is to act in ways we inherently know are right. Just as in the story at the beginning of this chapter, there is often more than one road, one choice to take, and the honorable choice isn't always the easiest one. It can be difficult sometimes to know which the "right" choice is, but I believe that if we take some time and look deep within, disregarding all of our cultural baggage around it, and apply the last lines of the Rede to it, we'll have our answers.

POSTURE OF POWER

If it works for you to do so, sit or stand, focusing your energy on the *sounds around you*. You may find yourself leaning toward the sounds, whether they're words coming from a person you're spending time with in a mundane setting, or the sounds of the city or nature's sweet song. Stay open to what is being said to you. Cup your hands around your ears, and hear how much clearer the sounds are. Try speaking or singing with your hands positioned thus. If you're inclined, speak the words in your heart as praise, a devotional to your gods and all of nature. Ground and center, and focus on your throat chakra and your own ability to speak. Breathe in vital life force energy and let it flow outward, as communication, as connection. Do not judge your words; just let them flow.

HOMEWORK

Make sure you do daily energy work of chakra spinning as outlined in the home-work section in the first-moon chapter of this unit. The throat chakra is a brilliant blue, and is located at the "hollow" of the throat.

   In your daily practices during this moon cycle, take a few moments to do some fire and air aspecting. Begin with an evocation: In your mind and spirit's "eye," feel the warm wind on your skin, inhale it into your lungs. Breathe deeply and fully, filling your lungs with the warm vibrant energy, knowing this is the energy of action, drive,

---

42. *Funk & Wagnalls Standard Dictionary* (J. G. Ferguson Publishing, 1978), 606.

and projection. Feel the energy, both within and without, and let it fill you. As you do so, take note of how like fire and air you are, how driven, how active, how warm and vital… and breathe. Feel the vitality of the life force surging through you, and allow yourself to revel in the energies.

Now allow yourself to feel the raw power of the fire and air energies within you, your ideas and your passions, your will and your causes, as well as the flow of air in and out of your lungs, and the physical manifestation of the emotions of love and lust, anger and Right Action, as well as spiritual bliss in your physical body. Now think about how fire and air manifest together elementally—together they create a blaze of passion, excitement, activity. Open yourself deeply and fully, filling your entire circle with this special and sacred energy that, combined, *is* the elemental energy of the God; the energy of drive, of action and intention. Aspecting is the act of acknowledging and feeling the energies of something that's merely a hair's breadth from our own energy. Take some time this moon cycle and think about the forceful drive energies that inhabit your every intention, that move and animate your every move, and know that these energies come from the spirit, both within and without.

Consider your connections. Take some time this moon and examine all the connections you have to others in your life as well as the connection you have with yourself. What is your brightest wish? What kinds of relationships would you have, if all was as you would wish it to be? Who would be in your life? How actively involved would s/he be? Who would you choose to walk away from? Why? How can your connections be healed or enhanced? What can you do to help yourself heal and grow?

Examine your shadows around connection, especially the connection you have with *yourself*. What are you communicating to yourself? Pay attention to the language you use in your communications with yourself. Are there judgments? I'll bet there are. Consider purging the negativity of your self-connection in some way, if desired, with this month's spellwork.

Write a personal Esbat. Begin brainstorming for the upcoming full and dark moons, decide what needs to leave or come into your life, and begin planning an Esbat ritual, including when it's most appropriate to do the work. Consider moon energies: What sign is she in, if any? What phase? Consider solar energies: Where are you on the Wheel of the Year? What time of day or night will you do the work? What day of the week? Consider other energies as well, such as whether Mercury or other relevant planets are in retrograde, your personal schedule, as well as your personal vibrance level (how good do you feel?) and the energies of your household (will you be able to be alone and undisturbed?).

Moon-tides work and devotionals: Don't forget to take some time each evening to get outside and look at (or contemplate the position of) the moon. Tune in to her energies; feel her power fill you. Remember to say your daily devotionals to your matron goddess(es) and patron god(s). Let their love fill you, let them show you how to become more powerful.

Read Anodea Judith's *Wheels of Life,* chapter 5—"Chakra Four: Sound." Do some of the exercises presented if you like.

Astral temple work: Take some time this moon to continue work on your astral temple. In your meditations, focus now on the doors. How many will there be? Doors, like windows, can symbolize how open you are. In your deep inner knowing, you can see and feel them. Are they strong and solid, carved with ornamentation or painted with runes and other warding symbols? Do they lock? Do they open? With or without passwords or keys? You've already set wards; do you need anything more? What about weather in your temple space? Will the doors be holding out cold and heat? Consider design, function, and usability as you cut holes for, and construct doors on, any and all levels of your temple you choose to.

10: The Sixth Moon—Understanding

> *You will never understand things until you trust them,*
> *for you inhibit what you doubt.*
> —Dion Fortune

MOON SIX—THE STORY

In the pre-dawn twilight, she rises. The Crone's Sickle, Hecate's tool and symbol of power. You feel the power rise in you even as her slender form clears the trees. So much you need to clear away, to discard in this rite, so much to try to understand. You have a friend who's going through many big changes in his life, and you want to be supportive, but there is so much of his experience you really can't relate to, and some of what he's doing is counter to what you've been raised to believe is "right." You feel uncomfortable around him now, at a loss for words, and uncertain whether he's acting in his own best interest. You cast.

After calling quarters and gods, you make your sacred entreaty. You ask for clarity, a cutting away of the muck and garbage of your culture, that you may come to understand the pure energy of your friend's new way of being, that you may be a better friend to him. In your mind's eye, you see Mighty Hecate, standing before the Great Tapestry of Being, handing you her sickle blade. Surprised, yet not wanting to insult the powerful

THE SIXTH MOON CORRESPONDENCES

Keywords: understanding, empathy, intuition, Right Action, discernment, the duty to truth

Energy: power-with/empathy

Chakra: brow/third eye

Chakra color: indigo

Element: water

Elemental color: blue or teal

Herbs and flowers: mugwort, rose

Incense: copal

Stones and metals: fluorite, sodalite

13 Harmonies: trance

Tool: journals and journaling

8 virtues: humility

Astral temple work: turrets and balconies

Shadow group: the Shadow of Blame

Energy keyword: empathy

Energy group: relationship energies—power-with

goddess, you reach out and take it, then realize that of course this is the only way. Your gods aren't about to do the cutting for you!

You heft the sickle in your hands, feel its weight and sharpness. You remember what Ruiz said about domestication and the Dream of the Planet. In your mind's eye, you begin to cut away the threads of the tapestry that appear to be laid over the original warp and weft. Carefully, so carefully, you slice through layers of what is becoming more and more obviously an overlay, and soon, the cleared layers reveal a field of pure power; a black night sky containing a billion stars. "Of course," you whisper, cutting away more and more layers to reveal the beautiful starry sky of the tapestry. "Of course. The gods gave us carte blanche. It's we humans who've made all these social mores and rules and taboos." As you clear the last of the overlay, your trance deepens and you see the underlying threads between the stars, as well as some threads from the stars... to you!

You realize then, even more profoundly than you already knew, that we are all interconnected, and that we are the creators of our own destinies, as well as the destiny of the planet... only... there's a deeper meaning still... Under all the thread patterns, under all those stars, you find you can now see an underlying energy pattern—a stronger current. Destiny? Karma? Fate? Underneath the stars that you now recognize as the lights of various spirits inhabiting the planet, underneath the energy threads and ley lines, lies a vitality that cannot be extinguished, the vibrant and surging power of Mother Earth, and like a light bulb coming on, you **know**. She will **always** carry on, will always and has always survived, in spite of what humankind has done to her, and she will **always** forgive our stupidity and exploitation, unlike us humans, who are largely unforgiving, sometimes even with our earth and our gods.

With this knowledge, you suddenly remember your friend. Now that the muck and mutter of humanity's petty rules and impositions have been cleared away, understanding seems quite achievable. No, his choices are not the ones you would make for yourself, but seeing his energy pattern and desires has made you realize this is the most logical and beneficial path **for him**. With that knowledge you finally and truly do understand. You know now that you can fully support him, and can even empathize to some degree, and so you now find yourself wishing for these changes on his behalf.

Gone are the doubts and fears you had for him even an hour ago, replaced by the light of clarity and understanding. You hand the sickle back to Mighty Hecate with a heartfelt thank you and come up from the meditation with a prayer for your friend's fulfillment in his new life—a deeply sincere prayer that leaves you tingling and glad of his changes.

THE ENERGY OF UNDERSTANDING

Thomas Moore, in his book *Soul Mates*, says that in order to understand something, one must "stand under" it.[43] "At the level of soul," he states, "the way to understand is to 'stand under,' to move closer and closer toward that which has our interest." A little later, he says, "... one way of doing it is to let the current passion or preoccupation get on top, to stand under it until it tells us who or what it is." So, just as in the story above, sometimes it takes a closer look at the underlying energy pattern, but

---

43. Thomas Moore, *Soul Mates* (HarperCollins, 1994), 148.

this requires patience and an openness not easily achieved by those of us who were raised in Western culture.

In our domestication, we're taught that to be open is to be vulnerable is to be hurt easily and repeatedly by anyone who wishes to take advantage of us. This attitude is not only untrue, but extremely unhealthy. We stay open, just as we practice forgiveness, for *us*, not for others. A heart that is closed off and full of fear sends out a clear message that the owner of that heart doesn't want to invite, communicate, or share love with anyone, and creates an energy pattern that perpetuates loneliness and sorrow. In addition, a closed heart *hurts*—from a point of view of darkness of despair, one can only stand on the edge of the crowd, observing the compassion, happiness, and connections others share. One may believe one is "interacting," but the connections lie only on the surface, and the kind of depth that is fulfilling to the soul is never achieved, because no one can get past such intimidating walls.

Sometimes, it's healthy to keep our hearts under wraps for a while—such as after we lose a love through either choice or death, but this is different from completely closing them off. Most of us were not raised with the slightest idea of how to conduct a healthy relationship. Quite the contrary; we're given such ridiculous notions by our culture that it's sometimes surprising to discover that some folks have actually made long-term relationships work. So taking some time off in order to heal our hearts in preparation to open them back up again is wise. Then, when we are ready, it's also a good idea to begin to practice a little discernment, which is not at all the same as being closed; it's about using our intuition and our minds to make better choices.

I once knew a woman who could best be described as "everybody's darling"—she was kind and accommodating, gave her all to the folks who came to see her in her line of work. As time went on, however, I began to see the threads: her great desire to be all things to all people not only exhausted her, but was in fact the indirect cause of many good people suddenly and unexpectedly leaving her life. Turned out that her lack of discernment kept a lot of unethical scoundrels in a very tight circle around her, which the more loving and caring and *ethical* people in her life had trouble penetrating. Eventually they would get tired of trying, and the relationships would fade or disappear, seemingly overnight. She would cry in pain over these losses, but never seemed to really connect the dots. There's an old saying, by Arthur Schopenhauer: "Everybody's friend is nobody's." So in the energy of understanding we must remember Hecate's sickle and our own bright blades of discernment; we must cut away what doesn't work or feed the energy of health in order to get to that starry field of potential. Only then can we truly pursue with clarity the Paths of our hearts.

USING DISCERNMENT

The sword of discernment can only help us if we take the time to listen to its subtle song. Those nagging doubts about the new friend in your life are there for a reason. Rather than blundering along, projecting our wishes and fantasies onto another, it's wise to stop and take a moment to breathe, assess, and truly "stand under" the relationship as it unfolds to see if it really is for our highest good. At this point, we can take a realistic look at the person we're developing a connection with and see them for who they truly are. Only then can we make a real choice to pursue the relationship or not.

Using discernment goes hand in hand with presenting ourselves truly, as discussed in chapter 7, the Power chapter, only this is the other edge of the blade, as it were. Remember that it's okay that not everyone will like us, and that it is not *for us* to worry about whether or not they do; all you can be concerned about is whether or not *you like the other person,* and whether or not you feel and intuit that the other person would be *good for you.* And *that,* ladies and gentlemen, **is** the sword of discernment.

USING OUR INTUITION

We're taught, from even before the Dedicant level in this religion, to honor our intuition. How do we make it stronger? The first step is in believing in ourselves. Ever tell yourself, "I have a funny feeling about this," whether it's about taking a different route to work or not getting involved in a project or relationship? How many times have we been sorry we didn't listen?

In the Basics chapter in *Dedicant,* I gave a few exercises designed to help one tune in and focus on their intuition. There are so many ways one can do this: the orange meditation; "guessing" color or Zener cards (or tarot cards or runes, for that matter); setting your phone so that everyone has the same ring tone and then "guessing" who's calling you without looking at the caller ID; following your hunches; and finally, writing it all down, to give your mind and spirit confirmation that you did, indeed, sense this particular thing correctly. Writing it down not only gives you a record of confirmed "hunches," but I believe this action also trains your mind to pay attention to such things in the future. Faith plays a big role, as does that sword of discernment—being honest with yourself about what you see and hear and sense and *know*.

A few ideas of other things you can do to enhance and deepen your psychic awareness are to continue to work with whatever divination method you've chosen, and especially to stay open to the feedback you get from others regarding the accuracy of your readings; continue to track and stay aware of yourself in your dreams; continue your energy exercises both alone, and if possible, with a trusted friend; and tune in to your psychic awareness to locate lost objects.

THE SHADOW OF BLAME

This second triplet of moons covers how we stand in the world: our attitudes, connections, and short- and long-term relationships. We've discussed how important honesty is, both with ourselves and in the way we present ourselves to others. This isn't always the easiest thing to do; we're raised on games and deceptions in this culture, so making (and keeping!) a commitment to honesty and truth can be a real challenge. So once again, we are called upon to look at the circles around us, but this time, we're looking at the shadows between the lights, as it were. These are the shadow energies of judgment, arrogance, self-righteousness, hypocrisy, control, deception, and abuse. It's all too easy to get caught up in blaming others for our life circumstances, but as people who follow a magical Path, as Witches who understand personal responsibility, we know that the creators of our lives are our*selves*, and that blame is an incorrect avenue to follow if we truly wish to heal and grow.

In our deepest and most intimate relationships, we are called upon to look at how *we* have been unkind, neglectful, dishonest or deceptive. Have we judged others based on our own perceptions of "right" and "wrong"? How have we judged ourselves or our worthiness in terms of relating with others? How have we shortchanged or sabotaged ourselves? Don't let these examinations cause you guilt or grief, as we are looking at them in order to heal them. But take some time now and look at your shadows around relationships.

I refer to this section as the "shadow of blame," as it is getting caught up in blaming others (whether people or our gods, or something else entirely) that keeps us from examining our own attitudes and actions. It may be a little hard to swallow, but we must accept the fact that we are where we are because *we've put ourselves there*. For whatever reason, our spirits have decided that we need to learn something, so we get to deal with that broken arm or broken heart or broken budget until we can figure out how to heal it. Staying focused on blame just keeps us in the cycle of pain and loss.

This is not to say that we don't all have very real issues and challenges. However, real healing only comes when we focus on finding and healing the *problem*, just as any good healer would do. What I've found helpful is staying open to the messages my gods send through other people in chance conversations; objects in nature; and through personal meditations, divinations, and dreamwork, while keeping the pointed intention of finding those keys and causes. I believe that once one finds the origin of a problem, one has in one's hands a great part of the key in healing it. But, as we must go back in order to find these keys, we of course see situations lost in memory that can be upsetting and unsettling, and it's easy to project our pain and fear onto the memory and become stuck in the cycle of blame rather than getting past that to the spiritual lesson we were trying to learn in the first place, and find the key. Sometimes this work can be overwhelming and deeply painful. In those cases, it's best to take it a little at a time.

For example, take an adult woman who was unwanted as a child. From the very beginning of her life, she was rejected. As her life unfolded, of course, her spirit gave her many opportunities to deal with that profound and immediate and total rejection by putting her in situations where she could either choose self-love or self-rejection. No, her mother didn't want her. That's a painful and deeply disturbing memory. She can choose to wallow in it, stay stuck in pain and fear and tell the world to "f-off," closing herself off to relationships because she "knows" they'll all end in pain and rejection, or she can choose instead to learn to stop rejecting her*self*, stop the self-sabotaging patterns that go hand in hand with self-rejection, and find the seed of love deep within that she can build into a healthy self-acceptance and self-love. I believe that finding our causes is just as crucial to healing our emotional ailments as it is to healing our physical ones. The trick is to focus on neither blame nor judgment once we find those keys, but to use them as valuable tools for healing.

THE BROW (THIRD EYE) CHAKRA

The third eye chakra is located between and slightly above the eyebrows, which is why it is sometimes referred to as the brow chakra. Its color is indigo—the deep purply blue of the night sky. Its Sanskrit name is *ajna*, which means "to perceive" or "to command." This chakra is correlated to our pineal gland, and its element is light. This is the chakra of our *intuition*.

Our intuition can be strongly connected to our ability to see, and to see on the inner planes. The word *clairvoyance*, according to Anodea Judith, means "clear seeing."[44] When we go within, such as in meditation, or when we open ourselves to observing energy patterns instead of projecting our own ideas and beliefs on the situation, we can receive very clear messages. The problem for many of us in the Western world is in overcoming our programming, our "domestication" as Ruiz calls it, and allow the images to be what they are. Interpretation from that point becomes a simpler matter, as we're allowing the light of truth to shine. Just as in the discussion above, our keys can help us wallow, or they can help us heal.

THIRTEEN HARMONIES WORK—TRANCE

It's been said that what we in Western culture refer to as "meditation" is actually trance. And while it's true that trance can be achieved in a number of different ways, I would have to say that the most common method is simply to deepen and relax fully into our meditations. As we go deeper and deeper within, we often experience euphoria—a sense of well-being, happiness, and contentment. This can deepen and expand even further the longer we travel on the inner planes.

Other nice ways to achieve trance include, but are not limited to, candle gazing, light and shadow play, color play, weaving, spinning, doing stitchwork, dancing, drumming, singing, chanting, having our hair combed or our skin lightly brushed with a soft cloth or scourge, listening to soft music, deep breathing, and light sex play. Some traditions include the use of the Mother's sacred substances such as ganja or other herbs and plants, but I recommend you be careful not to smoke too much ganja (which would tend to make you spacey or sleepy), and to only use the more intense substances with a guardian to watch over and assist you, and then only when you

---

44. Anodea Judith, *Wheels of Life* (Llewellyn, 1999), 298.

have a pretty good idea of what to expect both with the meditative experience and with how the body is going to react to the substance. All of these techniques can help take one's focus away from the self and move it toward the goal.

As we discussed in the Core/Ground chapter (chapter 5), trance dancing is fairly common in the Pagan community—just go to any drum circle and watch the dancers. As they circle the fire throughout the evening, they become more and more entranced. The drummers feed their energy, just as they feed the drummers' energy, and if you look closely, you'll see that many of the drummers are trancing too. I'm one of those folks—just can't trance dance, as I mentioned; I get too into it and get lost, and, well… I think the drummers I've fallen into will probably all say they're grateful I hung up my trance-dancing shoes.

Take some time this moon to experiment with trance and find what works for you. Start simply, with meditation, and then try some other methods. Note any differences in the depth achieved with various techniques.

TOOL—JOURNALS

As we discussed earlier in this chapter, often the best way to understand something is to "stand under" it. A helpful tool for that purpose is journaling. In the privacy of our own sacred books, we can explore all the avenues of a thing, all its perceived energy patterns, possible causes and outcomes, benefits and challenges, and in so doing, often find keys not only to how we feel about something, but also to why we feel that way to begin with. Is this something we can live with? If not, why not? Is it truly how we feel, or is it a domesticated belief? If we can go to our journaling without judgment toward ourselves, and just let the stream of consciousness flow, we can follow the many threads connecting our feelings and perceptions to any blocks we have in understanding ourselves and others.

Magical journals can be sections in one's grimoire, special books purchased because they "just felt right," cloth or leather covers (purchased or homemade) for blank books or notebooks that can be replaced in the cover when full, or inexpensive blank notebooks covered with hand-drawn or painted decorations. The only limit is your own imagination.

THE EIGHT VIRTUES OF THE GODDESS—HUMILITY

Humility, in my opinion, is in alarmingly short supply in some Pagan communities. A great many of the folks you'll meet struggle with a lack of self-esteem, which, at one extreme can manifest itself as a hesitation to do even the simplest ritual actions with power and authority, and at the other extreme can manifest as an arrogant posturing, which comes from (guess!) a lack of self-esteem. The prima donnas and posers often don't really think they're better than you; just as Linda Goodman says about the sun sign Leo's "private inner doubts of worth, well hidden beneath outward vanity,"[45] we can look at these folks as strutting their stuff, as it were, to try to convince people that they're better than *they themselves* think they are. This arrogant posturing is insecurity at its height.

To be humble is to have the attitude and ability of recognizing both our strengths and our limitations, understanding that we're not the end-all and be-all of all things Witchy (or anything else for that matter), while still having confidence that we do, indeed, know what we know, and that we have some good skills and ideas, even some damn fine ones. It's about a healthy balance; recognizing our strengths and weaknesses *as they truly are.*

POSTURE OF POWER

If it works for you to do so, sit or stand comfortably, leaning slightly forward, listening. Listen with your spirit, not just your ears. Open your arms out slowly, palms tilted slightly upward in a posture of receiving. Allow your mind to become still and your spirit to become settled into this posture, and listen! Listen to the sounds you hear, and then focus on listening to the sounds you *don't* hear. Listen for the gaps in the conversations around you, the stillness between raindrops or wind gusts, the sound of a silent snowfall. Let your consciousness be as open as possible, and then open it a little … bit … more. Allow yourself to acknowledge the divinity in yourself (and, in your public/social life, the person you are interacting with). This energy can be expressed by the Sanskrit word *namaste*, which means, roughly, "I bow to you," but that carries a deeper meaning conveying an acknowledgment of the Divine in

---

45. Linda Goodman, *Love Signs* (Mannitou Enterprises, 1978), 29.

both the person being greeted and the person doing the greeting. Try saying it to yourself, both in circle and in front of a mirror. Be blessed.

HOMEWORK

Make sure you do daily energy work of chakra spinning as outlined in the homework section in the first-moon chapter of this unit. The brow, or third eye, chakra is a deep indigo blue, and is located just above the eyebrows, in the center of the forehead.

In your daily practices during this moon cycle, take a few moments to do some earth and water aspecting. Begin with an evocation: In your mind and spirit's "eye," feel the cool water of a lake or river on your skin as your toes squish the mud of the bottom (as always, if you can get out to a lake and do this physically, all the better!). Feel the energy permeating the surface of your being, and know that you are made up of mostly water, your flesh, the flesh of the earth. Open yourself deeply and fully, filling your entire circle with this special and sacred energy that, combined, *is* the elemental energy of the Goddess. Know that this is the energy of rest, healing, repose, and the dreamtime; the energy of *receiving*. Experience the energy, both within and without, and let it surround and touch you. As you do so, take note of how like earth and water you are, how mellow, how loving, how cool and dreamy... and breathe. Rest in the feeling, bathing in the energies.

Now allow yourself to feel the solidity of the earth energies within you, your flesh and bones, as well as the flow of blood and other fluids in your physical body. Now think about how earth and water manifest together elementally—together they are slip, mud, clay. Our bodies, in many world mythologies, were originally fashioned out of clay by our gods. *Aspecting* is the act of acknowledging and feeling the energies of something that's merely a hair's breadth from our own energy. Take some time this moon cycle and think about the clay that is your very human body; how malleable it is, how easily it can be shaped and re-shaped with time and effort, how great its ability to remake itself, how miraculous its ability to heal.

Consider your ability to understand and empathize. How strong is this ability in you, really? No matter how much we may feel ourselves capable of these energies, they can *always* be improved. Think about the last time you had a disagreement with a friend or family member. Did you stay open to the other person's words and ideas about the situation? Or did you close yourself off to understanding by being defensive and certain of your "rightness" in the discussion? Next time, try to open yourself even more to understanding their side, even if you feel you are "right."

Shadow work: With this second triplet of moons, we've learned about the energies of *relating:* our compassion, our connections, and our ability to understand and feel empathy. Now it's time to look at the shadows around these energies as a whole: the Shadow of Blame. What needs to be re-examined in this realm? What still needs healing? Where are our blocks and what are our fears when it comes to our relationships with others? Personal responsibility is highlighted yet again, as we take ownership of our own role in how our personal relationships are played out. Once more, we're called upon to look dispassionately at our own behavior and shadows and to understand that this is not a time to judge ourselves, but to find the keys to the causes, which are ultimately the keys to healing.

As we learned about the energies of love and loving, we discussed the difference between compassion and pity, and learned that both energies have their place. Anodea Judith says, "Sometimes the most profound love is that which can simply let things be the way they are."[46] How have we pushed to have things be as we think they "should" be?

We also talked about what it is to have a Sacred Charge. How will we handle that relationship should it ever arise in our circle of friends or covenmates? We learned how important it is, as priests and priestesses of the Old Gods, to keep our health and well-being first when we have such a challenging responsibility, or we have nothing to give anyone, and that our health is more than just about the physical. How have we cared for our health in the five sacred realms? What still needs smoothing out or healing? What shadows do we need to chase around duty and obligation?

When we met with Hecate at the crossroads, did we choose the Path of Power by facing the shadows of our own attitudes and behavior in how we connect and relate to those closest to us? Or is it still a little too scary to walk down that Path of Thorns? We can remember that *courage is fear that has said its prayers,* and try again. We examined again the role of personal responsibility and learned that we can only change ourselves, which leads to a change in our relationships. We found the shadows, if any, that still lingered around our *word* and how important *truth* is in keeping our con-

---

46. Anodea Judith, *Wheels of Life* (Llewellyn, 1999), 201.

nections clear and healthy. How have we honored truth? We also discovered that two people can believe or practice magic in vastly different ways and still both be "right," as "right" is what's right for the individual. How have we judged others for being different from ourselves?

Finally, we were again challenged to question everything, and to use our swords of discernment to cut the threads of fear and insecurity in order to discover our own truest Dream and Path. How have we honored our intuition? Do we still need to heal our attitudes around our psychic abilities? Do we understand the difference between compassion and pity, and do we practice each of these energies where appropriate?

Take some time this moon to consider all of the above issues and to begin to clear and heal the shadows around them. Remember again that this is ongoing work; once we think we've "conquered" our shadows, they'll be more than happy to remind us they're still there, waiting to trip us up again! Once our connections with others are healed or healing, we'll be ready to reach out to our communities on a more expanded level.

Write a personal Esbat. Begin brainstorming for the upcoming full and dark moons, decide what needs to leave or come into your life, and begin planning an Esbat ritual, including when it's most appropriate to do the work. Consider moon energies: What sign is she in, if any? What phase? Consider solar energies: Where are you on the Wheel of the Year? What time of day or night will you do the work? What day of the week? Consider other energies as well, such as whether Mercury or other relevant planets are in retrograde, your personal schedule, as well as your personal vibrance level (how good do you feel?) and the energies of your household (will you be able to be alone and undisturbed?).

Moon-tides work and devotionals: Don't forget to take some time each evening (or day, depending on her phase) to get outside and look at (or contemplate the position of) the moon. Tune in to her energies; feel her power; let her love fill you. Remember to say your daily devotionals to your matron goddess(es) and patron god(s). Let their energies fill you; let them show you their love and truth as you express your love and truth to them.

Read chapter 7 in *Wheels of Life*—"Chakra Six: Light."

Astral temple work: Take some time this moon cycle to add any higher-level windows and features to your astral temple, such as turrets and balconies. These openings represent and can help us connect with our higher selves—sometimes called our "superconscious." Will they be large enough to host a ritual gathering, or smaller, for more personal rites and workings? Will there be some of each? What about those upper windows? Will they be clear, ornamented, stained glass, or simply open to the elements, with or without shutters on the sides?

11: The Seventh Moon—Devotion

When you are awake in devotion to divinity,
you abide in the timeless.
—Jennifer Reif

MOON SEVEN—THE STORY

You stand before your altar in the wee hours of the morning,
when all is still and dark. Lighting one black candle for the
dark moon and to honor your Lady, and one white candle to
represent the day's light that will grow today, in honor of your
Lord, you prepare to explore the Mysteries of these deities. You
breathe deeply and send your roots down deep, deeper, and
deeper still, down to bedrock. You want to be fully rooted, and
fully aware for the work you're about to do. The moon is new
today, so you know she'll rise with the sunrise, and although
*you can't see her, you can **feel** her in the sky, traveling toward*
you on the first rays of the sun. You chose this dark moon to
show your devotion to your gods as a new beginning in your
life, to herald an act that will solidify your commitment to and
acceptance of their guidance from this day forward. This is not
work you take lightly, or with your eyes closed. Some of the
lessons you've learned lately have been painful, yet you know
they've made you strong. You bow your head, grateful for the
blessings as well as the challenges, and then decide that this act

THE SEVENTH MOON CORRESPONDENCES

Keywords: commitment, duty, truth and love in accord, spiritual ardor, worship, reverence

Energy: surrender

Chakra: crown/bliss

Chakra color: violet or white

Element: spirit

Elemental color: white, black

Herbs and flowers: jasmine, violet, wormwood

Incense: frankincense and myrrh

Stones and metals: moonstone, pearl

13 Harmonies: meditation

Tools: the adoration; prayer books

8 virtues: mirth

Astral temple work: roof, rooftop spaces

Shadow group: the shadow of fame; the dark side of community service

Energy keyword: aspecting

Energy group: caring for our gods

alone is not enough. You kneel, open your arms, palms upward, and look up. Your altar is beautiful, as beautiful as you could make it this morning, to show your gods how very much you care, how deep is your ardor and commitment to this sacred Path. You feel both pregnant and empty; spiritually naked before your gods, as the cherished words from The Charge of the Goddess[47] ring through your heart and mind, "... before my face, beloved of gods and humankind, reveal your innermost self, and let your spirit soar!" You deepen into trance, settling back on your cushion, and begin your journey ...

---

47. See this book's appendix.

You wander down a winding path through the woods in the twilight, watching the shadow play between tree and bush; branch and bud. You feel your closest patron god at your side, guiding you, his strong presence a comfort in these unfamiliar surroundings. Up ahead, you see faint light coming through the trees, and you know your beloved matron goddess, too, is near. Soon, you see her before you, in all her glory, and with that very acknowledgment, you are on your knees before her, wide open to her messages and her wishes for you. Suddenly, you are overwhelmed with love; both the bright ardor you feel for her, and her encompassing compassion and caring for you. There's more, though: you also feel a surge of joy as she projects her very real gratitude and pride in your choice to stand before her today. She tells you the work you are doing is important, and will change the world in bright and beneficial ways. She speaks of tasks she wishes you to do, and energies she wishes you to embrace in order to become healthier and more powerful. Some of the things she suggests surprise you and you balk; you've got so many other things to do ... still, you listen respectfully, trying to think of how you can make it all work. You take as much time as needed to listen to her messages and guidance, willing yourself to remember all the agreements you make with her. Your patron god has words for you, too, words of truth and perception, duties and challenges, and you listen respectfully, nodding your agreement, though some of his requests, too, seem daunting. Still, you are committed, honored by their love for you and their trust in you; you will not fail them.

Finally, their counsel finished, you begin speaking the words you wrote especially for your most beloved deity this morning, expressing how much it means to you to have this deity's presence in your life, how important it is to you to follow their wise counsel. You speak of your intentions for the coming cycle, and pause only a moment to gather your strength and your courage. You take a deep breath, more certain now than ever that the act you're about to perform is indeed what you wish to do; what you've always known you'd do, when the time made itself known.

You pause only a moment to look deep into eyes that mirror your soul's own bright truths and deep longings. You draw your blade, and, bowing gracefully, lay it gently at your beloved deity's feet.

SURRENDER—THE ENERGY OF DEVOTION

The act of laying one's sword at the feet of another is a time-honored way of expressing a wish to serve, but it's a serious commitment, dear Initiate, so if you're ever so inclined to perform such a serious act, please take some time to ponder all the implications for—I'd suggest *at least* a season, preferably a whole cycle of seasons—before making such a commitment. For once it's made, *especially* if that commitment is made to a deity, there's really no going back. To lay your blade at someone's feet is to swear to them that you are their servant, but much more importantly, that you are their *champion.* It is a promise of loyalty and service to that being, and you are stating by doing so that you're prepared to do whatever it takes to defend, protect, and support that being, *no matter what.* And again, if this being you've just sworn such service and fealty to is a god or goddess, it also implies that you will heed even more carefully the things they guide you to and suggest as you walk this sacred road.

As their servant, sometimes your gods will ask you to do things you wouldn't necessarily choose for yourself. If you are told to do "A," for example, but you're too busy doing "B," "C," or "D," and you continue along your way, either telling them or not telling them of your intent directly, they will still be there, patiently waiting. And when you ask the next time how you may serve them, they will calmly, but firmly say, "Do 'A,'" and no matter how many times you tell them you *don't want* to do "A," you have other things you need to or wish to do, you have, indeed, laid your blade at their feet, and *they know that.* You *will*, I assure you, eventually and inevitably, do "A." I know: Artemis is patient, yet commanding, and as stubborn as I am, "A" still *always* happens, as soon as I'm tired of fighting, and then, all is well.

So at this time on your Path, you may want to refrain from any fealty swearing, as it were, though in many ways, the principles one learns as an Initiate are learned in preparation for just such an act, or at least we're beginning to look at (and perhaps starting to weave) that energy pattern. For one of the greatest and most rewarding ways we can show our devotion to our gods is *to surrender;* to listen to their guidance *and then actually follow it!* It's simple, but not always easy, this surrendering thing; a wise priest I know once said to me, "You have to pass through the gates of passion, love, faith, trust, knowing. It has to do with will. Surrender means no separation. Therefore, your will is to please them. You are one; the only things you surrender are your fears and doubts."

This is not to say that total surrender is the only way to express devotion. On the contrary, there are many ways, and total surrender takes time to be prepared for. Of course we aspire to hold our chosen deities in perfect *love*, but it takes moons, seasons, even years sometimes to get to that place of perfect *trust*, the depth of which is required before we can even *consider* laying down that blade.

At this point in your path, you've been doing daily devotionals. You've probably deepened enough in your faith and your connection to your chosen deities that you've begun to experience some blissful feelings, some highly charged energies of joy and spiritual passion; the energy of *adoration*. There may be times when you've felt a rush in circle as you've raised energy, or a tingling, particularly around the crown chakra, as you express your devotion. That's as it should be. Now is the time to allow those emotions to fill you up, overwhelm you, and encompass you as you connect and express your love for your gods. This is the easiest way to move into aspecting, and eventually, invocation.

THE CROWN CHAKRA

Sometimes called the bliss chakra, is located at or above the top of the head. Its color is violet or white, depending on your perception or tradition. Its Sanskrit name is *sahasrara* and it means "thousandfold," which refers to the thousand-petaled lotus that symbolizes it. This chakra is correlated to our pituitary gland, and its element is thought. This is the chakra of our awareness of and connection to the Divine.

As we journey to higher and higher states of consciousness and divine awareness, as we chase our shadows and become healthier and stronger, we also become aware of how like our chosen deities we really are. This, again, is not conceit or arrogance, but an understanding of our own strengths; our gifts. In chapter 8 ("Chakra Seven: Thought") of Judith's *Wheels of Life*, she discusses the millions and millions of connections, through sensory receptors and synapses in our bodies and brains, that make us much more sensitive to our internal environments than to our external ones, proving that it is *from within* that we learn the most![48] I couldn't agree more, yet it's interesting to note how easy it is for us humans to doubt ourselves. We constantly question our own abilities and intuition, and that's good to some degree, because questioning helps us find the truth, and to keep from falling prey to any player, or inner delusion, that comes along, but there is a point where we must open ourselves to our inner wisdom, have confidence in what we see and hear from the Divine, and let faith rule.

---

48. Anodea Judith, *Wheels of Life* (Llewellyn, 1999), 321.

THIRTEEN HARMONIES WORK—MEDITATION

Silence is the altar of God.

PARAMHANSA YOGANANDA

There are many, many different ways to meditate: repeating a mantra; gazing at a candle flame or other object such as a crystal or crystal ball; following a guided meditation led by another; chanting or singing into a trance state; or simply closing one's eyes and focusing on a scene in nature, a symbol, or even nothing at all. As you've likely been meditating for a while now, dear Initiate, now is a good time to consider trying some different techniques. In the October and November chapters you were (or will be) assigned *The Inner Guide Meditation* by Edwin Steinbrecher, which gives yet another viewpoint and technique: that of finding your inner guide. The idea behind any meditation technique is to allow one to empty one's mind of all outer influences and allow the inner wisdom to speak. This isn't always as easy as it sounds. Outer influences aren't always just the phone ringing or the buzz of traffic outside our windows. Outer influences can also seem to come from within: the chattering voice inside our heads, reminding us of all the tasks we have yet to complete by the end of the day, where we need to be in an hour, and on and on. Many of us also have a skeptic inside our minds, telling us that what we're trying to do won't work, that we're not good enough, etc. I sometimes refer to this as having "too many committees in my head."

The best thing to do, when all the nagging thoughts are trying to block us, is not to fight them, as that's just another form of distraction that will serve to keep those thoughts foremost in your mind, but to just *allow them their voice*, and then *let them go*—simply say to those thoughts, "Okay, whatever, of course..." or other such words that will allow you to just let them go on their way so you can get back to what you were doing.

This moon cycle, try some meditation techniques you haven't tried before, and see what works best for you.

TOOLS—THE ADORATION, PRAYER BOOKS

Up to now, dear Initiate, you've been practicing devotionals pretty regularly, possibly even adorations. The *adoration* is different from a devotional primarily in its intensity, and it can absolutely be used as a *tool*—both for facilitating a closer relationship with the Divine and for preparing you for the invocations you will eventually do. If you haven't yet written devotionals or adorations, now would be a good time to start. If you have already begun, take a look at the ones you've written. Remember that an adoration, like a devotional, is an expression of *praise and gratitude*; it doesn't ask for anything, with the exception of asking the Divine to hear you. An adoration goes beyond the devotional in *emotion* and *spiritual passion*, and the words you write for these expressions can overlap or be used interchangeably, as we can't always predict when our expressions will bring us to that deeply felt state. The idea is to be open to that depth of emotion, and to allow it to flow naturally.

Another tool I'd like to suggest along these lines is a *prayer book*. You can find special and beautiful bound books you can use as prayer/devotional books at most any bookstore or metaphysical shop, and there are so many choices! However, the important thing is the *content*. A fancy book is not going to mean anything if it's not used, whereas a simple spiral notebook the practitioner has drawn a nice sketch or written words of praise on the cover of might be a whole lot more powerful. Whatever you choose to use for your prayer book will become a valuable and beloved tool over years of use. You can also make homemade versions, similar to the ideas suggested for journals (on page 143) in chapter 10.

THE EIGHT VIRTUES OF THE GODDESS—MIRTH

It is tremendously important, dear Initiate, as you become more powerful (and more serious!) about your religion, to *keep a sense of humor*. I know it's not always easy. There is so much to learn, and the Initiate's program can be pretty intense with all the reading, practicing, and homework, but if we don't keep our sense of humor, we can become grumpy and snarky and life can lose a lot of its joy and meaning. Power is a wonderful thing, but it only goes so far. I'm reminded of a line said by a big, burly guy in an old comedy sketch: "I can lift 300 pounds over my head, and still nobody likes me!"

Now of course this doesn't mean that it's okay to blow off huge mistakes or ignore obstacles that must be taken care of. Instead, it means we need to try not to let life's challenges get to us too much, and to keep our seriousness and intense study and worship balanced with the lighter energies of joy and happiness, and especially *laughter*; and to find it in our hearts to laugh at *ourselves*. That's more powerful than you may imagine. When we can laugh at ourselves and let go of discomfort, we can get back on task much more positively and effectively than when we're letting anger drive us to take our aggressions out on the situation. So keep your humor! If you find yourself unable to laugh, take a day *off!* Go to the park and watch the kids and dogs play, or go to a funny movie, but *get out* of your home or office and away from your frustrations, and cut loose a little! Let the gods of mirth and humor help ease your heart and mind. You'll be amazed at how much easier it is to focus on work once you've allowed yourself a bit of slack time.

POSTURE OF POWER

If it works for you to do so, kneel on both knees, and open your arms, palms facing front. Allow yourself to open spiritually, receiving the love of the Divine. Then, project your love and adoration back to the Divine, and let the energy flow as your hands and arms move up, and out, rising up to the heavens. Be blessed.

HOMEWORK

Make sure you do daily energy work of chakra spinning as outlined in the homework section in the first-moon chapter of this unit. The bliss chakra is a bright violet-white, and is located about an inch above the top of the head.

Energy meditation—Aspecting: In our lesson this moon, which covers the energies of devotion and surrender, we discussed that there may have been times while doing your devotionals or adorations when you felt a rush or a tingling, particularly around the crown chakra. The first time I ever felt this I knew my matron goddess was "knocking at the door" so to speak; she was a hair's breadth from me spiritually and emotionally, preparing me for invocation (Drawing Down). The purpose of the following exercise/meditation is to prepare you, dear Initiate, for the same. If, in your aspecting work, you're feeling a strong pull toward invoking, by all means, plan a time when you can feel comfortable to go ahead with it, but please review the information on invocation in chapter 17, "Wholeness," and do not think you *must* do so yet—it is not assigned until the Adept Initiation chapters.

At this point, you've been experimenting with aspecting the elements. This moon cycle, dear Initiate, you will be aspecting your *closest,* most beloved deity *of the same gender.* I suggest you first work with the deity of your same gender[49] for this first exercise, as I feel it's easier to invoke from there. Prepare the space in your usual way, making sure to unplug or turn off phones, lock doors, and so forth, so you won't be interrupted. Light some candles and incense, and play relaxing music if you wish. Ground and center deeply, letting your connection to Gaia strengthen and sustain you... take some full, energizing yet relaxing breaths, in through the nose, out through the mouth...

You are in your power place, in the perfect season, time of day, and weather pattern that suits you best. Breathe deeply of the energy in the air around you, and cast a circle here, inviting the elements to watch over you. Invite any deities you wish to watch over you in this work, in preparation for the arrival of your most beloved deity... Remember the devotion you feel for your chosen deity, and invite him or her into your space with heartfelt words. Open yourself completely to the energy, surrender to the higher will of this god or goddess... Invite your deity to come closer. Don't try to force anything, just open yourself and allow it to happen. Now, focus on feeling the presence of the Divine. Allow the love and truth of your chosen deity to surround you, engulf you, uplift you... and now open yourself to **the possibilities of your own divinity**, *your own high energy patterns and truths... see and feel and know how very much like your chosen deity you really are... let all the common aspects of your connection touch your spirit, fill your heart... and breathe. Now take a few moments to understand how much this deity loves you and respects you, how grateful this deity is for your love and devotion... allow yourself to feel it acutely, and now open yourself even more... allow yourself to feel all of his or her devotion and admiration for you... understand on a deep level the very solid connection you have with this deity... and now, again invite your deity to come closer... and closer still... see the glow of your deity's chakras as they spin and spin, aligning with yours... there's not a hair's breadth between you now... enfold your deity in your arms even as you feel them enfolding you in theirs... and breathe.*

Listen closely to any messages you receive, and express your devotion to this deity if you wish, while still staying open to the energy coming in, letting it fill and surround you... love... truth... power... **power-with!** *Remember the concept of power-with and*

---

49. For trans people, I recommend working first with the deity whose gender *you most closely identify with*, then move into working with the other gender after you're comfortable with the first. Another option would be to work with a hermaphroditic deity, if you so choose, in your beginnings.

know that this deity is your staunchest ally, your deepest friend, a being you share tremen-
dous power (and a great many other things) with, a being who desires only the best for
you ... who loves you unconditionally, but who will never shrink back from telling you the
truths you need to hear and know. And again see how like this deity you really are ... and
breathe ... imagine their heartbeat, their breath, becoming one with yours ... allow those
truths and this energy into your consciousness, and know these truths are spoken with love
and compassion and absolute, unconditional love ... And breathe ... there's not a hair's
breadth between you ...

Take all the time you like to bask in this energy, to feel the depth of this connection, and
when you're ready, come slowly, gently, steadily back up from the depths, and open your eyes.

When you are finished, open your eyes and jot down any observations you made, even if they seem obscure. Ponder these energy patterns as you go through this moon, and use your personal Esbat to heal whatever needs healing in this area, if you wish. An exercise I find helpful in seeing myself in my gods is to take a piece of nice paper, and leaving a couple of inches empty at the top, make a list of all the qualities of my chosen deity. Then, when I'm all finished, I dare to write the phrase *I AM* (yes, in all caps!) at the top of the paper, and place it on my altar or other prominent place where I'll see it every day.

Consider your devotion to your chosen deities. Are you connecting with them on a daily basis? If not, why not? If so, how can you deepen and expand the connection? Take some time this moon cycle and ponder the depth of your closeness to your patron god(s) and matron goddess(es). How can you use the upcoming moon cycle to deepen or express your devotion?

Shadow work: Consider the shadows you have around your connection to your chosen deities. For many people, the depth of their connection to their personal gods is dependent on what they feel their deities are *doing for them*. This attitude of entitlement can really trip us up, but in many ways it's understandable, as we're taught by our culture to look only at the half of the cup that's empty. Whenever you find yourself unhappy with your lot in life, think about those who have it a whole lot worse than you do, and then re-examine your life, and count your blessings. Gratitude is the key to healing many of our emotional ailments. It's infinitely easier to have faith and devotion when things are going well, but it's often during the hard times when we most need our faith. Take some time this cycle to ponder devotion, entitlement, gratitude, lack, and abundance, and consider doing healing work in these areas, if necessary, with your upcoming Esbat.

Write a personal Esbat. Begin brainstorming for the upcoming full and dark moons, decide what needs to leave or come into your life, and begin planning an Esbat ritual, including when it's most appropriate to do the work. Consider moon energies: What sign is she in, if any? What phase? Consider solar energies: Where are you on the Wheel of the Year? What time of day or night will you do the work? What day of the week? Consider other energies as well, such as whether Mercury or other relevant planets are in retrograde, your personal schedule, as well as your personal vibrance level (how good do you feel?) and the energies of your household (will you be able to be alone and undisturbed?).

Moon-tides work and devotionals: Don't forget to take some time each evening (or day, depending on her phase) to get outside and look at (or contemplate the position of) the moon. Tune in to her energies; feel her power; let her love fill you. Remember to say your daily devotionals to your matron goddess(es) and patron god(s). Let their energies fill you; let them show you their love and truth as you express your love and truth to them.

Read chapter 8 in *Wheels of Life*—"Chakra Seven: Thought."

Astral temple work: Take some time this moon cycle to consider what "veil" your temple will have between you and the Divine, in terms of ceilings and roofs, skylights, and rooftop gardens. Will there be a special space up top for worship and stargazing? If your temple is constructed with a flat stone roof, this construction would be ideal for a beautiful garden area complete with plants that glow or bloom under the full moon. Will there be a telescope? Will there be a barbecue grill and entertainment equipment, or will you keep this as a worship-only space? Will there be more than one level, more than one purpose? What about those skylights? Where will they be placed, and how big will they be? Take your time this moon cycle to build and readjust these aspects of your temple as desired.

12: The Eighth Moon—Purpose

The purpose of life is to find your gift;
the meaning of life is to give it back.
—Author unknown

MOON EIGHT—THE STORY

You sit, humbled, in the middle of a circle of your most beloved patron gods and matron goddesses. They just suddenly appeared in your circle, right after you cast and called quarters. You had come to circle under this Diana's Bow moon tonight with a question, a Big Question. THE Big Question, so the presence of so many, while a bit surprising, is not altogether so. You raise your eyes to their loving faces, and notice there are still more deities standing behind them; some deities whom you've worked with before, some whom you've studied, still others you've only read a bit about and been intrigued by. The energy is palpable, and their intent is clear: they have an answer, an important message for you.

You are alert, yet relaxed, here in your power place, your most beloved landscape. The sky is glorious with color reflecting the setting sun, even as twilight ascends in the east. The slender waxing crescent moon, a Diana's Bow moon, follows the sun by only a few short hours at this time in her cycle, so she's high now in the pinkish sky, slowly slipping down the starry stairs in

THE EIGHTH MOON CORRESPONDENCES

Keywords: divine love, divine gifts

Energy: surrender

Chakra: hands

Chakra color: silver, green, gold

Element: air

Elemental color: pale blue, silvery-white

Herbs and flowers: lily of the valley, rosemary, angelica

Incense: ebony nights, past lives

Stones and metals: Herkimer diamond, silver

13 Harmonies: embracing (active reception)

Tool: the natal chart

8 virtues: reverence

Astral temple work: interiors; rooms and special spaces

Shadow group: the shadow of fame; the dark side of community service

Energy keyword: gifts

Energy group: the Divine—love and vocation

her path behind the sun. You are reminded of the old tale of Diana's passionate chase of her brother, Lucifer, the "Son of the Morning." You, too, have been passionately chasing something that's eluded you, and you, too, feel as though you'll be hard pressed to catch up. You hang your head to show your reverence, and also to help your mind to focus. You close your eyes.

At once, you feel the sublime power of the deities around you. Swirling bands of energy, both warm and cool, caress and tingle your skin, as colors both bright and dark, sparkling with power, fill your mind. You can hear a distant singing . . . or is it near? The soft sounds increase and decrease in waves, and you can hear your sacred name whispered throughout. Suddenly, gentle hands come to push you back into the arms of a beloved deity so that, although you are still sitting upright, you're leaning back into a divine body with warm arms and a comfortable presence. At that moment, your body completely relaxes, and the swirling sensations, colors, and sounds stop in a deep and abiding peace. You open your eyes to a much different scene.

In this scene, you are working happily at a task you most fondly enjoy. Whether you've ever done this particular thing or not doesn't matter—you know as you work that this is a gift, a sign from the gods that you have real talent in this area. You can feel the eyes of your gods upon you as you work, approving and applauding your choice here, suggesting an improvement there, and you are so tuned in that their will at once becomes yours. The words "highest ideal" spring into your mind, and you revel in the moment, but only for a moment; for suddenly, the scene before you changes yet again.

In the next scene, you are again working happily at a task you fondly enjoy, but this is an altogether different task, and you are again amazed and delighted at how good you are at it. Your chosen deities again whisper secrets to you about this work and how best to execute it, and their will, again, becomes your actions in merely a heartbeat, before the scene shifts yet again . . .

One by one, you go through various scenes where you're working at all manner of different things you enjoy a great deal, until all the ideas you've ever had about your purpose in life have been played out. You sigh with both contentment and frustration, for it feels so good to experience these things, but you still feel that you're searching, and you've been searching for so long. You still don't know for certain what your truest gifts are. With this very thought, a blank screen obliterates the scene you've been witnessing, and all is a black, blank space before you. You realize you can't even feel the beloved deity who's been holding you, although you can still psychically sense the connection. You know they're telling you that you have a choice, that your answer is yet before you, and that all you need do . . . is ask.

Immediately, you know what to do. Eyes still closed, you lean forward and rock onto your knees in reverence before the gods who you know still surround you, and slowly raise your cupped hands together, until they're above your head. Suddenly, all the swirling energy, colors, and music are back, louder, stronger than ever before, increasing in volume the higher you raise your hands, and then, just as suddenly, it all stops, cuing you to open your eyes. You do so, and at once, you know, and you smile brightly, for your hands are filled . . . with light.

THE ENERGY OF PURPOSE

In *The Charge of the Goddess*, we're told, "Keep pure your highest ideal; strive ever toward it; let nothing stop you or turn you aside." This, to me, speaks a great deal of one's divine purpose, one's greatest gift or gifts, which of course also speaks to me of service; how I will give that gift back to my gods (this is usually, though not always, done through serving one's community).

To find our purpose in life can be a real challenge, but I believe our chosen deities guide us well. I can look back on things I learned along the way that at the time I thought I'd never use. Using one small thread as an example, going to art school gave me skills to use later in my career as a professional cake decorator, which helped me to create some pretty awesome wedding cakes for the weddings and handfastings I've been honored to perform as High Priestess. To be able to provide a *magical* cake for the couples I've married is a true blessing and honor. In fact, art school gave me many threads that link back to various facets of my career as a priestess. As you look at your spiritual gifts in this course, you too will find threads linking back to things you've learned in life that connect to and expand upon the spiritual gifts you've been given.

In the Solar Wheel unit, we discuss many different types of spiritual gifts and callings, and one of the purposes of this course is to help you find those individual gifts. As in the story above, however, there may already be things you've pondered for a while, wondering if these really are your truest gifts. Only you and your gods can decide, as I always say, for this is your Path.

Regardless of what you choose (or are guided to choose), as in the quote at the beginning of this chapter, the meaning of life is to *give that gift back*. As the Adept level is the level of service, so the Initiate level is the level of *preparation for that service*. So now is the time to start thinking seriously about how you wish to serve your gods, and begin studying more about those gifts. The Solar Wheel lessons of course can help with that, as they outline many different ways one can serve.

THE HAND CHAKRAS

There are minor chakras in the hands and feet. I wasn't able, in my research, to find a corresponding color, but it seems it could be silver, as we receive with our hands, or perhaps green, since the hand chakras seem to be related to the heart chakra. The hands obviously project energy, too, so gold would work as well. Anyway, the hand chakras can be activated using a simple exercise: simply hold your arms out in front of you, with one palm down and one palm up. Now open and close your hands rapidly several times, say thirteen, for the thirteen moons in a year. Now reverse them and do it again. Repeat as desired. This opens the hand chakras.

To *feel* the energy, slowly bring your hands together, palms facing each other. You should feel a sensation of resistance. This is an excellent foundation for doing many kinds of energy work. You can (and should) practice making shapes: spheres, boxes, cones, moving on to more challenging amorphous shapes of your choosing when you get the basics down. Some other exercises include "turning" the chakras with a finger pointed at the palm from a foot or so away, and "growing" fingers by focusing on stretching them with the mind and comparing one hand to the other (which is done before the stretching, too, of course). It's helpful to have a partner or group to practice with, to both validate and expand upon the experience. Another valuable use of this energy is in self-diagnosis and healing: you can turn your palm toward your major chakras or other places on the body, to sense the balance and flow of the energy there, and then use that knowledge and energy to heal yourself. After all, we instinctively rub spots where we've hurt ourselves—ever wonder why?

THIRTEEN HARMONIES WORK—EMBRACING (ACTIVE RECEIVING)

We've heard it many times on the magical Paths: women naturally receive, men naturally project. This is understandable; by both nature and nurture, we are trained for it. In these next two chapters we'll be exploring that, and practicing a little energy work with it. Now, we've discussed a bit about the way the hands can project, to do the energy work above, but one of the nice things about having a partner or group to practice this type of work with is the validation, as well as the learning you can achieve in sensing energy. To practice receiving energy, then, one can do any number of things: in an energy group or with a partner, open one's hands to receive the energy mass the other person has created, and try to feel its shape; to open one's chakras to the other person and feel the energy they're sending, where it goes, and how it interacts with one's own chakras; to open oneself to nature or the gods and try to sense their messages as in the story that heads the chapter. And again, one can also attempt to sense and diagnose illness and injury in one's own body.

Remember too that active receiving is more than merely staying open to energy; it is an *active pulling of energy* toward you. The energy of receiving can be used to manifest just about anything. In fact, in many ritual actions, we are actually engaging this energy. For example, when we do many kinds of personal work, such as healing, money spells, or love spells, we typically light a candle or create a charm to wear on our bodies, which helps *bring that energy to us*, which is receiving. A physical object that can remind us of this energy, as well as help manifest this energy as a *tool*, is a cowrie shell (discussed in the April lesson).

TOOL—THE NATAL CHART

One of the best, most indispensable tools I've ever found for self-awareness is the natal chart, calculated and interpreted by a qualified astrologer. And by qualified, I certainly don't mean one should only go to an world-renowned astrologer with 150 years of experience. On the contrary, students of the art can be very good, too. I have been fortunate enough to have had mine done a few times, by friends who were learning. That they were all well qualified I have no doubt, as other than a disagreement as to my true rising sign (on the cusp, and therefore hard to pin down), the charts were basically all the same. The natal chart can show you so much about yourself, including avenues for your true vocation and spiritual gifts, that I believe it's a tool that should not be passed up. At the end of the Initiate Basics chapter, chapter 4, I said that you should begin saving up for, or considering how you *yourself* will do, your own natal chart. This would be the perfect moon for these sorts of explorations, while we're looking at our purpose and divine gifts. So, if you haven't had it done yet, please do, and if you have, you might want to spend some time this moon exploring it and re-reading the interpretation, see what fits and what doesn't, as well as how you can overcome some of your challenges and enhance some of your gifts.

THE EIGHT VIRTUES OF THE GODDESS—REVERENCE

You may wonder, dear Initiate, why we explored mirth in the chapter on devotion, yet we explore reverence in the chapter on purpose. This is because it is so easy, in our commitment and love for our gods, to lose our sense of humor, and it is equally easy, in our paths in which we pursue our purpose, to forget that these talents our gods have given us are, indeed, *gifts*, and should be honored as such. For myself, I know it is all too easy to fall into a trap of being ungrateful when times are hard, but the truth of it is that things would be a lot harder during those times if I didn't possess *and get to share* my gifts, and that is a great blessing to me.

This is part of why I stress the daily devotional, whether you do one or many throughout the day. Remembering where our spiritual joys and comforts come from as Wiccans not only does wonders for our dispositions but also helps feed positive energy into our lives and our world. Some of the simplest devotionals, said from the heart, can be the most profound, such as merely thanking the gods of the sun, action, and drive for another beautiful day, or the triple goddess for a restful or profoundly dream-filled night, the earth mother for nutritious fresh food, and so forth.

Devotionals aside, however, showing reverence can take many forms, from reducing our energy footprints and working to heal the planet to showing gratitude for the gifts we're given, to providing Witchy services, such as open rituals, classes, and workshops in our communities. Finally, the best way I know to show reverence is to listen to what my gods wish of me and to act in accord with those wishes to the best of my ability. This is not to say that I always do this. Yeah, I'm stubborn—this we know. But I also believe doing my best to surrender to their will each day is a great way to show reverence.

POSTURE OF POWER

If it works for you to do so, resting comfortably on your knees, cup your hands together in front of you as in "the story" earlier in the chapter, as though someone's going to hand you a big bowl of water. Extend your arms slowly, opening your hands slightly, with an attitude and energy of gratitude and openness to the gifts of the Divine. Take a moment and ponder the light and energy that fill your hands, both in the meditation and in life.

HOMEWORK

Make sure you do your daily energy work of chakra spinning as outlined in the homework section in the first-moon chapter of this unit. The hand chakras may be silver, green, gold, or another color—what do they look like to you? They are located right in the center of the hands.

Energy exercise—Aspecting the opposite gender deity: At this point, you've been experimenting with aspecting the elements, as well as deity. This moon cycle, dear Initiate, you will be aspecting your *closest*, most beloved deity *of the opposite gender*. I suggested you first work with the deity of your same gender for the previous moon cycle to help you prepare for this very different energy.

Prepare the space in your usual way, making sure to unplug or turn off phones, lock doors, etc., so you won't be interrupted. Light some candles and incense, and play relaxing music if you wish. Ground and center deeply, letting your connection to Gaia strengthen and sustain you... take some full, energizing yet relaxing breaths, in through the nose, out through the mouth...

You are in your power place, in the perfect season, time of day, and weather pattern that suits you best. Breathe deeply of the energy in the air around you, and cast a circle here, inviting the elements to watch over you. Invite any deities you wish to watch over you in this work, in preparation for the arrival of your most beloved deity... Remember the devotion you feel for your chosen deity, and invite him or her into your space with heartfelt words. Open yourself completely to the energy, surrender to the higher will of this god or goddess... Invite your deity to come closer. Don't try to force anything, just open yourself and allow it to happen. Now, focus on feeling the presence of the Divine. Allow the love and truth of this deity who is very different, yet very much the same as you in profound ways, to surround you, engulf you, uplift you... and now open yourself to **the possibilities of your own divinity**, *your own high energy patterns and truths... see and feel and know how very much like your chosen deity you really are... let all the common aspects of your connection touch your spirit, fill your heart... and breathe. Now take a few moments to note and understand the differences in gender, in gender energy patterns, and observe how much this deity loves you and respects you, how grateful this deity is for your love and devotion... allow yourself to feel it acutely, and now open yourself even more... allow yourself to feel all of his or her devotion and admiration for you... understand on a deep level the very solid connection you have with this deity... and now, again invite your deity to come closer... and closer still... see the glow of your deity's chakras as they spin and spin, aligning with yours... there's not a hair's breadth between you now... enfold your deity in your arms even as you feel them enfolding you in theirs... and breathe.*

Listen closely to any messages you receive, and express your devotion to this deity if you wish, while still staying open to the energy coming in, letting it fill and surround you ... love ... truth ... power ... **power-with!** *Remember the concept of power-with and know that this deity is your staunchest ally, your deepest friend, a being you share tremendous power (and a great many other things) with, a being who desires only the best for you ... who loves you unconditionally, but who will never shrink back from telling you the truths you need to hear and know. And again see how like this deity you really are ... and breathe ... imagine their heartbeat, their breath, to become one with yours ... allow those truths and this energy into your consciousness, and know these truths are spoken with love and compassion and absolute, unconditional love ... And breathe ... there's not a hair's breadth between you ...*

Take all the time you like to bask in this energy, to feel the depth of this connection, and when you're ready, come slowly, gently, steadily back up from the depths, and open your eyes.

When you are finished, open your eyes and jot down any observations you made, even if they seem obscure. Ponder these energy patterns as you go through this moon, and use your personal Esbat to heal whatever needs healing in this area, if you wish.

Consider your purpose throughout this moon cycle, and trust yourself and your gods to show you the way to best share it when you're ready.

Shadow work: Consider your shadows around *receiving.* They may have threads tying themselves to your ability to also receive messages from the gods about your spiritual gifts, as well as your ability to feel or show reverence, all of which can keep you from your true purpose. What are you not allowing yourself to have, and how does this energy manifest? More importantly, what must be done to clear it so you may move forward?

Write a personal Esbat. Begin brainstorming for the upcoming full and dark moons, decide what needs to leave or come into your life, and begin planning an Esbat ritual, including when it's most appropriate to do the work. Consider moon energies: What sign is she in, if any? What phase? Consider solar energies: Where are you on the Wheel of the Year? What time of day or night will you do the work? What day of the week? Consider other energies as well, such as whether Mercury or other relevant planets are in retrograde, your personal schedule, as well as your personal vibrance level (how good do you feel?) and the energies of your household (will you be able to be alone and undisturbed?).

Moon-tides work and devotionals: Don't forget to take some time each evening (or day, depending on her phase) to get outside and look at (or contemplate the position of) the moon. Tune in to her energies; feel her power; let her love fill you. Remember to say your daily devotionals to your matron goddess(es) and patron god(s). Let their energies fill you; let them show you their love and truth as you express your love and truth to them.

Begin reading James Hillman's *The Soul's Code: In Search of Character and Calling*. Try to have it finished by the end of the following chapter.

Astral temple work: At this point in our astral temple work, we're going to be considering the rooms and how they're broken up within our temples. How many rooms will there be? Which rooms will be devoted to rest, to cleansing, to nutrition, to spiritual pursuits? Will there be separate wings or floors for private and shared spaces? Will there be access from one room to another, or will all be connected by a main hall? Finally, how will the rooms look and feel? Will they be cozy or expansive? Richly decorated or plain and simple? The choice should be what you most desire, whether "practical" or not. What would make you most comfortable, and feel most like you belong in this space?

13: The Ninth Moon—The Path

When I give food to the poor, they call me a saint. When I ask
why the poor have no food, they call me a communist.
—Dom Hélder Câmara

MOON NINE—THE STORY

You stand strong and proud before your gods, humbly open to
the messages they wish to give you, on the edge of a beautiful
natural area where you like to go walking. The waxing quar-
ter moon, high in the western sky, reflects the vivid pink and
orange sunset while crickets and birds herald the gathering twi-
light. Deeply grounding and centering yourself into your Tree
of Life, you visualize the circle where the sphere of light around
you bisects the ground, and allow it to move with you for your
working today. Today's ritual, you've decided, will help you
choose your direction in life through the medium of a walking
meditation. Taking a deep breath, you focus on the circle follow-
ing your movements, and begin.

As you walk, you feel your body fall into a steady rhythm of
breathing, stretching, stepping, swinging your arms comfortably
and naturally, and these rhythms combine to help you enter a
light trance. You consciously filter the sounds around you into
the background, focusing on your breathing, your pace ... Soon,
you will come to a crossroads, and you've decided ahead of time

THE NINTH MOON CORRESPONDENCES

Keywords: the spiritual warrior, service, courage, destiny, "living the dream"

Energy: meaning, confidence, honor

Chakra: feet

Chakra color: brown, red (close to earth), gold (for god energy)

Element: earth

Elemental color: brown, green, gold

Herbs and flowers: cinnamon, wormwood, vervain

Incense: frankincense, Damascus rose

Stones and metals: topaz, gold

13 Harmonies: projecting

Tool: labyrinth

8 virtues: honor and humility in balance

Astral temple work: paths and grounds, larger gardens

Shadow group: the shadow of fame; the dark side of community service

Energy keyword: service

Energy group: power-with the Divine—service

to allow your body to go where it will as you open your spirit to divine messages and your mind to the creative ethers.

So many decisions to make this moon cycle; so much that could prove crucial to your life and your happiness. So much of your energy is bound to duty, so much to survival; where will you find the energy to **thrive**? Where will you go from here? Thoughts keep swirling around in your mind, and you let them pass right on through... telling your gods with your heart and spirit that these are the issues you most need answers to tonight. The random thoughts come less and less often as you walk, focusing your attention on the beauty around you... the green earth and bright sky... you remember what Ruiz said about the mitote (see glossary) and acknowledge that there has been a **cacophony** in your mind of late, with so many decisions and so much to do, so much stress and need, and... oh for some peace! Laughing at how easily your mind nearly slipped into chaos again, you open yourself once more to the experience, keeping the rhythm of your breath and your walk...

The crossroads comes and goes, and you walk steadily on in the direction you chose there. Twilight deepens, as does your trance, and you see the first stars. In your mind's eye you can see that you're surrounded by shadowy gods, watching over and protecting you, guiding you... even as you think of guidance, you focus a moment on your feet and now you can feel the chakras near the arches more acutely, as if they've only just now become activated, but you know it's just that you've never tuned in to them before. With this new sensation, you realize suddenly that your feet... are actually guiding you! As though they know where to go—all on their own! You open yourself to receiving: messages, guidance, newness, divine gifts. As you walk, you begin to notice symbols and energy patterns in the deepening shadows and emerging stars. You can hear messages on the breeze, **between** the sounds. Your feet keep turning onto paths you never expected, and you just keep watching and observing, opening yourself to the divine messages you crave. As you walk and deepen into your experience, your Life's Journey somehow becomes clearer, more... sacred. Ahead lies another, unexpected crossroads, a much darker one, with less defined paths leading in a few different directions. You look up at the stars and smile as a gentle breeze plays across your face, adding to the magic of the night.

At that moment you realize that you, too, are sacred, and that you can shape and mold your life to be whatever you most wish it to be, for you are a powerful Witch and spiritual warrior, and you have vitality and energy to spare! You know much more clearly now what it is that you need to do. Whirling on the spot as if in answer to yourself, you begin walking in a Whole New Direction, opening yourself even more to your gods, and to the promise and the Mystery of such a new life, determined to train your mind to follow along.

THE PATH OF THE SPIRITUAL WARRIOR— THE ENERGIES OF HONOR AND HUMILITY

As we walk our spiritual Paths and learn more about our shadows and our light, little by little, small threads of our own truths come into our energy patterns, weaving themselves into a healthy balance. At this time, we've developed a heightened awareness of ourselves and the world around us. We've become more psychic, and we've likely done a bit of public service, either in the form of helping with a public ritual or workshop, or perhaps we've just been available for someone who needs some support or counseling. We've talked a bit about helping people, and that it's always a good idea to ask if they desire your help first, as they may or may not feel comfortable with our kind of help or our religious beliefs.

The honor and humility required to offer such help means you're confident in your abilities, yet you know your limits. It's important, too, as we help others, to make sure we're offering the help *they need*, and not simply what's easy, convenient or comfortable to give them.

Imagine a woman (let's call her Joan) who's just experienced a deep loss: her lover of several years has gone away on a spiritual journey, possibly indefinitely. Her friend (we'll call her Amy), over a period of several weeks, continually tells Joan she's giving her "space" to deal with her very difficult emotions. Joan tells Amy repeatedly that she's not the kind who needs space when she's hurting—quite the opposite. Joan tells Amy frankly that she tends to shut down; isolate; curl in upon herself, and that's when she most needs a friend, support, companionship—someone who cares to reach out to her, in order to pull herself out of her despair so she may heal. But Amy isn't listening. She simply doesn't possess the love or compassion required to pull herself out of her own domesticated beliefs to see what's truly needed, in spite of Joan's very clear requests. This works to Amy's detriment, of course, as it always does when we make assumptions (remember the old adage; when we "assume," we make an "ass" out of "u" and "me"). For to *give* support and care is a great gift, almost as great as receiving such care, and to withhold that from someone who needs it often causes problems within the relationship. The final outcome: Joan will leave the friendship behind, as she felt abandoned by Amy when she most needed a friend.

So, what we need to be looking at in terms of service is taking the high road—humbling ourselves enough to ask, instead of assuming, what's needed. This is one of the hallmarks of true clergy; of a sincere priest or priestess. If you have a friend or community member in need, remember that it requires much more compassion and humility to simply ask, and then give, your friend what he needs than it does to simply make assumptions and throw a placebo at him, or worse, give him what *you yourself* would need, were you in his "shoes." In many cases, it would be better to do nothing at all than to do the above actions. Even if you think you can do little to help, it is your duty as his friend to at least try. Remember that we create our own reality, so watch those negative affirmations. If you think your help isn't going to be good enough for your friend, I'll guarantee you it *won't* be, so don't even go there! Your confidence should be stronger than that by now, and it it's not, perhaps this moon cycle would be a good time to work to improve it.

Once we've made some progress in achieving awareness, we will be able to "See." Awareness, or "Seeing," simply means observing the truth *as it is*, without assessing or judging a situation. The responsible priest will then act (after asking!) on what's needed, where appropriate. A spiritual warrior practices awareness in every moment of every day.

Now, there's a difference between a soldier and a warrior. When folks speak of the spiritual warrior, they're talking about the energy of the battle of the Self with the self. You are engaged in that battle, dear Initiate, every time you do your shadow work. Remember how, in *The Four Agreements,* when Ruiz speaks of breaking our old agreements, he says that we must sometimes *stalk our intentions* to *fight our parasites.* Only then can we experience true freedom. Stalking our intentions is not easy; we are *so* good at deluding ourselves! Stalking means examining our true motivations behind all that we think, do, and say, and weeding out that which no longer works for us.

What is true freedom, really? For many it's the ability to be comfortable being ourselves without fear or apology. Now of course, we, in our domesticated world, all have certain people in our lives whom we feel more comfortable being ourselves with than others; these are usually our close friends and mates, and for some lucky folks, our families of origin. But some folks aren't that fortunate, and so this freedom can be difficult to achieve. So it's time now, as we begin to define, create, and walk our spiritual Paths, to make decisions to be more true to ourselves; first *with ourselves*, then with people who know us well, and when we're ready, taking more and more risks to reveal our personal truths as we expand out into the circles around us. Most importantly, always, is being honest with ourselves about who we are as well as who we wish to be. Stripping away false obligations and pre-programmed energies will take time and patience. Be gentle with yourself in this work.

The honor and humility of the spiritual warrior also speaks to *owning your power*. At this point in your path, you're over halfway done with the *Thirteen Moons* section of this program, so you know the importance of chasing your shadows as well as the power of affirmations and positive thinking. A wonderful affirmation I heard a few years back was spoken in answer to my inquiry as to how a friend of mine was doing. He said, "Great! I'm *living the dream*." I thought he was being sarcastic at first, until I realized he actually meant it; he'd had a turn of good fortune, and was grateful for it, so he was actually affirming the positive at the same time as he was healing the negative in his life with this simple yet powerful affirmation. As we now know, dear Initiate, such positive affirmations have a way of *creating the very energy* they speak of, so using them can have a beautifully fulfilling snowball effect! So if you choose to use this amazing affirmation, make sure you never say it sarcastically, as that can have an opposite, and detrimental effect. Remember, always, your *intentions*!

Owning your power also means *giving your word sparingly and adhering to it like iron*, as we've discussed many times on this sacred road. You may think the little promise you keep forgetting about or putting off is nothing, but you must remember as we walk this Path of the Wise that *we program ourselves all the time*, so if you keep making promises you don't keep, remember this action is stripping you of power the longer those promises go unfulfilled. Pay attention to your words and actions! How many times do we promise we'll do something or help in a certain way, only to decide later that we're just "not that into it"? Then we decide it's okay not to keep this promise because _____. But it doesn't matter what the excuse is; it's still just an excuse. Remember, you are *programming* your mind and spirit to take you (or not take you) *at your word*! If you want your magic to work, for your spirit (and the gods) to know you mean business when you say the words "So mote it be," then you must be cognizant of, and make good on, all of your promises, no matter how "big" or "small."

THE SHADOW OF FAME—
THE DARK SIDE OF COMMUNITY SERVICE

This third triplet of moons focuses on how we relate to the Divine, in terms of our devotion to them, our divine gifts, which give us our spiritual purpose, and honoring and walking the path they lay down for us. This shadow work pulls the current triplet of chapters (moons 7–9) together, as these chapters are more focused on the Divine. Meditation on, as well as contemplation of, shadows around how we believe or don't believe divine messages, hunches, intuitions are all called for at this time. It's also a good idea to examine in which ways we do or do not rebel against the path our matron goddesses and patron gods lay down before us.

In the February chapter, I speak of arrogance and how damaging it can be to both your public rituals and your future as a priest/ess working with your peers in public rites and other activities, should you choose to do public rites as part of your spiritual calling. We discuss that the reason we do public works is not for our communities to bow down in service *to us* in our imagined greatness, but for the glory of our gods and the benefits of that sacred and vital community connection, to *serve our communities* with our callings and our gifts.

There's another extreme: humility that's carried to the point of reticence in standing up and acting as that Hub of the Wheel that is being the leader of a public ritual, either because of low self-esteem issues or a misdirected sense of duty.

Imagine a woman who wanted so badly to serve her community, and was quite capable of doing so, but in her public rituals, she would stop and start so often to explain—in extreme detail—what she was doing and why, that the energy never really *flowed*. In addition, she would often spontaneously ask folks who had no prior experience with or knowledge of magic or Paganism, to do ritual actions most traditions would only allow Initiates to do, such as standing at center and taking the HPS's role while this reticent priestess would step back and simply observe. Now, I'm not saying these actions are necessarily *wrong*—rituals of this nature can serve a purpose (educating the non-Pagan public, for example), and many folks would certainly enjoy them. But the energy in such rituals would never really get off the ground to do its work; rituals with this "instructional" quality tend to feel more like a class than a magical working. There could be no power raising, as the energy would be scattered, and it would tend to become somewhat... flattened out by the end, as these instructions can take a rather long time, and folks often get tired and bored.

And so we must approach our public works with confidence, not arrogance, and humility, not hesitation. It's a difficult balance sometimes, which I also believe makes it important to wait until we're really ready, but to also push ourselves a little if we're waiting too long to get our feet wet. The right time is something only you can decide.

But why should I surrender?
Doing as we're guided by our gods can be a challenge sometimes. We discussed at length the energy of surrender in the chapter on devotion and how hard it can be to

do as our matron goddesses and patron gods ask if we have something else in mind. This can lead to a rebelliousness that can work to our detriment as spiritual warriors. The shadows around our stubbornness (read "arrogance"!) can indeed trip us up, keeping us from our true purpose. This can result in feeling confused and/or without any real sense of purpose. Trust me, I know: I've mentioned that my matron goddess, Artemis, has told me more than once that I am one of her most stubborn priestesses. And, honestly, I must admit the things I get stubborn about are always the things that come from ego, arrogance (i.e., insecurity), and wanting to be right. Bowing to her greater wisdom has been a challenge at times, but it's always worth it in the end.

So the shadow of surrender, then, at least for me, is all about *trusting her wisdom* and opening my heart to accepting the fact that the path she lays down for me is *always* to my betterment and growth as a person and a priestess. By the time this book is published, it will be forty-five years and counting since that little girl did rituals to her Lady in the field across the street. Forty-five years of learning, over and over again, to surrender, and a good nine years since I laid my blade at her feet. Perhaps this lesson will sink in soon.

It can be lonely at the top

Whether we as priests and priestesses are "at the top" hierarchically or figuratively, leading a coven, doing public works, managing a busy life and devoted solitary practice, or something else entirely, our spiritual practices and duties can often keep us isolated from our peers, and that can be lonely indeed when we are in need of support or help of some kind. As a teacher, I have had many offers of both financial help and emotional support from my students in troubled times, but it's not appropriate for a teacher to accept such, in my opinion (more on that in the *Adept Initiation* section), as, more often than not, accepting this type of help, however heartfelt, from a student ultimately leads to both the student's and the teacher's detriment: What if the teacher can't pay back the loan, or uses the money in a way the student didn't intend? What if the teacher reaches out to the student, and the student is emotionally cool or absent? It could make things really awkward later. This is, of course, different from accepting assistance with presenting ritual, building community, or any type of less personal help. For the community leader, too, sometimes the connections we make are all about the business of presenting the Sabbat/public ritual/event, and the time one would normally spend getting to know another is spent running and working one's butt off and there's really no time or energy for those connections to deepen. For very busy priests and priestesses, this can be quite isolating as well.

It's important, then, for you, dear Initiate, as you get closer and closer to the next gate, to make sure you have a strong support system in place. For if you do get involved in public works (and you certainly will *in some way* give back to your community), your time will become… *condensed*, so to speak, and large amounts of public service activities will both energize *and* drain you. Then, every precious moment with your support system will count. Make sure you schedule regular time with your closer companions, as well as quality "you" time, in order to keep your energies up.

Keep your sense of humor

"Mirth and reverence, mirth *and* reverence" is the mantra. Don't sweat the small stuff. When I first started leading a coven and doing large public ritual, I was a crazed maniac the day of the rite, running to and fro, making as much stress and work for myself as possible, adding small touches to the decorations here, changing the ritual so it would be "just so" there, and in general being a whirlwind of highly stressed, focused activity. I still do all those same actions now, only without the emotional stress and panicked feeling. I love getting up early on the Sabbats and cooking and decorating for the upcoming event. It's even more fun if coveners or friends come over and help, as we chat the day away getting ready for the celebration, so we're always excited and mellow by the time it starts. Remember to ground. Remember Murphy's Law: if anything can go wrong, it will, so always, *always* have a Plan B. Remember, too, that for each and every ritual you present, whether solitary or for ten or one thousand people, there will be really cool things you'll want to remember to do again, and there will be not-so-cool things you will have learned to avoid or improve upon in the future. Trouble-shoot your rituals, every time, and understand that each one is a learning experience. How'd that go again? Oh yeah: *Don't sweat the small stuff*. What's important is the *heart* of the thing. Is your heart connected to your gods? Then it's all good. Beyond that, as the saying goes, it's *all* "small stuff."

…But I didn't really want a purple elephant!

As a spiritual leader, there will be many times when folks will want to give you something you don't necessarily wish to receive, but please remember that allowing yourself to receive their offerings is a *gift to them*. Especially when it comes to receiving help (with the exceptions of the more deeply personal and potentially problematic financial or emotional help, of course). Some folks have shadows around receiving help with even the most overwhelming life issues, letting their pride get in the way of accepting assistance. This can often feel or appear to the one offering that you're saying you think you're too good for their help, or think you're above it all, somehow. As clergy, we need to recognize that those we love *need to feel needed* in our lives, and try to stay open to the idea of receiving. If you haven't done your shadow work around receiving, or if you're still not open in that area, you might wish to do some more shadow work to heal these energies during this moon cycle.

In conclusion

Remember that honor and humility are about making your gods and community *more important than yourself* on occasion. Most days, actually, once you become a community leader of any flavor. When someone comes to you for help or advice, it's important to tell them what you know in a respectful manner. I don't care if they shock you by telling you they use a plastic kiddie cup to cast a circle. So what if you've never seen it done before or don't think it'll work? It's *their* truth, and if they want to share it with you, as a priest/ess of the gods, first of all, you should be *honored by that*, and secondly, you have a sacred duty to be open-minded and receptive. After all, there may very well be something important about that kiddie cup (or that practitioner!) that you just don't know. It's in your best interest to listen to others; remember that sometimes strangers bear messages of the gods! Remember that no matter how humble a person's background or how squeaky brand-new a person's Path, we all have the potential to learn from *everyone*. My grandfather used to say, "Learn as much as you can about as much as you can." I would add "from as many sources as you can," keeping in mind that even the humble earthworm has something important to teach us. Only by being open-minded to the stories and experience of others can we truly do honor to gods and community.

THE FOOT CHAKRAS

The foot chakras are located near the arches, in the middle of the feet, just inside the surface of the soles. The appropriate color could be gold, for the spiritual warrior/God energy, or brown or black, for the earth. I like red, too, as the closest major chakra is the root, which is red, and red is action and drive, so it seems appropriate for feet.

These are considered "minor" chakras, but I believe that, just like the hand chakras, they're much more significant than we give them credit for. Take some time this moon to tune in to your foot chakras, and record what you learn.

THIRTEEN HARMONIES WORK—PROJECTION

As we study and learn more about ourselves in terms of our spiritual Path and how we will walk it, we are engaging active (which many of us Wiccans label "male") energies. As such, now is the time to be looking at how we project our energy. Men have a natural tendency to project. Historically, they are the hunters, the aggressors sexually, and even in these "enlightened" times, most often take the main "provider" role in families. When men start working with energy, too, usually they find projecting their energy to be much easier (sometimes a bit too easy) than women do. For the woman Witch, then, it becomes even more vitally important to practice projecting her energy magically, in order to become more powerful, as well as more adept at handling its direction. If you haven't begun a practice of projecting energy, ladies, now is the time to do so. If you have a friend you can practice with, that's great, but if not, you can still practice, and there are as many ways to practice projecting energy as there are energy forms.

One simple method is to push energy out of your hand chakras, to try and move something lightweight, such as a crumpled piece of paper or a small bit of something hanging. My first experiments with this were with a cloth model of a hot air balloon I had hanging in my bedroom. If you have a friend to practice with, another idea is to set up blind tests where you project energy toward one of their chakras, and have them tell you when (and where, and how!) they feel it. Then, of course, you can add more creative touches to these simple exercises as you become more skilled.

Therapeutic touch is a kind of energy healing I learned about at a women's retreat in the early 1980s. At least, this is the term the teacher used for the energy work we all learned in her amazing workshop. This action is quite simple: just open up your hand chakras (as you learned to do in the previous chapter on page 164), then slowly move your hands toward the subject until you feel her aura. Once you get a sense of your subject's aura you can then begin moving your hands over her aura in systematic strokes, feeling for holes, temperature or vibrational differences, rough spots. Once found, these energy "vacancies" can be smoothed out by running your hands over the affected area, and then shaking out the energy into an open area of the grass if this is done outdoors (best), or in an unoccupied area of the room if indoors, with the intention of grounding and dissipating the energy thoroughly.

TOOL—THE LABYRINTH

Labyrinths are wonderful meditative devices. I have only limited experience working with them, but the experiences were nonetheless quite moving. One kind of labyrinth is the walking kind—a path set up so that one can walk quietly in a contemplative state, letting one's body fall into that vital meditative state in order to quiet down and let wisdom come.

The other kind are the finger labyrinths found in many metaphysical shops, which literally let one's fingers do the walking through the simple pathway that twists and turns but is always steadfast and safe. If money is an issue, and you want to practice this work, it's perfectly acceptable to render one on paper or other artistic medium. Labyrinths inspire confidence by helping us to see the certainty we sometimes need in our spiritual Pathwork; that all roads lead to center, and home, and that all really is well in our worlds, even if only for this one timeless moment.

THE EIGHT VIRTUES OF THE GODDESS—
HONOR AND HUMILITY IN BALANCE

Much of what we discussed above in the shadow work section have to do with holding these energies in balance. At the extreme level, honor without humility can often present itself as arrogance, and humility without honor can cause one to be a virtual doormat for anyone to wipe their feet on. Keeping these energies in balance, then, means that we *own our power*: we know what we are capable of, as well as what we still need to strengthen. This can be a tough lesson, especially for women. Believing it when others tell us we are powerful is not conceit or arrogance; it is simply our own personal truth. Powerful people in this culture still aren't always perceived positively, so opening ourselves to our power means coming to terms with those shadows as well. Remember that "powerful woman" does not equal "bitch," and that "powerful man" does not mean "oppressor" (or any of the other negatives you may have been programmed/domesticated with), and repeat after me: "I accept and own my power. My power is growing daily! I am powerful!" For best results, repeat daily.

POSTURE OF POWER

If it works for you to do so, stand tall. Hold your arms up with elbows bent in a "power walking" stance. Lean forward on your dominant foot as though you've just begun a long, strong stride. Feel the power surging through you, and the readiness of your body to begin moving. Then, go for a walk and get some fresh air! Blessed be.

HOMEWORK

Make sure you do daily energy work of chakra spinning as outlined in the homework section in the first-moon chapter of this unit. The foot chakras may be brown, red, gold, or another color—what do they look like to you? They are located in the center of the feet, near the soles (i.e., on the bottom).

Energy exercise—Invoking air: By now, you should be well versed in evoking and aspecting the elements, so ground and center in your usual way, and go through the steps of evoking and then aspecting the element of air: Imagine yourself in a circle outdoors, with a gentle breeze that becomes stronger and stronger. In your mind and spirit's "eye," feel the breezes around you as they come closer and closer, feel the energy of air billowing like a soft sheet in the summer sunshine, touching your skin, your mind, your spirit… connect with and engage the energy as you relate it to all that's airy in you… Your mind is spinning on bright creative ideas, and the more you spin on these intellectual exercises, the harder the wind seems to blow. The wind spirits rise up around you as your creative ideas rise up inside you. Hear and open to the cacophony of thoughts as they come closer and closer, eventually penetrating your mind, not overtaking it, but permeating it with incredible imagination! Feel the energies of air, like the bright sunrise on a fresh spring morning, charging you up with a million desires, to ponder, to develop, to create! Connect with and engage the energy as you relate it to all that's airy in you, as well as the sharpness and clarity of your mind and spirit… as you aspect this gentle energy, allow it to begin to penetrate. A helpful way to start is by simply inhaling… as you inhale, visualize and feel and know this air energy; feel the breath flowing in and out of your lungs, the fresh creativity of your mind, and as you aspect this intelligent energy, allow it to begin to penetrate and fill you. Now visualize and feel and know that air energy is penetrating your body, your mind, your spirit... A helpful way to start is by simply inhaling... as you inhale, visualize and feel and know that air energy is penetrating your body, your mind, your spirit... feel the air energy settle into you as you become lighter and lighter... as you... become... air.

Practice this meditation throughout the moon cycle.

Consider your spiritual Path. Where have you been? What triggered your transition from your previous spiritual beliefs to this Path of eclectic Wicca? However difficult your past may have been, it's likely there were events or conversations, energies that you can recognize and honor yourself for. Remember that having pride in who you are is a balance of both honor and humility. Try saying, "Blessed be my feet, which have brought me to these ways," while truly allowing yourself both credit and gratitude for all that you've learned, however challenging those lessons might have been; after all, you've accomplished that learning! Now, ground and center, breathe in the energies of the Earth Mother and Sky Father, and feel the pride and power of the spiritual warrior you truly are. Finally, focus for a time on *where you are going*. What are your spiritual goals? What is your highest ideal? Imagine you can accomplish anything you wish to—because you can! You have your whole past as proof!

Shadow work: This third triplet of moons has all been about the *shadow of fame*, the dark side of community service, pulling together the energies of how we feel about our gods, our purpose, and our spiritual path.

Remember, always, that the shadow of fame is really just another manifestation of the shadow around the Path of the Spiritual Warrior—the battle of the Self with the self. How do you present yourself in your public works and/or interactions? What are your priorities? Are you more interested in presenting large public rituals so you can show off, while your coven or solitary practices fall by the wayside? Conversely, are you reticent to do public works, content to leave that responsibility to others? Overcoming these shadows, then, requires utter self-honesty and a discipline and commitment to truth, even if the truth hurts. Only then can we hope to heal the shadows of our own religion and come to a healthier place.

Finally, we also must look at our own personal shadows again around our daily work. Are we avoiding it? If so, why? If not, what could we do to make our daily practices more real, more immediate, more satisfying? If time and energy are not allowing us to feel as though we have time for even this most simple of workings, what can we do to open up that time and energy in our lives? Remember the *mitote* and try to see if you have shadow energies swirling around you, creating confusion and "too many committees in your head."

Take some time this moon cycle and consider what needs to heal in these shadow realms, perhaps using your upcoming Esbat to do work to that end.

Write a personal Esbat. Begin brainstorming for the upcoming full and dark moons, decide what needs to leave or come into your life, and begin planning an Esbat ritual, including when it's most appropriate to do the work. Consider moon energies: What sign is she in, if any? What phase? Consider solar energies: Where are you on the Wheel of the Year? What time of day or night will you do the work? What day of the week? Consider other energies as well, such as whether Mercury or other relevant planets are in retrograde, your personal schedule, as well as your personal vibrance level (how good do you feel?) and the energies of your household (will you be able to be alone and undisturbed?).

Moon-tides work and devotionals: Don't forget to take some time each evening (or day, depending on her phase) to get outside and look at (or contemplate the position of) the moon. Tune in to her energies; feel her power; let her love fill you. Remember to say your daily devotionals to your matron goddess(es) and patron god(s). Let their energies fill you; let them show you their love and truth as you express your love and truth to them.

Continue reading The Soul's Code: In Search of Character and Calling, by James Hillman, finishing it this cycle.

Astral temple work: It's time now to think about how you will choose to floor your temple. Will there be hardwood or stone floors? Will they be covered with throw rugs or thick furs? How about a more modern finish of deep plush carpeting? Will there be throw pillows on some of the floors? How will you furnish your temple? What style or shape the chairs and couches?

More importantly, how will the *paths* around the temple look? These are the paths that will guide you to this sacred space. What would you like them to look like? Feel like? Perhaps they'll be simple, narrow dirt tracks that create a minimum of distraction from the gardens and grounds. Perhaps they'll be cobblestone or wider tracks, maybe even concrete, or pavement, or something even fancier, like marble or slate. Will they go straight toward the temple, or will they wind and wind around, so that the temple is actually at the center or end point of a maze or labyrinth? However you wish these surfaces to look and to wind is up to you.

14: The Tenth Moon—Expansion

The path of total freedom is the path of total responsibility.
—Common Wiccan saying

MOON TEN—THE STORY

Silver full moon at apogee in the summer sky. Full power of earth, moon, and sun. You, too, are at "full power" as you have finally come to a place where you feel confident, balanced, and so grateful for all that you've learned, for how much you've grown. You gather your tools around you, lying them reverently on your earth altar, in their proper places. Checking, then double-checking, to see that all is ready, you finally quiet yourself a moment, and stand, fully aware, at center. With mind, heart, intention, you cast.

At once, the air shifts and your awareness is profoundly heightened. Suddenly, it's all so clear; your whole life, the Big Picture. You've won some confidence from chasing and subduing, at least for the time being, a great many of your shadows. You can feel them, held at bay, at the edge of your consciousness, in the landscape around you, way out on the perimeter in ... well, the shadows. You smile, your thoughts lingering on your life for only a few moments when suddenly, you are acutely aware of, indeed, sharing a point of consciousness with a tiny spider, hurrying homeward with a small speck of food.

THE TENTH MOON CORRESPONDENCES

Keywords: enhancing and growing power; fate; truth; Right Action; magnification; prayer; bliss; pushing boundaries; outstretching; faith; flying (astral projection); illumination; force; freedom; opening the gateways; the path of excess; ideas; perfect trust

Energy: action, expansion, spiritual bliss, enlightenment

Chakra: liberating current

Chakra color: violet-white, magic-circle blue

Element: fire with air

Elemental color: gold

Herbs and flowers: African violet, sandalwood, ganja, other herbs and plants used in sacred journeying

Incense: frankincense, cedar

Stones and metals: gold, amber, clear crystals

13 Harmonies: Opening the Gates

Tool: the staff

8 virtues: mirth and reverence in balance

Astral temple work: ascending stairways, "lifts"

Shadow group: the Shadow of the Path

Energy keyword: crescendo

Energy group: Pathworking, moving forward with awareness

Then, your consciousness shifts, and you're as one with the speck of food... then, your consciousness shifts again, and you are as one with a single cell in that speck of food, then a single cell in the leaf in the tree above the spider, then you are the leaf... then, thousands of leaves... then the tree... you tune in more, and more, feeling and sharing a living, breathing consciousness, a spiritual connection with: a mountain lion; a sparrow; a wolf; a snake;

intertwining energies, becoming one, yet individuated, like small threads that make up a larger cord in a much larger tapestry. You stretch your consciousness further, touching and connecting… interweaving… becoming. You are both the fish in the river and the river itself, then you are as one with the forest… the mountains around you… you feel yourself grow larger and larger, until your body encompasses the entire valley, skirted by the ocean… and you realize you are as one with both the whales and the plankton; both the shoreline and the tiny grains of sand… then you expand more and more until you encompass the region, then the land mass, the hemisphere, the planet…

You begin to soar, then, limitless, both at one with and simultaneously swimming through the stars and nebulas, the All… and all the wisdom and truth you so crave are here with you, in you, yours to touch, and hold, and keep…

FREEDOM: THE ENERGY OF EXPANSION

What makes you strong? What feeds your energy; makes you feel more wholly able to be "you"? These are the questions we ponder when we think of freedom. For some, freedom is all about money; "If I could just win the lottery, I could do anything I wanted." Well, take a moment to ponder that. What *would* you do if you had buckets of money? For others, it's about work; vocation. Mark Twain said a man is happiest in work that is, for him, the most like play. What is "play" to you? How would you make your living if you could do anything you wanted? For many on this Path, freedom is about spirit. How deeply connected to your deities would you like to be? What is the attitude and countenance of a true priest or priestess? How does that set you free? For still others, it's about love. How would you feel if you had the love(s) you most desire in your life? What would that look like? How would you express yourself to your loved one(s)?

For most of us, freedom is all of the above, plus much more. Expand your mind! Think about *all* the possibilities! Who would you love, what would you hold sacred and important, where would you work (*would* you work?), when would you wake each day, how would you spend your time, and most importantly, *why* would you do all of the above? What are your motivations and causes? In *The Charge of the Goddess*, the Lady states, "Keep pure your highest ideal. Strive ever toward it; let nothing stop you or turn you aside." Take some time this moon and ponder that highest ideal; what does it look like? How does it feel?

With these thoughts in mind now, expand your consciousness outward even more, as in the story above. Consider the interconnectedness of all things, and let your mind soar forward a few years. How do you see yourself? What will you have accomplished? Where do you want to be? At this time of expanding awareness, it's good to begin thinking seriously about your life and where you would like for it to go. Remember you are a powerful Witch; becoming more so with every moon. Your only limit is your own imagination. Do not censor yourself or "should" on yourself! Instead, free your mind for the time being, and let yourself dream.

CHAKRA LORE—THE LIBERATING CURRENT OF THE KUNDALINI

The kundalini serpent moves up the chakra system, weaving in and out between the spinning wheels. As it moves upward, we become aware of the energy rising in us, and we tend to focus on our upper chakras. Indeed, the very energy of many of our spiritual actions activate and highlight these chakras. For this reason, many folks tend to get kind of stuck on the idea that the upper chakras (and the ascending current of the kundalini) are the only "truly spiritual" ones. This is not correct, however, as we know that body, mind, spirit, passion, *and* emotion are all vital parts of us and must be held in balance. Indeed, as the Goddess gives us in *The Charge*: "Mine is the ecstasy of the spirit, and Mine also in joy on earth." Clearly, this is why we have both a descending and liberating current. For this moon, focus on your liberating current, sending those thoughts up and out to reach your highest ideal. Next moon, we'll be doing something with that!

It is interesting to note that, just the opposite of common Wiccan beliefs, in the Hindu tradition, it is the female who rules the action-filled, ascending current, and the male who rules manifestation. However we perceive this energy, the liberating current is expansive, forceful, light, and active.

THIRTEEN HARMONIES WORK—OPENING THE GATES

I worry that drugs have forced us to be more creative than we really are.
—Lily Tomlin

From Gerald Gardner's own Book of Shadows, I quote: "Incense, Drugs, Wine, etc. Any potion which aids to release the spirit."[50]

There is so much controversy on this issue in the writings of other Witchy authors and teachers as well as in the attitudes and actions of many leaders in the Pagan and Wiccan communities that it can truly boggle the mind. The sheer hypocrisy of such folks who adamantly insist on following certain Witchy or Shamanic *teachings* yet state absolutely and unequivocally that one must never *do* as they *did* (i.e., use "drugs" such as ganja, psilocybin, or other herbs or plants to achieve deep trance—to "release the spirit"), insisting that these substances are either "dangerous" or "lower" forms of releasing the spirit (as opposed to chanting or drumming or anything else) can be disheartening, to say the least.

Well, I'm here to say otherwise. We are all intelligent, thinking adults here, and I'm not going to insult your intelligence by suggesting you should do as I say, but not as I do. Spiritual journeying with natural substances such as psilocybin, datura, peyote, and the like, is a valid and time-honored practice, and, yes, I have done such journeying on occasion, as well as acted as guardian for coveners (Adepts and Masters, all) who did the same. While I do not insist upon or even necessarily advise you to do such practices, I certainly do not forbid or invalidate them in any way. I think such practices have their place, and that, used in moderation and with reverence, they can be amazingly useful and healing. However, I will state that if you are planning to use such substances for your journey work, in my opinion it's best to have some experience with both *the substance* and *the practice of journeying* as separate energies before you attempt them *together*. In addition, you need to be fully prepared to deal with the consequences of such actions. And the importance of a helper to act as guardian for you cannot be overstated. It's wise to have someone to both look out for you as well as to attend you so that your whole focus can be on the journey itself. You won't want to have to "pop out" and get yourself a glass of water, or a blanket, or put more

---

50. Janet Farrar and Stewart Farrar, *A Witch's Bible* (Phoenix Publishing, 1996), 52.

incense on the burner. Your guardian can also take notes for you if need be, or help with divinatory readings if this is something you feel pulled to explore at such a time.

In addition, folks who are already very experienced with a particular substance may find themselves wishing to "step it up" a bit for the deeper journey work; in this case, a guardian is an even better idea. If one starts seeing darker aspects of one's self that scare or confuse them, having someone present who knows what they're doing and who cares about their well-being can be, literally, life-saving.

If you chose to experiment with these practices, dear Initiate, take great care! If you have never done such before, examine deeply your motivations for doing so. These journeys are not simply opportunities to get high and call it a spiritual experience. After much serious thought, find someone who is experienced with such things to ask questions of before you make any final decisions, and for your own best interest, get a magical Adept to act as guardian for you. Again, I am not at all advocating that you take a spiritual journey with ganja, psilocybin, or any other of the Mother's sacred substances; I'm simply stating that if you should choose to do so, make sure you take very good care of yourself in the process.

THE PATH OF EXCESS

I suspect most humans enjoy overindulging in something or other every now and again, as we tend to be hedonistic beasts. In this chapter, as we deal with the energies mentioned above, it's important to look at our *indulgences*. Specifically, our *overindulgences*, as they relate to energy and magic.

How often do you like to tie one on? Is alcohol your indulgence of choice? Ganja? Or are you one of those rare folks who *never* get inebriated? Maybe you eat too much sugar, to the point of going on a sugar high (I've done this, more times than I can count!). Perhaps you like to drink so much caffeine that you get yourself wired. Then again, maybe you simply cannot drive a car, eat a meal, or relax after sex without smoking a cigarette. Maybe you're one of those folks who push themselves so hard when studying something new that they frequently operate on very little sleep. Workaholic, much? My suggestion to you, in this moon of Expansion, is that you consider your indulgences and excesses, and how magically skilled you are while under the influence of those energies. Not so much? Join the club! Most of us are trained to avoid all mind-altering substances while learning to use energy, with good reason. We simply are stronger, better magicians when we're sober and clear-headed. However, if we are to be the *best* magicians we can be, we must acknowledge those times when we're *not* on our game, not 100 percent "present," and so it's a good idea to have some practice with those energies as well. I personally have learned that I can barely concentrate while under the influence of (too much of) the Mother's Sacred Herb, so practicing energy work while in that state is something I try to remember to do on occasion, just in case it's ever needed.

For example, let's say you've spent a winter's evening out at a bar with your best friend, and you're both a little tipsy. As you're leaving she suddenly slips on the icy steps and twists her ankle. In order to best help her, you would likely wish to do some energy work to help ease the pain and swelling in her ankle so she can walk to her designated driver's car or catch a cab home (because, of course, you wouldn't let her drive tipsy, now would you?). Another scenario could be that perhaps you're a little high on ganja and your dog gets into a tussle with the neighbor cat, leaving him scratched up and sore. You would likely wish to do some energy work on his wounds after you've cleansed and treated them, both to ease his pain and to help them heal better. In both of the above scenarios, if you've never done energy work while under the influence, you could conceivably panic and not only be ineffective in your work, but perhaps even cause greater pain with your hesitation and blundering. In order to *be* the best we can be, then, it's a good idea to practice magic sometimes when we are *not* at our best, in order to prepare for such emergencies.

My suggestion to you this moon, then, dear Initiate, is to enjoy getting a bit inebriated, *if* you are one of those folks who like to do so from time to time (or go sleep-deprived, or over-caffeinated, or whatever your personal indulgence or excess is), and then practice various forms of energy work, from basic aura smoothing techniques such as therapeutic touch (page 181), to intense bright healing streams, chakra work, etc., so that you can become more practiced doing helpful energy work in these types of situations.

Please understand I am *not* advocating the use of ganja or alcohol (or anything else!) for folks who never indulge in such; what I am advocating is the *practice of energy work in all possible states* the practitioner *regularly experiences* in her day-to-day life, in order to become the best magician she can be.

Addiction—The shadow of excess

For some folks, the excesses they indulge in no longer become pleasant escapes or indulgences, but rather habitual practices they do without thinking: The man who automatically mixes himself a scotch on the rocks every day upon arrival home from work; the woman who smokes a bowl at exactly 4:20 every day; the student who automatically starts every morning popping a tab on an energy drink are all *following habits*, not making conscious choices. For some folks, the habit becomes so automatic and mindless over weeks, moons, and years that the indulgence of choice becomes something that they no longer control or even enjoy. The substance controls them, and not the other way around, which of course takes the entire idea of "choice" away. In many schools of thought, the very definition of addiction is something one cannot *not* do.

For many folks, and with many substances, trying to control or quit the habit is next to impossible without some kind of help. There is no shame in seeking and using such help. There are support groups and mentors of all kinds who can help with overcoming addiction, and let us not forget the very great power of the gods in helping us to overcome these shadows as well.

For myself, it wasn't until my health was severely threatened that I could overcome my sugar addiction. From there, the road was simple, though not easy, but with her love as well as the loving support of my partner, I managed to get through my one-season "experiment" as well as the resulting "experiment on my experiment" (see the July lesson), which showed me that sugar is indeed a true addiction for me. As always, we must be ever mindful of our shadows, lurking just beyond our vision, or they will surely trip us up.

TOOL—THE STAFF

From the beautifully carved and polished, gemstone-encrusted walking sticks to more natural-looking pieces of driftwood with a few symbolic items attached with twine or leather, the staff is an awesome symbol of the God, moving forward, male energy in action. Just as we look to our patron gods, we can use the staff as a guide over rough terrain; we can feel the way ahead with it; and we lean on it when we're not strong enough to make it on our own. We can also use it as a super-charged wand, if we consecrate it as such; I would suggest adding metal and crystals to help conduct the energy if you do so.

THE EIGHT VIRTUES OF THE GODDESS— MIRTH AND REVERENCE IN BALANCE

A poem has been going around the Internet for years and years, written by that wonderful writer "Anonymous,"[51] which I often joke is the story of my walk with the Goddess. For me, it summarizes perfectly what balancing mirth and reverence (and personal responsibility!) is really all about:

Butt Print in the Sand

AUTHOR UNKNOWN

One night I had a wondrous dream,
One set of footprints there was seen,
The footprints of the Goddess they were,
But mine were not along the shore.

But then a stranger print appeared,
And so I asked Her, "What have we here?
This print is large and round and neat
But much too big to be from feet."

"My child," She said in somber tones,
"For miles I carried you—alone.
I challenged you to walk in faith,
But you refused and made me wait.

"You would not learn, you would not grow,
The walk of faith, you would not know,

---

51. There has been one claim, by a fellow named Sam Glenn, that he authored this poem, but upon further investigation I learned that he simply found one version and "revised it" and then folks started claiming he "wrote" it. So the author and origin of this piece is still unknown, as well as whether it started out as a Pagan or a Christian piece. In my humble opinion, it sounds much more like something a Pagan goddess would say to a reluctant follower than something the Christian god would.

So I got tired, I got fed up,
And there I dropped you, on your butt.

"Because in life, there comes a time.
When one must fight, and one must climb,
When one must rise and take a stand,
Or leave their butt print in the sand."

And so, yes, we must take our spiritual Path seriously—for our soul's progress is serious business! But part of taking our Path seriously is taking very good care of *ourselves*. Humor and laughter are powerful medicine, especially for those of us who are dealing with the stress of living at survival level in these troubled times. Make sure you keep your sense of humor and try to laugh heartily and loudly as often as possible. It's good for you!

POSTURE OF POWER

If it works for you to do so, hold your hands palms together in prayer. Many "classic" prayer gestures comes to mind here, especially this one where we hold our hands pressed together in front of our heart chakra, fingers pointing upward as the kundalini rises to the heavens above. This posture has deeply ancient and obscure origins that predate the Common Era (CE) by millennia, and it is believed to be effective because:

1. The positive and negative energy forces in our left and right hands are "neutralized" when we bring them together in the center of our body. Some say there's a nerve running along our breastbone in the center of the chest, and pressing our "neutralized" hands on this point stimulates a nerve called the "vagus nerve." This nerve causes energy to run upward, altering our brain waves, which can induce trance.

2. Holding our hands in this position, in ancient times, symbolized touching the testicles of a religious leader (or even the inner thigh or penis of one's deity).

3. It was a gesture used by the ancient Romans to symbolize submission to the shackling of a prisoner's hands with vine or rope. In those times, a soldier could avoid immediate death by joining his hands together this way when captured.

4. It symbolizes surrender.

5. It symbolizes the joining together of the "higher," more spiritual self with the "lower," more worldly self.

6. It is the joining together of two extremities—the feet of the Divine, with the head of the worshiper. The right palm denotes the feet of the Divine and the left palm denotes the head of the worshiper. The Divine's feet symbolize the ultimate solace for all sorrows.

Finally, through this research I have come to believe this gesture can pull energy from both the liberating and manifesting currents of the kundalini to produce and channel power, sending our wishes, like a wand would, directly from our hearts to the Divine. However, I can understand that for lots of folks, this classic prayer gesture has been so overused by a religion that tormented and oppressed them that they wish to have nothing to do with it. In this case, you might wish to try another classic prayer stance—simply open your arms, palms upward, and look up. This will work to initiate that rising energy as well. Finally, if you find that neither of these gestures/stances work for you, make something up! For this is *your* Path, and when you send prayers and energy to your gods, it should always be in a way that you find personally satisfying, powerful, and true to your heart and spirit's intention.

HOMEWORK

Continue your daily energy work, checking on your chakras regularly, adding your mindfulness to the ascending current of the kundalini, making sure all your chakras are clear and bright, and that the energy runs smoothly.

Energy exercise—Invoking fire: Ground and center in your usual way, and go through the steps of evoking and then aspecting the element of fire: Imagine yourself in a ring of fire, flames ever so close, yet you are not being burned. Instead, you simply feel the heat; intense, escalating heat. The flames rise around you as your passion and conviction rise inside you. In your mind and spirit's "eye," feel the flames as they come closer and closer, eventually licking your skin, again without burning, but with intensity! Feel the energies of passion and fire like the bright sun on a hot summer day, heating up your skin, your mind, your spirit… connect with and engage the energy as you relate it to all that's fiery in you… feel the warmth of your body, the creativity of your mind, as well as the depths of your desires... as you aspect this intense energy, allow it to begin to penetrate and warm you. Now visualize and feel and know that fire energy is penetrating your body, your mind, your spirit... feel energy of fire settle into you as you become lighter and lighter... as you... become... fire!

Practice this meditation throughout the moon cycle.

Consider your indulgences. How does the use of them affect your spiritual work? Do you need to practice using energy while in an altered state? If so, you might wish to begin setting that up. Conversely, if you are someone who never really enters an altered state, you may wish to simply consider how you use energy, and practice raising energy, feeling it flow up through your chakras as the kundalini serpent does, soaring to the sky.

Shadow work: it's time to look more closely at your indulgences, habits, "vices," and addictions. Remember that anything can be an addiction (from chocolate to sex to tobacco to morphine), and do not minimize the effect that substance may have over your life! A question to ask yourself is who's in control—you or the substance? Is this indulgence or habit something you are able to *not* do? How does that serve you? If you have no substance attachments, take some time and think about other habits you may or may not have and consider changing things up a bit, so that you are making conscious choices rather than following a habit or addiction. If you do find that you're addicted to something, ponder strategies for helping yourself overcome that addiction. Remember, too, that there is no shame in getting help with ending that addiction. And of course, please remember to be gentle with yourself.

Write a personal Esbat. Begin brainstorming for the upcoming full and dark moons, decide what needs to leave or come into your life, and begin planning an Esbat ritual, including when it's most appropriate to do the work. Consider moon energies: What sign is she in, if any? What phase? Consider solar energies: Where are you on the Wheel of the Year? What time of day or night will you do the work? What day of the week? Consider other energies as well, such as whether Mercury or other relevant planets are in retrograde, your personal schedule, as well as your personal vibrance level (how good do you feel?) and the energies of your household (will you be able to be alone and undisturbed?).

Moon-tides work and devotionals: Don't forget to take some time each evening (or day, depending on her phase) to get outside and look at (or contemplate the position of) the moon. Tune in to her energies; feel her power; let her love fill you. Remember to say your daily devotionals to your matron goddess(es) and patron god(s). Let their energies fill you; let them show you their love and truth as you express your love and truth to them.

Re-read the section titled "Liberation and Manifestation" pages 31–41, as well as chapter 10—"How Chakras Interact" in **Wheels of Life** *by Anodea Judith*. Take the chakra self-test, if you like.

Astral temple work: Take some time this moon to continue work on your astral temple. Now, we're going to look at the many (or few) levels of our temple, and make some decisions as to how we'll get from one floor to another. Will there be stairs? Will they be wide, with shallow treads, or steep and narrow? Will there be any spiral staircases? Inside or outside the temple? Will your temple have more modern conveniences, like elevators and escalators, going up to the roof, or even higher, up to the sky? Take some time this moon cycle and build these important sections of your temple.

15: The Eleventh Moon—Fruition

The sower may mistake and sow his peas crookedly;
the peas make no mistake but come and show his line.
—Ralph Waldo Emerson

MOON ELEVEN—THE STORY

*Your meditation brought you deep this dark moon, much deeper than you ever expected to go. As you cast your circle, however, you could feel it: could feel your darker gods reaching out to you with an odd sort of... measured urgency... their pull was compelling; undeniable; wholly real—you simply cannot **not** answer this call, yet there is a subtle underlying energy to their beckoning; the energy of meticulousness, of slow and careful... measuring. You look around you in the darkness of your inner landscape and see, all around the perimeter of your circle, like home-canned produce in colorful canning jars, all that you have manifested to date in this cycle.*

What have you created? Are the contents of these jars beneficial to you or to others? Are there jars with broken or abandoned dreams? What about the things you yourself have abandoned or denied? Look closer—look into the darkness between the spaces. What do the shadows around these energies have to say? How about the darker deities—what do they have to tell you about these patterns? Take some time now and

THE ELEVENTH MOON CORRESPONDENCES

Keywords: manifestation; receiving/receptivity; proof; listening; home and hearth; the occult; Mysteries; culmination; limitation; meditation; boundaries; structure; form; perfect love

Energy: manifestation, receptivity, pulling

Chakra: manifesting current

Chakra color: black, brown

Element: earth with water

Elemental color: silver

Herbs and flowers: balm of Gilead, dandelion root, Echinacea root

Incense: myrrh, magic temple

Stones and metals: silver, hematite

13 Harmonies: returning through the Gates (control)

Tool: the cauldron

8 virtues: beauty and strength in balance

Astral temple work: secret passages and slides

Shadow group: the Shadow of the Path

Energy keyword: skills

Energy group: Pathworking, manifesting with love

ponder your actions and intentions in the past cycle, your choices and your completed works. And now, within this space, this place that is not a place, in this time that knows no time, find yourself floating, weightless, in the vast darkness, surrounded now by even more of your creations, not just in a circle, but in an entire sphere all around you ... you can now see the Greater Picture, the completed works of your life; perhaps some energy patterns can even be seen from beyond your current life into former ones ...

Just as the last moon had you expanding your consciousness into the bright waves of action and drive; of soaring heights, so this moon heralds the time to look at going down deep into your consciousness and inner Mysteries, to make some real-life choices for the betterment of your soul.

*Your inclination at this point is probably to run away from this stark and sudden assessment of your actions and your future Path, but you know this question will lie before you until you choose to answer, no matter how long you wait, for your gods are infinitely patient, and stern enough that you know there is no escaping this lesson. And even floating here in the vastness of the Mystery, you choose, like the spiritual warrior you are, to **stand**.*

With that very thought, you are, again, standing on solid ground, though the sphere of your various creations still whirls and dances around you. Under your dominant hand, you feel a shape manifesting. You look toward it. Lit from inside with an eerily commanding force is a set of scales. You wave your hand over one side, allowing your consciousness to fill the tray with your own perceived worth, tipping the scale downward. Sighing with the resignation of the dutiful priest/ess, you take the jar nearest you, and spill its contents onto the other tray, to see how the scale balances out.

*Yes, you repeat to yourself, your gods are infinitely patient, and stern enough that you know this lesson must be learned, this exercise **must** be fulfilled. You record your findings in your grimoire, which you miraculously find next to the scales, then take another jar from the whirling mass around you, smiling in spite of the fear of what you may find here, for your courage is fully awakened now; you know your gods are with you. Determined, you look courageously, then empty the jar onto the tray.*

DISCIPLINE—THE ENERGY OF FRUITION

"What we think about, we talk about, we bring about" goes the saying, and as Witches, we know this to be true. Whether in the form of positive (or negative!) energies, we definitely manifest the things we say, especially if we say these things a lot! For most of us, these "affirmations" are often negative: "I never get ahead," "I'm so sick and tired of...," "I'm broke all the time," "No one cares," and so forth. Even the statement, "I want ____" can be a negative affirmation, as the word *want* implies *lack*. I was actually guided by my Lady a few years ago to avoid using this word (that's a tough one to untrain!). As Ruiz clearly points out in *The Four Agreements*, we've been domesticated so well that it can be quite difficult to break these habits.

We must agree that in order for us to accomplish anything in life, discipline (control!) is required. We get up every day, go to school or work to earn the money (or the education) required to keep a roof over our heads (or to learn how to) for another day, or we, as the homemaker, get up and clean and cook and prepare and see to things in order to run the household. Or, if we have a dream or aspiration, we understand that it is we who must do the required work to accomplish that dream, etc., etc. Likewise, dear Initiate, you are going through this course, doing the exercises and reading, expanding your mind, in order to learn and to manifest change in your own life and the lives of others you wish to help.

In the hedonistic culture of the Western world, exercising discipline can be difficult, as we are so often tempted, even *shamed* on occasion, into abandoning our Path in favor of a momentary pleasure, often from the lips of those who love us and claim to wish us success: "Oh, one little cookie won't kill you," our friend says when she hears we're trying to abstain from sweets; "You can sleep in *later*," from another friend who wishes to keep our company much later than our new school or work schedule allows. And if this unintentional sabotage our loved ones tempt us with seems formidable, it is nothing compared with the sabotage we so often and willingly inflict upon *ourselves*. "I'll start my exercise program tomorrow," we say, or "I'll put some money into savings *next* payday." Or, to quote some of my in-real-life students, "I'm going to wait and do *all* of my homework at the *end* of the year and a day." I just laugh and shake my head, because I'm human, too, so I can relate to time stresses, as well as the very real tendency for our excuses and rationalizations to go on and on.

As we know, however, nothing can manifest in our lives without discipline. My dictionary defines *discipline* as "(1) Systematic training of subjection to authority; especially the mental, moral, and physical powers by instruction and exercise. (2) The result of this; subjection; habit or obedience."[52] Later in the paragraph, it mentions training and education. In other words, teaching through repetition. It's also interesting to note that the word *disciple* has the same Old French root as does *discipline*.

A few years ago, I was fortunate enough to attend a lecture at PantheaCon by John Michael Greer, just after his book *The Long Descent*[53] was published. He was talking about the times to come and the many changes we would likely be going

---

52. *Funk & Wagnalls Standard Dictionary* (J. G. Ferguson Publishing, 1978), 363.

53. John Michael Greer, *The Long Descent: A User's Guide to the End of the Industrial Age* (New Society Publishers, 2008).

through as oil supplies and oil-related resources dwindled. He told the audience that the best thing we could do for ourselves was to learn some good old-fashioned skills like bread baking, organic gardening, spinning, and weaving, to name a few. When it came time for the question-and-answer period, a member of the audience asked him if he should be putting money away against the coming times, to shelter him and his family against sudden misfortune. Greer patiently repeated what he'd said before, that the querent should *learn skills*.

A few questions later, another member of the audience asked, "So should we be setting aside gold and other precious metals and jewels?" Greer, again, very patiently stated, "No. You should *learn skills*." I had to bite my lips to stifle a chuckle. Clearly, many members of the audience didn't want to have to go through the uncomfortable process of disciplining themselves in order to learn something new, but would rather simply throw money at the problem, in true American hedonistic fashion.

Learning the skills required to survive the end of the industrial age, just like learning the skills needed to work magic effectively, requires discipline. It's not something you can just throw money at or expect someone else to do for you. These are skills you must learn for yourself.

"The upward current brings us transcendence, the downward, immanence,"[54] Anodea Judith states of the descending current of the kundalini, and this makes a great deal of sense on many levels. Magically, we draw down the power of the upper realms whenever we consecrate a tool. We imbue the tool with the power of the Divine, making it sacred. So, too, are all of our manifestations. In some magical schools of thought, everything, from mundane to highly magical, everything is considered sacred, and this can certainly be true for those following the Wiccan Path.

CHAKRA LORE—
THE MANIFESTING CURRENT OF THE KUNDALINI

As the kundalini serpent moves downward, we become aware of the energy of fruition, of culmination, completion. Sometimes it's hard to focus on the lower chakras, since the upper chakras are the only ones that truly matter in some schools of thought, as though giving our attention to survival, individuality, sexuality, and personal power are seen as "less than" or "unspiritual," but again, we know that spirit

---

54. Anodea Judith, *Wheels of Life* (Llewellyn, 1999), 355.

permeates everything, that spirit is alive in our highest dreams and rituals as well as in our ability to get out of that bed every morning and do something toward achieving our highest ideal.

For this moon, focus on your manifesting current, sending your thoughts down and down, to see what you are bringing to fruition in your life. As in the meditation above, you can look into the energy patterns of what you've created to see what still has place and purpose in your life. Continue to be mindful of all of your chakras, and send healing energy to the ones that seem sluggish or out of balance.

THIRTEEN HARMONIES WORK—
RETURNING THROUGH THE GATES (CONTROL)

The Path of Control includes the energies discussed above, as well as fasting, control of the body through yoga, the breath, the blood, and postures. Sexual abstinence can also be an avenue for control—building and conserving energy for magical or other uses. In some more traditional systems, control is done through the use of the cords—tying them in certain ways controls the flow of blood, which can help induce trance. This, of course, would have to be done by another person, so it's not the easiest practice for a solitary Witch. Control can be explored through sexual abstinence or orgasm denial such as was explored in moon two with the discussion of the Great Rite. Finally, and most importantly, control is used in meditation, ritual, spellwork and daily life when we concentrate on our goal, letting no other thoughts intrude. This isn't always easy! But for us to reach that essential place "in the center," we must be able to practice that essential control.

As you've worked through these chapters, dear Initiate, you have been learning control: in your meditations, your trancework, your work with discipline and general energy work, possibly even through work with the Great Rite, and you will learn more in the next moon chapter with visualization, as well as the following one, on invocation. The importance of control is even illustrated in the quote in the beginning of this chapter; one must have control to sow those darn peas in a straight line. In addition, the energy of control can be enhanced with the practice of control in other aspects of your life. As we know, dear Initiate, being Witches is something we are, not simply something we do as a hobby or whim. So everything we do is touched and interwoven and enhanced by everything else we do. Even the Path of Excess as explored in the last moon chapter can teach us much about control. Imagine trying to concentrate your focus and control the energy when you're all pumped up on too much caffeine or drunk on alcohol and your friend has just been bitten by a dog. That takes *control*!

TOOL—THE CAULDRON

The cauldron is a great tool for manifesting the energies of receiving. Made to hold water, earth, air, or fire, the cauldron is often thought of as a tool for the center, spirit. As such, it is a tool of the Goddess, and transformation.

The cauldron, like the chalice, is considered a goddess tool. Round and deep like a womb, it's decidedly female, although it can and often is used for sacred fires, among many other things. Cauldrons can be used to hold water for scrying or blessing, for floating roses or expressing gratitude such as in a Mabon or Samhain rite. It can be used to hold the ritual fire (put some earth in the bottom, though, and keep the fire relatively small, or it'll be too hot to handle), acting as a receptacle for change as the practitioner burns scraps of paper representing fears, such as in a Beltane or Litha rite. The cauldron can hold earth for blessing and later planting seeds or seed crystals programmed with wishes, such as in an Ostara rite. My big cauldron has also been used for lighting several candles at once, sending prayers to loved ones on Imbolc, and the smaller one, for making camp meals at festival.

More than anything else, however, the cauldron is a tool of *transformation*. Remember the tale of Cerridwen and Gwion Bach, and how just one drop of liquid from her cauldron (whose name is "Amen," by the way), made one intelligent beyond imagining; when he licked his finger after the boiling liquid popped him, this began the process that made him Taliesin the Bard. This is a classic example of the transformative energies of the cauldron.

Cauldrons come in many sizes and materials, and there is a vast selection to choose from. Most commonly, they're made of cast iron, but some are made of copper or brass. If you choose to purchase a cauldron, you can find them in all sizes, from the smaller ones in occult shops usually used as censers or brew pots, to the bigger ones found at camping supply stores, to really huge ones you can sometimes find at festivals and renaissance fairs.

If you decide to purchase a cauldron, just remember to keep it *seasoned* if it's cast iron. To do this, simply heat it up, and then coat it with a little oil or shortening. It's important to add the fat while it's hot so the fat can penetrate the surface of the metal. Then, let it cool completely, and rub the excess fat off with a towel or paper towel. Repeat the process until the fat you're rubbing off is clean. If the cauldron you've purchased is used and rusty, such as my big one was, you may have a bit more of a challenge. You'll have to scrub the rust off with a scratch pad and hot soapy water before you season it. Some schools of thought say never to use soap on cast iron, but I have done so occasionally over the years with both my skillets and all four of my cauldrons with no detrimental effect. However, I *never* soak them, and I *always* dry them completely and immediately, re-seasoning if needed. With the more stubborn rusty cauldrons, you'll probably have to do more seasonings to get them fully re-conditioned, as you'll likely be pulling out rust for a while, but it will get better! Eventually. I had to do my big cauldron over the fire in my back yard three or four times, as it was so big, and so rusty. Finally, you'll want to season the outside of the cauldron, too, and again if it's a large unit, you may want to do it over a fire or even in the oven, wherever it fits best.

THE EIGHT VIRTUES OF THE GODDESS—BEAUTY AND STRENGTH IN BALANCE

Keeping the energies of beauty and strength in balance as we walk the Path of the Wise can also take some discipline, but more in terms of our thought patterns than any physical manifestation. Beauty can be hard to spot in ourselves, especially if we buy into the Western world's perception of beauty and are also a woman who's older than twenty or weighs more than 110 pounds (i.e., most of us!). Strength, too, can be difficult to see in ourselves—again, *if* we buy into Western culture's perception of strength and are also a man who isn't made of steel.

It is my considered opinion that the truest beauty radiates out from within, and to see this beauty in ourselves can sometimes take a great deal of inner strength, especially if we have very many shadows looming in these realms. Like it or not, men are still expected by our culture to be smart and athletic, the big breadwinners who never cry or show emotion, except for the emotions connected to sexuality or anger, and to be sexual automatons who perform perfectly, who "just know" what their lovers want so they can give it to them on a silver platter. Women, of course, are still expected to look like Barbie dolls, run to do a man's bidding, and be sexual machines who never say "Yes" to anyone but their husbands, whom they are expected to never say "No" to. Yes, these unhealthy and unbalanced attitudes are changing, but very slowly. We can help to change these perceptions by refusing to buy into them, and by being the change we wish to see around us. Take some time this moon cycle and look at the beauty and strength that is real both in yourself and in all of the people you know. Everyone possesses these qualities to some degree. Strive to find and celebrate them in yourself and in others you know.

POSTURE OF POWER

If it works for you to do so, sit with your arms out in front of you, with your hands positioned at slight angles to each other, ready to push down and manifest energy, as if imbuing a large tool with magical power. Feel the energy flowing from your hands as you manifest change! Don't forget to breathe.

HOMEWORK

Continue your daily energy work, checking on your chakras regularly, adding your mindfulness to the descending current of the kundalini, making sure all your chakras are clear and bright, and that the energy runs smoothly.

Energy exercise—invoking water: Ground and center in your usual way, and go through the steps of evoking and then aspecting the element of water: in your mind and spirit's "eye," feel the cool mists around you as the mist turns to rain. Step into the pool before you, and let yourself sink in up to your neck. Feel the deliciousness of the cool water as it caresses your skin, your mind, your spirit... connect with and engage the energy as you relate it to all that's watery in you... feel the fluids in your body, the blood in your veins, the tears and sacred sexual emanations, the emotions and depths of love and longing, as well as the compassion you hold for yourself and others... as you aspect this powerful energy, allow it to begin to penetrate. Visualize and feel and know that water energy is penetrating your body, becoming as one with your emotions, your spirit… feel the water energy settle into you as you become more and more fluid, as you become one with the pool, as you… become… water.

Practice this meditation throughout the moon cycle.

Consider working to bring a dream to fruition. What is most important to you this cycle? Likewise, now is a good time to think about your accomplishments to date, and to give yourself credit for all that you've accomplished. Looking back over all the shadow work you've done thus far in this course is a good place to start.

Shadow work: Again, on the topic of fruition, now is a good time to look at your shadows around what you've manifested this moon cycle, season, year, or your life. Do you allow yourself to feel good about your accomplishments, or are you constantly pushing yourself, never allowing yourself to enjoy what you've brought about? Conversely, are you one of those folks who are great at starting a project or course of study, but rarely finish? Now is a good time to look at why those energies are present in your life. If there's a block, you could use the upcoming Esbat work to try and find and heal that block.

Write a personal Esbat. Begin brainstorming for the upcoming full and dark moons, decide what needs to leave or come into your life, and begin planning an Esbat ritual, including when it's most appropriate to do the work. Consider moon energies: What sign is she in, if any? What phase? Consider solar energies: Where are you on the Wheel of the Year? What time of day or night will you do the work? What day of the week? Consider other energies as well, such as whether Mercury or other relevant planets are in retrograde, your personal schedule, as well as your personal vibrance level (how good do you feel?) and the energies of your household (will you be able to be alone and undisturbed?).

Moon-tides work and devotionals: Don't forget to take some time each evening (or day, depending on her phase) to get outside and look at (or contemplate the position of) the moon. Tune in to her energies; feel her power; let her love fill you. Remember to say your daily devotionals to your matron goddess(es) and patron god(s). Let their energies fill you; let them show you their love and truth as you express your love and truth to them.

Read Anodea Judith's *Wheels of Life*, chapter 9—"The Return Journey."

Astral temple work: Continue this moon to work on your astral temple. This time, let's focus on the descending pathways, slides, and secret passageways. Perhaps there are even poles like firefighters use, to quickly go from the top floor to the bottom. Secret passageways can be a fun and exciting element to put into your temple, giving a sense of mystery and magic to an already magical place. Will they wind round and round a great turret, or go straight down from the upper realms to the lower? How many of these passages will your temple have, if any? Your only limit is your imagination and personal tastes.

16: The Twelfth Moon—Overcoming

Oh, so you hate your job? Why didn't you say so?
There's a support group for that.
It's called "everybody," and they meet at the bar.
—Drew Carey

MOON TWELVE—THE STORY

You pace restlessly in your magic room, preparing for your evening's work. The full moon, brightly visible in your open window, glows silvery white just before the earth's shadow begins to gobble her up. You planned your rite to begin in this exact moment, the moment the moon begins to slip into the shadow of the earth, marking the lunar eclipse. You timed it all just right, but now ... you're not so sure. Now, this important working that seemed so certain, so right to execute with this lunar eclipse, seems ... silly. Petty. Inconsequential.

Vacillating between your last-minute candle color change and the original plan, you find yourself suddenly uncertain of ... everything, suddenly insecure about all of your pre-ritual decisions, and you dash from one room to the next, trying to beat the clock in order to have everything prepared on time, but for what, exactly? And why?

"What am I doing?" you ask yourself when you catch yourself removing ritual items you just added to the altar moments

THE TWELFTH MOON CORRESPONDENCES

Keywords: getting around obstacles; dancing with our shadows; the energies of both failure and success; staying the course; breakthrough; catharsis; opening to the Divine

Energy: chasing the shadow of spirit

Chakra: all in balance

Chakra color: rainbow

Element: water

Elemental color: silvery blue, deep teal, black

Herbs and flowers: gardenia, angelica, carnation

Incense: dragon's blood, lavender

Stones and metals: amethyst, silver and gold in balance

13 Harmonies: "Seeing"/visualization

Tools: chime/bell

8 virtues: power and compassion in balance

Astral temple work: tunnels, underground passages, catacombs

Shadow group: the Shadow of the Path

Energy keyword: standing

Energy group: Pathworking; the showdown with the Shadow

before. You question whether this is really the right time for this work, really the right action to take with this issue. You look to the sky. The earth's shadow is now a prominent "bite" on the moon's bright countenance; of course this is the right time. The shadow's grip on your consciousness is the telling sign; if it weren't fighting for its survival already, you wouldn't be so nervous. Of course, you realize, this is the Shadow's energy talking!

Just as suddenly as your uncertainty came, it vanishes. You make your final preparations with more confidence, and chuckle at how easy it was for you to question yourself, how easy it was to assume you weren't doing things "right," and then laugh out loud, for this lack of confidence is exactly why you're here.

You think about all you've studied, all the shadows you've chased to date. In your beginnings on this Initiate's Path, you worked with the core shadows of survival, sexuality, power. Then, as you became stronger, you took on more of your own Mysteries, and worked with the shadows hovering over your personal relationships, and made real decisions regarding your priorities; your care and love for your intimates. Then, you chased the shadows of this Wiccan religion in your own mind and heart, made decisions regarding your priorities on the long road we all share as a religious subculture. You remember how much it's helped you to look at your own mistakes, for if you couldn't admit where you'd been wrong, it would be that much harder to see and believe in yourself when you've been right. You begin to feel strong again; sure. Yet... there is still a hesitation, for this is a deep working that involves connecting with your darkest shadows yet. The time to heal these energies is now, and you're ready, so ready to finally **Overcome.**

It's time. You look out the window and breathe a deep breath of renewal, inhaling purpose, confidence, strength. You exhale doubt, uncertainty, vacillation. You notice that the earth's shadow nearly covers the moon now, and you again breathe deeply of the cool night air. Your gods are with you. You remember that courage is fear that has said its prayers. With a final prayer to your most powerful patron god(s) and matron goddess(es), you cast.

"Earth and moon, dark and light, lead me to my Mystery," you chant, over and over, as the shadow of the earth glides over and covers the moon, leaving the room in near darkness, and the Shadow... comes.

The Mystery of your particular Shadow's manifestation is a secret known only to you, but you spend much time with this Shadow, learning its energy patterns, its ways of manifestation, its sacred name. Once you have obtained this shadow's name, you know it will be easier to overcome it in the dance of the spiritual warrior; you know it will eventually pass into a form you can more easily dance with; keep at bay. As long as you never hold the illusion that you do, indeed, have complete control, for you know that this is the nature of our Shadows—to own them is to Dance with them in an energy pattern of give and take, of grasp and release, for our shadows never really die; they simply become more manageable.

In your work, you battle long and hard, hearing the Shadow's arguments even as you state your own. You strike an agreement with this most fearful, desperate shadow form. You agree to come back and dance with it, learn it well, understand it by **standing under it**, as *you learned to do in the moon chapter "Understanding," in return for the secrets it tells you, which will ultimately give you better control over this dark force in your life. You come to understand that **all of life** really is an energy exchange, and that our shadows are not forces to be feared, lashed out at and blindly assumed vanquished, but rather they are forces to be honored, respected and understood, for this is the only way we can ever hope to dance with and therefore overcome them; to make them our allies. You remember the old adage "Keep your friends close but keep your enemies closer," and with this very thought, you realize that Overcoming, and therefore, Wholeness, is a Sacred Journey, and not a destination.*

As you wrap up your work, you see that the shadow on the moon has slipped all the way across, and she's clear and whole again now, shining down on you. You breathe deeply of her energy, letting her fill and uplift you even as you earth the power, acknowledging again that you are a strong and vibrant spiritual warrior, at least as strong as that damn Shadow.

THE ENERGY OF OVERCOMING

In this discussion of Overcoming, I would be remiss if I did not cover some ideas on how to overcome The Hated Job. I remember reading a few years back that something like 80 percent of all Americans hate their jobs. (I would imagine the statistics are similar in all Western countries.) How convenient it would be if we could all just trade places—instead of simply "meeting at the bar," as in the quote above. Maybe then some of us would enjoy a little fulfillment!

I have had more than enough experience with this, myself. At one particularly difficult job, there was so much stress and miscommunication, in addition to a lot of practices that seemed rather "shady" to me, that eventually I got to a point where working there was making me physically ill. I woke up crying almost every day, stressed and fearful about what I was going to get yelled at about, or how closely I was going to be asked to skirt the law. Finally I dreamed one night that my boss smiled at me—for the first time *ever* in six months of working for him—only to tell me I was fired. At that point, I knew I had to do something about it.

Following are suggested strategies, most of which I think can be adapted to help a Witch deal with *any* extremely difficult or overwhelming life situation, not just a difficult job:

Daily practices for Overcoming

Remember to breathe! Deep and easy: in through the nose, out through the mouth. Count to four as you inhale power, purpose, and calm; pause for the count of two, then exhale doubt, uncertainty, fear while counting again to four, pause for two, and repeat. Adjust the number you count to whatever works best for you.

Keep up with your meditations and devotionals. Remember that the Lord and Lady love you and want you to be happy. Connection with beloved deities helps keep us strong and mindful of why we're here.

Exercise, water, and proper nutrition! Physical energy helps so much when the psychic "arrows" start flying! Exercise can be a great release for pent-up frustrations.

Guard those chakras! Especially the solar plexus and heart ones. The most beneficial posture I've found is this: hold the right shoulder with the left hand, covering the heart chakra with the left forearm, then hold the left elbow (or just above it) with the right hand to cover the solar plexus chakra with the right forearm. This can of course be reversed if the opposite is more comfortable. This helps us hold our power and love energy to us, and prevent it from spilling out when those darts and arrows of negativity and nastiness start flying. You can also cross your legs to help guard the root chakra, if the energies are also threatening your foundation.

Take a three-minute vacation. In some jobs, breaks are basically not allowed. Never mind the employment laws; the less ethical employers always find a way around them. So, for this exercise, sneak away if you have to. Go outside, focus on your Tree of Life, ground and center, and breathe. If you can't get outside, hide in the bathroom if need be, and try imagining yourself in the mountains, by a beautiful river, in the company of those who know and love you. Let that energy feed and nurture and fill you for at least a few minutes.

Immediately before entering the building in the morning, focus on your Tree of Life, and shield, shield, shield!

Immediately after leaving the building at night, force the energy of negativity from your being and command it to dissipate, stating, "I refuse to take this garbage home with me!" Keeping a touchstone in your vehicle can help a lot (in my situation, my brother had crocheted me a beautiful scarf, which I would hold to my heart while thinking about his gentle arms around me. It helped a lot that it also smelled like his cologne).

Open to those who would give support and comfort. Your partner; your family; your close friends; even co-workers who are going through similar issues with "The Job" can lend a shoulder, which can really help.

Use affirmations! I am smart. I am competent. I *rock*! These can help you remember who you are, and that you are *not* "The Job." Don't let them define you!

Drink deeply the nectar of every happy moment. Encourage yourself to open to the positive in your life. Count your blessings. That may sound corny, but sometimes allowing ourselves to focus on the positives in our life can be just the uplift we need to get through until quitting time. Do not use this to minimize your pain, however, or to blunt the urgency of finding a way out. Keep moving toward eliminating the cause of your unhappiness; and add to your list of blessings that you are a resourceful person who *will* find a way out.

Use ritual, if need be, to find a way out. You'll know when it's time to break out the Big Guns! Has The Job become something you have the hope of fine-tuning to your liking, or do you feel stuck there, that The Job is something you must silently endure? Ask yourself, then, for how long must you endure this? To what end? Why?

What I finally did, when I reached the end of my rope, was to take a twisted, gnarled piece of tree root I'd found on the property of the above place of employment and, in ritual, dressed it with banishing oil, stating that I was banishing "twisted and gnarled corruption, cruelty, and dishonesty from my presence." Then I flung the heavily anointed and energetically imbued root into my fireplace and watched it burn. Even during cakes and wine, I had hopes that what I'd been hearing, witnessing, and intuiting at work was all just a big misunderstanding on my part, that the place I worked wasn't *really* corrupt, that the man I worked for wasn't really a crook. I knew if this was so, then nothing would come of my spell. But in my heart, I knew. Of course I knew; I'd had the precognitive dream a moon or so before, which still haunted me. Immediately after the spell, I must say I at least felt safer, more relieved. And for good reason; after all, the corruption was not going to leave the place I was working! I was fired less than thirty-six hours later.

*Allow yourself to **not** care so much.* In addition, do your bliss, whatever that is, every day. Even if it's only for fifteen minutes. This can help so much to keep your mind off the thing you're working so hard to overcome, give you a break from it.

In conclusion, I believe people need *three basic things* in order to break out of survival mode and begin walking a path toward true happiness, success, and fulfillment. These are: love (self-love first, then possibly the love and support of a good friend or partner); good (or improving) health; and satisfying work (whatever that means to us)—all lower chakra energies. If any of these things are out of balance, we can't get a foothold on our lives and will continually feel as though we're standing on shale.

The shadow of Overcoming—the falsehood of perfect serendipity

Life's changes and obstacles can also be difficult to overcome, especially if those changes seem to be taking us in a direction opposite of where we wish to be going. Many of us have fallen prey to the common New Age belief that if we're on the "right" path, all doors will suddenly and miraculously open to us, we'll meet all the "right" people, in all the "right" places, and our life will be blissfully easy and laid out for us, like a smooth and plush red carpet. Yeah… not so much. Sorry. Life and spirit just don't always work like that. What about those tests our shadows and our gods give us? Perhaps some of our goals are *supposed* to be difficult to reach, in order to stretch us and make us stronger for when we get there.

As we work with our shadows and learn what we must do to overcome them, other shadows are guaranteed to rear their ugly heads as well. In fact, going through a Gate (such as any Witchy or magical ROP, or wedding, rebirthing, or croning rites, to name a few) can often test us, and life can seem to bear down on us pretty hard, creating more and more obstacles to our growth and success. Does this mean, in accordance with the belief from above, that we are *not* on the right Path? On the contrary, it can absolutely *also* mean we're being tested and tempered for other obstacles that may lie ahead. Our gods are not so unkind as to not prepare us for our life's journeys, so we must accept the fact that sometimes a hard lesson simply means more hard lessons are coming, and our gods want us *prepared*! This is not a negative, nor does it mean the gods are cruel. On the contrary; it simply means that life is a series of lessons, just like school, and we can't possibly grasp calculus before we know basic math. So yes, our lessons get increasingly more difficult, in order for us to stretch and grow.

It's easy when working on shadow issues to become overwhelmed and end up frustrated. Even more overwhelming sometimes, is that we lose patience with ourselves and then end up even more frustrated. Just as we need to take care not to be too hard on ourselves, we must also be certain we're not feeling sorry for ourselves. Ralph Blum, in his description of the rune thurisaz, states, "If you are undergoing difficulties, remember: The quality of your passage depends upon your attitude and upon the clarity of your intention. Be certain that you are not suffering over your suffering."[55]

And so our biggest obstacle to the Shadow of the Path is that good ol' black-and-white thinking so many of us are trained in, which makes us see ourselves in only those terms. We're either victors or we're losers, and all of our suffering, all of the things that happened in our childhoods, as well as the mistakes we made in our adulthood, come to bear on the Great Scales we use to measure, judge, and sentence ourselves with. How many times must we pay for our mistakes before we feel we deserve our own forgiveness? In equal measure, how brightly do we wear our scars, like badges of honor, as justifications for all our misdeeds, all of the pain we inflict upon others?

It is time now, in this last triplet of moons, to also look at our black-and-white thinking in terms of the world and our place in it. How often do we put someone on a pedestal, and when they fall (as they, being human, inevitably will), we withdraw, or suddenly find fault with all they say or do? How often do we wear those scars, assuming others have had such better lives than us they can't possibly know the depths of true pain (i.e., *our* pain)? I actually heard someone at a festival tell a group of people gathered around a fire that they couldn't possibly know what it was to _____, because the other people didn't have the exact same experience she did. This is dangerous territory to tread, dear Initiate! For to be so arrogant as to measure your pain against another's with some sort of cosmic ruler set to *your* standards alone is bad enough—but to do so with a group of strangers whose experience you've no idea about is a great way to alienate those who could possibly help you overcome that pain in the first place!

Balance. The Path to Overcoming is all about *balance*. Coupled with the very real truth that in order to truly overcome we must first recognize that our shadows will always be right behind us, ready to grab us if we slip, and being ever mindful that we replace old, unhealthy thinking patterns with more positive ones, our gods and guardians can begin to lead us on our Journey to Wholeness.

CHAKRA LORE—ALL IN BALANCE

This last couple of moons don't have specific chakras to study, but it is a good idea here to discuss daily practices, and checking in with the state of health of our chakras is a

---

55. Ralph Blum, *The Book of Runes* (St. Martin's Press, 1982), 126.

good step to add. You've been doing chakra work all along this moon progression, dear Initiate, developing good habits and learning how it feels to tune in to these powerful energy centers. Going forward now, it's a good idea to spend a little time every day, either before or after your devotional work, to just run through them, sweeping your vision over each chakra in turn, checking to make sure they're clear and spinning brightly. If you see any "mud" clinging, you'll know there's work to do in that area. It's also a good idea to observe in your inner eye your kundalini serpent in terms of both the manifesting and the liberating current, making sure all is smooth and healthy there, too.

THIRTEEN HARMONIES WORK—VISUALIZATION

In this moon, with the emphasis on seeing ourselves truly as part of Overcoming, it's a good idea to discuss *Seeing* in general. Visualization and psychic vision are both skills you've been working toward enhancing since Dedicant level, dear Initiate, so likely these skills have been becoming stronger as you've progressed on your journey. As a way to make magic, visualization has been used in probably every Witch's spell since time immemorial, as *Seeing* the work done is a big part of making it happen.

How can you improve these skills? Are you still tracking your dreams and coincidences? What about meditation? Is that still a regular part of your life? If not, why not, and if so, what can you do to deepen and enhance the experience? Take some time this moon and see what you can do to enhance and sharpen your psychic vision and visualization skills.

TOOLS—CHIME AND BELL

The chime is a wonderful tool to use to demarcate various phases of a ritual. It, along with the bell, is also a wonderful tool for alerting the faerie world that magic is taking place. For each phase of the rite, you can ring a bell or strike a chime, which sends shivers of anticipation through the entire group and faerie world surrounding you.

The use of a chime is also a good way to add substance and weight to other aspects of ritual. For example, I've used a chime for many years in my Samhain rites, as I do a Crossing ritual for my students and friends nearly every year, and the chime is a wonderful way to honor the spirits who come to visit with us during these sacred rites. As each name is stated, the chime is rung once, clear and strong, and then the person honoring that spirit speaks for a moment about them until it's time for another spirit to be "chimed in" to the circle.

Chimes and bells of a smaller variety can be sewn onto our ritual garb or threaded onto our magical cords, which subtly mark our passage in between the worlds, like sending a greeting to the fey whenever we garb up or hold circle.

THE EIGHT VIRTUES OF THE GODDESS— POWER AND COMPASSION IN BALANCE

To hold power and compassion in balance, dear Initiate, is in large part exactly what you're doing by walking this Initiate's Path. You have come so far in honing your power as a Witch, chased some pretty daunting shadows, and have become skilled in working with energy. To balance that power with compassion is to recognize that not everyone in your life (or in the world!) is as strong as you are, so there will be times in which you'll be called upon to help others.

Having compassion is the art of recognizing when others are in need, as well as understanding that not everyone is capable of asking for help. That's where the delicate balance of power and compassion comes in. For example, maybe you have a friend who is broke and injured and having a hard time making it on her own. To have a balance of power and compassion would be to perhaps invite her over for dinner fairly often and to send her home with the leftovers, which would help her out without damaging her pride. Of course it's not always this simple: often the need is more spiritual than physical, more magical than mundane, but you're a clever Witch, and I know you can find ways to help, keeping your power and compassion in balance.

POSTURE OF POWER

If it works for you to do so, relax completely where you sit, confident and receptive in your place and power, and in the presence of the Divine; opening yourself to her (or his) will and energy. Allow yourself to hold a comfortable posture as you open your arms and place your hands palms upward on your knees. Breathe in the essence of the Divine.

HOMEWORK

Make sure you do your daily energy work of chakra spinning as outlined in the homework section in the first-moon chapter of this unit. Take care now to examine all of your chakras, as well as both the ascending and the descending kundalini serpent. Heal, or begin work to heal, whatever's amiss or seems unhealthy. Don't forget to give some thought to the energy patterns around the cause once you're finished with your meditation.

Energy exercise—invoking earth: By now, you should be well versed in evoking and aspecting the elements, so ground and center in your usual way, and go through the steps of evoking and then aspecting the element of earth: Imagine yourself in a circle of fresh clay, surrounded by fertile fields that have just been plowed. The scent of the earth surrounds you and fills you with solid, steadfast energy. As you rest against the soft clay, you feel your body sink in a little, making a comfortable impression in the surface.

In your mind and spirit's "eye," feel the energy of the earth all around you as you sink more comfortably into the cool, wet clay. Connect with and engage the energy as you relate it to all that's earthy in you… Your muscle and bones suddenly take center stage as you realize her flesh is the hard packed dirt and clay, her bones, the rocks. Your little earth cocoon seems to grow closer around you, comforting, conforming to all of your curves and angles. Connect with and engage the energy as you relate it to all that's earthy in you, as well as the physical reality of your body and your ability to manifest… as you aspect this solid energy, allow it to begin to penetrate. A helpful way to start is by simply inhaling… as you inhale, visualize and feel and know this earth energy; feel the solidity of your body, its ability to act as ground, and as you aspect this stable and grounding energy, allow it to begin to penetrate and fill you. Now visualize and feel and know that earth energy is penetrating your body, your mind, your spirit… A helpful way to start is by simply relaxing… as you relax, visualize and feel yourself sinking deeper, feel the earth energy penetrating deeply into you until you… become earth… going deeper and more solidly grounded with every passing moment.

Practice this meditation throughout the moon cycle.

Consider what you must Overcome throughout this moon cycle, and trust yourself and your gods to show you the way to best do the work when you're ready.

Shadow work: In light of the above, it is time now to consider your shadows now in total. What still must be done to bring your spirit and your life to balance on the road to Wholeness? Take some time now to examine all the places and spaces, all the energies surrounding where you are "at" in your life. Are you happy in your chosen vocation? What about your spiritual gifts? Are you truly following the Path of your Heart? What about your home life? Are you happy with your mate, your roommates, your family? If not, why not, and what can you do to change things in order feel that you have overcome these shadows? Close your eyes and imagine the perfect life. What does that look like to you, and what steps would it take for you to accomplish your highest ideal? Of these shadows, what do you feel is most pressing, and what can wait? Sometimes a little prioritizing is in order. This might be a good moon cycle to do some spiritual housekeeping, as we near the end of your year and a day, dear Initiate. So ask yourself, what are the blocks to my achieving wholeness? And what is your role in attaining such? This is the perfect time to plan an Esbat for just such work!

Write a personal Esbat. Begin brainstorming for the upcoming full and dark moons, decide what needs to leave or come into your life, and begin planning an Esbat ritual, including when it's most appropriate to do the work. Consider moon energies: What sign is she in, if any? What phase? Consider solar energies: Where are you on the Wheel of the Year? What time of day or night will you do the work? What day of the week? Consider other energies as well, such as whether Mercury or other relevant planets are in retrograde, your personal schedule, as well as your personal vibrance level (how good do you feel?) and the energies of your household (will you be able to be alone and undisturbed?).

Moon-tides work and devotionals: Don't forget to take some time each evening (or day, depending on her phase) to get outside and look at (or contemplate the position of) the moon. Tune in to her energies; feel her power; let her love fill you. Remember to say your daily devotionals to your matron goddess(es) and patron god(s). Let their energies fill you; let them show you their love and truth as you express your love and truth to them.

Read Dion Fortune's *The Sea Priestess*, paying particular attention to her words about invoking the Goddess.

Astral temple work: At this point in our astral temple work, we're going to be considering the shadows of the space. Go deep underneath—is there a crawl space or basement? A full floor underneath? How about under that? Are there tunnels or dark passages? Waterways? Catacombs? Let your imagination be your guide to the shadows that inhabit your temple.

17: The Thirteenth Moon—Wholeness

Serenity is not freedom from the storm,
but peace amid the storm.
—Anonymous

MOON THIRTEEN—THE STORY

You stand in the center of what appears to be a vast plain covered by a swirling fog. To one side is the sun, shooting the last rays of light onto your inner landscape, turning the fog a delicate pink at your feet even as crimson, orange, and gold fill the sky. To the other side, the full moon is rising, pulling night's dark cloak of stars up with her as she shines with his reflection. You reach out a hand to each of them, feeling their energies acutely as they face each other in perfect balance across the sky.

"Yes," you muse; you can feel it: Balance. The energies of your life these past several cycles have been coming into balance ... here, the space where you listen to them; there, the space you pray. And here, the space where you exert power and passion: your altar. Other spaces are dedicated to work, love, health, friendship, more ... You have chased your shadows, pushed them back to a comfortable distance and healed much, while holding true to the knowledge that you must be ever vigilant to keep those shadows at bay. So much has changed ... so

THE THIRTEENTH MOON CORRESPONDENCES

Keywords: balance, being as one with the universe, interconnectedness

Energy: healing on all levels

Chakra: all; entire kundalini and chakra system as a whole

Chakra color: all/none

Element: all in balance

Elemental color: rainbow

Herbs and flowers: white sage, white roses; and any/all as desired or needed by practitioner

Incense: frankincense and myrrh; cinnamon; vanilla; any/all as desired or needed by practitioner

Stones and metals: amber and jet combination; moonstone and lapis combination; silver and gold

13 Harmonies: invocation

Tool: the nexus; cord and knotwork

8 virtues: Love and Truth in accord

Astral temple work: altars; shrines; personal power places

Shadow group: the Shadow of the Shadow

Energy keyword: primed

Energy group: shadow chasing

much remains the same, and you know, or are beginning to know, who you truly are. Moreover, you find that you like that person very much.

The fog at your ankles continues to swirl as night descends. The trees around you darken into shadow, and you raise your arms to the moon as she glides (rather rapidly!) to a halt overhead. Your trance deepens as you prepare yourself for her message…

She speaks of the shadows and the light, how you must keep all in balance by understanding that **true** balance is never static, but rather dynamic; that stillness is not about stagnation, but instead, like the rune Isa, it is that pregnant pause before acting, and wholeness, and the achieving of it, is never a place we arrive at for more than a few brief moments, for to keep all in balance is a continuous flow of energy, and becoming whole is always achieved in the actions of the journey, not at a place one rests at the end.

You have become conscious of your own inner nature, your essence, and in these past few seasons, you've realized that what you've wished so fervently to **become** in your life is already within you... in your very soul. That seed was planted when you were conceived, fine-tuned throughout your lifetime thus far, and now it's become crystal clear to you that every day of your life, every leg of your journey, has brought you closer and closer to your highest ideal—your brightest wish of who you can become.

Even as you acknowledge this, you remember the shadow work you've been doing, and you can look back and see how defiant you were, how sure of yourself and your causes, how much it hurt to face down your own very real flaws, and ultimately, how battling your shadows has made you so much more humble yet so much more confident—all at the same time! You are simply amazed at how much more open you are now, and this humility, you realize suddenly, gives you an inner confidence unlike any false bravado you've ever mustered, stronger than any prayer you've ever uttered. You know your **Self** now; your inner strengths, your limits, **and** your gifts. You know what you most desire, how to heal yourself, and how to find the Paths that will help you grow. You know what kinds of relationships you need in your life, which ones will nourish your spirit, and which ones will drain you of power. You know when to advance, when to wait, when to retreat, and when it's best to run away screaming... or at least, you now know a little better how to gauge these energies.

... As she shines her light on these deep inner truths, the fog parts and you look down into a silvery moonlit landscape of mountain peaks and deep valleys, and suddenly, you realize you've been **standing** on one of those mountain peaks—a very narrow one! You can see that even the gentlest nudge, the slightest shift in your footing could have sent you tumbling, ass over teakettle, down the mountainside. You laugh out loud and deliberately tilt the angle of your outstretched arms, deliberately rocking your own balance and sending yourself rolling down the grassy hillsides, landing gently, as you knew you would, face up on the valley floor. In that moment of stillness, there is no doubt in your mind; they are here. All of your guardians, your matron goddesses and patron gods—everyone. They surround you in the bright *meadow and the deep shadows, shining down on you and supporting you from underneath. You smile, breathing out gratitude and hope, trust, love and sweet surrender, and open your arms again, laying them softly in the grass. With all your respect, you mutter the ancient words of both longing and understanding that magical adepts have uttered since the beginning of time—a whispered prayer and an affirmation of unconditional love: "We are one!"*

WALKING IN GRACE—THE ENERGY OF WHOLENESS

There are many definitions of "grace" from a spiritual point of view. What I wish to address here, what I believe may be a good starting place from a Pagan point of view, is the state of feeling so acutely aware of our *connection to the All* that there is *no separation*. This, to me, is what being in a state of grace means. We are as one with the tree in our back yard just as we are as one with our lover, our neighbors, our Lords and our Ladies. We can feel their joys and support their dreams; we can feel their pain and have compassion for their causes, even if those causes are not ours. We are beyond judgment and rationalization, defensiveness, or the need to manipulate or control, and do not operate from a place of ego.

Ralph Blum, speaking of initiations (and another one is coming right up for you now, dear Initiate!), says that the forces of change are *powerful* at these times, and that what is achieved isn't easy to share. This we know: deepest Mysteries are extremely difficult to articulate, and attempting to do so can rob these experiences of power. That's exactly why this *Thirteen Moons* section and all the personal work at Initiate level is so completely solitary: because these *are* our own personal Mysteries. As Blum so eloquently states, "After all, becoming whole, the means of it, is a profound secret."[56]

And so, much of what we are learning at this time cannot be shared, but the results of this work are sometimes abundantly clear for those around us to see. For when we are determined to heal ourselves, everyone we love benefits from our actions. Now, I'm no expert on what being whole means, nor do I think anyone is. We're all merely travelers on this sacred road. However, as fortune would have it, I have had a few of those wholeness *moments*. So I offer here a partial list of telling signs that you may be experiencing a "Wholeness Moment":

---

56. Ralph Blum, *The Book of Runes* (St Martin's Press, 1982), 96.

Signs of wholeness—a partial list

- Living somewhere above survival level financially
- Being comfortable in your own skin, being honest with yourself about your sexuality
- Owning your power: walking with both honor and humility
- Experiencing *true* compassion (it's easy to feel compassion for the cuddly bunnies, but what about the junkyard dogs?)
- Speaking your mind, asking relevant questions rather than making assumptions, being impeccable with your word
- Trusting your intuition; believing in yourself and what you know
- Devotion to your gods; seeking to understand and act upon their will for you, above and beyond any personal wish or whim
- Knowing and using your spiritual gifts; allowing yourself to receive gifts from others
- Having a plan of action and sticking to it; walking the Path of the Spiritual Warrior
- Being able to focus your energy and concentrate amid distractions
- Manifesting love by forgiving others as well as yourself
- Taking time out to work on your issues, only to discover you haven't any, then laughing out loud—long and hearty, with total self-respect and love—at yourself for your own follies and failings
- Surrendering to the will of your personal gods, without resentment and with *acceptance*

As you can see, each of the entries on the above list relates to a moon chapter. This has been my formula for my personal journey toward wholeness, though I took it in a "hit-and-miss" order until now, and certainly didn't know it as such at the time. I hope it has helped you on your journey, dear Initiate.

At this point, you should be feeling a strong connection to your personal deities, as well as a deep respect and love for yourself. These studies were designed to bring you to a place of receptivity in an attempt to invoke, or Draw Down deity for the first time. We have gotten your shadows under control, shown you your higher truths and love, "flooding" your vessel with your love for your gods through the adoration, your love of yourself and the connectedness between you, so you should be feeling "full to overflowing" at this point—so much so that you can hardly help but invoke. Although invocation is not required for this chapter, we will discuss invocation in depth here.

CHAKRA LORE—NONE AND ALL

By now, you should be fully aware of how to tune in to your chakras in order to clear and heal them, energize them, and keep the kundalini flowing smoothly. Make sure you keep tuning in to them periodically, and keep a balance of order and vibrance.

THIRTEEN HARMONIES—INVOCATION (DRAWING DOWN)

General overview

There are many teachers who believe that invocation is "the heart and soul" of Wicca, and as such, require this act of their students before allowing them to ascend or to traverse certain Initiatory Gates (which Gates those are will vary depending on tradition). Other teachers and traditions hold that invocation is merely the act of inviting the Divine into the magic circle (but as we know, that isn't really invocation, but rather *evocation*), so they have no specific requirement for students to perform this sacred act. I personally am of the belief that Mystery experiences such as Drawing Down, vision quests, sensory-deprivation experiences, and the like can be deeply spiritual, awakening, and life-changing acts because of what one learns during such times, and all are valid ways to come closer to the Divine. Invocation, however, is probably the most prevalent form of Mystery experience one practices in this religion, so this is what I've been training you for all along, dear Initiate, as you well know.

In my travels on this sacred road, I have met many different priestesses and priests, all of whom handle invocation differently, and I daresay there are just about as many different ways to invoke deity as there are individuals. One dear priestess I knew back in my early days said that when invocation is immanent, one feels "very large." Another wise priestess I once knew taught me about the different levels of invocation and how important daily devotionals are to the big picture in this process, as they are instrumental in helping a priest/ess to become closer to one's chosen deities. A priest I once knew taught me about the differences in the ways that men and women invoke deity. He didn't present his method as such; it just suddenly hit me one day when I was teaching a student about different techniques that the energies of *opening out* vs. *inviting in* can speak very clearly to gender difference. Yet another priestess taught me about chakra alignment, and still others have taught me so many things about invocation in particular, and magic and spirituality in general that I'd have to write another book to describe them all.

Throughout the years, using the advice of my dear fellow Pagans, I've learned and practiced and honed my techniques, and then, to my delight discovered even more as I Drew Down my beloved Artemis, who has always been my primary teacher and guide, who then gave me further, more personalized instructions. Your matron goddesses and patron gods will help you as well, dear Initiate; all you need do is ask them.

By now you should be well versed in the process of both invoking the elements and aspecting deity, so you're but a hair's breadth away from invoking, if you haven't already done so spontaneously. As you are fast approaching Adept initiation, if you would like to go ahead and try it this moon, you are more than welcome to, but remember the attempt is required prior to your Adept Gate (note I said the attempt; many people don't actually invoke on the first try, so don't sweat it), so you may wish to save this practice for yourself for your ordeal.

Preparatory considerations

Some good dietary advice to use prior to invocation, given to me by a friend, which my Lady Artemis expanded upon, is to eat lightly the day of, as well as to abstain from red meat for at least three days prior to invocation. I know one priestess who can eat red meat five minutes prior to invocation, however, and it doesn't seem to affect her adversely, but for most folks, I think red meat tends to make the body feel heavy, especially as it takes something like three days to digest. In addition, an invocation tea[57] can help induce a feeling of euphoria, which can assist greatly in relaxing the body and the mind so one can enter trance more easily. Mugwort, a prime ingredient in my invocation tea recipe, wears off rather fast, which is nice, as once the practitioner is "down there" in deep trance, one tends to *stay there* for the most part, so the dreamy effects last just long enough to help the practitioner go trancy.

---

57. The recipe is in this book's appendix.

A period of sexual abstinence can help, too, especially if one's energy tends to be low anyway, as I learned in my lower energy periods. Holding our sexual energy in or, rather, channeling it to other areas of the body can help build energy nicely for this important work. If you're bold, you might try not only abstaining, but also actually building the energy for a couple of days as described in the section on the Great Rite (page 77). The important consideration here is not to "spend" your energy on orgasms, though you will likely wish to later that night.

Moderate sleep deprivation can help as well, but take care not to go so far with it that you're sleepy and sluggish when it's time to begin. Know that you have a lifetime to practice these ideas and see what works best for you. In addition, what works best for you will quite likely change as you grow in your power and skill as a Witch.

Levels of invocation

The levels we reach during invocation (and the often resulting performance of Oracle) vary widely from individual to individual. From personal experience, as well as the conversations I've had with other community leaders who provide this service regularly, I've found there are three general levels. The first level—one I stayed at for years—is one that feels like a deep meditation, and for a long time, I was afraid to allow the Goddess to open my eyes—I thought I'd "lose" her if such happened. Finally, I became more comfortable with that, and I found that I only half-saw the querent in front of me. What was much more fascinating was this ... *picture* of words appearing in my inner landscape (literally—these brightly glowing words seemed to "float" over a background of the mountains in a night sky), which I simply read to the querent when performing Oracle. When in solitary practice, the feeling was similar to a deep meditation, and I would often be led to automatic writing as she required.

The second level is deeper, and the visualization of words and landscape disappear. At this level, although I still maintain awareness, it feels as though she is in the "front seat," so to speak. She totally takes over my mouth and speaks freely, whether to me (in solitary practice) or to the querent (when performing Oracle). Unlike the first level, which allows more recall, at this level there is very little.

With the deepest level, although there is little recall, I am still aware during the process. I've also noticed that many folks' bodies heat up considerably during invocation, as the presence of the Divine speeds up the vessel's vibrations, which produces a great deal of heat. I've often joked that the depth to which I go in my invocation seems to be directly proportional to how much I freeze the second she departs. I'm usually cold afterward, but when I've invoked very deeply and especially when I've performed Oracle for a considerable amount of time (an hour or more), it always feels like there are no comforters thick enough, no teas hot enough to take away those deep chills. Usually, however, by the time I'm on my second cup of tea, I start warming up. There's a recipe for a good warming and grounding tea in the appendix as well.

Other logistics

Some other things to keep in mind in preparation for your invocation rite are *lighting, physical comfort,* and *keeping distractions, both inner and outer, to a minimum.* Keeping light from going directly in your eyes can help considerably with beginning this work. I recommend keeping the light, even moonlight, at your back, and perhaps even wearing a hood. You want to sit or slightly recline in a position that is most natural and comfortable to you, without becoming so comfortable you fall asleep. Your regular meditation posture usually works very well, at least in the beginning. Also consider the temperature, whether outdoors or indoors for this work. You want to be neither too cold nor too warm. Lastly, distractions can come from anywhere, and of course your focus should be strong enough to allow you to stay the course, but the more you can do to help yourself ahead of time, the less energy it'll take to ignore those distractions, which means more energy you'll have for the work.

For example, once, when I presented a Women's Mysteries event in the Pacific Northwest in high summer, we found a beautiful mossy site near a small creek for the invocation space. Knowing how much mosquitoes love my skin, I made sure to spray my chair and comforter thoroughly with insect repellent well beforehand, so the chemical smell wouldn't be present, though the repellent was. Inner distractions can be as multiple and varied as the practitioner, so sometimes soft chanting or prayers, even soft instrumental music in the background, can help with this also.

Tools for invocation

First of all, just as with any aspect of Witchcraft, the most powerful tools you can use for invocation are your breath and your body. Tools enhance and expand, and of course, store energy the more you use them, but it's best, in my opinion, to perform magical acts without them at first, and then, once a tool is obtained, to still perform magic without them once in a while. It keeps us from getting so dependent on tools that we can't perform without them. Additionally, there will be times, once you've practiced invocation for a while, when you'll spontaneously invoke. I've done so during especially powerful meditations, while reading *The Charge* to a class once (as the Goddess had a special message for one of my students), and during rituals, both solitary and with others. So, as wonderful as our tools are, it's good to remember that *we* are still the best channels for that energy.

Some folks like to use special *crystals*, held either point upward, toward the sky or moon, or point downward, toward the solar plexus chakra, effectively channeling that moon or sky energy into their power center. I personally do the point downward method, and when she enters, I usually spontaneously drop the crystal, so overwhelmed am I by her amazing presence.

Additionally, many folks have special *garb* and/or *adornments* just for invoking, such as clothing that reminds them of the Godform they'll be assuming, such as leather loincloths or leggings for those who wish to invoke a fertility god; special gowns, robes, or hand-embellished veils for certain deities or archetypes; circlets such as High Priests and High Priestesses wear; and so forth. All these tools can help create that special "I am your vessel between the worlds" atmosphere, which can expand and enhance the experience. For myself, I consider the special veil and circlet I wear as her tools, not mine, which makes them very special indeed.

The actions of invocation

As you ground and center yourself just prior to the act of Drawing Down, it is often beneficial to read or recite devotionals or adorations. You've been doing them for a while now in this course, dear Initiate, so they should come readily to you. Some folks even like to write and recite personal invocation prayers as a prelude to the next step, which is highly appropriate, as is singing, chanting, or simply sitting in stillness while others sing or chant softly in the background.

One of the best, most moving and effective tools priestesses in this religion use to Draw Down the Goddess is to recite *The Charge of the Goddess*. Some folks have *The Charge* read to them while they open themselves to the energies, but I personally find speaking *as* the Goddess helps me a great deal to acknowledge myself as her vessel, and to be more receptive to her descent, so I highly recommend memorizing and reciting your favorite version, as least for your first few times. For priests, I recommend using any version of *The Charge of the God* they find preferable. My versions of both *The Charge of the Goddess* and *The Charge of the God* can be found in the appendix.

Many folks use their own words and prayers for invocation, however, and some small few use none at all. *Energetically*, there are also many techniques that help one to focus on the energy:

ALIGNING YOUR CHAKRAS

This is as simple as it sounds. Stand or sit facing your deity. Visualize his chakras spinning in time with yours. See the chakra colors and energy as the space between you closes. As he comes closer and closer to you, see ropes or threads from each of your chakras radiating out to connect with each other: root to root; base to base; solar plexus to solar plexus, etc. By the time they're all aligned, he should be coming in. If not, invite him in with your energy.

OPENING IN

Visualize yourself (or physically do this—even better!) sitting quietly under the full moon. Open yourself completely to the idea of the Goddess's (and the moon's) energy penetrating you from above. Allow her to come in; invite her. You'll likely feel a great tingling in your upper chakras, from bliss on down, as she descends. If you're working with an archetype that isn't a moon goddess (such as Gaia) or a specifically *full moon* goddess (such as Hecate), you can still use the opening in (and moon) energy, just visualize your goddess coming *into* your body from her own realm.

OPENING OUT

An old acquaintance of mine once told me that for him, invocation isn't so much allowing one's gods *in*, as it is about allowing one's gods to come *out*. For this exercise, you can do just that. As you breathe from your grounded and centered place, acknowledge to yourself and your god that he is indeed, within, and then open yourself to the idea of *letting him come forth*. You can even start with your arms crossed as though holding him in, and then open your arms in the symbolic gesture that allows his energy to come out.

Interesting to note: The *opening in* technique was taught to me by a woman, and it's the method I feel most comfortable with. The *opening out* technique was taught to me by a man. As men naturally project and women naturally receive, it seems a valid way to start, in my opinion.

BECOMING THE FURNITURE

No matter whether you use one of these techniques, a combination, or some other method entirely, there will be a point where you will strongly feel the presence of something *other than* within you. At this point, it's a good idea to let that entity know they're welcome to be there by settling your energy into the background, so to speak, and allowing them to use your body and voice. I call this "becoming the furniture," as I am the one in the back seat now, acting as physical support for the Divine. I usually visualize—and *feel*—myself sort of melting back and becoming one with the chair.

Performing Oracle

After we've invoked deity successfully a few times, many of us are moved to perform Oracle (or the Divine makes that decision for us!) as a service to both ourselves and our communities. I don't recommend jumping into this right away, however; allow yourself to get used to simply holding the energy at first. Performing Oracle can be a bit tricky; the first few times I did it, I kept trying to control what the Lady was saying (I tend toward this when out of practice, too), as her messages aren't always what the seeker wishes to hear. Above we spoke of some different levels and different ways the Oracle information can present itself to you. However those messages are given to you, whether in line with the above or in some other way entirely, it's very important that you allow the words and energies to come forth and be spoken. Don't attempt to second-guess the Divine! Just let it out. There have been many messages I've delivered, blind with tears, because I couldn't help but "listen in" when it was someone I was personally close to, but it's best to avoid this if you possibly can. Either way, however, the messages typically fade to nothing within minutes of the deity's departure.

Ending actions

Remember to ground thoroughly after invoking. This is very important. Also, it's a good idea to have some things prepared ahead of time, such as a thick blanket (if you're like me, and freeze when the Divine leaves, or conversely a small fan, for those who get overly hot), a cup of hot tea or cold water at the ready, a hearty food choice such as grainy bread and pure juice for cakes and wine. If you drink alcohol or smoke ganja, it's best to wait a good while, until you're thoroughly grounded and have eaten something substantial (as in an actual meal), before indulging in these, or you could fly too high.

Last of all, make sure to ground thoroughly. Did I mention that? **Earth that power!** It bears repeating: **Earth that power! Earth that power!** *Ground, ground, ground!* Once, when I was especially depleted after a prolonged period of performing Oracle, I just up and decided that I needed to pull energy in, rather than ground it out. Made sense, as I was so depleted, right? Hahaha. Not so much. I pulled as much energy as I possibly could into my body, but I kept a cap on it at my bliss chakra. Within mere moments, I was flying so high that my heart was racing, I felt giddy and excited, and if I remember correctly, I started babbling nonsense and laughing hysterically, my eyes welling up with tears. My spirit daughter and my boyfriend were nearby, so I told them what I'd done, which made me laugh even harder, sending tears rolling down my cheeks! They were all business, though, and immediately laid their hands on me, sending the energy down and down, getting me grounded. Within minutes, the symptoms stopped. Then, they had great fun teasing me for the rest of the evening. It's a good thing they were there, though, or it might have taken a lot longer to bring myself down.

A final word

Of course, it bears mentioning that anything you hear or manage to remember hearing from (and saying to) someone while performing Oracle is a sacred secret and therefore a sacred trust. *No one* should ever know what was said save you and your querent without the querent's express permission! This goes for your helpers as well. More often than not, however, the words and ideas that flowed through you while the Divine was using your body will fade from your memory within minutes, unless you have some sort of personal stake in them.

TOOLS—LOVE AND TRUTH IN ACCORD: THE NEXUS

A nexus, as my astrologer defined for me many long moons ago, is the combined energies of Divine Truth and Divine Love, the energies of the Lord and Lady, respectively, twined together to form a much stronger energy bond than the sum of its two parts. I've since been exposed to many other definitions of the word, from band names to scientific discoveries. My dictionary states that the word *nexus*, from the Latin, means: "A bond or tie between the several members of a group or series; link."[58]

---

58. *Funk & Wagnalls Standard Dictionary* (J. G. Ferguson Publishing, 1978), 855.

As we walk this Path of the Wise, the best way to keep a healthy, dynamic balance, in my opinion, is to honor and respect both our male and our female sides, our light and our dark, our active and our receptive energies. When these principles of love and truth are out of balance within us, I believe this is when dis-ease within ourselves originates, for love without truth can be coddling and coercive, and lack understanding. Truth without love can be mean-spirited and distant, and lack compassion. Balancing both of these principles, then, can lead to not only greater personal spiritual health, but also to stronger and healthier relationships with others.

When we use energy in ritual, we are weaving together the energies of the elements, which in turn combine to create the "male" and "female" aspects of the Divine, which then combine to create this nexus of truth and love in accord. These energies combined are the most powerful force in the universe; what we use to create change in our lives. We need no physical tool to represent the nexus; for *we* are that tool, both male and female, active and receptive. However, if we are to choose something to represent this dynamic energy, a twisted rope or cord comes immediately to mind, such as we use in *knotwork*.

Knotwork

There are a few types of magical cord and knotwork, some of which you may already be familiar with. The first is simple spellwork with a cord: you tie temporary knots into the cord in preparation for the thing you're building (or destroying), repeating that step usually nightly, such as "with each knot, I remember how strong I am," and then when it's time to do the spell, untying the knots; using the same example, you would then state that you now *own* your power and can feel it coursing through your veins. Other knotwork of this type can of course be used for health and healing spells, prosperity work, love spells, and more.

The second kind is based on the first, but is more complex, and is meant to last. This would be your Initiate's Sacred Cord (or your Sacred Cord for any level). This cord is woven with all the symbols and colors of your spiritual Path thus far, and is highly charged with energy and magic, as you made it, or will make it, in circle, with intention and focus, and have worn (or will wear) it in circle many times with your ritual garb.

A third kind of knotwork is the kind used in binding magic, and it is meant to be permanent. This type of knotwork is usually done to prevent those who would harm from doing further damage, such as binding a rapist or murderer, for example. If you dare do this type of spellwork, remember that a piece of your spirit will also be bound to this person, as you are the Witch wielding the power for the working, so make sure you are willing for this to happen! Remember the Law of Threefold Return and keep your ethics intact. A reading (or several!) is in order prior to any working of this nature.

BALANCING THE EIGHT VIRTUES OF THE GODDESS

Once again, we're visiting that healthy and oh-so-sought-after energy pattern of balance in this chapter on Wholeness. It goes without saying that the eight virtues of the Goddess are energies to strive for, yet it's important to note that with these energies, too, there is reason to caution against the black-and-white thinking that states we must have *all of them* in balance *at all times* in order to be whole. Yes, and no. Again, wholeness, and the means in which we get there, is deeply personal, and it is always a journey, not a final resting place. We only get to bask in that sweet place of Perfect Wholeness for a little while before life again demands our attention, swinging us off balance yet again to handle another challenge. And that is as it should be. We are never finished learning our life's lessons; to be finished would mean we were finished here, too, and the Divine, just like any good teacher, sees our strengths and our accomplishments, and by them, determines when we're ready for the next lesson, which is of course more difficult than the previous one.

Likewise, it is unrealistic to expect ourselves to always maintain a perfect balance of the sacred energy *pairs* (i.e., beauty and strength, power and compassion). One thing that helps me to accept the above as well as to move closer to that balance is to recite *The Charge of the Goddess* in its entirety, or to simply repeat or chant the segment of *The Charge* in the line above (beauty and strength, etc.). This act especially helps me during times when I feel frazzled or overwhelmed, as does simply hearing *The Charge*. In fact, memorizing your favorite version of *The Charge of the Goddess* (or, if male, your favorite version of *The Charge of the God*) is part of your homework for this last moon lesson, in preparation for Adept initiation, so it's a good idea to look at your favorite version and begin that work *now*.

POSTURE OF POWER

The easiest one yet, if it works for you to do so, is to simply stand as you normally would, yet more precisely *in balance*, lightly on your feet, running energy through your chakras, feeling the elemental energies surrounding you as you focus on that balance, the moon and earth tides, while your spirit is totally open yet totally protected, knowing your own power and that your gods walk with you.

HOMEWORK

Continue your daily energy work, checking on your chakras regularly, keeping them brightly spinning and healthy, as discussed in the previous chapter on Overcoming. This is a good exercise to practice fairly regularly as you move forward on your spiritual path.

Meditation—Aspecting into Invoking deity: Please do the following aspecting exercise in preparation for invocation, which is fast approaching. If you feel ready to try invocation at this point, good for you! Remember that there are many paths to invoking deity, as we've discussed, so start with what seems most comfortable to you.

Before you begin, make sure you won't be disturbed. Turn off your phone, leave a "Do Not Disturb" sign on your door. Prepare the room by lighting a favorite incense or some candles. Get a light blanket to keep nearby in case you need it.

Sit comfortably in a favorite spot. Close your eyes. Ground and center. Acknowledge your personal guardians and gods, and project a circle around you. Breathe deeply and steadily.

Let your focus become dreamy and not fixed on any one thing, other than the deep roots of your Tree of Life. See the little points of light you are so used to pulling in through your roots, gathering around those root tips now, ready to be drawn in... you breathe through your tree as always until your body is filled with light, until your branches overflow and drip sparkling light onto the dark earth below you, to be pulled back in at root tip. And breathe.

Now think about your closest matron goddess or patron god (if you're a man, or feel more connected to male energies). See this deity clearly in your mind as their spiritual presence takes form before you... you've been connecting with her, aspecting with her all this time, but tonight, you feel the bond even more deeply, as the energy between you melts... remember the love and devotion you and this deity share... feel it pour from you even as you feel the energy of her love for you swirling out from her sacred form, surrounding and engulfing you. Let the energies of devotion and love fill the space between you, as always . . .

Now feel her acutely in your heart and mind . . . express your devotion . . . open yourself to her energies, her love and devotion to you, her precious child . . . Just take a few moments to embrace and bathe in the glory and wonder of this deep and sacred bond . . . your devotion to each other . . . and breathe . . .

Now feel your deity come close, closer . . . now she's touching you, palm to palm, cheek to cheek. There isn't a hair's breadth between you. And breathe.

And now, as you come to the place of noting how like this deity you are, feeling the sameness intimacy and now the lines between you blurring between you, see her chakras spinning in time with yours . . . feel the energies sing in your body as each chakra tunes itself to her bright energy, her higher vibrations . . . and breathe . . . now, open yourself even more. Feel her holding you so tightly you begin to blend . . . until you are one. Accept and understand and hold that energy, for as long as you like . . . you are right on the verge of invocation.

If you feel ready, begin to recite The Charge of the God/dess *. . . allow yourself to embrace your deity in the most intimate way possible: to Draw their willing energy Down into your body. Invite this deity to come in and become one with you in whatever way they and you find most comfortable. And breathe . . .*

*Hold this energy **gently** for as long as you like, being sure to work with your deity on how long or short the exercise should be, within the parameters of your own comfort zone. When it is time for your deity to leave, let them go with love and honor.*

When you are ready, open your eyes, stretch, and jot down the things you learned while you were deep. If invocation did occur, you will likely be fairly depleted. This manifests differently for everyone (for example, her presence makes my body very hot, so that when she departs, I usually find myself freezing and in need of hot tea and a thick blanket). Please take good care of yourself by doing a thorough grounding! Also make sure you have comforts available, such as a warm blanket, and some good, earthy, grounding food and drink.

Consider performing an invocation. Memorize your favorite version of *The Charge of the God/dess* (or some devotional prayers, adorations, or other words that have meaning for you), in preparation for invoking.

Shadow work: Examine what shadows remain in your life that could affect your spiritual Path. You are a spiritual warrior now, and as such, you must be ever mindful of those shadows (especially the ones you think you have completely under your control!), which will try to trip you up if you don't keep them in the corner of your mind's "eye." Remember, always, that staying on top of your shadow work is one of the many paths to spiritual (and often physical, mental, and emotional) vibrance! Keep dancing with them and let them know, always, just exactly who's boss! Good luck!

Esbat work—as always, keeping in mind you have an initiation coming up. You may wish to do work to prepare for that Gate. Consider moon energies: What sign is she in, if any? What phase? Consider solar energies: Where are you on the Wheel of the Year? What time of day or night will you do the work? What day of the week? Consider other energies as well, such as whether Mercury or other relevant planets are in retrograde, your personal schedule, as well as your personal energy level (how good do you feel?) and the energies of your household (will you be able to be alone and undisturbed?).

Moon-tides work and devotionals: Don't forget to take some time each evening (or day, depending on her phase) to get outside and look at (or contemplate the position of) the moon. Tune in to her energies; feel her power; let her love fill you. Remember to say your daily devotionals to your matron goddess(es) and patron god(s). Let their energies fill you; let them show you their love and truth as you express your love and truth to them.

Read Anodea Judith's *Wheels of Life,* chapter 12—"An Evolutionary Perspective."

Astral temple work: Now, we focus on the Big Picture—standing back and looking at our temple, seeing its strengths and weaknesses with love and truth in accord, understanding we can modify, change, or rebuild it anytime we want to… take your time this moon cycle to work out and fine-tune all of the details. Make it yours in every possible way.

Now your temple is complete. All that's left at this point is moving in, dear Initiate! Open your arms and heart and embrace your spiritual home!

PART
THREE

ATTUNING THE VESSEL:
THE SOLAR WHEEL

THE SUN

The sun is the center of our solar system and, at about 4.5 billion years old, has been around about as long as the earth has. It is the primary source of our light and heat, and without it, all would die. Described as an "average" sized star, the sun is so huge that it could contain within itself more than a million earths. That is, if it weren't so hot and had discernible boundaries. And wasn't filled with toxic gases.

The sun also sends out a steady stream of particles that make up what is called "solar wind." This wind blows at a rate of about 280 miles per second, and occasionally sends out *solar flares*, which are connected to *sun spots*, or cooler places on the surface of this 10,000° Fahrenheit star.[59]

The sun pulls on all the planets in our solar system, and the earth rotates around it in a long ellipse, coming to a halt at the solstices (the word, oddly enough, means "sun-standstill," not "earth-standstill") for about three days before we begin the long journey around him again. The sun, which represents the God, speaks to us of differentiation and separation with the bright light that creates sharp and distinct shadows. With all of his fiery activity, he speaks to us of action and drive, inspiration and illumination. His is the realm of day, and work, and prayer and doing-ness.

So this Solar Wheel unit, dear Initiate, will teach you, in a little over one solar cycle, how very much like the god you are, how the actions you do will in many ways define you and your spiritual path, help you become your own ideal of a spiritual warrior, and will show you ways in which you may wish to connect with and serve your gods by serving your local (or not so local!) Pagan community.

NAVIGATING THE SOLAR WHEEL UNIT

As stated in the "Jumping on the Wheel" segment in the beginning of this book, for the Solar Wheel lessons, you'll be starting with the current or upcoming month. A good guideline to follow is to start with the *current month* if today's date is on or before the 10th of the month, or to start with the *upcoming month* if it's past the 10th, as this gives you time to prepare for the upcoming Sabbat. All you need to do then is follow the wheel around the year month by month.

---

59. "Sun," *National Geographic.com*, http://science.nationalgeographic.com/science/space/solar-system/sun-article/.

The Solar Wheel lessons are more outwardly focused, and will prepare you for the service work you will begin in earnest at Adept level. These lessons will cover holiday lore, energy of that time of year, and a tool that relates to the energy pattern. We'll also explore ideas regarding our *spiritual callings* or gifts in the *Pathwork Focus* segments—these are ways in which we may someday wish to serve our communities. In addition, there will be ideas for *Pathworkings*—ways in which we can attune ourselves to our regional energy patterns, and of course there will be homework. Homework will include essays, ritual writing, and suggestions for a lightworking or spell for that month. There will also be reading assignments and suggested grimoire work.

If you took the Dedicant course, you will have already written a half-set of rituals (the lesser ones); however, if you got your Dedicant training elsewhere, you will have those rituals assigned in the monthly lessons also—just look for the words, "Write a _____ ritual, if you've never written one before" in the homework sections.

So now is the time to act! Just choose which monthly lesson you would like to start with, and from there, begin working your way around the Wheel.

18: The December Lesson

Man is in part divine; a troubled stream from a pure source.
—Lord Byron

YULE—THE STORY

In the wee hours of the morning, you can hear little except the wind in the chimes outside the window and the muffled sound of the occasional car going by. You stretch your consciousness to the spirit realm as even the subtlest of the night sounds are shuffled to the back of your mind. Deeper and deeper, you settle into your meditation, sending roots down into the rich black soil a hundred feet below, two hundred, three ... hundred ... down and down ... to bedrock. You breathe deeply of the dark silence, opening yourself to the Mystery. Suddenly, you find yourself facing a great wheel. The Great Wheel. You see symbols of your life, intermingled with the symbols of the Sabbats, some that are precious to you, and some that you still have much to learn about. You take some time exploring your favorites first, and your heart fills with joy when you notice all the symbols and memories from past years that make up the scenes before you. Finally, you look toward the top of the Wheel, to the place of the current holiday. Yule. The ancient word for "wheel." You acknowledge that this is the place on the Wheel where endings and beginnings are highlighted, magnified. Exalted. You ponder

THE DECEMBER LESSON CORRESPONDENCES

Focus: Yule

Energy keywords: dark and light; yin and yang; hope; new beginnings; rebirth

Tool: grimoire

Pathwork focus: the Historian's Path

Herbs and flowers: oak and holly; all evergreens; poinsettias

Incense: frankincense; cedar

Stones and metals: jet; obsidian, both black and "snowflake"; hematite

Overarching energies: blank the end; blank the beginning

Radiant energies: hope

Sun enters: Capricorn

this energy, then lean closer to examine the dark symbols and markings on this part of the Wheel.

At first glance, you see nothing but faint etchings and a small golden dot in a vast and darksome field. Then, as you draw closer, you can see that some of the etchings are as deep as canyons and the little gold dot is actually … a seed. As if in response to your curiosity, the seed becomes larger in your field of vision, just like you're zooming in on it with a camera. As the seed becomes more clear, you can see it's actually a cluster of billions of tiny golden seeds, all filled with potential, and purpose, all vibrant with the energy of youth, all new and exciting, and no small sum of them appear exciting, yet … challenging! You look just to the left of the seed cluster. Hidden in the deep crevice of an earthy symbol, you can see symbols of fulfillment and culmination, lined up all in a row. These, too, shine with golden light, but they have a different energy, the energy of fulfillment, of pride and satisfaction, of completion.

Many of the symbols you recognize as things you've accomplished this past year. Several of them fill you with pride in your accomplishments—some of the actions you took this past *year weren't easy, but they were essential to your growth. Your chest puffs out a bit as you take a deep, full, and satisfied breath, sighing with contentment as you slowly exhale. But your mission here isn't about resting on your laurels. You know it's about looking ahead.*

Looking again at the myriad of golden shining seeds, you breathe deeply and will yourself to relax. There is no hurry here. You can see that this place on the Wheel is filled with the magic of choice and change, of ending a Path or beginning one, and even Paths that you are currently following will take a new turn when the Wheel clicks again after the solstice. You look at one of the deeper grooves, one that is shaped like a symbol for a change you wish to make and again slowly release your breath. As you do so, you are filled with a profound and deep respect and awe, for your consciousness is sinking deeper and deeper into the symbol's grooves and meanings. Silence engulfs you, and you are suddenly alert, calm, and aware that you must make fully conscious and careful choices in this magical place, for this is the place of deep and profound change. You know that whatever you choose to begin today will take time and care to fulfill, and that the energy will connect to you on a fundamental level and will not be easily released, for you are deep in your own consciousness, where the most powerful changes take place.

You take all the time you need to examine these bright and shining seeds of potential, and when you're ready, you choose a few to add to your goals for the coming year. You hold them in your hands, shining with gold, silver, and a myriad of colors. You breathe on them to give them life, and smile when a little flutter in your solar plexus tells you these choices are choices of **power***. Breathing deeply again, you remember the Sun God, and all of his bright energy. Holding fast to your exciting new changes, you emerge from the meditation slowly, floating easily and deliberately to the surface, ready to embrace the fresh new year.*

THE ENERGIES OF LIGHT AND DARK: HOPE AND FEAR

The energy of Yule, as we know, encompasses both endings and beginnings. It is the turning point where dark gives way to light and, as such, can be a turning point within. The table of correspondence for this chapter describes the overarching energies as "blank the end; blank the beginning" because this energy is that tiny, still fraction of a moment, that pregnant pause on the Wheel of the Year between the moment when all is culminated, measured up, fulfilled, and the moment when all begins again. It is the breath one takes before jumping off the high dive; the idea, still unformed, as it rushes into our creative consciousnesses; that stillness that tells us we must stop to listen and perceive and prepare for what's coming next, for all is blank, nothing is decided—yet. Like the solstice itself, we are in "pause" mode, waiting to begin again.

Lots of folks are disappointed with the whole idea of the winter holidays because of the commercialism of this time of year, but if we can strip away the outer trappings of the holiday and look to the realm of the gods, to the energy of the season, and to our own inner landscapes, we can see that Yule is a time of embracing the Mystery of the dark as well as the hope engendered by the return of the light, the hope of renewal. As the Wheel turns from dark to light, so this time of year can be a chance to create our lives anew, to take a new turn in our Paths.

The Ancients undoubtedly began the tradition of bringing a tree into the home and decorating with lights in order to acknowledge and celebrate the evergreen God and the return of the light. They may even have felt they had a hand in turning the Great Wheel, doing the above actions as an assurance that the light would come again. And as we Pagans have gone through time, we've adopted many of those ancient practices, added our own, and supported the energy of renewal through our faith and our actions. Sure, many folks don't even realize why we bring a tree into the house, decorate with lights, or speak of Father Time and the Newborn Babe at this particular time of year and no other, stating that "Jesus is the reason for the season." However, knowing that Jesus was born in the spring, as well as knowing what we do about Yule and the newborn Sun God, assures us in our belief that *the season is the reason* we celebrate as we do. These traditions and practices have remained through hundreds of years as heralds of the returning light. Is it because folks simply *choose* to do so? Because it's "tradition"? Possibly, but I submit these practices and beliefs have held strong because we have triggers in our ancestral memories that are automatically tripped this time of year, and our spirits respond, alerting our minds and bodies to participate in the dance of energy around us.

This time of year is about remembering and acknowledging the darkness, and moving toward the light—the faith and the hope—that can pull us out of it. Hope is indeed something that will be needed in times to come, as we face the end of the industrial age. It's not something most of us wish to look at, but the reality is that it *is* coming, and the time to begin preparing for it is *now*. John Michael Greer writes, "There's a rich irony... in the common dismissal of the lessons of spirituality as 'magical thinking,' because magical thinking is exactly the form of human thought that deals with the realm of motivations, values, and goals that technical and scientific thinking handle so poorly."[60] These wise words say to me that we *can* have hope, even as we face the uncertain times ahead, and that we can use spirituality and magic to improve our own situations and to find like minds to pool resources with, to help others and to receive help in turn, if necessary. In my opinion, we need a balance of both the practical and scientific, and the spiritual and magical, in order to most effectively deal with what's ahead of us.

Of course, there are many schools of thought out there on what might happen, and while it's true that no one knows for certain how things will go, the one thing we do know is that great changes are coming and not all of it will exactly be comfortable. Predictions have been made for all kinds of scenarios, all kinds of difficulty, from moderate fuel rationing and food shortages, to total fuel depletion, rioting over resources such as food and water, to outright war.

Many prominent and respected authors have written on the subject, and it behooves us to study up on these possibilities, so that we may prepare ourselves and our loved ones. What we can do, in addition to learning some useful skills, is to keep hope alive, in part by doing just that—we tend to feel much more hopeful if we're prepared in some way, if we feel we have some skills and resources. We can also learn or relearn some new (to us) useful *older* skills, going back to the basics our parents and grandparents knew intrinsically, such as: making basic home repairs and improvements; how to diagnose and heal ourselves (this is covered much more extensively in the July lesson when we talk about becoming our own healer); how to cook from scratch; how to sew basic garments or at least to mend them; how to make bread (without using that silly bread machine!); basic organic gardening; and for us omnivores, it's not a bad idea to learn to hunt or fish and to effectively process our kills.

I believe the best wisdom is to hope for the best, but plan for the worst, to the best of our ability. We just don't know if by some miracle someone will come up with a new energy source that doesn't require petroleum to create, or if the world as we know it will come to a screeching halt tomorrow. This is not a time to panic and lose sleep over what might be, but to take the responsibility to be smart about our choices and our connections, and to face the future with courage. Remember, too, that courage and fear are not opposites; as they say, courage is simply fear that has said its prayers.

---

60. John Michael Greer, *The Long Descent* (New Society Publishers, 2008), 204.

In light of that, we would also do well to work on deepening our connections to our loved ones, as we'll all be helping each other in the times to come. Tolerance and compassion, if not already staples in our consciousnesses, need to be cultivated, and petty differences will need to be ironed out. In addition, it behooves us to open our hearts a little more to others, to at least tolerate, but better—to accept and embrace our differences, for it's been proven by nature that diversity, not homogeny, is key to a species' survival. I've mentioned before, my friend Moonstar's advice, "You must *make* your friends before you *need* them." Profoundly wise, this advice can not only make life a bit sweeter, but it could also quite possibly help keep us alive. Just as the Ancients traded one skill or resource for another, so may we also in the future, which means our friendships will become even more important to us as a community. In addition, deepening our connections to our chosen deities can go a long way to strengthen and uplift us for what's ahead. Indeed, time has proven that faith is a strong medicine against despair.

I realize my words have been a bit dark, but this is the time, not only on the Wheel of the Year but also on the Greater Wheel of our lives, to be looking ahead and making decisions regarding our futures: as individuals, as family groups, and as a community. And indeed, dear Initiate, you must know that there is always the seed of darkness in the light (which is why many folks get a little depressed this time of year—and that's okay), just as there is always the seed of light (such as hope brings) in the darkness. May our faith support and sustain us in the year and the times to come.

TOOL—THE GRIMOIRE

The grimoire, as you may well already know, dear Initiate, "a (usually mediaeval) book or 'grammar' of magical procedures,"[61] or Book of Shadows (BOS), is one of the most important and potentially powerful tools you can own. Like a good cookbook, it can store recipes for anything from magical oils to medicinal salves and extracts, to recipes for your favorite ritual cakes, and even wine or mead. Like a journal, it is a record of magical and spiritual study and progress, as well as a record of emotions and insights into life and personal growth. Like a dictionary or thesaurus, it's a quick look-up for symbols, colors, ideas, etc., that you may want to use in your next ritual,

---

61. Janet Farrar and Stewart Farrar, *A Witch's Bible* (Phoenix Publishing, 1996), 321.

as well as a record of dreams, coincidences, readings, and rituals. And, if you're like me, like most busy Witches, you don't probably keep it up so well. This month would be a good time to update it. With an up-to-date grimoire you can much more easily troubleshoot, track, or plan just about anything in your Witchy life.

It is generally held in the Wiccan religion that it's best to write everything in your grimoire by hand, but I believe in today's busy world, especially once one initiates, it's not always practical to keep to those guidelines. In addition, there are many ways and styles you can adopt for this most important tool, from a single blank, bound book you only write in by hand, to a fancy leather embossed cover with interchangeable filler books, to a file or group of files on your computer system, named as such.

Another great way to keep your BOS was revealed to me by a student of mine, years ago. She was an herbalist, so she kept her herbal grimoire in her kitchen, where she prepared her herbal formulas; she kept her dream grimoire in her bedroom on her bedside table; her meditation grimoire in her meditation room; and so on. At the time, my whole grimoire was on my computer, plus a fairly hefty stack of notes and bits of herbs, pressed flowers, typed-up rituals, songsheet copies, and tiny scraps of paper with ideas scribbled on them. I was inspired by her idea, so I bought myself a few blank books. Most of them were fairly plain, but I splurged on a couple of really fancy ones, and now my grimoire is a combination of the above, kept in a special case I built and painted for it, along with a now *really* hefty stack of notes, etc., all neatly filed and waiting to be typed up into my computer grimoire or transcribed into the bound books. (I must admit, being an incredibly busy Witch, this stack of notes has been waiting a long time!)

Whatever you've decided to use, or will now decide to use, it's best to keep it as up to date as possible, as it can be a great resource to you for many years to come.

PATHWORK FOCUS: THE CALLING TO THE HISTORIAN'S PATH

History is a fascinating subject to many people, and religious history can be even more so. The origins of our beliefs, how they affected the ways of the world from ancient to current times, and their strong ties to the origins of Christian thought can expand your mind in ways you never imagined. I haven't always had this opinion. Other than a short period of time—when I was a freshman in high school, and lucky enough to have a teacher who could present history in a manner that didn't put me right to sleep—I spent most of my life bored to tears with the topic. I can remember doing research for my first novel. I can't remember exactly what it was that I was looking up on the microfiche in the basement of the Colorado State University library, but it took hours of poring over, which eventually ended in my *snoring* over, these tiny little squares of film. Yes, literally. When I awoke (from a rather loud snort), I was *so* glad that I was alone in the room! I decided then and there that the distaste I had always felt for history had grown into an aversion so deep that I would never again attempt to write a novel with any historical references whatsoever.

Then I discovered Marion Zimmer Bradley. Diana Paxson. Margaret Murray. Gerald Gardner. Dion Fortune. And Robert Graves. By researching religious history and reading some really good authors of both historical fiction and nonfiction, I realized I didn't have an aversion to *history* at all. I just had problems with the way some people presented it. History is so much more than dry facts and figures—it is the story, or stories, of the *lives of our ancestors*! And that's exciting! Being a storyteller at heart, I am a sucker for a good plot and good writing. This is what keeps it interesting, even if the author just isn't.

The person who chooses to follow the Historians' Path should be able to sift the wheat from the chaff, so to speak. Even the most brilliant of writers will have a fact or two out of place, and really, with a lot of historical information, especially that which goes really far back, much of the information is simply speculation. So, just like studying Wicca in general, one must be constantly aware of that common thread that runs through all good work and eventually serves to tie it all together. If one author says that the sky is red, and seventeen other authors say the sky is blue, you can pretty well rest assured that the sky is, indeed, blue. This is an oversimplification, I know. But the Wiccan historian must be willing to read the snoozer authors as well as the more creative ones, not be blinded by a superb writing style, and measure all that she reads against her own gut and her own mind. She must be able to discern the truth, and only by reading many different books and learning many different viewpoints can she hope to reach the objectivity required for this kind of discernment. And I don't mean just the authors with a Wiccan point of view. I mean lots of authors, lots of historians, all with different life experience and viewpoints.

The Wiccan historian must be able to truly understand the color of the lens each author uses to present the material, and take it all with the proverbial grain of salt.

Only then can he truly serve his community by keeping us all on our toes, correcting the misinformation and presenting the truth. That he must use tact and diplomacy to do this should go without saying, but considering how easy it is for us humans to fall into the trap of Supreme Know-It-All, I think it bears repeating: When you act like an ass, no one will listen, no matter how knowledgeable you may think you are. If you choose your words carefully, keeping in mind how you would wish to be spoken to when incorrect about something, you will gain many friends who not only like you, but will respect you as well. Arrogance only serves to distance you from the community you will eventually wish to serve.

If, after reading this, you decide to explore further, you would do well to go ahead and start collecting both scholarly and poetic works by historians *now*. Make sure you are aware of the biases and beliefs of the author, and read several sources for your information. To this I would add: Thank you, and welcome. Your community needs your brains, your passion for this work, and your compassion for all of us who don't have the calling to this particular Path. Good luck, and Blessed Be.

INITIATE PATHWORKINGS

Go for a holiday walk! Bundle up if it's cold in your region, and as you walk, notice how the light has changed, how the sounds have changed, become higher, sharper. The shadows, too, are sharper at this time, as the earth is so close to the sun. Breathe deeply of the fresh air and know that it is filling you with clarity, newness, ideas. When you get home, jot down any new ideas or changes you wish to make in your life.

Buy yourself a Yule gift, no matter how small. You deserve it! Especially if you're the kind who always does for others, make a commitment to yourself to get a special treat—a nice crystal or stone, a book you've wanted, or a music CD with goddess songs—whatever would make your heart happy to use and see in the coming year.

Take extra special care of yourself during the insanity of the season. While partying and enjoying the festivities around you, remember to eat healthy and get plenty of rest and water, take all of your medication on time—it's easy to forget when one is caught up in all the excitement and hustle-bustle. Give yourself special healthy treats, like a cup of a favorite tea, a hot bath, or an early-to-bed night.

Go deeper in your moon work at this time, perhaps focusing on the dark moon and your inner Mysteries. Know that you are strong, and capable of handling whatever comes up.

Do a Dark Time meditation or divination. The Dark Time energies can expand and enhance our meditations and divinations a great deal, so now is a great time to tap into these energies before the light starts growing again. Ponder all possibilities, willing yourself to have the *Courage to Dare* to see the deepest truths of your own Mysteries.

Give yourself a time-out. If you are the kind who usually gets depressed during the holiday season (or if you're going through a difficult period of time, which the holiday season exacerbates), allow yourself an hour or an afternoon (or a whole day, if need be) to *wallow*. Take to your bed and focus on what's depressing you. Now, this is not to say you should stay in this place and avoid your problems forever, but that it's okay, healthy, even, to take some time to let yourself go through the process of mourning, to allow yourself to feel depressed, to go into the depths of this particular shadow in order to find the keys to heal it. Keep some paper and a pen or pencil by you and, throughout the process, write down whatever you're feeling. However, now is not the time for analysis. Now is the time to simply allow yourself to *feel*, so please don't censor yourself or minimize your situation. Then, after your allotted time is up and your list is complete, go before your altar. Ask your chosen deities to help you turn these energies around. Rewrite, where appropriate, the negative thoughts as positive affirmations, and use them whenever the negative thoughts threaten to creep in. It's also a good idea to burn or bury the paper with the negative "affirmations" on it, giving your problems over to the care of your gods.

Make a list of all the things you love about the winter holidays, and then make a list of all the things you don't love. Make a decision to turn around those things you don't love, or come up with ways you can avoid those energy patterns, in order to truly clear out the negative and so more fully enjoy the positive energies of the season.

HOMEWORK

Write a Yule ritual, if you've never written one before (such as if you took my Dedicant-level course), from grounding and centering to opening the circle. Be sure to include altar decorations, cakes and wine choices, and what you'll serve for the feast afterward, if applicable.

Make a list of your personal thirteen laws, rules, or edicts. We all have things we say we'd "never" do, or things we say we "always" do. Think about your personal goals, morals, ethics, values. The Christians have their Ten Commandments. What are your personal guidelines for your life? Aim for thirteen, but more or less is fine, too.

Read **A Witches' Bible,** *chapter XI—"Yule, 22nd December."* Also read Part II in *Drawing Down the Moon.*

Lightworking: endings and beginnings

Take some time this month and ponder the things that need to end in your life so that a new cycle may begin. Plan spellwork, either in conjunction with your moon work or as a separate ritual, and then use the talents and skills you've learned thus far on your Path, dear Initiate, to create something wonderful and new for yourself.

For your grimoire

Begin (or continue) a table of correspondence for darkness, earth, winter, and the Dark Time.

19: The January Lesson

At the heart of Darkness, there is Light; at the heart of Light,
there is the Mystery. Ours is not to question the gods,
but to surrender to their will.
—The Great Goddess Brighid
(as spoken to Thuri in meditation)

IMBOLC[62]—THE STORY

You come up from your meditation slowly, holding fast to the
ideas you were given while you were deep. The room is dark
except for the single white candle in the cauldron before you.
Tiny crystals glitter on the sand in the bottom of the cauldron,
reflecting the brightness of your thoughts and ideas. Imbolc. In
the belly. The seed-place. You pick up one of the little crystals,
remembering, and hold it in your dominant hand, sending the
energy of creativity and focus, power and passion, of one of the
things you wish to "plant" in your life into the crystal's core,
"programming" it with your intention. You breathe on it, then
kiss it to seal the spell, and place it in a special bag of black silk,

---

62. *Just as in Dedicant, I offer the Imbolc lesson in January, dear Initiate, because the*
holiday comes so early in February, and I wish to give you plenty of time to study
and prepare for your holiday celebration.

Focus: Imbolc

Energy keywords: in the belly; the seed-place; deciding

Tool: quarter energies—candles and holders

Pathwork focus: the Stone Whisperer's Path

Herbs and flowers: peppermint; white sage; white roses

Incense: pine scents, nag champa

Stones and metals: platinum, blue topaz, diamond

Overarching energies: planning the garden; choosing seeds

Radiant energies: learning; interacting

Sun enters: Aquarius

to await planting time. You repeat the process with the others until all have been programmed and place the little bag in a special place on your altar.

Next, you take a small colored candle from your altar, and carve it with a symbol of your wish for a loved one, then light it from the white candle and secure it in the sand. You repeat this process for all of your loved ones, sending prayers and wishes for love, happiness, security—whatever each of them needs. Soon, there are candles in all the colors of the rainbow surrounding the larger white candle in the cauldron. Chanting over them, you feel powerful, filled with such hope and deep love that it sings in your power center; your solar plexus. You visualize your family and friends healthy, whole, prosperous, and at peace as you chant, sending the energy higher and higher until it peaks, and then shooting it into the candles.

While enjoying your ritual cakes and wine, you hold the images in your mind, drifting… and the power and positivity you raised fills your heart and spirit with the absolute certainty that your magic will hold, that all is well. Satisfied, you finish your ritual and open your circle, letting the candles burn down into a lovely colorful mess in your cauldron. Later, you will take some time to scry the patterns in the wax in hopes of gaining insights on how best to help those loved ones who have the most dire needs. For now, you are content to simply watch, and ponder the meaning of the growing light and hope in the air.

THE ENERGY OF THE SEED-PLACE

Imbolc reveals to us the first visible stirrings of light since Yule. As we look around us, we can see the shadows again beginning to lengthen as the days become visibly longer (in the Pacific Northwest, where I live, the days are already over an hour longer than they were at Yule), and even though in many regions we're still in the heart of winter, the earth tides catch us up, and our thoughts turn to spring. This energy is at once youthful, vibrant, and bright with promise, yet still untried, still in form. The experienced Witch can harness that energy to choose the "seeds" he will plant at Ostara. I refer to Imbolc (which means "in the belly") as "the seed-place" because it's the time of Mother Earth's gestation; while all around us appears dormant, underneath the soil, in the bellies of many animals, and in our own hearts and minds, new life is stirring. It is the time and place where we make solid choices about what we wish to plant, and later harvest, in the year before us. This can be symbolized in ritual by taking small crystals, just as in the story above, programming them with our purpose, and allowing them to "gestate" inside a cloth bag (or simply wrapped in cloth), such as silk, which won't let the energy out, until we're ready to release our wishes on the wind at planting time.

This day is also known as Brighid's Day (pronounced "breed" or "bride," not to be confused with her watered-down Christian counterpart, St. Brigit), and is a celebration of this Celtic goddess's triple aspect of healing, smithcraft, and poetry. Brighid means "fiery arrow,"[63] or "bright arrow"[64] which makes sense—as her talents and attributes have much to do with passion and fire. In ancient times, her worshipers celebrated her day by visiting her numerous wells, making Brighid's crosses and corn dollies, which they would lay in a "bride's bed" along with a priapic wand to symbolize the god of fertility.[65]

By its very nature, then, this Sabbat is all about creative energy. If we look at the Wheel of the Year, it is the place between Yule and Ostara, between earth and air,

---

63. Janet Farrar and Stewart Farrar, *The Witches' Goddess* (Phoenix Publishing, 1987), 206.

64. Patricia Monaghan, *Goddesses and Heroines* (Llewellyn, 1998), 74.

65. Thuri Calafia, *Dedicant: A Witch's Circle of Fire* (Llewellyn, 2008), 83–84.

the deep dark of rebirth and the idea in form; a time to open up to *possibility*! We honor Great Brighid by honoring our own creative sides, and solutions to problems we once thought insurmountable can come, swift as light, to our consciousness if only we dare to think outside the box.

For the experienced Witch, as you most certainly are becoming, dear Initiate, Imbolc can be a time of great power, for this is the first thrust of energy after the Dark Time. If you've been keeping up on your shadow work, Imbolc energy can feel like a great sigh of relief, like a tremendous burden has just been lifted from your shoulders. Still, there is reason for keeping our awareness sharp; we are still pulling out of the darkness, and with any new pattern we try, the old ones will try to hold on to us. Being cognizant of the fact that our shadows are always behind us can actually help a great deal in staying one step ahead of them. The minute we think we are "healed for good," those shadows will jump in and grab us again.

So as we watch our physical shadows grow longer, we can hold this awareness in our consciousness even as we awaken from winter's long sleep, shake off our lethargy, and look to the east for earlier sunrises, longer days, and new inspiration from both this powerful goddess and this uplifting Festival of Light.

TOOLS—QUARTER CANDLES AND HOLDERS

At first glance, candle holders may not seem like a very powerful magical tool, but when you consider the many ways we use candlelight in ritual as well as *the months and years* we Paganfolk tend to use the same candle holders for in every ritual, they definitely can be. We use candles and candle lighting when we call quarters, call deity, and work spells, so it follows then that the candle *holders* we use again and again for these purposes, far more than simply demarcating the directions, these little, seemingly insignificant tools gather abundant energy over years of use, and they hold the candles that produce the flames that call the spirit energies, which makes them *powerful*!

Additionally, *you* are a vessel for that energy every time you call quarters, dear Initiate. As we know, with magic, as with so many other things in life, you get out of it what you put into it. In our beginnings, ritual is more simple: it's a pleasant experience, where we say (or hear) beautiful and poetic words, feel some excitement as the cone of power is raised, and we creatively engage in perfect love and perfect trust to understand that we are indeed creating change as we use and thoroughly enjoy that level of energy. Once we've practiced a little, our magic can become a much more serious business. There is a depth we begin to achieve even now, and "calling quarters" becomes much more than just beautiful words and a level of excitement; we are evoking (and for a few folks, *invoking*) these elemental energies, which we then *hold in place* with our intent, our spirits, and our bodies, our concentration and focus, throughout the rite. As we practice using energy, it naturally follows that we begin to *feel* it, and therefore, control it more, too. Our tools take on a new resonance as well, and even the seemingly ordinary items—such as our quarter candle holders—become powerful tools that hold special energy and meaning.

As far as the *type* of candle holders Witches use, the materials and design vary widely, from simple (or elaborate!) silver or crystal candlesticks for deity, to the vast variety of colored glass holders for votives or tealights for quarter candles, to plain "jar" or "seven-day" candles and/or clear glass holders that the practitioner decorates herself. This can be done easily, with a little glue or glass stain, and some imagination.

To decorate a jar or seven-day candle, you need only find four of them in elemental colors that speak to you personally, and then create a drawing or set of drawings, and attach the picture to the glass with a little non-toxic craft glue.

To decorate a clear glass holder with glass stain is a little more complicated. To do this, you'll want to first create simple elemental drawings: waves for water, flames for fire, pine sprigs for earth, and feathers for air—that sort of thing. Then, tape the drawings on the inside of the glass as a pattern, and paint over all with glass stain. Glitter makes a nice addition, if you're the "glittery" type. You can get little assortments of basic glass stain colors at your local hobby shop for a couple of dollars. An option I like using is the crackle glass holders, which I feel add to the energy by reminding me of the "crackle of power," besides just being really sparkly and beautiful. If you choose to use candle holders that have been decorated with glass stain, remember to use extra caution when cleaning them, as the stain can come off pretty easily. Another idea, if you're so inclined, is to use acid etching to create the design on the glass. Check your local hobby store for the correct techniques.

Other ideas I've used in the past are to roll beeswax of elemental colors, incorporating herbs and stones that speak to the particular element within the layers. I've placed crystals and/or stones along the wick and on the outside of the candle (making cutouts for these can be a beautiful and symbolic touch), and essential oils and pinches of herbs in the layering. Be careful to use *very* small sprigs if you use herbs—

the first ones I made used large sprigs near the wick, which went up like roman candles when the herbs caught on fire, causing the smoke alarm to go off and coveners to run around frantically, trying to find something to put the candles out with! Yes, it was hilarious—once the crisis was past—but still, you won't want to make this a habit. Also remember to always use only pure, natural essential oils for anything you will burn; if you use synthetic oils, they will smell like plastic when they burn.

As far as which colors you should use, there are many good systems out there, such as Bonewits', [66] mine, [67] and the "standard" Witch's colors, which can be found in many books, as well as on simple charts that you can find in almost any occult shop.

PATHWORK FOCUS:
THE CALLING TO THE STONE WHISPERER'S [68] PATH

Do you hear the rocks breathing in quiet forests? Do you feel the pulse of their slow, steady energy, or the high frequency of a crystal's bright song? Does it make your heart pound to hold malachite? Do you find that rose quartz soothes you? That hematite grounds you? You might be feeling a calling to some of the Mother's sacred treasures—crystals, gemstones, rocks.

The Witch who follows this path will have a vast store of things to study, things that will enhance his spellwork and everyday life, bring relief from stress and unhappiness, and promote the healing of both body and spirit. He will undoubtedly possess a great many stones himself, for he will be drawn to them, and people tend to give gemstones to those who love them. They just seem to sort of… gravitate to them. I know this, because ever since I was a little girl, I have collected stones. I never knew back then why they sang to me so acutely, but I know now. They are fascinating stores of very specific energies, both in their general energy patterns, such as fluorite being a stone to help intellectualize the emotions, and in patterns specific to each individual stone—the stone's deva. Each stone has a purpose, then, and you can discern

---

66. Isaac Bonewits, *Real Magic* (Samuel Weiser, 1971), 122–24.

67. Thuri Calafia, *Dedicant: A Witch's Circle of Fire* (Llewellyn, 2008), 86–89.

68. I made this term up based on the information I found on dog whisperers and horse whisperers, who are known for their innate ability to engage the energy and understanding of these special animals. It follows, then, that a "stone whisperer" would have the same innate understanding and talent with stones.

what that purpose is with a little quiet time and energy work. Just ground and center and hold the gemstone in your left hand (left receives, remember), and project your energy from your right hand *through the stone* in the form of a questioning, an openness to receiving the stone's energy or message. Just do this for a few moments, then let your mind go blank and observe the words you hear or pictures you see. That should give you a sense of the stone's energy, or deva. Once you know the general energy of the stone through its deva, you will know kinds of things would be compatible to program the stone to do for you.

I have long studied gemstones for their spiritual properties, and I never feel that I have enough time to devote to these amazing and wonderful gifts from the gods. A dear friend of mine from long ago who refers to himself as a "rockhound" says he feels much the same way. He teaches gemstone workshops at one of the festivals I used to attend regularly, and you should see the way his eyes light up when he talks about them! He can look at most stones and immediately tell you many things about them, from the way the Mother made them to what they are good for in terms of healing and psychic strengths, as well as what part of the world that particular stone is likely to hail from. He taught his gemstone workshop at one of my Circles Dedicant classes as a guest speaker several years ago, and we had such a lively discussion! He brought many samples and even gave each student a gemstone from a big jar he had with him. It seems that stones are one thing many Wiccans have an interest in to some extent.

If you are feeling a calling to study gemstones more deeply, I suggest you start with a few stones at a time, as you can afford them, from your local rock shop. I recommend checking out the rock shops first; the occult shops, unfortunately, sometimes charge much more, so compare carefully! I have found that even within one small town, prices and quality can vary widely. The next step would be to get yourself some good books, both for the spiritual properties, such as Melody's *Love Is in the Earth* or Scott Cunningham's *Encyclopedia of Crystal, Gem & Metal Magic*, and for the geological properties, which most retailers of stones could recommend.

INITIATE PATHWORKINGS

Go for a holiday walk! It's so good to get outside in the blustery weather and tune in to the Mother. Open yourself to the energies of the season, and try to imagine what's going on under the soil. Let the winds of change call to you from across the season, pulling you forward, urging you to hear the earth tides that are Ostara, Beltane, Litha. See if you can warm yourself up by focusing on the hot summer sun, and then come back to today, letting the cold, clear light of Imbolc refresh and revitalize you.

When calling quarters next time, try focusing even more intently on the energy of each element. Remember your interactive elemental work. Know that you are the vessel and the tool of the gods, and that you are *holding* this energy, just as much as the candle holders are the vessel and tool of your circle. Be blessed.

Visit a rock shop and see if the energies of stones and shells speak to you. Buy yourself some "seed" crystals for use in your Imbolc rite, if you choose to, programming them as the seeds in the meditations above, and store them in silk or a human-made fiber to hold the energies in until you're ready to "plant" them.

Get outside at night sometime this month and observe the crescent moon. The old farmer's trick of imagining the slender crescent as a vessel or dipper for water can tell you if it's time to plant in your region: if it looks like it will hold water, it's not time yet, but if the water will spill out the end and "water" the earth, it's time.

Feel the earth tides. In your meditations, as well as your ordinary life, take a moment to tune in to the energy of the season. Feel the rush of power that is the first stirrings of light, and allow yourself to ride that wave. Let it fill and vitalize you, knowing that you are a sacred child of the gods, and your power is budding and building, too.

Focus on your own awesomeness. If you're one of those less confident Wiccans, take some time and think about how far you've come in your personal Path, how much you've grown. This is a great way to build confidence. Acknowledge how much more powerful you are today than you were a year ago, and hold that truth by saying to yourself, "I am a priest/ess of the God/dess. I can do anything I wish to. I am powerful!" Say it out loud. Now. No, I can't hear you. Say it *louder*! Say it loud enough that I can hear it all the way out here in the Pacific Northwest—that's right: shout it out! Because you *are* powerful, dear Initiate. Trust in that.

HOMEWORK

Write an Imbolc ritual, from grounding and centering to opening the circle. Be sure to include altar decorations, cakes and wine choices, and what you'll serve for the feast afterward, if applicable.

Read chapter IV—"Imbolc," in A Witches' Bible *and Part III in* Drawing Down the Moon.

Lightworking: choosing seeds

Take some time this month and ponder the energy of the seed-place. Plan spellwork, either in conjunction with your moon work or as a separate ritual, and then use the talents and skills you've learned thus far on your Path, dear Initiate, to make decisions regarding what you might wish to plant in your life this cycle. Purchase some small crystals, and read their energies, if you like. When you feel ready, program them with your purpose, and then hold them in a pouch made of silk or human-made fiber until planting time.

For your grimoire

Continue (or begin) a table of correspondence for candle magic and colors. Try to think of some unusual applications and situations where you would use a color not usually thought of for a particular thing (for example, I usually use red for healing, but a few years back a friend was badly burned, and I felt red would just add to the pain, so I used light blue to cool down the wounds for a few weeks, switching to red only after the burning pain was past, focusing on healthy red tissue building and re-forming).

20: The February Lesson

Community isn't a name for a fancy assortment of fan clubs.
—John Michael Greer

COMMUNITY—THE STORY

In the bright light of a clear breezy afternoon, you finish the last actions of cleaning your home, and suppress a squeal of excitement. They're coming, all of them—the people in your life you hold most dear. Now for the fun part: the decorating and prep work for the ritual and feast. As luck would have it, you were able to find every single item you envisioned for this rite, from the altar cloth, flowers, and greenery to the special stones and crystals each person will use in circle and later take home as a gift and a remembrance of this most special evening. You start with the beautiful new altar cloth you found at a second-hand shop, a lovely, soft scarf with a pattern that totally connects to the work you're doing. You run your hand over its cool, slippery surface, smoothing it over your altar. Next comes the greenery, at the back of the altar, and you smile as you add a few of the funny, twisty branches you found in the field where you like to walk. Next you add flowers, breaking a few of them up and scattering the petals over the branches and greens in the back. Perfect. Your heart races and you check the time again, reassuring yourself you needn't hurry. No one will be here for hours,

*even the sweet friend who always comes early to help. You wouldn't let her this time, telling
her this day's celebration is your gift to your family.*

*Family. A warm glow spreads through your solar plexus, and you nod to yourself. Yes,
these wonderful people are indeed your family, as you remember the old saying, "Friends are
the family you choose." You think about each individual person in your chosen family, how
your relationship with him or her came to be, how the two of you have nurtured it over the
time you've known each other. You smile brightly, thinking of how much they all like each
other, how it warms your heart to hear them talking and laughing together, so deep is your
joy in their joy for each other. Tears spring to your eyes all of a sudden, and you laugh out
loud. The altar set-up complete, you go to your kitchen to begin your preparations for the
feast.*

*You tried to choose a little something from each person's list of favorites, and you're con-
fident you did well. From appetizers to dessert, there will be delicious surprises and special
treats for everyone, including yourself. Rather than being daunted by the work and expense
required to pull off this celebration, you're actually glad to have something to do, some way*

to spend all of your excited, abundant energy. You chop and sauté, slice and dice, mix and mash, and open packages. You place the purchased items as well as your carefully prepared goodies on your best serving dishes, and soon you have a spread Great Gaia would be proud of, complete with main dish, sides, appetizers, and a fabulous dessert. By the time you're done, you're a little tired, but you want everything to be perfect, so you tour your dwelling, both indoors and out, to be extra sure everything is in its place, to be extra sure everyone will be comfortable and well accommodated. Satisfied, you go back outside and sit down, breathing deeply of the fresh, clean air, relaxing, grounding, and centering yourself slowly, smoothly. Everything is ready, you think contentedly, and it's a good thing, too, for the moment you open your eyes, you see the first of your chosen family arriving, and you jump up, heart racing with happiness, to greet your spiritual sibling with a warm smile and a welcoming hug.

THE ENERGY OF COMMUNITY

We're hearing an awful lot about building community these days. People are becoming more aware, more awakened, and they want to connect to the greater whole, to feel like they have something to contribute, like they're important to their communities, like they belong. In some Pagan communities, there seems to be an old, extended family feel, with little infighting or compartmentalizing, but in others, it can seem that some folks are really saying, "I want to build *my* community, in *my* way, on *my* terms—here, follow *me* to true enlightenment!" and then when things don't follow their ideals and plans, they are quick to abandon their projects *and* their fellows, stating that the community has somehow "failed" them.

So at this time, dear Initiate, we are called upon to look at what exactly is "community" and whose responsibility it is to build it. Is it the exclusive province of some self-appointed grand master? Some great metaphysical figure or guru or BFWHPS?[69] No. It is *us*, people, and it is *ours*.

From your local Pagan community in any city or town, to the larger communities of American Pagans, European Pagans, or even Pagans worldwide, *community* is made up of each and every one of us, with all of our individual talents and challenges, quirks and foibles, hopes and dreams. The people you see around you, in your circles of family and friends, your covens and your local Pagan festivals *are* our community—and it can

---

69. A humorous term coined by an old friend and prominent community leader I knew years and years ago, meaning "Big F-ing Witch High Priestess."

be so much greater than just the sum of its parts. Each of us, who are here to help shape and build it, play an important role in nurturing a healthy loving community, family, tribe.

So I submit that instead of allowing, much less expecting, any one leader or group of leaders to "fix" it, we can, and must, build our community ourselves. First, by adding our own unique contributions, and then balancing that action by standing back and letting someone else add theirs, weaving all the threads of the community together, allowing it to evolve organically into what it inherently needs and wants to be, what it's *destined* to be. Whuuuut? Let the community... build *itself*? My gods, this is *heresy*!

It is the responsibility of each of us to help our community thrive, in any way that we can. My personal belief is that it starts with two people, and only two. These would be yourself and the person you're connecting with at the moment. It is up to *us* to treat our fellows with respect, welcome, and compassion. Do we have to all get along? Not just no, but *gawds*, no! That's not realistic. But we must recognize that this task is not for "someone else" to do—no matter what our personal feelings are, we must understand that treating each other as vital, important members of our little subculture is *fundamental* for laying the foundation of a solid community. And, dear Initiate, once we've become Wiccan clergy, it becomes our sacred duty and *responsibility* to exhibit respect and compassion to our community. Bruce Springsteen put it very well in a 2009 interview in *Rolling Stone*. He was talking about bands, but I think his words can easily be applied to any group. He said, "The trick in keeping bands together is always the same: 'Hey asshole, the guy standing next to you is more important than you think he is.'"[70]

And so we must recognize that we're *all* important—we *all* have something to contribute, and the only way our community is going to grow strong is by each of us, as individuals, standing up and taking the responsibility to strengthen it. How can we do that? By opening our hearts to each other, by *welcoming* each other, and not waiting for "someone else" to do it! By listening to and respecting each other, by treating others just as the old Golden Rule suggests: *as we would wish to be treated.* This means we don't "trad-bash." Most Pagans would agree that Christian bashing is extremely uncool, but many of these folks will then go on to make disparaging remarks about folks whose traditions are a hair's breadth different from theirs. Just

---

70. David Fricke, "Bringing It All Back Home," *Rolling Stone*, February 12, 2009.

the other day, I read a post on a social network website describing Wicca as "the Christianization of Paganism," and that was about the nicest thing the woman said about Wicca (*and* Wiccans) in her post. We forget sometimes how hurtful and how damaging such narrow-minded attitudes can be. And so we must always strive to treat our fellows on this magical Path with dignity and compassion, recognizing that no *one* of us can build our community by ourselves, because our community belongs to us *all*.

Prima donnas and posers

On the flip side, we have those who would happily appoint *themselves* Grand Master or BFWHPS. (I'm sure none of them are reading this book!) Keeping our dignity when dealing with such individuals can be a real challenge, but it's imperative that we do so, especially when we start doing public works. I remember a public ritual I did long, long ago, in a galaxy far, far away... I had agreed to allow a man I didn't know very well to be my High Priest for the rite. He was very popular in the community and was experienced in public works, so I agreed to meet with him and see if we were compatible. At the meeting, I was very impressed with his intelligence and compassion, his knowledge and his stated commitment, and drove home confident that I had made the right decision regarding his participation.

Long story short, I *didn't* make the right decision. Looking back on it, so many years later, it's pretty funny. But at the time... oy! He missed the read-though, even though we had rescheduled it twice to accommodate his schedule. He showed up two hours late, drunk and empty-handed, for the rehearsal and potluck meeting, and *at that time* decided to change his lines (something I encourage those who help me with public rites to do in order to sound more like themselves, but *at or before* the first read-through). While we all waited. What he changed was relatively minor, so we all rolled with it, but a couple of my other helpers gave me the fish-eye, and after he left they all expressed strong concerns over how sober and committed he'd be on the day of the ritual. I defended him, stating that he was a solid, respected member of the community, and I was certain he'd be fine.

On the day of the ritual, he was, again, drunk, though thankfully not late. We did a dress rehearsal, and it went... okay. He was clunky, but there wasn't much I could do. I prayed he'd be better in circle. The ritual began. The folks calling quarters and doing other roles, some of them my star students, shone brightly as the rite progressed. When it came time for the heart of the ritual—when the High Priest and I were supposed to take turns speaking, bouncing the verbal ball, as it were, back and forth five or six times, to stir up everyone's energy for the very dramatic next segment—my worst fears were realized. He started his second set of lines after I said my first, and then he … just … kept … talking! He completely steamrolled me in a Grand Showboating the like of which I had never before seen in my Witchy life, going way off topic and pushing his own personal agenda, stripping the ritual of any meaning it originally had, cutting across all of my lines and actions until he came to the lines going into the dramatic part that began the raising of the cone of power! And so of course, there was no turning back from that point. I could tell by the wide-eyed stares of my helpers and the "Whatthef—?" mouthed to me by one of them that no one knew what to do. Thank the gods those wonderful people were quick on their feet, so there was only a tiny hiccup in the flow of the rite in the eyes of the participants.

What to do at that point? Well, I'm always asking my students what they think it means to "act in a manner befitting a priest/ess," telling them that they are the only ones who can define that for themselves. "We have to be able to look ourselves in the face," I tell them, "so we want to make sure we act with dignity in *our own* eyes, which are the only eyes, ultimately, that truly matter." So for me, in that moment, although my strongest desire was to bring the ritual to a screeching halt, grab him by the shoulders and shake him, asking him just exactly who he was and what he'd done with my High Priest, I could really only roll with it, and try to hold and build the energy we intended to raise, as I could see the folks gathered there didn't have any idea what had changed, if anything, and we were, after all, in service to them. So, although the ritual was a success on the surface—in the eyes of the participants—the intention of the work utterly failed, because of all the slashes he cut in the fabric of the energy. But honestly, it wasn't entirely his fault. The sad truth is that it's really hard to raise any kind of *real* magical energy in a public rite, as the people are total strangers to each other, often having never done any kind of energy work before (and certainly not together), and so the chances are iffy at best. And, obviously I chose very badly, but, being new to that particular community, I didn't know. Still, I'd wanted to try, as it was for an extremely good cause. After the ritual, one of my helpers told me this man was notorious in the community for both showboating rituals *and* showing up drunk. Great! If only I'd known!

And so again, we must take responsibility for the actions we do to serve our communities, remembering always to think through to all possible consequences of our actions. Presenting public ritual is *not about us!* We are serving our *gods* with these actions, and in doing so, we are also serving our communities, as well as setting an example for the priests and priestesses who will eventually follow us down this sacred road. So it's not a good idea to think about watering down our rituals because it's "just us," as many an unprepared covener has stated to me when they failed to follow through on their ritual commitments. Neither is it a good idea to "pad" our public rituals just because they're public and we'll be "seen" by someone special or important to us, as was once suggested (and insisted upon) to me by a venue owner whose shop I once worked out of when she learned that the local press would be there. And, gods forbid, my dear Initiate, please refrain from correcting others in public. As a spiritual teacher, I have long believed in reflecting starlight in my students; that is to say, I reprimand in private and praise in public, not the other way around. And those folks who go around "correcting" all and sundry (you'll see them—unfortunately it seems every community has them), will remind you not to be that way, either—for it is *always* awkward, *always* demeaning, and it alienates people in a big way.

Remember how beautiful it is to be in that sacred circle, dear Initiate, and you can't go wrong. There, you're connecting with the Old Ones, and when you're helping others to find that special connection for themselves, it lifts you up higher, too. It is so touching to help facilitate that connection for those starry-eyed loving souls! So for me, service is and always will be about glorifying the gods we serve through serving our communities, however small or large our contributions may be. May we honor them by revealing the dignity and beauty of this sacred Path, in both our actions and our rites, no matter how "big" or "small."

Pagan festivals

Ahhh, festival season. The time of year most Pagans anticipate with great excitement and joy. There are so many of them, all over the country, from the smaller, more cellular-type mini-festies one finds in the Pacific Northwest, such as Spiritual Anarchist's Beltane; Northwest Fall Equinox Festival; Sunfest; and others, to the really big, kick-ass ones, such as Dragonfest (Colorado); Starwood (New York); and PantheaCon (California), which is a conference but feels just like a ginormous indoor festival, to name just a few. To find festivals in your area, just get online and search, using your favorite search engine. More often than not, Pagan festivals and mini-festies are educational, enlightening, uplifting, fulfilling, and both revitalizing and exhausting all at the same time. One runs from workshop to workshop at the bigger ones with never enough time to see and learn it all, from ritual to intensely uplifting ritual, sending one's spirit soaring to heights never even imagined. One can meet new friends, lovers, teachers, students, and business associates at such events, as they encourage networking and camaraderie, as well as supporting individual and group practices. There are usually merchants with more eye-poppingly amazing and magical wares than one can possibly buy, beautiful ritual garb and artwork, magical brews and medicinal ones, too, to help with whatever ails you.

Some festivals have early registrations, which is why now, in this time of growing light, it is time to start thinking about and planning which one (or ones!) you'd like to attend. If you've never been to one before, I highly recommend considering it—you will learn and grow by leaps and bounds just from the sweet energy of having so many like-minded folks around you, and you will sleep like a baby, if for no other reason than you've been running so hard.

Intentional community

There's a lot of interest in intentional community throughout Pagandom these days, and the interest is growing. This could be due to a vital need in many of us to find a deeper connection to more than just a mate or nuclear family, to share more of ourselves and our lives with more of those we love. For many of us, especially those on an earth-based Path, it's also about getting back to nature, back to the land, to a cleaner and greener life. This increased interest probably also has a bit to do with some of the changes many see as imminent in the world—many folks believe that we are better off forming family units and clusters in a larger connected community, in order to better navigate through an uncertain future.

To say that the folks involved in any intentional community should be compatible and in accord should go without saying, but it's a good idea, if you are interested in such, to begin giving some serious thought to your dreams and wishes in this realm. What kind of family would you choose? What would be the advantages and disadvantages of such a lifestyle for you? Would you want to live with a bunch of folks in the same house, or go together and purchase a chunk of land, with each person or family unit living in their own dwelling? Urban or rural? What would the community do to make money? To feed itself? To succeed, whatever that means to you? There are many established communities, and more of them forming every day. Just perform an Internet search with the phrase "intentional community" to begin exploring in your area. Remember that not all of them welcome visitors, so proceed without expectation.

Polyamory

Many folks these days are discovering polyamory. The word, coined by Morning Glory Zell, from the Greek *poly* and the Latin *amor*, means "many loves," and describes a "lovestyle" of romantic involvement with more than one person concurrently. Polyamory is thought to be one end of the nonmonogamy spectrum, with swinging on the other end. Swinging is focused, many believe, on recreational sex with or without emotional intimacy, whereas polyamory is generally held as being more focused on emotional intimacy with or without sexual expression. In the Pagan subculture, no style of loving is seen as any "better" than any other, any more than loving an opposite-sex partner is any "better" than romantically engaging with a partner of the same sex.

In any discussion of intentional community, it's important to address these ways of living and loving, too, as polyamory and alternative ways of loving are much more common with intentional communities of any flavor. Lots of poly folks have a cherished ideal of living with more than one romantic partner, which flows naturally into the creation of an intentional community, however small or large. I love the way Raven Kaldera describes polyamory in the subtitle of his book as "Becoming a Tribe of Hearts,"[71] for even if one doesn't identify as nonmonogamous, the very act of living with more than one person whom one cares about, is, indeed, an act of forming that vital *tribe of hearts*. I believe for *any* intentional community to work, there has to be love involved: love for the home and hearth, as well as the land, yard, or garden; love for one's sisters and brothers in the home community; love for one's ideals and dreams in this realm; and most importantly, love for one's *self*. And of course, if one is involved romantically with others who are also romantically involved with others, there would ideally be a lot of *compersion* to go around to keep things in harmony and balance.

---

71. Raven Kaldera, *Pagan Polyamory: Becoming a Tribe of Hearts* (Llewellyn, 2005).

Compersion, a term commonly used in the poly community, roughly translated, means "joy in another's joy in another." When folks tell me they're considering polyamory, but just can't understand how polyfolk manage the twin beasts of jealousy and possessiveness, I ask them how they feel when they introduce a couple of good friends of theirs to each other at a party, for example, and then later hear them laughing and talking and having a great time together. If it melts their hearts and brings them joy to hear such wonderful sounds, I tell them that's exactly what compersion is all about, and that's the ideal many poly folks strive for. Does it always happen? Goodness, no! Poly folks are human, too. But this is the ideal. Kaldera puts it well: "To us Pagans," he says, "polyamory is about having passionate attachments to more than one person, and learning how best to handle that without sacrificing one bit of the intensity. It's about learning to handle riding the wild horse, rather than exchanging it for a tamer one or deciding that these horses are just too much trouble." If you think you might be interested in what a polyamorous lifestyle has to offer, I highly recommend his excellent book, especially for Pagans, for he addresses in a clear and concise way the difference between approaching polyamory from a spiritual, as opposed to a secular, point of view.

If you do decide you'd like to explore polyamory, please keep your motivations for doing so very clear in your mind. Living as a poly person doesn't necessarily mean you'll "get more" (sex). Quite the contrary; folks who seek sex for sex's sake are often looked down upon in the poly community (who generally refer to that behavior as "polyfuckery"), but if your heart truly is inclined toward loving more, it can mean that you'll get a heck of a lot more *out of life* than if you don't pursue it. It's not a magical formula to take all your problems away; life is filled with challenges. Just as with any big lifestyle change (such as choosing to come out as gay), you'll simply be trading one set of problems for a *better* set of problems. There are several other great books on the subject, too, such as Deborah Anapol's *Polyamory: The New Love Without Limits*. In addition, most cities and towns have support groups and social networks for polyfolk—just do an Internet search on "polyamory," and you'll be surprised how much information you'll find.

Covens

No discussion of community would be complete without a discussion about the smaller, more nuclear community of the coven. A coven can be many different things, depending on the needs and desires of the individual group, so if you should decide at some point, dear Initiate, to get involved with or form a coven, there's a lot to consider. Some covens are quietly reverent, focused on worship; some covens' focus is on public works; some covens are teaching covens; some covens are simply groups of friends who mostly get together to feast and party; still other covens are deeply committed to becoming proficient at magic and energy work. Some covens meet once a week, some meet only once a month, and still others only a few times a year. Some covens work skyclad; other covens wear robes. Some covens have very hierarchal structures, with leadership keenly and solidly defined, and still others are so loosely structured you can't tell from one minute to the next who the High Priestess is.

If you'd like to join a coven at some point, a good time to be making decisions about what you want in a coven is now, before you meet a bunch of people you'd like to practice with whose focus maybe isn't the same as yours. And if you're currently in a coven that isn't meeting your needs, you might consider moving on, or getting involved with an *additional* coven. Not all coven leaders will allow this, but many of them do. I once knew a woman who was in three covens. The first one she joined was very loosely structured and rarely did ritual or any kind of energy work, so she got frustrated, checked with the leaders, who had no problem with her getting involved with another one. She ended up joining two more, which rounded out her needs nicely, as one was more energy-work focused, and the other was more deeply spiritual. This woman could have continued her search for "the" coven to meet all of her needs, but what she found made her happy—a sort of "polycovenry," if you will. So that's another choice you can make about your personal Path. In my opinion, spiritual growth is way more important than ego or hierarchy, so I believe a person should pursue what brings him the most fulfillment and joy, providing he isn't burning himself out with too much activity. Rest and dealing with mundania, as boring as those things sound, are important, too.

If you should decide to join a coven, or to form a coven with like minds, do not be daunted if the person or coven you're asking to join turns you down at first. Many folks believe very strongly in the "three times the asking" rule. This isn't a game, but rather it's a time-honored way to assess the seriousness of the individual. In my experience, it allows the HPS and potential covener to really be sure of each other, gives the HPS time to see that you're really serious and confident (or else you wouldn't have the courage to ask more than once), and to feel you have something to contribute. I also highly recommend working with the chosen group for a while to make sure it's a good fit, keeping in mind that old adage that in life it's often much easier to get *into* something than it is to get *out* of it. So take your time, use caution, and make sure of what you truly and genuinely desire in a coven before you make a commitment to it. I definitely recommend a "trial period" of a year and a day before deciding.

The thing to look for in any coven, in my opinion, is compatibility—like minds and like purposes (if the potential group's main focus is partying and you want to do serious magic, it's *not* going to work!), and above all, *long-term contentment*. Sparks and rockets are all fine and good, but the bottom line is whether you feel energized or drained whenever you leave these people's presence. Trust your observations and emotions; they're very telling. Again, take your time. Finding the right group can take effort sometimes.

COVEN CHECKLIST

1. Does this coven have rules and traditions that are compatible with my magical style? Consider: meeting times, skyclad or specific garb requirements, ritual procedures, tools required, meal and other expenses.

2. Does this coven impose rules regarding my personal lifestyle outside the coven, and if so, how do I feel about that?

3. Do I feel I can grow as a priest/ess in this coven? Will the leaders of this coven guide my study, and do I want them to?

4. Is there opportunity and encouragement for covenmates to spend quality time together outside of coven activities in order to bond, to become close, that they may discover their shared power?

5. Do these people seem to genuinely like and support each other, or do they snipe at one another behind their backs?

6. Is one-on-one time available with the coven leaders? Is it required? I recommend at least a quarterly meeting with the HP/S to discuss one's progress on one's Path and in one's coven.

7. How are the leaders of the coven regarded? With admiration, respect, disrespect, fear? Do they have an undue amount of power in the group (either too much or too little)?

8. Are the leaders consistent? Do the rules apply to all members equally?

9. Is there "permission" to speak freely, to offer your opinion on coven matters or in general conversation?

10. Do you genuinely like these people? Do you feel comfortable with them? Does this group make you feel energized and powerful, welcome and important? Or, conversely, do you feel drained and frustrated, invalidated and ignored? How do you feel when you leave their company?

11. Are rituals and celebrations closed to certain coven members and open to others (inner circle/outer circle structure)? How do you feel about that?

12. What about privacy issues? Are the things you say to someone in confidence held in confidence?

13. Does this coven have a "three times the asking" rule? Have you asked thrice yet?

TOOL—THE INNER PRIVATE NAME OF POWER

Many Wiccans and Pagans choose a name of power when they start along a magical Path. Many more wait until initiation, or later. Some never choose a magical name at all. I spoke at length about magical names in the February lesson in *Dedicant*,[72] as I've always been fascinated by nomenclature, both in the meanings and in the reasons people choose the names they do.

It's important to many Witches to have a magical name, because, much more than a tool used to create anonymity in the mundane world, we see magical names as tools for building personal power as well as a deeper connection to our gods; thus the magical name becomes a *name of power*. The private, inner name can be even more of a source of power and connection than the outer, public, or "festival" name is, though those names are powerful too. Shared with few others or no one save our gods, our private inner name speaks of our highest aspirations for ourselves, and as such, can charge us up when we go before our gods, as they are the ones who know us most truly. Indeed, many people's inner names (as well as many people's festival names) are given to them by their matron goddesses and patron gods, through meditation, divination, dreaming, or one of those mysterious "aha" moments—unexpectedly, and without warning.

---

72. Thuri Calafia, *Dedicant: A Witch's Circle of Fire* (Llewellyn, 2008), 108–13.

If an inner power name is something that calls you, feel free to open yourself to that possibility, and ask your personal deities to help you find or choose one. The inner name can be found in as many ways as the public name can. Remember, however, that these names are intensely personal and private, are names of deep power, so you will want to consider carefully whom you share it with. My private name, for example, is known only to one other person on this planet besides myself, and the spelling is known only by myself and my gods. So consider all of these factors when choosing, and may your intuition guide you well. Be blessed.

PATHWORK FOCUS: THE CALLING TO THE BARD'S PATH

To say that this Pathwork focus is close to my heart is a real understatement. The calling of bard can refer to either storytelling or the role of musician, or both, as in old times.

Long ago in Celtic Europe, the noble bard was not so noble, however, as his role was simply that of entertainer, and not educator. In fact, in Ireland the nobility as well as the Ollaves looked down their collective noses at him. The Ollave, a highly specialized and educated role requiring the recitation of basically any myth or story at any given time, was the "respected" storyteller, and the twelve-year course of training was grueling.[73] These men (no women allowed! No, sir!) were grilled and drilled in their ability to remember all the stories accurately, usually in more than one language, and they had to tell them in an entertaining fashion. A mere bard was looked at as simply the amusement, often telling bawdy and humorous stories, as opposed to the highly intellectual and lyrical poet-myths of the ollaves. The bard was the storyteller to the common folk, the average people.

Nowadays, a bard can be anyone who wishes to share their storytelling or musical talents with the Pagan community. This person can be the skilled musician who shares songs written both recently and long ago, the musician or author who writes new versions of the old tales, or the musician or author who writes about the Pagan life from a modern perspective.

To say that there should be enthusiasm and joy should go without saying—most folks who pursue either of these avenues love what they do. Both fields can be dis-

---

73. Robert Graves, *The White Goddess* (Noonday Press, 1948), 457.

couraging to try to make a living at, however, and if that is what one wants to do, it's a good idea to keep in mind that it is indeed a long road.

The storyteller would, one hopes, give the Pagan world good stories about what Witches are really like, dealing with our types of challenges in the real world, and perhaps how we do magic to help us overcome them. It would be great too, to have stories for young Pagan readers, telling tales based on our mythos and our world, complete with moral lessons that help mold character and build confidence in children and young adults.

Songwriters, especially the more progressive types, are always welcome in our community too—there are many people who like a more modern sound, music they can relate to. Many of us love the old classics, and the older instruments such as harps and zithers, and the bards who can belt out those tunes can teach us much of our history and our selves. Many more songs have been written in the last decade or so, which focus on worshiping the Old Gods, and it's wonderful to hear and learn them as well. In addition, many of us like to dance to a great beat or hear more modern themes in the lyrics, so it's also wonderful to hear songs with a more progressive sound. It would be awesome to have more Witchy music, more songs we can all relate to, more chants and simple tunes to use in ritual too. Happily, more and more musicians are coming to bless our ears daily with the sweet sounds and rhythms we hold dear. Perhaps you will be one of them. If you are, good luck and have fun! I'm sure you will be very well received. So get out there and make some music! We're waiting for you with our dancing shoes on!

INITIATE PATHWORKINGS

Go for a long walk and feel the growing light! While walking, ponder the Dream of the Planet and your own domestication. What would you change? What's holding you back?

Write your own Book of Law. What holds true for you? What would you change for the better? What beliefs and energy patterns are you holding on to that run counter to your own book of law?

Explore your community! Take some time this month and talk to others who are from a completely different mindset and life- or love-style from your own. If you are solitary just now, try and see if you can talk to someone who is either currently in or who has been in a coven about his experience. If you are in a coven, try to see if you can have a conversation with a solitary Witch, or someone in a coven vastly different from your own.

Keep exploring your community! If you are monogamous, for example, speak with a polyamorous person about what they feel makes the poly life work better for them, or vice-versa.

And keep exploring your community! If you live alone, visit someone who lives in a large family or communal-type situation. Find out if there are any successful intentional communities in your area, and see if you can go visit.

In all of these conversations, be sure to keep an open mind regarding the other person's experience, remembering that we don't have to desire a particular lifestyle in order to understand and support it.

And still keep exploring your community! Try to get out to a large public ritual or two, to see what others are doing, and make some decisions about attending a festival, however large or small, in your area.

Make some decisions about whether or not you would like a private, inner name of power, and then meditate on how you will choose it, if you decide this is important to you. If you already have one, take some time this full moon or one in the future, and chant your name, building its power.

Think about whether or not you would like to be in a coven or spiritual group, or to work with a magical partner. Examine the coven checklist on page 280, and add any questions you feel are important to ask yourself should the time come when you'd consider getting involved in a coven. Strike any that don't work for you. Keep the list and when the time comes, remember to *use* it!

HOMEWORK

Write an outline for a public workshop or ritual you would consider presenting, including both where and how you would like to present it. Then, be brave! If you feel ready, follow through and schedule that wonderful offering with your local metaphysical shop or festival committee member in charge of such things.

Write an essay titled: How I will serve my community. Expand the essay with the concept of personal responsibility by asking yourself, "What does my community still need?" and write with the idea in mind of why it's your job to provide it for them.

Read Drawing Down the Moon, Part IV.

Lightworking: sending up a beacon

Sometimes it takes a real effort on our part to find our communities, covens, magical partners, or even just folks of "like minds." Take some time this month and think about the community you would like to connect with. Then, go to a rock shop and buy a small crystal cluster—it needn't be big or expensive. Take some time to focus on the types of people you would like to draw to you, and ponder how strongly those same qualities live in you. "Like attracts like," remember. Plan spellwork to draw those like minds to yourself by using the crystal as a beacon, just like the floodlights car dealerships send up to advertise sales and such. Visualize the beacon panning the skies just like those floodlights, shining your beautiful, bright light, drawing people to you who wish to find a friend or magical partner *just like you*! Be blessed in these new relationships; nurture them and help them grow. Use the following chant, if you like:

> I'm sending up a beacon
> To pierce the darkest night
> A kindred spirit awaits you here
> Beneath this shining light!

For your grimoire

Begin (or add to) a table of correspondence for *covens*, and another one for *community*. First, jot down ideas regarding what these things mean to you, then make a list of what you feel an ideal coven or community is or could be. Now add the word *family* and make both lists for that word, too. How do they compare?

21: The March Lesson

Knowledge speaks but wisdom listens.
—Jimi Hendrix

OSTARA—THE STORY

You stand outside in a sheltered area near your home, watching the wind blow through the trees. It's been raining off and on all day, and the wind is now kicking up in earnest. You remember the expression "a blustery day" from your childhood, and smile a little at how blustery today is becoming; how blustery your life has become. You think about the necessity of this weather in the grand scheme of things: how important it is for the new spring seeds to be scattered, how timely and conveniently the rain comes to water them in their new homes. Soon, they will take root, and blossom in to new plants, flowers, trees. In your mind's eye, you can see them in full blossom with the sun pouring light down on them from above. The wind gusts and blows rain down your neck, sending delicious chills down your spine. You feel refreshed, alive, so full of energy and purpose and drive that you laugh out loud. This spring day is blustery indeed; you can almost see the seeds themselves being blown around.

You, too, have seeds to plant in your life and your inner landscape, and you take a moment to ponder them, remembering that this time of year, this holiday of Ostara is all about balance, equilibrium, change, and staying the course once change has begun. Confident you can find a way to heal even the most unbalanced aspects of your life, you cast.

As you call your guardians and gods, you reflect on the past season's highs and lows. You are ready to face your future, to smooth out and balance all that has been out of whack in your body and your life. You state your intentions and breathe deeply, focusing on the rhythm and power of your breath, inhaling the energy of the wind and of the season; the energy of True Change and Right Action. You begin chanting to raise your cone of power. As your chant grows in strength and power, it seems as though the storm has taken its cue from you, for the wind swirls around you, faster and faster, whipping sharply, threatening to rage out of control. You step forward, into the storm it seems, and raise your arms. You call out to the elements and your personal gods to join with you in your intention and purpose, and the wind rises still higher as your chant becomes an eerie wail, surprising you in its strength and urgency. You move your arms in giant sweeping motions, calling up the Winds of Change, calling up Fertility; Spring's Promise; Right Action, that your dreams may take hold, grow, and blossom, and you can literally **feel** yourself directing the flow of energy even as the wind succumbs to your power, flowing in the direction you send it as you evoke and then invoke the air powers, channeling it to work your will. Your power reveals itself to you then; at the mere thought of sending a gust toward a particular direction, you see a large bush bend to your will ... and you know. You KNOW. You are powerful! You laugh out loud, expressing exuberance, triumph, satisfaction, and the power peaks. Suddenly, rain and wind come together in a mighty wild and wet gust, showering you with moisture before softly dissipating, then falling down gently all around you.

In the momentary stillness you pause for only a few seconds to ponder your working, wondering how long until you'll know the answer to the questions and ideas you brought forth in your rite. You ask for a sign. Gathering up your tools and other items, you feel the energy of the storm rising up again, though much more gently as it moves off toward the east to scatter nature's seeds in the next county.

As you wrap up your rite and gather your belongings, you take a closer look at the ground nearby. Unfolding still, but clear as day, you see the unmistakable sign you asked for: the bright glistening petals of Spring's first flower.

THE ENERGY OF CHANGE

As you went through your Dedicant training, dear Initiate, you learned all about Ostara and the energies of spring. You know that springtime can be a really great time to bring needed changes to our lives, as it's that halfway mark between the dark gestating idea-forming energies of winter and the bright vibrance and action of summer. The God is in his most active phase in the light half of the year, and we can tap into those energies of drive, thrust, and action, and allow that forward momentum to carry our magic for those changes. We can tap into that energy, just as in the story above, to enhance our personal power as well as to loan power to our workings. Take some time this month to embrace the wind. You may be surprised at what you'll learn.

Now that you've gone around the Wheel of the Year as a Wiccan at least once, you're likely feeling more attuned to the energies around you. Perhaps you've noticed the changing of the seasons more than before or maybe the energies just hit you more profoundly. Ever notice how many fresh new ideas you seem to get in the spring? It's been said by many that "ideas are in the air," and as travelers on this magical Path, we hold this to be true. For how many times have we had a brilliant inspiration, and then a little while later, heard the same idea uttered from the lips of another? I believe the very air is full of creative energies that, if we but open ourselves to them, can inspire us to greater visions, motivating us to artful change.

We are all incredibly creative beings with the potential to change the world, if we will but allow those winds of change to move through us. We all have the potential to bring fresh new ideas into form. How we choose to express that energy is up to us, whether it's in the form of learning a new craft, coming up with a complex mathematical formula, or writing a timeless symphony.

By now, dear Initiate, you've begun working with the elements, and, depending on where you are in your moon work, may have aspected or invoked them, so the story above rings even more true for you. Remember your power, and allow yourself to know comfort in that truth.

The energy of change is also about having faith in our own creativity. How many times have we done something, whether it's artwork, cooking, mathematics or some other creative act, and then discounted our worth by stating that it's "not good enough," or that we "should" do this or that thing to make it so? Stop "shoulding" on yourself! Yes, it's good to strive for excellence, but sometimes we get carried away with our striving to the point that nothing is good enough in our own eyes. Try to be realistic with yourself, and love what you've accomplished. Only then will it be possible to create better and more beautiful works.

TOOL—THE BREATH

In most any school of magic or mystery, the breath is emphasized. More specifically, control of or focus on the breath. When we gather together for circle, we often start out with a group breathing exercise. In through the nose and out through the mouth. This helps center and calm us, but it also helps us to tap into and build energy for the magic we're about to do. The breath can also be a good measuring tool in circle: "Pause for five breaths," or "Take one full breath between these actions," for example. Breathing deeply helps us clear and cleanse our lungs, in addition to preparing us for what's coming next.

Breathing is ingrained in us as an automatic function—we don't have to consciously inhale and exhale, as our lungs do these actions for us, so we don't tend to think much about it. However, as years go by, we forget to breathe deeply, to our detriment both magically and in terms of our physical health. It's been said that we use something like a quarter of our lung capacity.

For this month, and this airy season, try focusing on your breath more, and breathing more deeply. Try a simple inhale, hold, exhale, hold exercise with your breath. This is one of my favorites, as it's both calming and energy-producing, encouraging us to breathe more deeply and fully. Start out by taking a deep breath, filling your lungs completely (but not uncomfortably so) while slowly counting to three... or four... or more. Then, hold your breath at the top of the inhale for half as long as you just counted. Then, exhale for the same count as the inhale, and hold at the bottom of the exhale for the same half count. So the pattern would be 4-2-4-2, or 6-3-6-3, 8-4-8-4, etc. Try incorporating deep breathing into your Ostara rite and other rituals and spells this season, and beyond.

PATHWORK FOCUS: THE CALLING TO MAGICAL CRAFTER'S PATH

There is such a myriad of artwork and crafts that one can do to serve the Pagan and Wiccan community, that to go into too much detail here would require another book. Some of the many options worth considering are: beadwork items; medicine bags; tooled leather items such as large bags for carrying ritual items to ritual sites away from home (though these can be made from fabric as well); wands; ceramic or other decorative type chalices; seasonal wall decorations; stained-glass items large and small reflecting our beliefs and mythos; altar pentacles; earth dishes; and so much more.

Another item you might consider for your spiritual calling to craftwork is the noble altar cloth—we see a lot of beautiful scarves that many people use as such, but we don't really see a lot of cloths specifically designed as altar cloths. They could be so beautiful and meaningful, with symbolic embroidery or beadwork that would set them aside from the mundane world. You could do special colors to match the elements, seasons, even specific holidays or types of workings.

In the same category as the altar cloth, but not quite the same, would be nice, absorbent small cloths about the size of a napkin, perhaps also embroidered on the edges, but plain in the middle for functionality. These could be placed on the altar so one would have a convenient cloth for wiping the blade after a salt-water or wine blessing, to catch spills, or to use as a hot pad for taking the lid off the censer. I have made a few such cloths for use in my own practices, and I've found them to be pretty handy.

Another idea for magical crafting, which I've personally noticed missing from the occult stores and festivals I frequent, are small, cleverly designed wooden cabinets that can be used as portable altars, as well as larger ones for at-home altars. If you're good at woodworking, and decide to try your hand at providing these, it would be a good idea to provide plenty of variety. Different-sized, wall-mounted cabinets can be hung in a pantry or a meditation room as a place to hold incenses, oils, or any Witches' brew in that "cool, dark place" most herbal formulas require for long-term storage.

A person with a calling to magical crafting could also make candles, candle holders, even sculptures of gods and goddesses of many and varied cultures. Pretty much anything you see for sale at your local occult shop—and even more importantly, anything you *don't* see there—can be an option for you to try, and a way to eventually serve your community. Jewelry making is another option, although that market, I must say, is pretty full.

Really anything you feel you are good at, craftwork-wise, could be used as a way to give back to your community. Remember to consider all incomes, however—finer items made from expensive materials can command a really large price, thereby keeping the average person from being able to purchase such a thing without a lot of saving up. You can do plainer designs to keep costs down, and do the fancier ones for your less financially challenged customers. Remember, too, that the more unique your product, the more demand there will be for it. There are so many artists and craftspeople, but many of them are doing the same things. Study the market, see what's missing. Then, if you already possess the knowledge to fill this place in our community, begin. If not, there are lots of craftwork books in the hobby stores and libraries that will instruct you, or you could always take a class.

The sacred clothier

Falling neatly under the heading of *Magical Crafting* is the calling to creating ritual garb. *Sacred clothiers* are always needed in the Pagan community. There are so many different and wonderful things one can make and wear as ritual garb! From leggings to cloaks, boots and hoods, to robes and gowns—all are needed. One thing one does not see on the merchant's racks too often, however, are the simple cotton tunics many people wear as "everyday" ritual garb. Many people like to make their own garb, as they can add special stitches as a spell, but they can also add those stitches later, to a garment that has already been made. For most of us, if it were possible to find them, we would never make our own tunics or robes, or anything else. And knowing a Witch had made my garment, although I would always doubt the sincerity of anyone trying to sell me a "ritually made" garment, would still be a comfort. It would also be nice to be able to special order certain "extras," like a tiny pocket for a lighter or my crib notes!

If you choose to make magical crafting your Pathwork focus, you can gift yourself, your spiritual friends, and your community with your beautiful work. If you have enough passion to pursue this as a way to make a living, that's even better! Your community needs your creativity and talent to help us express our spiritual selves in our homes and in our daily lives.

INITIATE PATHWORKINGS

Take a holiday walk! Engage the energies of spring and bright new beginnings. Even if you're in a difficult place in your life right now, know that the earth is turning, the world is changing, and that you are a powerful Witch who can have whatever you choose!

Practice breathing. It sounds simplistic, but it can be so healing and revitalizing! Try it! In through the nose, out through the mouth, deeply and like you *mean* it!

Check a farmer's or Witch's almanac or astrological ephemeris to find out what day the vernal equinox lands on this year, and then plan your Ostara rite for that day, if possible. If you can't do your rite on that day, try to at least acknowledge it in some way, even if only to go outside, breathe deeply, and say words of welcome to the spring.

Allow creativity. Learn something different; go to an art show or craft fair and study different artistic techniques, even if you're not looking to create the same thing. Looking at art can inspire and prime your own creativity. Allow new ideas to take form in your mind, and then have *the courage to dare* to try them!

Expand your mind! Go somewhere you've never been before, blank your mind, and open to the ideas in the air. See what comes to you.

Go out on a windy day and focus on nature's need to scatter seeds. Think about what "seeds" you've been scattering, and make some decisions about those seeds. Which ones will you nurture? Which ones will you allow to go fallow? Which ones would you like to pull back? Put your arms up into the air and feel yourself channeling the air energies.

HOMEWORK

Write an Ostara ritual, if you've never written one before (such as if you took my Dedicant-level course), from grounding and centering to opening the circle. Be sure to include altar decorations, cakes and wine choices, and what you'll serve for the feast afterward, if applicable.

Make a list titled "Things I can do to help the earth and reduce my energy footprint," and then begin incorporating those practices into your daily life.

Read chapter V—"Spring Equinox, 21st March," starting on page 72 of A Witches' Bible.

Lightworking: flying

In your dreamwork, allow the possibility of astral projection in a lucid state. Take some time to consider how that would feel and look to you, and then plan a nocturnal spell to affect your dreaming. Be patient with yourself; this takes practice to accomplish. Try not to "try" to fly, but rather simply allow it to happen. Repeat as desired, but give it a few times before expecting flight to occur. There are many good books on the subject if you need ideas for getting started.

For your grimoire

Begin (or continue) a table of correspondence for the element of air. Also track your breathwork, astral projection work, and any other "airy" themes such as creative project ideas and new beginnings you would like to create.

22: The April Lesson

*Let me seduce you into exploring the most sacred and juicy of all
the mysteries—the connection between Sex and Spirit.*
—Lola Babalon

BELTANE[74]—THE STORY

*You rise from sleep on a warm spring night in late April. You've
had a dream, a profoundly erotic dream, which was surprising to you in both its scope and its urgency. In the dream, you
were doing things you'd never really imagined yourself doing
before, in ways you never thought of, and your delight and heat
were ... palpable! In the dream, you were so highly aroused and
the heat was so intense that you knew you must express this
energy immediately or go completely insane. The heat of your
passion itself was what woke you, and you're still trying to tell
your organs to relax. "Fat chance," you tell yourself, for you're
wide awake, the dream was highly provocative, and it's nearly
Beltane, after all. You think about all the delightful ways you*

---

74. I offer the Beltane lesson in this chapter, because although a great many
Pagans view Beltane as May Day, many others, including myself, view Beltane
as May Eve. There are many definitions and schools of thought as to what the
word *Beltane* actually means, and therefore, when Beltane actually occurs. For
myself, the defining question is this: If the young people in ancient traditions
went out to gather flowers overnight to "bring in the May," how could they
possibly be doing that once May has already arrived? So in my books and in
my classrooms, I present Beltane as April 30th, the Eve of May.

THE APRIL LESSON CORRESPONDENCES

Focus: Beltane

Energy keywords: love and lust; sacred sexuality

Tool: cowrie and crystal

Pathwork focus: the Sexual Healer's Path

Herbs and flowers: rose, tulip, damiana, ganja

Incense: Damascus rose, ebony rose, patchouli

Stones and metals: amethyst, malachite, silver and gold

Overarching energies: planting early crops

Radiant energies: sharing

Sun enters: Taurus

could *expend that energy and then go back to sleep, but you feel there's more to the dream than that—although it was intensely erotic, it compelled exploration, as it was so unfamiliar, yet so familiar in a way, too, because the things you were doing felt so right, in spite of their newness—and boldness—to you.*

You decide to meditate, and almost as soon as you're grounded and centered, you're whisked to a scene on the ocean's shore. The moon is nearly full, and nearly set, which means the hour is quite late, as she rose late in the afternoon. You stand on the shore, facing the ocean, feeling the energy of her might and her glory. With the ebb and flow of the tide, with every surge of water and sound rushing to you, you can feel a vast and mighty power, the power of the Primordial Mother, and as the tide comes in and the energy rises … you find yourself relaxing into a dynamic balance, arms open to receive, and you open yourself completely to her. Suddenly, you feel filled with power! It's as though each rush of her energy toward you is filling you with her sacred goddess energy, until you feel you, too, are a goddess in your own right. With that very notion, you're whirled around to face the forest.

The energy of the forest at first glance seems almost oppressive, certainly it is challenging; willing you to accept … no, to **receive** *… and you feel the rise of energy again, but this energy is more like a pulsing, a throbbing … pointed, and direct, and your Goddess energy* is awakened to this energy, and your libido is singing, bright shivers of desire and heat deep inside you; pulling, encircling, insisting, demanding, yes, actively receiving and embracing your god who stands waiting in the shadows. With that knowledge, you realize that this is the very nature of the Dark God, to wait, to command the moment, to demand attention to his sacred purpose and pleasure, but yet ever to wait, ever the Gentle Savage.

With the pulsing energy of the shadows in the trees, with every surge of electric, erotic promise whispered by your own hidden Mysteries, you can feel a deep and darkly compelling force, the power of the Primordial Father, and as the tide comes in, his energy, the energy of the fertile forest, reaches forth, practically piercing the silvery night with dark eroticism. You acknowledge the passion, and the power, of such a demanding desire, and you relax again into that dynamic balance, arms open to receive his energy, and suddenly, you're again filled with power! It's as though each throb of his ... force toward you is filling you with his sacred god energy, until you feel you, too, are a god in your own right. With that very notion, you're whirled around to face the ocean again.

Just as you were feeling the energy of the Goddess's desire for the God, so **now** you feel the energy of the God's desire for the Goddess, and the whirling, swirling currents of love and lust and arousal and desire are flowing around you, whispering secrets and mysteries of life and sex and your own sacred secrets ... you open yourself to the energy as it swirls around you, ebbing and flowing in and unto itself, until male becomes female becomes male and the energy and the desire and the fulfillment of all your deepest darkest fantasies is revealed to you and you can accept and hold any and all of them you care to. Your power surges with that of the primordial deities in a dance so high and so dark and so deep that you feel your body encompasses the entire shoreline and your mind—the entire sky, and you **actually** believe for a moment, **just** a moment that you understand men ... or women ... or both. The absurdity of the idea hits you and you laugh out loud. This act sobers you enough to stop the dance of erotic energy long enough for you to see down the shoreline.

With the crashing spray of a large wave, you see a shimmer. Squinting, then rubbing your eyes to make sure you saw correctly, you peer more closely. Yes, that's a goddess, all right, coming out of the water, all light and shimmers and softness and pulling aching need, oooh yes, that's her, all right; you just know it! Just as you know if you ventured a step toward her, she would vanish, dissipate into nothing. Then, you see a gathering of darkness at the forest's edge, and out of those woods, you see him taking form, all shadows and leaves and dark hard driving energy. They approach each other; a sacred dance as old as time, and you *realize the images you're seeing are just symbols for the energies in the air all around you, the energies of the season, the energies that are sweeping you up and inviting, compelling you to dance ... and you surrender to yourself and open yourself to the glory of the truth of your deepest sexuality ... the rightness of it, and the power you hold within it.*

And with your acceptance of this truth, you feel a tremendous rush of both erotic power and magical power rising within you, surging in you, in your heart, in your spirit and your body, causing **more** *surging in places ... just awakened in you ... and in this dark and shining light your body sings and your spirit knows its deepest truth ... the truth of your own power, and the power of your desires. Your gods urge you to accept this truth with love. You have the power of all your desires ... you can hold and bend and shape that power and you can do with it as you will, and as you have the courage ... to dare!*

What then, Witch, will you dare to bring forth this Beltane?

BELTANE ENERGY—SACRED SEXUALITY

As a Wiccan priest or priestess, dear Initiate, you must know that your personal responsibility is greater now in terms of how you affect those around you, simply by virtue of the fact that now, you're becoming more trained in the use of energy. Once we know how to use energy and become more and more skilled at it, it is my considered opinion that we not only tend to forget how much power we have, but we also often forget how easily we can, sometimes even unconsciously, manipulate the energy regarding those objects of our desires. Not convinced? At this point, you may or may not have had an experience in your Witchy life where you were pondering a bit of spellwork for a day or two, mulling it over in your mind, making plans, when suddenly you find that the thing you were planning your spellwork to manifest ... *has manifested!* If this hasn't happened to you yet, don't worry, it will. And so, it is because of this that I urge a bit of caution in the sexual realms. Even the staunchest monogamist is going to be tempted at some point in her life and it's best she be prepared and honest with herself should it happen.

Imagine, you're suddenly in the company of someone you find compellingly, deliciously attractive, but for some reason or another you can't ethically pursue the connection. Do you want that person to *feel* your energy and desire? I should think not, especially if it's very strong. The responsible Witch takes a moment (or several, if the girl has really rocked his world) and shields himself before having contact with his friend. If he's very attracted, or can tell that she is, too, he might have to shield himself more than once during the conversation! This principle goes double for Pagan festivals—especially Beltane ones, where the sexual energy is high and the clothing items and lights are low. Responsible Witches like us have to consider how very easy it is to manipulate energy and resolve not to do it, however inadvertently, by taking precautions to *shield*.

Beltane energy can also be used, as in the story above, to go deeper into our own Mysteries, for this is a time of year when the veil is thin, just as at Samhain. Witches who have curiosity about the darker sides of their sexuality may want to take some time exploring these avenues, too. Darkside issues in terms of sexuality can include fun, positive, and exciting things, like exploring our kinks and proclivities, touching on the edge of our personal taboos and boundaries, perhaps, and even going beyond, either in meditations or in explorations with willing partners who are of like mind. If this is challenging, remember the words of the Great Mother from *The Charge of the Goddess*: "All acts of love and pleasure are My rituals." Our gods don't want us to feel guilty about this compelling and sacred primal drive—they want us to *celebrate* it! But for many of us, this is difficult. Remember our domestication: "We're not 'allowed' to do *that* in bed!" By whose rules, and by what right do they make these rules? Remember this is *your* body, and *your life*! Listen to your inner goddess and god, open to their wisdom, and acknowledge the truth of your sexuality for *you*, and for no one else. How you choose to express it usually depends on others, of course, but no one can tell you your desires *themselves* are wrong.

Beltane Mysteries can also be about healing from sexual abuse or trauma. Many of us have had nightmare experiences (current statistics show one in four girls and one in every six boys by the age of eighteen[75]) of someone sexually molesting or abusing us. For many folks, these horrific experiences hinder, and sometimes prevent, the possibility of having a fulfilling sex life. In these cases, sexual healing is in order, and it can take many forms: setting up pictures of our abusers and screaming at them, renouncing them and any control they once had over us, breaking the bond and the karma magically; peaceful rituals where we simply yet irrevocably cut ties to those who have hurt us; lightworkings either by ourselves or with a partner, using energy work to form pathways to healing, for example, running one's hands over the entire

---

75. Darkness to Light website: http://www.darkness2light.org/KnowAbout/statistics_2.asp.

body, projecting healing energy into the most traumatized places, such as the genitals and the brain; creating paper masks and banishing them in a pointed rite, such as the mask dance in the October lesson in *Dedicant*,[76] and much more. The important thing to remember, again, is that our sexuality is a gift, and it is ours and *ours alone* to give. If you've had that energy robbed from your spirit this way, healing work will help you become stronger and more fulfilled.

Finally, in any discussion about healthy sexuality, we must also take a look at the idea of celibacy. In the Pagan subculture, it can be really daunting for those folks who are experiencing a period of celibacy for spiritual (or other) reasons, or for folks with low or no sex drive, especially this time of year, to be surrounded by a bunch of sex-crazed Pagans. Folks with high drives and a lot of interest in sex can certainly make the less sexual among us feel they're not as accepted or understood with our constant flirtations and innuendos, frank discussions, and genuine surprise when we hear of someone's lack of interest in sex. From folks who are in the process of healing sexual traumas, to the very real occurrence of folks with low sex drive in general, we must understand that there is nothing whatsoever wrong with not having an interest in sex, and make an effort to make folks feel welcome in our circles of friends and community no matter how kinky (or unkinky) we think they are.

TOOLS—THE CRYSTAL AND THE COWRIE

Perhaps some of the most blatantly sexual tools a Witch can use for her spellwork are the simple crystal and the cowrie shell. For magic such as love spells having to do with a heterosexual union, you might want to use these together; for gay or lesbian relationships, you may wish to use two crystals, or two cowries; for polyfolk, there would of course be multiples in varied combinations.

The *crystal* has long been held as a projector of energy, and so it relates to male energy especially well. Whether you consider the crystal a tool of the east or the south, this wonderful little tool can be used to project your sexual (or any active) energy by holding it in your hand as you fire your cone of power, or as a receptacle for that energy to be used later, as a magnifier for charms and poppets (usually the small "seed" crystals work best for this), or simply as a blatant symbol of the male in a Great Rite or other working. Love spells for many years have involved projecting energy out into the

---

76. Thuri Calafia, *Dedicant: A Witch's Circle of Fire* (Llewellyn, 2008), 253–54.

cosmos, sending up a beacon for the right person to find the Witch doing the spell. Whether you are male or female, crystals work great for projection-based love spells. Now, to *pull* love or lust *toward* you, there's another option.

Blatantly female, the *cowrie's* smooth sides curve around, leading to the opening, which has a natural pulling curve that leads straight into the depths of the shell. I've used cowries many times in this capacity: to draw a lover toward me, to invite an established lover into a sexual encounter, to draw customers to an ex-friend's metaphysical shop (no, we didn't program them with sexual energy, but with female, nurturing, mysterious, and most importantly, strongly *receptive* energy, which would of course, draw people into the shop), and to draw a myriad of other energies in other circumstances. Sold at rock shops, cowries come in a variety of sizes and colors. Not only has the cowrie been used as a (female) fertility symbol for millennia, but certain of the smaller ones were also used extensively as currency in West Africa and the Mediterranean for many years as well.

PATHWORK FOCUS:
THE CALLING TO THE SEXUAL HEALER'S PATH

More and more these days, we are finding Pagans who help heal people's sexuality. These services can be offered in a myriad of ways, including teaching about sacred sexuality, doing sexual counseling or sexual surrogate[77] work, teaching and practicing sex magic and Tantra, and much more. This work can be quite challenging in an unhealthy culture like ours.

Cutting through to the truth about human sexuality is not an easy task, as the field is overrun with so much *opinion* (disguised as "expertise"), which is unfortunately often judgmental, whether on the side of the puritanical or the kinky, or somewhere in between. In *The Charge of the Goddess*, we are told that "All acts of love and pleasure" are her rituals. If we hold these principles to be true, if we believe sexuality can be sacred, then we need to stop judging each other, or trying to make each other into our own little molds. Seeking a compatible lover is one thing, but it is not *anyone's* job to tell others how to have or enjoy sex! As we discussed on pages 75 and 76

---

77. The common belief is that a sexual surrogate is someone who "substitutes" for a client's partner, in order to facilitate sexual healing.

in the Pride chapter (chapter 6), *no one* is the exclusively appointed or anointed guru of *anything* in our little subculture, and that would include "correct" sex talk.

While I agree that individuals should *absolutely* use the words that carry positive meanings for them, I also believe that the words and actions of sex are highly personal and individual, and that if someone enjoys the word "_____," for example, finds it erotic, positive and stimulating, to use this word neither diminishes nor denies the dignity of either the act of sex or the body parts involved. Of course, hearing your lover refer to your genitals as something you find ugly is going to be like throwing a bucket of ice water on them, but equally so are some of the words popular authors suggest, if one finds them clinical, flowery, or just too ridiculous to be taken seriously.

If you are interested in becoming a sexual healer, I suggest you keep a very open mind and continue to expand that mind of yours, taking into account the very wide variety of your Pagan client base, and you will surely succeed in being respected and beloved of your clients.

Another way to look at sexual "service" in terms of sexuality is, for example, in the BDSM community: in Domination/submission (D/s) play, often the sub is referred to as "serving" the Dom or Domme. This is a form of service one could perform on a spiritual level in a few different ways. For one, as a way to achieve sexual trance. Other ways could include ritual workings to repair or enhance the relationship between the individuals involved.

Finally, we're hearing a bit these days about folks who wish to serve their communities with the act of *sacred prostitution*. While I have limited knowledge of these practices, I can definitely see how they might be used as a way to serve community (as these types of interactions are highly personal), so I can definitely imagine the need, as so many folks have sexual baggage. As Paganism is vast and varied, the things we can do to serve our gods through serving our communities are widely varied, too. If it is your wish and desire to serve your gods through a desire to help people heal their sexuality, I say, more power to you! Just make sure you practice safe sex to keep yourself and your clients safe, harm none, and do as you will! Be blessed.

INITIATE PATHWORKINGS

Go for a holiday walk! See how many examples of fertility you can find taking place around you. Open yourself wide to the energies, and see if you can feel what it's like to be a flower, opening to the sun; an eagle, coupling while plunging dizzily fast to earth from a great height; or a big cat, clawing his way onto his lover's back … or something radical: your truest self!

Push some boundaries. Take some time this month and think about your own inner Mysteries in terms of your sexuality. Then, go exploring! Surf the web, check out some library books or films, and rediscover yourself sexually! Try something new!

Take a long, luxurious healing bath with sweet scents and healing herbs, and let all the old thought patterns and labels that no longer fit you as a sensual and sexual being just drain away with the bathwater. Then, rinse off clean and begin life anew!

Make some May wine for your Beltane rite: Toss approximately one pint of sliced strawberries and two to three small handfuls of crushed sweet woodruff (reserving the flowers to float on top) into a punch bowl, and cover with one to two bottles of champagne. Fabulous! Raspberries work great, too (some traditional recipes call for lemon slices and regular white wine with the sweet woodruff). If you wish to have a bit stronger fruit flavor, crushing a little of the fruit you place at the bottom of the bowl works well, too, as does drizzling a little honey over the fruit an hour or so before adding it to the bowl.

Make some "hot" peach cakes for your Beltane rite: You'll need 6 peaches (or one 29 oz. can of peach halves), ¾ cup butter, 2¾ cups flour, 1 teaspoon cinnamon, ½ cup organic brown sugar, and a dozen raw, unblanched almonds.

For the pastry, cut the butter into 2¼ cups of the flour until mixture resembles fine crumbs. Add enough water to make a stiff dough, and shape into a ball. Set aside. Mix the remaining ½ cup flour, the cinnamon and the sugar in a small bowl.

Roll out the dough and cut into circles about ½-inch larger than your peach halves all around. For each peach cake, dip one peach half into the flour and cinnamon mixture and place on dough disc. Cut another disc of dough, slightly bigger, and lay this over the top of the peach, using water and pinching to seal. Now you should have a pastry-covered dome. From the top of the dome, cut a slit down one side, almost but *not quite* all the way to the bottom. Insert a raw almond, pointed end up, into the top of the cake (trust your intuition to tell you exactly *where*), and dust the top of the slit with cinnamon sugar. Bake these wonderfully blatant and womanly cakes at 375 degrees for about 20 minutes, or until the edges are golden brown. Just like what they represent, they are best served hot and with plenty of cream! Enjoy!

For a fun "male" version, I like to purchase those slender cream-filled cookies, melt some milk chocolate, and dip the ends a few to several times, letting the chocolate cool well between dips so that it builds up. Tasty and fun! These can be especially erotic to make with a partner, seeing who can shape the warm chocolate in the most provocative way.

HOMEWORK

Write a Beltane ritual, from grounding and centering to opening the circle. Be sure to include altar decorations, cakes and wine choices, and what you'll serve for the feast afterward, if applicable.

Read chapter VI—"Beltaine, 30th April," in A Witches' Bible, *and Jamake Highwater's* Myth and Sexuality.

Lightworking: making peace with our sexuality

Take some time this month and ponder your sexuality. Plan spellwork, either in conjunction with your moon work or as a separate ritual, and then use the talents and skills you've learned thus far on your Path, dear Initiate, to create a ritual to make peace with your sexuality. Try a cleansing bath as part of, or the main action of, the rite. Use a cowrie and crystal to help balance the male and female sides of your sexual expressions. Ask yourself what the truest part of your sexuality is, and ask yourself what your deepest sexual fantasy is. What are your ideals? What are your fears? Do not judge yourself, just let your mind go to the place of truth and love.

For your grimoire

Continue (or begin) a table of correspondence for sex and sexuality. Be sure and include any darkside issues.

23: The May Lesson

*If the Goddess is seen as the supreme metaphor for Nature itself,
life-creating and life-taking, then the God is the metaphor for
the life-energy that undergoes these transformations... He is the
living and dying aspect of Her whole.*
—Nicholas Mann

THE GOD—THE STORY

*At sunset on a rosy, sultry evening, you sit quietly in trance,
contemplating the coming summer season, all the inner work
you've been doing, and the outer, community service work you
wish to do. You know that the time to serve your gods is coming,
and you wonder what forms your service will take. You'll do
your mandatory volunteer shifts at festival of course, but you
feel the drive to do more, to become involved, to take action and
give something back, as you're so grateful for your life and all
that you've been given since starting this Path; you feel so connected, have become so protective of the earth and her sacred
places. Something prideful and strong and warrior-like rises up
in you, and you can feel your chest puffing out in your conviction to protect, to preserve, to devote yourself to the earth's service. The feeling is at once both familiar and foreign; the need
to experience your warrior energy is wholly new, yet you know*

Focus: the God

Energy keywords: drive; projection; owning our path

Tool: priapic wand

Pathwork focus: the Guardian's Path

Herbs and flowers: yarrow, mistletoe, oak

Incense: Forest blend; Druid's Grove; frankincense

Stones and metals: topaz; gold; amber; sunstone

Overarching energies: main planting time

Radiant energies: action

Sun enters: Gemini

your personal deities can help you understand the most appropriate ways to serve, to find your gifts and to share them with your community.

Your trance deepens as you ponder these questions, opening yourself to receiving messages, guidance, gifts. "My Lady," you whisper, "I am open to receiving. Show me the ways of my gifts."

At once, a swirling mass of light and dark, of color and magic, pierces the clouds around you, and suddenly he appears. There, on the edge of the forest, half in shadow, half in light. Where the sunshine hits him, he appears radiant, illuminated, bright; rays of light emanate from his golden hair, streaking out around his entire body toward the rivers, the mountains, the open field where you sit. Where the shadow hits him, you can see antlers, furry legs, and a magnificent erect phallus that emanates the fertile and fecund Mysteries of desire, flowing out through the dark forest, out to the world, to you where you sit. Along the impressive rack of antlers, you can see gold, like glitter, wherever the sun penetrates through the thick canopy of leaves above him. On the bright side of his body, you can see no antlers, but a velvety darkness wherever his body creates a shadow from the sun.

"You cannot get to Her but through Me," he says without speaking, yet his voice resonates clearly in your mind. He holds out his hand, his obsidian eyes sparkling with challenge. You rise.

"Guide me, my Lord," you beseech him, and he reaches out his hand. You feel the warmth and passion of his love as you slip your hand in his, and together, you walk into the dark forest. Though darkness was falling outside the thick forest, it was still fiery bright with the sunset, so the sudden blackness of the dense trees gives you pause. There is no time for your eyes to adjust, however; not if you wish to keep up. You make the decision to trust him, and squeeze his hand in a tighter grip. He presses back in reassurance, increasing his pace.

On and on, through a sliver of moonlight and shadow you travel as your eyes slowly adjust. On and on, the trail twists and turns, dips and gently rises. He never lets go, but rather urges you onward with his warm, strong hand. You fall into a trance state from the rhythm of the hike, and time passes rapidly toward midnight. The shadow of the forest deepens; you struggle to see, yet you will yourself to trust him.

The wind around you howls, cats screech, and you swear you can feel his intent, smell his sex, hear his thoughts. As you rely more and more on radical trust, you become confident enough to let go of his mighty hand, content to rush along behind him on the whisper of his gait. On and on you travel, until there is no light, no glimmer, not even a lighter shade to the darkness around you. Your courage begins to fail, and . . . is the path still here, below your feet?

"My Lord?" you call out hesitantly, and your voice seems to echo in the depths of blackness around you. "Are you still with me?"

The answer, "I am **always** with you, child," rings inside your mind, causing you to wonder—was that his voice, or just the imaginings of a hopeful heart? The hairs on the back of your neck stand up, but you know you can brave the darkness because you know, deep inside, that he is, indeed, with you. Of course he's with you; there is no need to question. You whisper a reminder to yourself: "Courage is fear that has said its prayers," and the tingles of fear subside. You know he will make good on his sacred promise of protection and guidance, and besides, you tell yourself, you are strong, and capable, certain of your place on your Path.

With that very thought, a silvery glow begins to take form before you, and your matron goddess manifests. Beside her, you see your beloved patron god, holding out his hand to hers, meeting her fingertips, palms facing toward you. A bright light begins to glow between their

hands, and the light grows larger and more powerful with every breath of interest and excite-
ment you breathe, and then lo! There, before you, is your answer as, together, they show you
yourself*, acting in their service, showing you your potential, and your shining spiritual gifts.*

TRUTH—THE ENERGY OF THE GOD

As our guide and guardian through the darkness, the God is the bright (and sometimes subtle) glimmer that keeps us moving forward, in courage and in trust. Just
like the sun on a bright summer day, god energy shines a light on that which we
seek to understand, showing differentiation and individuation in all that we see. In
our dreams and meditations, he appears as the authority figure: grandfather, father,
teacher, patron, as well as the keeper of rules and of time. He is the Watcher in the
Shadows and the Bringer of Light.

When we seek to understand the truth of something, he gives it, unvarnished,
clear-cut, flat-out, yet we often interpret that truth with the buffers of culture and
nurture, holding fast to our personal denials and fears, as it's not always easy to accept
the truth. Sometimes, dear Initiate, the truth is difficult to hear, and even more difficult to bear. But our patron gods can help us with that.

More God Energies—Protection and Projection

When we raise and fire energy in circle, that energy is of the God, because these are
active energies, or *actions* (whereas meditation, for example, is of the Goddess, because
it's a *receptive* energy). This, you certainly know by now, dear Initiate, and we also
understand the dynamics of projecting and receiving being what we in this religion
refer to as male and female, respectively. On page 181 in chapter 13, "The Path," these
energies are discussed in detail. And as we grow as Witches and build our power, we
must take care to use shielding in order to avoid inadvertently manipulating others
with our desires.

It's been said more that once that one cannot get to the Goddess but through
the God, and we hold this to be true, for in our religion the God is action, motivation, drive, so we *must* engage that energy if we ever hope to get to her wherever she
resides, whether we see our gods as our guides through the forest path, or simply our
ability to put one foot in front of the other intuitively, and bravely, in the darkness
outlying the Gate to the Mystery.

It is also true that we cannot get to the God without the Goddess, for to find him, we must be willing and open to receive him, as he is, in all his power and glory. Nicholas Mann states, "I believe that only by passing through the realm of the Goddess will men be able to release the old patriarchal definitions of the sacred masculine and move into a new definition. Only the feminine has the power to destroy the old patriarchal worldview. Only the feminine has the power to birth the new man."[78]

So it all comes back to the sacred balance of the Divine Feminine and the Divine Masculine; action and reception; yin and yang.[79] The seed of darkness is always present in the light, and the seed of light is always present in the dark.

I believe we who seek to understand the God in general, and the Dark God in particular, owe Nicholas Mann a great debt of gratitude, for his work has been instrumental in uncovering, and thereby helping us to understand, the true nature of the Dark God, freeing us to understand the nature of his Mysteries more deeply, thereby finding ways to face our fears more bravely, and to come to know our own darker gods and goddesses, enabling us to celebrate our Mysteries and our richest sexuality more fully and joyfully than ever before.

TOOL—THE PRIAPIC WAND

The priapic wand was covered briefly in *Dedicant*[80] in the Beltane chapter. It's also appropriate to discuss in a chapter on the God, as it is so blatantly male. Named for Priapus, the Roman god of procreation, these sacred tools are most commonly made from a small branch topped with an acorn or crystal. Horsetail, which to my eye looks just like river reeds (this prehistoric plant grows by water), has a beautiful and ornately detailed "head," rendering the individual stalks natural priapic wands in and of themselves. The one I harvested (leaving an offering of a few strands of my hair) lies on my altar even as I write this, drying. I'm excited to see how it turns out. Anyway, the priapic wand can be used in fertility and sexual rites of any variety. If a woman wishes to get pregnant, for example, she can use this wand to project energy to her womb to give it a boost of fertility energy in preparation for a sacred sexual act, such as a Great Rite. If a woman (or a man!) is seeking a lover, the priapic wand can

---

78. Nicholas Mann, *The Dark God* (Llewellyn, 1996), 109.

79. Pronounced "yahng" to rhyme with "long" (not "yayng" to rhyme with "tang").

80. Thuri Calafia, *Dedicant: A Witch's Circle of Fire* (Llewellyn, 2008), 155.

be placed on the altar in a variety of creative ways in order to project this energy out into the ethers to draw the right person close.

My recommendation for these types of spells is to use that unvarnished truth and honesty both in the rite and then again later, upon meeting potential lovers, in order to be crystal clear of our intentions and desires. Only want a one-night stand? A friend with benefits? Make sure you make your intentions clear! Looking for a serious relationship with someone who loves and desires sex as much as you do? Put it out there! Perhaps your particular wish is for a BDSM master or slave. Now is the time to speak up, both to your gods and to your potential mate. Nothing is worse than drawing a lover whose intentions are at cross-purposes to yours. As the saying goes, "bad sex is worse than no sex at all."

PATHWORK FOCUS: THE CALLING TO THE GUARDIAN'S PATH

More and more, we are seeing men and women taking up the role of guardian, a sort of spiritual warrior or champion of Witches, who watches over our ritual circles and spaces. These special people are those who feel a calling to protect, to guard their friends and loved ones who are in circle, and therefore open to the starlight vision, that they need not worry about intruders, either physical or psychic. This role is sometimes filled by the High Priest, but as more and more eclectic covens spring up without a High Priest, it's clear that the role of guardian can of course be filled very well by women who feel this calling.

In the coven, traditionally, the High Priestess takes the main leadership role. She is in charge of making the rules, sees to it that coven activities go off smoothly, schedules events and healings, counsels and teaches, runs the coven, and does all the leftover work that no one else wants to do. It follows then, that the High Priest typically takes care of the High Priestess, loans his helping hands, and acts as protector and guardian to both the HPS and the group. When I had a female life partner and coven co-leader, we called this role "guardian" as a way to express the role in a more egalitarian fashion, rather than "priestess number two" or something equally demeaning.

The guardian's duties and obligations in a coven setup under this structure, then, can of course be the same as those of a High Priest; she would take the "male energy" role of calling the God, sometimes directing the cone of power, grounding her High

Priestess during invocation, etc., if the coven followed a more traditional pattern with these duties.

The role of a female *or* male guardian as folks who watch over the outer perimeter for public rituals is a comforting thing as well. This is also a role I can see becoming more important as the years go on. I can see how reassuring it would have been in old times to have had guardians or sentries of some sort, walking the outer perimeter of the ritual space while the ritual went on, to ensure safety and lack of interruption. As Wicca grows and thrives in our culture, I think there may very well be more need for qualified individuals to take up this role once again. Can the Burning Times come again? That's a question for open debate. I do know that as Wicca takes more and more people into a saner, healthier religious world view, the less healthy practitioners of some religions will (and have) become rather disruptive upon discovering folks in circle in woods and mountains and other natural settings (not to mention their own back yards![81]), whose only aim is to interrupt the flow of our practices (at best), becoming loud and belligerent, even violent sometimes, trying to halt or ruin our experience (or worse), because they know that these religions are losing their grip on the people's power and control of their own lives. I, for one, think I would feel much, *much* safer with a HP or guardian on watch over any group rite I had going, especially in some urban parks.

A still bigger-picture perspective on the energy of this Pathwork focus, and even more of a heart's path undertaking perhaps, is that of *Gaia's Caretakers*. Beyond the duty we all feel as Pagans to take care of the planet, these people are often called upon to participate in a deeper and more active role in the earth's guardianship. Their duties call for more vigilance, an awareness of world events, and a passion and a drive to protect and serve her as priority one in their lives. These folks, both women and men, are often in leadership roles in the mundane community as well as the magical ones, heading up tree-planting projects, highway and campground cleanups, and other replanting and earth-healing works, and a small few are even employed in those vital earth-guardianship roles (though they're not referred to as such) from within the mundane structures of government and corporate America. These bright and noble

---

81. Oh, yes, my darlings, people sometimes do crazy things. Once, during a Litha ritual in my back yard in Colorado, my neighbor decided to just up and use his side of my back fence for target practice with his pellet gun. I was lucky to have a strong, brave covener present to go out the gate and ask him to stop while I kept the ritual running.

guardians are also often called upon to serve in more mysterious and secret ways, known only to themselves and their fellow guardians and gods. These folks often feel a great passion for Gaia, and are deeply committed to overseeing her growth and health. They see themselves as very much her guardians and protectors, and will fight for her well-being with everything they have in them. They are shining, noble, angry people with an inner light that is beautiful and terrible to behold. They are usually very aware of her processes—from growth cycles of native trees and grasses to how long certain things take to biodegrade, what will, what won't. They also usually know what Mother Earth needs in order for healing to occur in her more scarred places.

And fierce? These are her staunchest and most ardent protectors! They will put her before any other, so take care that you walk softly upon your Mother, for if you don't, her guardians will be certain to bring it to your attention in a profound and eye-opening way!

INITIATE PATHWORKINGS

Get outside and embrace the sun! Take some time to feel the warm embrace of the Sun God while engaging the energy of inspiration, illumination, truth and change. Feel and know and acknowledge to yourself how like him you are.

Embrace the darkness, too! Toward evening, look to the gathering shadows in the landscape in your area, between the leaves and branches on nearby trees and bushes, and open yourself to the energies of the Dark God, engaging guidance, protection, and your richest sexuality. Imagine yourself holding and projecting these energies. Remember to breathe!

Take some time this month and think about your ability to be assertive. Do you speak up for yourself? If not, why not? By the same token, look at your ability or tendency to be aggressive. Has that been effective in your life? If so, how has it helped?

Spend a day in prayer. Speak to your patron god(s) of your own personal truths, and unburden yourself of your troubles. Take a long walk while doing so, and acknowledge and honor your more active and analytical "male" side; your thoughts and perceptions, your choices and decisions, your warrior self who protects and guides. Talk and talk and talk yourself out, and then perform a goddess function, for balance: *Listen!*

Honor yourself with truth and trust. Speak to someone you respect and trust about some of your personal truths, especially if you've been wishing to do so for some time.

Contact and engage your own inner spiritual warrior. Ask yourself which direction you will go next. Write down some of these ideas, in the form of setting goals and planning. Napoleon Hill wrote, "A goal is a dream with a deadline." If you like, write up this quote and hang it somewhere prominent in your home, for inspiration.

HOMEWORK

Write a God devotional or adoration for a patron god or favorite archetype.

Read **The Dark God** by Nicholas Mann.

Lightworking: honoring our male side

Take some time this month and ponder your own male side (as we on this Path think of male energies). Plan spellwork, either in conjunction with your moon work or as a separate ritual, and then use the talents and skills you've learned thus far on your Path, dear Initiate, to honor those energies. Allow yourself to feel the energies of action and drive, and the intellect to inspire you to a greater vision and version of yourself.

For your grimoire

Begin, or continue a table of correspondence for male energy, as well as one for god energies. Compare them. How are they similar? How are they different?

24: The June Lesson

Imagination is more important than knowledge. Knowledge is limited. Imagination encircles the world.
—Albert Einstein

LITHA—THE STORY

It all connects now, makes so much sense. In the escalating heat of a late June afternoon in an open field in your area, you watch as the sun reaches his zenith. You open your arms to the culmination of the sun's glory coupled with the earth's response, feeling the waves of passion and power in the air rise like an inferno in you. The energy that inspired you at Imbolc, that you chose to nurture at Ostara, that rose in you in a dance of fertility at Beltane and both escalated and stabilized in May with your studies of the God's bright energy, is now blazing and pooling in you, in your solar plexus, the center of your will, to be released today, Litha, the summer solstice.

You think of how you blazed with passion on your Dedicant's path, of how much fire you had in you back then, of how that fire's been tempered a bit now with the coolness of the Lady's touch, by going deep within in your personal work. You've spent some serious time now, testing your own heart, chasing shadows, conquering demons, and scarier still: owning your own worth. You recognize that the fabric of your life is never going to

Focus: Litha

Energy keywords: abundance, creativity, will, passion, success

Tool: will

Pathwork focus: the Smith's Path

Herbs and flowers: sunflower, daisy, all "sun-shaped" flowers, rose, cinnamon, ginger

Incense: cinnamon, dragon's blood

Stones and metals: ruby, copper, diamond

Overarching energies: growth

Radiant energies: radiating

Sun enters: Cancer

be perfect; just a tangled jumble of threads that weave and connect smoothly in spots, need repair in others, and are patched and scarred in places you try not to show. But you have your will, and on this hot summer day, you also have your very real courage. So much more courage than you ever had, ever thought you'd have. And you know just **exactly** what to do with that energy.

You cast. The sun beats down. You call your guardians and your gods to hear you. Today, you will reach for a dream, a dream you've long cherished, which you dared not ever believe could be real for you, dared not ever hope for. But your time on this path and your meditations and readings have been clear; you are here to learn some Mysteries today of Light and Dark.

In the shadows of the trees at the edge of the field, you sense a presence, and in your mind's eye, you see him; the Shadow God, the Protector. This gives you assurance for what you're about to do. This work is totally secret, yet, for it to be completed correctly, it must be done in the sun sweet brightness. You know the Dark God will keep anyone from straying near the field until you're finished. Breathing deeply, you focus. You think about all the time you've spent daydreaming about this cherished wish: how many hours, days, weeks, even years have gone into building the energy pattern, yet how much time has also gone into dismissing your deepest wish as mere fantasy? Not for you? Unattainable? Ha! Suddenly, a few weeks ago, you asked yourself why you've always held this belief. Why have you never believed you could have this bright goal? Suddenly, you asked yourself why **not?** Why couldn't your dream come true for you? Today, you begin the process of making that happen.

THE ENERGY OF WILL

Your entire Dedicant's year, dear Initiate, was spent learning about your will, how to use your will; how to hone it. Now, during your Initiate's year, you're putting much that you've learned into practice. But just as this time of year is about the brightness of the sun, so it is also about the depth of the shadow. At this time, you are called upon to take a moment to look at the shadow side of will.

As Witches, we often forget our own power or how much what we do affects people. There are times, I would imagine, when you find yourself, just like I have, in situations of high stress and somehow all of your Witchy training leaves your mind for a brief second (or much longer!), and you fall into your domesticated training and panic! These are the times when we most need our will, yet it seems to have failed us. It's times like these when it's good to have reminders. I have used many different things in my long career, some of which were effective, and some of which were not.

Power jewelry, which we've briefly touched on in the March lesson's Pathwork focus, and in more detail in *Dedicant*,[82] can serve as one of these reminders as well as carry energy to your purpose. The most effective results will be achieved by using a new or long-unused piece of jewelry, for the simple reason that if you've been wearing a piece for years and years, you're going to associate it with other memories than the energy you're going to be charging it with, simply because you have been wearing it. Take the item and cleanse it in the usual way, then when you're ready to charge it, give it its purpose: "You will serve to remind me of my power/my matron goddess/my Path/my sacred duties, etc., whenever needed," or something to that effect.

Other reminders can take the form of symbols or words we write in strategic places. Years ago, I worked as a cake decorator in a grocery-store bakery, with a woman who was fond of screaming at any co-worker who irritated her. She would shoot these nasty arrows of negative energy at people, and when they came my way, if I wasn't properly shielded, they would cause me to feel tired, drained, ill. We weren't allowed to keep

---

82. Thuri Calafia, *Dedicant: A Witch's Circle of Fire* (Llewellyn, 2008), 163–64.

beverages behind the counter because of health codes, so I kept an insulated water bottle in the stockroom behind the bakery. To help me *remember I was a Witch* (we forget our power sometimes!), I drew my personal sigil on the bottle's insulating sleeve, along with the word *Remember!* underneath it. Whenever I went to the back room for a drink, I would remember to shield. It helped a lot. I've also drawn runes or written words on my skin, clothing, and pieces of notepaper as reminders for certain crucial events and confrontations in my life. The runes, of course, serve the additional function as protections in and of themselves. So remember your power, dear Initiate; remember your will. With a little creativity, you can keep yourself strong in bad situations with similar reminders.

THE ENERGY OF ABUNDANCE

Abundance can also be a theme for both ritual and meditation at Litha, as this is the *coming to fruition* time of the year in many, many regions. The idea of nurturing abundance is difficult for many of us, as we are still indoctrinated with the early church's admonition that in order to live a truly spiritual life, one must live in poverty. A common thing one hears in the Wiccan community is the phrase "need, not greed." I take exception to that, for I believe there is nothing wrong with wanting more. Abundance is our *birthright*! There is more than enough, if we only tap into it. Problem is, many of us don't feel we really "deserve" it, as we are still in that old mindset, and I believe that's at least part of why so many Pagans have financial struggles. I've even heard some of my personal friends say they feel "guilty" for having more when others are lacking. I also had an acquaintance, years ago, express delighted surprise over my joy in his fantastic new promotion. He said that most of his friends (who made considerably less than him, like I did) got jealous, angry, and upset when he told them about it. These attitudes are *not* in our best interest!

To be jealous of another's blessings is invalidating and mean-spirited at best, but it also sets up an energy pattern of loss and entitlement, along with feeding energy into the "us vs. them" mentality we were raised with in this culture. We are, in effect, telling the universe that we think of money as a negative thing. Look at the abundance around you, and be *glad* that those who have it do! Open yourself to receive by believing you deserve it as much as others do. It's hard, really, with the way we look at money in the Western world, to overcome these negative beliefs and stay open to the possibility of abundance, but it's in our best interest to make the effort.

It's also self-destructive to allow ourselves to feel guilty for what we have worked hard for, or to feel we're not "deserving" of abundance in any way. To do so is to negate our worth, and to tell the powers that be that we *desire to be poor.*

So a couple of things we can do to heal this poverty attitude is to affirm to ourselves that "no one deserves abundance more than I do." And of course, keeping in mind that we are all incredibly ethical people, we understand that *everyone* deserves abundance as much as we do. There is really no reason that all of the beings on this planet shouldn't have all that they want or need. I know that only a tiny percentage of the American population holds and controls the largest percentage of the wealth, but I'll bet most of those folks "at the top," so to speak, never doubt they deserve that wealth! No, no one deserves abundance more than us. We *all* deserve abundance equally. Now, say it: "No one deserves abundance more than I do." Louder. Say: "I deserve all the wealth and prosperity my heart desires." Or simply say, "I have plenty," or "I'm rich," or "I have all that I desire or need." If we all truly learned to understand and hold fast to these truths, who knows where those percentages would be in a few years' time?

A PROSPERITY SPELL

In today's uncertain times, many of us are struggling to make ends meet. In addition to doing the everyday task of going to work (or looking for a job, or running a business), which can seem futile, even hopeless, when what we're doing isn't making those ends meet, it can help to do spellwork to help ease our current situation. A good attitude to have whenever we're pondering such spellwork is an attitude that reflects the above—that we *all* deserve abundance, no one of us deserves any more so than any other, which makes it easier to embrace the phrase, "No one deserves abundance more than I do."

For this spell, you'll need to gather together several herbs and some silver coins (I use dimes), as listed below. You'll also need a large non-metal (remember—metal grounds out the magical properties of herbs), preferably glass bowl, and a glass jar or plastic bag to store the mixture in. Read through the entire ritual and make a list of everything you'll need.

Ideally, you'll want to do this work on a full moon if at all possible, in an earth sign, but the need at hand may require you to use a different moon. Use your best judgment. The first time I did this spell was a quarter moon in late winter. I've done it several times since, on various moons, as I find my loved ones need this spellwork and the resulting powder as much as I do in this crazy economy.

Cast your circle and call your guardians and gods in your usual way. You may wish to address your current financial need, and why you feel they should help you in this magic. The more heartfelt and immediate your passion and wording are, the better. Then, as you add each item to the bowl, read the line attributed to it. This process, of writing a poetic dialogue addressing the herbs, was taught to me by a student (I learn so much from my students!), and over the years, I have found that when I do my herbal spellwork this way, I'm able to stay much more focused and charged with energy *myself,* which of course adds a lot of "oomph" to the Witchy brew itself.

In the following recipe, I've used patchouli oil as well as cedar oil when I was out of the herbs. Both of these oils have lovely scents, and they give the powder a rich earthy fragrance. I usually add silver, gold, or green (or all three!) glitter, too, just for fun. When portioning your batch out for storage, be sure to add a silver-colored coin or two (I use dimes) to each container. I believe gold-colored coins, such as the Sacagawea coins, if available, would enhance the powder as well. As neither of these coins contain the metals referred to, the enhancement, I believe, would be purely from the energy projected into the mix by one's own associations with the coins, as well as the belief in our money system by all the hands who have touched those coins thus far. I also believe a small piece of the *actual* metals, if you have such on hand, could enhance the powder through both their inherent energies plus the associations we would make with our minds.

This powder can (and should!) be sprinkled anywhere money can come into your life: thresholds; cash registers; mailboxes; computers (be super careful!); telephones; vehicles; and of course, *yourself*. If discretion is required, the powder can easily be made into an infusion or oil.

MONEY-DRAWING POWDER SPELL[83]

Oats build a strong foundation
For money, riches, and wealth
Allspice brings in lots of luck
To enhance financial health
Sage will manifest wishes
Of abundance and treasure to come
And lemon balm ensures success
From below, around, and above
Patchouli enhances many things
Especially earthly treasure
Cedar adds a spark of fire
For riches beyond measure!
Pine nuts lend a helping hand
To ensure abundance is mine
Sandalwood brings wishes home
To make prosperity thrive!
Echinacea seals this spell
By the power of three times three
May this money powder enrich my life
By my will, so mote it be!

TOOL-WILL

As a Dedicant, you learned to use your will, but it's probably been made clear to you by now, dear Initiate, that far from putting that study aside as you began this Initiate's Path, you have continued to refine, temper, hone, and wield it more efficiently and successfully than ever before. Your will, along with the courage to dare, is the foundation of your magical power. Remember always that your will *is* indeed a tool, and it must be used and cared for in order to function at peak performance. You do this by continuing your shadow work, your lightworkings, too—for these teach you so much of the good you have inside yourself; by continuing to honor the Sabbats, and by loving yourself

---

83. This spell of mine originally appeared in *PanGaia* magazine, May 2008.

passionately! For only by loving ourselves truly can we truly act in our own best interests, becoming the vessel in the long run that will spill out and feed our loved ones, our communities, and our world.

PATHWORK FOCUS: THE CALLING TO THE SMITH'S PATH

A smith is someone who fashions things out of metal. A silversmith is, in essence, a jeweler, and a blacksmith works with a forge, making blades and casting things out of iron. Both folks can serve the Wiccan community by creating pieces people will find meaningful and powerful. And with Wicca so solidly and rapidly on the rise in Western culture, it is getting easier and easier to find things that in former decades were rare, if not nonexistent. Some items are still hard to find, however, and for both types of smiths, it's a good idea to look around and see what *isn't* being provided, and create work that has something different and special to offer.

For the silversmith, it is wise to remember that it's still a little difficult, though not impossible, to find nice, affordable circlets for priestesses, but it's practically unheard of to find circlets for priests. The priest's simple circlet, for Adept or higher level, should be of copper or gold (or the more affordable brass, perhaps) to represent the Sun God, or silver perhaps would be suitable for representing the Dark God. The High Priest's crown or circlet could have a sun on the front or antlers on the sides, and maybe even a fire or air meander running the length of the metal band. One hardly ever sees these, except on rare occasions when someone has either made their own or hired one made.

Another thing one rarely sees many of are the bracelets that High Priestesses are traditionally reputed to wear. To find something suitable in the mundane can be difficult. The bracelet can be anything the woman is personally attuned to, but frequently priestesses want a triple moon design, even their power animal or a matron goddess theme. But many designs one sees in the mundane world, while often beautiful, just aren't that symbolic or meaningful. Many priestesses prefer malachite or moonstone, lapis, amethyst or another semi-precious stone rather than amber, and amber most certainly abounds. While I respect the tradition of waiting until one is a High Priestess until one wears amber, I personally am not that connected with it, so for me the search for a bracelet has been a long one.

A silversmith can provide the Wiccan community with jewelry that represents our spiritual beliefs in so many ways, in spite of the fact that we seem to be inundated with rings, necklaces, earrings, etc., but the above items could be a way a person could serve her community with something that is a little more unusual. There are many more things the silversmith could provide, if she just looks to see what *isn't* there.

A blacksmith forges blades that can be used for a few different magical purposes, such as athames, coven swords, white-handled knives, and crescent blades. There are a lot of blacksmiths in our community, so the challenge for this craftsperson is going to be to providing, again, something unusual. These days, for both of these crafts, a working person's price would also be of great benefit to the community. Certainly, we all have to make a living, but it is important to remember the gift of service too. There are so many things one can do to make a beautiful blade—different shapes and flowing lines, kris blades, and Damascus, all make this most personal tool that much more special and rare. Our blades become such a part of us after so many years of use that we want them to be highly personal and resonant to begin with, so that we can add our energy to that.

The white-handled knife should be beautiful, too, but it should also be functional. Many Witches use these blades to craft magical items, so we need something we can manipulate easily, like a craft knife, with the flexibility of an exacto. Carving candles would be so much easier then!

If the Smith Pathwork focus is something you'd be interested in, a good place for a jeweler or silversmith to start would probably be to take a jewelry class to see what kind of talent you have. For a blacksmith, classes are more difficult to find. You could probably find information at a local library on how to make your own forge, or you may be able to find an apprenticeship with someone. Be blessed.

INITIATE PATHWORKINGS

Go for a holiday walk! As you walk on or near Litha, open yourself to the sun's rays, and feel the energy of the Sun God as he fills you with brightness, inspiration, action. Allow him in, filling your whole being with drive, action, confidence, sharpening and honing your will.

Go on a picnic or go camping—get out of town. It's summer, for crying out loud! Enjoy it! Be blessed.

Chant the chant of the Magus (page 99) seven times, or in multiples of seven, a number sacred to the Sun God, at sunrise, either on or near the solstice. Feel your entire being fill with power and sunshiney-good energy!

Ponder the gold in your life. Allow your thoughts to wander from time to time to what the "gold" in your life really is.

HOMEWORK

Write a Litha ritual, if you've never written one before (such as if you took my Dedicant-level course), from grounding and centering to opening the circle. Be sure to include altar decorations, cakes and wine choices, and what you'll serve for the feast afterward, if applicable.

Make a list of personal spiritual goals, including how you'll go about achieving them.

Read God of the Witches *chapters 1–4*, by Margaret Murray, *and A Witch's Bible chapter 7—"Midsummer, 22nd June,"* by the Farrars.

Lightworking: prosperity and abundance

Take some time this month and ponder the energy of abundance. Plan prosperity spellwork, either in conjunction with your moon work or as a separate ritual, and then use the talents and skills you've learned thus far on your Path, dear Initiate, to create the money-drawing powder from this chapter. Don't go broke on ingredients—remember a little goes a long way. Be sure to decorate your altar with all the colors of money, as well as all the things you feel symbolize prosperity.

For your grimoire

Begin a table of correspondence for your own personal passions. Remember that a passion is an emotion you feel so strongly it becomes a physical feeling. First, list the category, such as anger. Then list all the things that really make you angry, and why. What makes you so mad you shake? Rather than looking at anger as a "destructive" emotion as we are so often taught, think about how anger, many times throughout our history, was a catalyst for *change*. In other words, someone got pissed off enough to do something about it! Now take a look at your list and decide what you are angry enough about to work to change, and what you simply can't muster the passion to do anything about (which means those ones aren't really valid anymore, and are best made peace with and then discarded). Make some decisions about which of these things need spellwork or healing, or other actions to get them out of your system. Continue this table of correspondence for passion by next tackling your *political passions*, your *spiritual passions*, and your *sexual passions,* as well as *any other passions* you find personally appropriate to list and explore. Try to look at these strong feelings you have as neither "negative" nor "positive," but simply as being normal parts of life. Then, decide which energy patterns are serving you and helping you grow, and which are no longer needed in your life.

25: The July Lesson

Make the most of me, for I shall last only one year.[84]

—Joan of Arc

LUGHNASADH[85]—THE STORY

Sacrifice. Giving up. Releasing. Letting go. These words and concepts fill your mind and heart, swirling around you in the bright summer sun as you cast your circle. This clear, hot day, just like the summer, is beginning to wane, heralding many more harvests than today's first fruits of the season, and the harvest of the grain. On your altar are your offerings: the first, juicy ripe tomato, slender stems of just-ripe herbs, a baby cucumber, some bright green lettuce. On your feasting table are more of these tender vegetables, along with fragrant hanks of the first herbs of the season, awaiting your presence.

Sacrifice. You ponder all that you have given up in order to gain this beautiful harvest: time, effort, energy, the first sleepy moments of the day each day as the sun rose, which found you checking on your little garden, pulling weeds, nurturing growth, watering your precious babies before heading off to days filled

---

84. Margaret Murray, *God of the Witches* (Faber and Faber, 1952), 132.

85. Just as in *Dedicant*, I offer the Lughnasadh lesson in July, dear Initiate, because the holiday comes so early in August, and I wish to give you plenty of time to study and prepare for your holiday celebration.

with work and… even more sacrifices. You breathe deeply of the scents of the earth, still fragrant from where you tilled the soil under this morning in an effort to keep down weeds. All is as it should be, here in the garden, in these cherished moments under the sun.

Your thoughts turn to Lugh, the hero-god of the Tuatha de Dannan, and how much he gave up for his people, including his very life at this time; this Sabbat, to go into the grain. Grain. You snicker a little at how unlike today's uber-hybridized grains are from the grains of our ancestors. Wheat isn't even wheat anymore, and corn's byproducts have been found to be some of the greatest health toxins of the modern world. Your thoughts turn to the fine line between what we perceive as "real," what is hidden behind the veil, what has been kept from us as a people, and what you've learned thus far as a Witch and priest/ess. More Divine Victims come to mind: Joan of Arc, William Wallace, even the Christians' Jesus gave their lives for their land and their people. These thoughts of sacrifice swirl around you as the earth tides grab at you, pulling you toward Samhain, and the last harvest. You understand even more fully now how all is connected, how all must rise and fall, how all must be born, grow, peak in glory, decline, and meet their deaths so they may be reborn once again.

You call your elemental guardians, your personal gods, and your Higher Self, speaking of your love for them; your emotions escalating in your gratitude for all you've been given.

*You ponder how willing your sacrifices were and will continue to be, for that which is most important to you, most vital, including your personal health and that of your loved ones. A tear escapes your eye as you affirm to your gods that you understand life is about so much more than mere survival, so much more than just what we **get**; life is very much about what we give as well. You thank them for all you've been learning since beginning your journey on this sacred road, which seems so long ago now. The sun reaches the horizon, bringing brilliant color and glory to the sky as you tell them that your celebration today is to simply express your deep and very real gratitude, asking for nothing in return for what you've been given, and it occurs to you that this is exactly how our gods give to us as well.*

You remember a favorite line from The Charge of the Goddess, *and you whisper it aloud, in reverence and humility, "…for behold, I am the Mother of all things, and My love is poured out upon the earth." With this line, you spontaneously pour all but a tiny sip of the wine in your chalice, all but a few crumbs of your cakes onto the rich and sacred soil, offering **yourself** as the recipient of the usual smaller libation this time, as you reverse roles and give the lion's share of your sacred treats to your gods, a real-life symbol of your own willingness and joy in the gifts they have given, which you, in turn, give back in their service.*

SACRIFICE—THE ENERGY OF THE HARVEST

Just as in the story above, dear Initiate, we know that in order to achieve anything worthwhile in life, from the tiniest container garden on an apartment balcony to the purchase of a much-desired magical tool to a career of just about any flavor, sacrifices can and must be made. After all, there's only so much time and energy in a day. Additionally, many of the things you've likely done to further your personal spiritual growth, from the reading and exercises in this book to helping out with public rituals and more, all require time and energy and a certain giving up of other activities in order that these things may be achieved. At this time of year, these things are especially highlighted, as the sun is waning even as the heat in most regions is peaking in strength, gardens are bursting with life and setting and ripening fruit, and farmers are beginning their grain harvests. As in the story above, if we're tuned in to the earth and moon tides, this time connects quite easily to the energies of the waning and death aspects of the year, and Samhain will pull us, just as surely as the earth rotates, toward the final harvest, the harvest of herbs and meat.

But now is just the beginning of our abundant harvest, and the first fruits are ready for the picking in most regions. Indeed, many herbs can be harvested again and again before that final harvest; before winter sets its icy grip. As such, it is time to explore all things herbal, so herbal medicine takes a central role in the energies around us, especially as Witches become more aware of our own health and healing. In the very act of healing ourselves, more sacrifices must be made; sacrifices of time and energy to study health and healing, herbs, and our own bodies' individual quirks and patterns, as well as the occasional sacrifice of the more convenient (and often addicting!) junk foods, in favor of good nutrition and healthier choices. Time also must be sacrificed in the making of our own herbal medicines. We'll explore more on these topics in a moment.

No discussion on the nature of sacrifice would be complete without at least touching on the role of the Divine Victim. As we grow as Witches, we become more comfortable with the darker Mysteries of decline, death, and sacrifice. In *God of the Witches*[86] by Margaret Murray, as well as in the novel *Lammas Night*[87] by Katherine Kurtz, the idea of the Divine Victim is explored in depth. Both women talk about the belief that in ancient times in Celtic Europe, kings were essentially thought of as *the God incarnate*, or at least took the role of the God, and as such, were sometimes required to give their lives for their land and their people.

As the God incarnate, the king must be ever vital and strong, so when a king began to show signs of health problems or old age, he was sometimes called upon to give his life in this way, spilling his blood on the land that it may thrive. Even more often, these divine sacrifices were called for as a way to help save the land and the people from outside threats, such as invasion or starvation. The sacrifices made were usually voluntary, and were honored and honorable acts that were planned carefully, typically coinciding with the Greater Sabbats, in seven- or nine-year cycles. Now, there are many who question Murray's work, and I'm not saying she had all the answers, but her conclusions regarding the Divine Victim in *God of the Witches*, to me, are compelling. And Kurtz's *Lammas Night* illustrates the whole concept of the Divine Victim in a well-written and beautifully bittersweet manner. When you read

---

86. Margaret Murray, *God of the Witches* (Faber and Faber, 1952).

87. Katherine Kurtz, *Lammas Night* (Ballantine, 1983).

this intense novel, or, more to the point, when you come near the end of it, you will need an entire box of tissues!

The point is, dear Initiate, that as you grow and become stronger in this religion, you will often find it necessary to make personal sacrifices as well. As a member of the Wiccan clergy, giving back to your community through your spiritual gifts as explored in these solar chapters as well as a myriad of other ways, you will find yourself giving up much of your personal time (and energy!), and sometimes the time you would spend with family and friends as well. Depending on how you will choose to serve your gods, that time can become extensive. I can personally attest to this; at various times in my life, I've run myself ragged to present public rituals and other public events, for example, when those events, as they occasionally will, found me with little to no help. You will find that some folks are quick to pledge and promise, but are then reluctant to follow through, leaving you holding the bag. And, as the presiding clergy, it will be up to you, as I often say, to "suck it up and be the priest/ess." There is a reason that in ancient times, covens were ideally run by a "Maiden." I believe it's because an unmarried woman will have much less pulling at her than, say, a mother with four children, three in-laws, a couple of dogs, a cat, and a husband to also devote her time and energy to.

I remind you of these things, dear Initiate, not to scare you off, but to help you keep a realistic picture of what you're getting yourself into once you begin to serve your community. As you likely well know, there are times in life when one volunteers for a project of any kind, thinking they will have loads of help, only to realize they're the most reliable (and sometimes the *only* reliable) volunteer in their little group. This is one of the many reasons I am always admonishing my students to "give thy word sparingly but adhere to it like iron." My best advice to you in these cases is to try to pace yourself, plan only what you think you can handle alone, and always, *always* have a Plan B. Although the bliss of serving the gods is indeed its own reward, if one is not completely spent at the end of the day, the knowledge of having done our best becomes a much more satisfying feeling. Keeping our energy level intact makes it a lot easier to volunteer for the next Sabbat, festival, workshop, etc., which is one of the many reasons why I have become such a strong advocate of safeguarding our personal health through becoming our own healers.

BECOMING YOUR OWN HEALER

Health is not simply the absence of sickness.
—Hannah Green

One of the biggest reasons I feel it's so necessary to take these proactive measures in our personal health is because our healers, however good they may be, cannot possibly know everything there is to know about us or our bodies, or about the diseases they are treating, every time, without fail. Although I was admonished repeatedly as I grew up that we must always tell the absolute truth to our doctors, and still hold that good advice to be true, we must first and foremost be honest with *ourselves*, especially as this honesty relates to our health.

Sometimes, we forget to tell our healers important details, and sometimes, our healers forget (or fail) to tell us. For example, when I was diagnosed with osteoarthritis in my knees, I was told by the doctor I consulted that the best thing I could do for my aching knees was to walk. I was not told *why* walking was helpful, nor was I told that the damage is irreversible (meaning I damn well better take this condition *seriously* and act *immediately*!). Of course, as a Witch I know that *nothing* is "irreversible," and continue doing energy working to this day to re-grow the cartilage that's chipped off. However, I was not told *anything at all* about what osteoarthritis is or how it works, or that one of the worst surfaces a person can walk on is concrete. I was not told that further damage is highly preventable if one simply gets regular exercise and takes glucosamine daily. I learned all of this information from my own research,[88] through reading as much as I could about it, from talking to others with the disease, and by "experimenting" with my own body. And why shouldn't I experiment on my own body? That's exactly what our physicians and healers do. Lest you think otherwise, dear Initiate, remember that it's called "the practice of medicine," not "the mastery" of medicine! When I first moved into my apartment upon my arrival in Portland in the summer of 2006, I could barely climb the stairs to my third-floor apartment, the pain in my knees was so intense. Through applying the knowledge I found, by Yule of that year, I was *running* up those very same stairs!

---

88. One great resource I found was Barry Fox and Nadine Taylor's *Arthritis for Dummies* (Wiley Publishing, 2004), particularly the chapters on osteoarthritis.

Another reason I believe it's crucial that we become our own healers is that healers can sometimes be … remote, unavailable, and sometimes they simply disappear from our lives.

Now all of this is not to say we should be our own healers *to the exclusion of* consulting with any others, *ever*! What it means is that we need to be more involved in our own health care, more educated, more proactive. There's that ol' personal responsibility again! And yes, good healers can absolutely be helpful guides on your path to health and wellness. The thing to remember is that they are simply that: *guides*. I believe we need to take our health into our own hands, and not just blindly abandon our care to those we consult. Sometimes these guides have our best interests at heart, and sometimes, they simply want to herd us through their offices as quickly as possible in hopes of a new Ferrari or a quick exit to home and family. What I mean by this is that we must recognize that our health is *our* responsibility, and although I am a big advocate of getting a good healer's opinion, we need to remember that it's their *opinion* we're paying for, not their *omnipotence*. Anytime a doctor or healer tries to play "god" with your health, remember: you're paying good money to have that done to you!

The third, and certainly not least, of the reasons I believe we need to be our own healers is that health care, especially non-allopathic health care (since insurance pays little to nothing for those beloved "alternative" modalities we Pagans so love) is *expensive*! So we need to try to do what we can for ourselves. A good place to begin is with a foundation built on a healthy diet, reasonable exercise, fresh air, and lots of water.

Nutrition

Jethro Kloss, a pioneer in the natural foods movement and author of *Back to Eden*, said, "There is today a greater menace to civilization than that of war. The name of this menace is Malnutrition. We eat too much, and most of what we eat is poison to our system. *Half of what we eat keeps us alive, the other half keeps the physician alive*" (italics mine). He also said, "As most of our diseases can be traced to improper food, the medicine for all ailments is a correct, well-balanced diet." In addition, he admonishes that refined white sugar "drains out all the mineral salts of the blood, bones, and tissues."[89]

---

89. Jethro Kloss, *Back to Eden* (Lotus Press, 2004). Originally published in 1939.

I agree with these statements, as I've personally witnessed as well as experienced the profoundly healing quality of a healthy diet and moderate exercise. I became interested in natural foods and nutrition in high school, when I made the acquaintance of a girl—let's call her Emma. Emma and I were friends for several years, and through her I learned about Kloss's work, whole grains, the importance of fresh vegetables and fruits, and how much better the body feels with an all-natural diet. That interest never waned. I have come to believe that my love of natural whole foods, water as a favorite beverage, and my enjoyment of and interest in good cooking has played a significant role in keeping me from many of the devastating diseases and problems many folks experience by the time they're my age.

To date, I have never been hospitalized, had a major illness, or undergone surgery. Most people, upon meeting me, guess my age at about fifteen years younger. This is not to say that I don't have my issues; I was diagnosed, two years ago as of this writing, with pre-diabetes and hypothyroidism, in addition to the osteoarthritis mentioned above. But I feel that because I generally *don't* ingest a bunch of chemicals (except for all that refined white sugar—in the past!), and *do* keep a relatively healthy diet, drink a lot of water, try to make sure I get out in nature and move around a bit once in a while, and, most importantly, have become my own healer, that I now enjoy much better health than I did at half my age. However, I know there is still *a lot* of room for improvement, and that is why I'm on this path of personal healing. Following this section are the steps I believe are important for achieving this end.

Before you start, I suggest you get yourself a thick spiral notebook (or set up some other system) for tracking the progress of your health. I recommend, at the very least, keeping one section for pertinent notes, another section describing your current ailments and future concerns, and a *big* section for tracking your intake (food, water, indulgences, and supplements) and output (exercise, work, energy work, bathroom habits such as *you feel are applicable and relevant,* and any other "output" activities, such as donating blood or plasma), allowing a lot of room for notes regarding the all of the above. Keep in mind your own personal preferences, so that you can set your system up in a way that is user-friendly and non-cumbersome, or you won't stay with it.

To give an example, at the beginning of each day's tracking section, I draw a little box and then divide it into eight to twelve sections near the top for my water consumption, so that every time I finish one of those vital eight-ounce glasses, I have only to make an "X," which takes about point ten seconds. Above the box I put "1st" so I know when I started drinking water for the day. I also track my whole food carbohydrates (WC) separately from my processed carbs (PC), such as my homemade, honey-sweetened spelt bread, by tally. I note my supplements with simple letters as well (such as a large *G*, instead of writing the entire word *glucosamine*). I also track my ganja use, and any alcohol consumption, on the rare occasions that I drink. Your notations will, of course, be different, as they will be tailored to you. Then, I simply note the approximate time of consumption and the item notes themselves, leaving space open for how that item makes me feel later. Most days, no extra notes are necessary, but some days, there are a lot, such as on the days I fall off the "no sugar" wagon, as it were. Therefore, I don't try to keep any kind of "standard" to the format such as one page per day. I simply use what's needed, and start the next day's entry where the previous one left off.

The point of all this tracking is to help us understand how our actions and habits affect us, not to become slaves to the system. By using a simple tracking method such as this one, and by keeping pertinent notes, you will be able to easily see if, for example, every time you ingest _____, that you feel _____, and you'll be able to adjust your health-care decisions based on that information, which ultimately will *help you feel better*.

Step one: Expand your mind!

Open yourself to possibility. Think outside the box. Allow yourself to understand that no *one* author, teacher, or healer has all the answers for you and your personal path to healing. Some books I highly recommend to help you in your journey:

Back to Eden, by Jethro Kloss (mentioned two pages back). Although this book is a bit older, there is still much wisdom to be gained within its many pages, and certainly much food for thought. I believe what Kloss says about malnutrition is quite true. Consider the all-too-common phrase "Obesity in America is epidemic." I have begun to seriously wonder if the reason so many of us are obese (myself included) is because our bodies are screaming for proper nutrition, and try as we might, we're not getting it, due to the fact that so many of our foods are polluted by the chemicals the USDA not only allows, but now also frequently *requires* in the processing of our food: namely petroleum-based fertilizers, antibiotics, and hormones in meat and milk, and corn byproducts. So we eat and eat, to try to satisfy a hunger for nutrients, without ever actually meeting that need in our bodies. This leads me to my next recommendation.

The Omnivore's Dilemma, by Michael Pollan, explores nutrition in a whole new way, following our food back to its origins, which is often a chilling journey. His book is essential reading for anyone who cares deeply about their health and wants to know the truth about what's in their food. The only drawback is that the reader learns through this work the rather uncomfortable yet very real truth that in order to eat the way Pollan recommends, one must make a *sizeable* income.

You Can Heal Your Life by Louise Hay. This book explores our many ailments and the possible mental or emotional roots of those ailments, offering positive affirmations to help counter the shadows around many unhealthy thought patterns, giving hope and positivity to help us heal.

The Invisible Woman, by W. Charisse Goodman, explores the experience of being a larger woman in Western culture, bravely looking at this experience with open eyes about many aspects of Western culture's attitudes toward women, and uncovering the thin veneer of "concern" many in the health care professions exhibit to cover their very real aesthetic prejudices against people of size.

Fat Is a Feminist Issue by Susie Orbach. For anyone who has ever had a problem with overeating (although the book is focused on women, these issues can, and do, affect men as well), this book offers valuable insights and exercises to help us understand why we do what we do. I highly recommend this book to all over-eaters and those who love them (so most of the Western world's population!).

Eat Right for Your Type by Dr. Peter J. D'Adamo. The idea that we are indeed individuals is explored extensively here, and although the book is focused on the four main blood types, the ideas are fascinating, and it's not a big leap to take these principles and fine-tune them to one's own personal issues, tastes, and preferences, creating dietary guidelines that are, indeed, *individualized*.

So much of what ails us is brought about through faulty dietary habits. It follows then that much can be healed through *good* dietary habits. I'm still learning this one, to be sure. To get started, in addition to the books above, many of which can be found at your local library (or through an inter-library loan), I suggest checking out a few basic books on nutrition, and, if you can afford to, buy one that has tables outlining the various nutrient contents of basic foods, to help you in your plans.

I most heartily recommend *not* using the Internet or, worse, trusting *anything* published by the USDA as your *only* source of information. As we well know, any*one* can publish any*thing* on the Internet, and if you're just starting out, it can be hard to find, much less discern, the truth. Additionally, keep in mind that the USDA and the largest "fake food" corporations are pretty much in bed together, which renders this agency utterly biased, and therefore completely unreliable. They created the highly erroneous and laughable "food pyramid," after all, and we now know how unhealthy a carbohydrate-based diet is. Remember that the USDA has a vested interest in the consumption of grain.

I most heartily *do* recommend keeping in mind that, although we're all members of the human race, we are still, ultimately, *individuals*. I give the ideas presented in D'Adamo's work, as well the ideas found in traditional Chinese medicine (TCM), as great examples of how we need to look at our own bodies and health *individually*, and trust our own body's innate wisdom and uniqueness, in order to heal properly. TCM takes into account body weight and size, gender, age, and many other factors before any medicines or treatment plans are prescribed, as opposed to Western medicine's standard approach of "Take two aspirin and call me in the morning" for everyone regardless of any of these crucial factors.

Healthful eating can be a real challenge in today's economy, as many of us simply cannot afford to eat optimally. Yes, our health is vitally important, but most folks can't afford to buy organic everything and only eat grass-fed beef at prices that are frequently double, or even triple, the price of what "regular" beef costs. So, we must do our best with what we have, and strive to make the best choices we can. Sometimes this means learning to cook and bake from scratch, eating a little less volume in order to eat higher quality foods and meats, focusing more on fresh local produce, and learning to make our own medicines, preferably from fresh herbs we've wildcrafted or grown ourselves.

Finally, I encourage you, dear Initiate, just as I do in all things Witchy in this often-confusing realm of health and nutrition, to investigate *many* sources, educate yourself thoroughly, and then, ultimately, make your decisions based on your own knowledge, power, and intuition, as well as the wisdom of your own body. Be sure to enlist the aid of your personal gods, guardians, and guides in making final decisions about your choices, in order to best help your body heal, flourish, and begin to thrive.

Additionally, I would caution you against swallowing any information hook, line, and sinker, especially if the source makes grandiose claims or suggests the path to health means giving up (or eating solely from) *an entire food group*. Study many different viewpoints, and pay attention to your intuition when you do so. What advice seems *sound*? What *feels* right to you?

Remember to engage the energy of gratitude when you sit down to eat. For some folks, this means giving thanks in the form of prayers and praise to their gods, asking them to bless the food they're about to eat. For others, it means using energy to imbue the food with healthy energy, perhaps even to remove any impurities it contains. I've recently begun a practice of *thanking the food itself* for giving its life that I may live and thrive. It just occurred to me one day to thank all those living beings that gave their energy (or their lives) that I may eat … so I thank the broccoli as well as the chicken, the milk as well as the herbs. I offer gratitude to the farm worker as well as the grocer, and I say, "Thank you" to my beloved as well as to myself for helping to purchase or cook the food. Of course, I thank Great Gaia and all of my gods and guardians in a simple prayer that lasts only about thirty seconds. Last of all, I thank my dog for *not* begging while we eat, as a hopeful and positive affirmation. I began this practice several moons ago now, and it just keeps feeling right. Whatever works for you is the right road, but remember it's always best to do such things *mindfully*, and not just say rote words or do actions you're not really paying attention to. We must live intentionally, dear Initiate, in the present moment.

Step two: Assess your general health

Brutal honesty required. Please, however, remember to be compassionate with yourself. This assessment is not to be used to judge, harangue, or beat yourself up in any way, but to simply get to the heart of the matter; to find some causes, so that you can work on healing the *problem*, not just masking *symptoms*. Remember how important we've decided truth is in determining what's best for you. Ask yourself all the important questions, including, but not limited to:

How do you really feel here lately? Do you wake up every morning fully rested, filled with energy and a feeling of promise and hope? Do you breathe deeply, move easily, feel clear-headed and vibrant? What is your skin like? How about your hair, your nails? What are your bathroom habits like? How about your ailments? How do you sleep? Do you dream? What do your dreams tell you? Aches and pains? Where?

Why? How about when you come down with a cold or flu—how long does it take you to recover? How often do you get sick—do office bugs pass you by, or do you seem to catch everything that comes along? What are your indulgences like? Smoke tobacco? Ganja? How much? Do you cough a lot? How do your lungs feel? Do you drink alcohol? How much? How about water? How much? Milk? Are your sinuses clear, or "cloggy" when you ingest dairy? Finally, assess those dietary habits. How much junk do you eat, really? Remember that chips from the health food store may not contain the toxins others do, but junk is still junk! What about fresh fruits and vegetables? All of this goes into that vital assessment. Think about these things, and make some decisions as to what you would like to improve, and why. Take some time and jot some of these ideas down.

Step three: Gather information

Here's where a few consultations with physicians and healers comes in. I understand that many of us are broke, and in these troubled times, it's hard to scrape the funds together to see just *one* allopath or healer, much less two or three. However, I must stress that with something as important as your health, scraping those funds together could make the difference between vibrance and, well, *less than* vibrance. Do you really want to go there? Just as we can't always find lost items without the help of "another set of eyes," sometimes one healer will miss something another healer (or you!) will find. In these consultations, I urge you to see at least one healer who is *not* an allopath. Western medicine can sometimes be invasive, incomplete, and leans toward treating the *symptom* rather than the *problem*, keeping you in a cycle of drugs, drugs, and more drugs, often with devastating side effects. Remember, no matter who you see, a true healer *listens*, shows *compassion*, and is interested in actually helping the patient.

Step four: Gather even more information

Learn about herbs and herbal medicine. Herbs have been around for millennia, yet our sadly misguided Western culture often refers to herbal medicine (and acupuncture, which has been around for over five thousand years, by the way) as "alternative," stating that the efficacy of these methods "have not been proven by science." I think this is hilarious, because what do we think the last two hundred thousand years have been, if not one Grand Scientific Experiment, which "proves" the effects of herbs?

Now this is not to say one should never use allopathic drugs, for they certainly have their place. I believe we simply need to know as much as possible about whatever it is we're taking, and that quite often, there's an herb that will prove to be just as effective, but without the unwanted side effects.

Yes, there's a lot of incomplete information on herbs out there, as well as conflicting information, but the truth is that there's incomplete and conflicting information about allopathic medicines, too. Take some time and peruse the herb books at your local library. Ask some folks who know about herbs which books are their favorites, and take a look at those, too. Then, when it's in the budget, pick up a few different ones so that you'll have cross-references for your information, and again, trust your intuition as to which herbs will work for you and which ones will not. Please also study the cautions regarding what not to mix as far as which herbs will counter other ones or play havoc with your allopathic medicines as well.

Step five: Learn to make your own herbal medicines

Most herbalists will tell you that the best, most effective medicines come from fresh, organic herbs. In your herbal studies, take care to note that sometimes, different parts of a plant will require different preparations, and quite often, affect different ailments or different parts of the body.

One of the easiest ways to ingest an herb is to make a simple *tea*. Just like those good ol' black and orange pekoe teabags you grew up with, the herb should steep for three to five minutes.

An *infusion* takes longer—for this you will place one ounce of herb in a quart jar and cover it with a quart of boiling water, and let stand for eight hours or overnight. This obviously is a much stronger brew, and the dosage can vary—depending on the herb and the ailment, your body weight, and resistance (or non-resistance) to medicine—from one tablespoon to one cup.

A *decoction* is a water-based brew as well, and is usually recommended for barks and twigs, as it takes a little more effort and energy to extract the constituents. A decoction is typically simmered for thirty minutes to an hour.

An *extract* is made by soaking the herb either in alcohol (often called a *tincture*), vinegar, or food-grade glycerin. Glycerin-based extracts can be tricky, though. Although they can be much more palatable than the alcohol-based ones, they can be exceedingly frustrating to make. The first time I made glycerin extracts, I used way too much herb for the amount of glycerin, and they were impossible to shake. I ended up going and buying more (and then more!) glycerin, in order to achieve the right consistency. It was frustrating, yet highly amusing! I ended up adding a little alcohol in the end (25 percent by volume), to give the mixture more "stirrability," and that helped a lot. Based on these experiences as well as my experience with ginger extract in glycerin (below), I'm coming to believe glycerin works best with fresh herbs.

Anyway, with any extract, it's recommended you "cover" the herbs with your liquid until it's approximately one inch above the herbs, then shake well (you'll need to stir as you go with glycerin ones), and store in a cool, dark place for six weeks, shaking once or twice daily, then strain and use.

My very favorite glycerin-based extract is ginger. I have found ginger to be a remarkable ally for just about anything involving the digestive tract. And it tastes good! I have actually mixed a little ginger extract with some sparkling water for upset tummy, which is reminiscent of times as a child, when drinking ginger ale made me feel so much better (no, it doesn't taste the same; it's similar, but a *lot* less sweet). To make this awesome extract, simply peel and chop fresh ginger root, drop it in your blender, cover with food-grade glycerin, and whirl. Let stand in a cool, dark place for six weeks. If you don't have six weeks to wait and need relief *now*, try ginger tea.

To make a *hot infused oil*, cover the herb in a high-quality pure oil, such as almond or olive, place in a double boiler, and cook for three hours. You can achieve the same results with a crock pot, but increase the cooking time as you would for food; I usually cook mine on low for thirteen hours.

For a *cold-pressed oil*, simply cover the herbs as you would for an extract, and let stand in a cool, dark place for six weeks, shaking daily. Then strain off the oil, place fresh herbs in the jar, cover with the herbal oil, and repeat. Strain and use. Continue to store in a cool, dark place.

To make an *ointment*, gently heat your strained oil on low heat, and add a few shavings of beeswax, stirring occasionally. Once the wax has melted, lift your spoon out of the mix and let the sample cool. Test the mixture on the spoon for thickness, adding more beeswax as desired.

For a basic *cream*, simply add a bit more beeswax until it's a thicker consistency.

A *poultice* is a mash of fresh herbs, and a *compress* is simply a tea- or infusion-soaked cloth. Both of these formulas are applied directly to the wound.

You can also make *capsules* of powdered herbs, though a lot of herbalists will tell you this is one of the least effective ways to ingest them. However, I have been making my own capsules for years with great success. There are wonderful little capsule makers available in most herb or natural foods stores for a reasonable price. Watch the price of the gelcaps, though! The prices vary widely from store to store. I personally purchase mine from the website owned by the company I got my capsule maker from, and they often have specials, so that helps the budget considerably.

Please keep in mind the above is a *very basic* overview. You will want to consult your own herbal books and/or herbalists for more exact procedures and details. Remember also that you are a Witch, dear Initiate, so imbuing your medicinal brews (and foods!) with your awesome *magical energy* as you're making them, or even going the extra mile and actually casting a circle and making these items *ritually*, gives an extra boost of healing power to anything you create.

Step six: Plan your experiment

Once you have a good idea of what you'd like to try, make a solid game plan, set a timeline, and stick to it. Remember that it will take a while for the body to respond. For example, it took about six weeks before I started noticing the effects of my experiment with eliminating wheat, corn, and sugar. It took a full four months for me to see changes with Ryan Drum's recommendations[90] of eating five to ten grams of mixed kelps per day, and now, I don't need to take nearly as much. So we must be patient. Remember, always, that you are worth it!

Step seven: Become your own experiment

Again, if you have problems with the idea of cautiously conducting an educated experiment on yourself, remember that's what our healers are doing *every time we consult them*. Still, this Path isn't for everybody, and if you would just rather not have to go down this road, simply disregard this exercise. It's your body, after all, and what you choose to do with your personal health is up to you. But if you do wish to pursue becoming your own healer, please remember to take baby steps at first. Don't go out and spend buckets of money on pounds of herbs you know little about, use only my overview here for your techniques, and dump all your allopathic meds down the toi-

90. Ryan Drum, "Thyroid Function and Dysfunction." Online at http://www.ryandrum.com/thyroid1.html. ©2005–2011.

let! Take things a little at a time, and see how your body feels before taking the next step. Be gentle and compassionate with yourself. Remember that it took a long time for us to become ill or less than healthy; it will take time to determine what's working and what isn't, and for healing to begin to take place.

Step eight: Awareness, communication, documentation

Again, being gentle and compassionate with yourself, track *everything*! Communicate with yourself honestly about how you feel. Tell such loved ones who are capable of being supportive of your experiment about what you're doing, and why. It's good to not only have that understanding and support, but also to have someone who knows what's going on in case something happens. For example, if you were in a car accident, it might be nice to have someone in the know to tell the police that the bag of green stuff in your car isn't an illegal substance, or to tell the doctors that you're taking Siberian ginseng in case they want to give you a barbiturate, as, according to some herbalists, the effects of the two together can increase each one markedly.

Write everything down! Not every little detail of your every move—just enough so you'll know what you did and approximately when, and the results thereof. Otherwise, you'll never know if you're experiencing insomnia because of the herbal blend you took at bedtime or the pot of coffee you drank that morning.

Step nine: Review, revise, refine your experiment

As you go through this process, you will learn much, and you will change your game plan anywhere from a few to many times. Remember to give your experiment a chance by taking the time you need. Remember that simples are often the best way to start, adding others slowly as you learn what works (and doesn't work!) for you.

Step ten: Experiment on your experiment

Sometimes we need to back up a step or two to confirm to ourselves that our experiments and theories do, indeed, hold water. And that's okay. Sometimes the confirmation we receive can be mind-boggling, as it was for me.

For myself, probably because I am such a huge sugar addict, I had to retest my theories at the end of my three months "just to be sure," or so I deluded myself into thinking. I planned my experiment in order to see how I would do with incorporating a small amount of sugar back into my diet over the course of a weekend. What I learned was that, true to the nature of any addiction, there is no such thing as a "small amount" of sugar for me. As they say in Alcoholics Anonymous, "One is too many, and a thousand isn't enough." During the "free weekend" I assigned myself, although I told myself I would make my sugary treats last, eating them only on weekends over several weeks while keeping to the original experiment during the week, I ate the entire supply, which was considerable! By Sunday night, I was sick to my stomach, feeling toxic and "spinny," my hot flashes that had finally come under control were raging *out* of control, I was insomniac, and, worst of all (though it was great for the learning part of the experiment), when I went for my morning exercise walk on Monday, I couldn't do more than a third of my normal laps, as my legs were stiff and achy to the point that even the post-exercise stretches that usually felt oh-so-good actually *hurt*. Well, of course. As Jethro Kloss stated so truthfully, refined white sugar leaches all the minerals and salts out of the body!

As I was rounding the corner of my last lap, agonizingly slowly, I saw a clear picture in my mind of a bowl of strawberries, sprinkled with refined white sugar, and the result upon returning to that same bowl after five minutes or so—a bowl of somewhat limp slices and a boatload of fruit juice, because *sugar pulls all the moisture out of the fruit!* So it stands to reason that it does the same with our muscle tissues, and when there's no moisture, kids, there's no suppleness! By the gods, did I learn that one! I also remembered vividly that I'd been up to urinate seven (*seven!*) times during the night before, so there's where all that vital moisture went. Yet still, as I look back on that weekend and think about the Swiss chocolate … yep! I'm craving sugar like crazy! Refined white sugar (which I now write in my notes as RWS to help me remember that it's a *chemical*, and a toxic one at that), for this particular body anyway, is bad, *bad* news!

Step eleven: Lather, rinse, repeat
Continue refining, documenting, studying, and questioning. As you go along, you will undoubtedly need to make decisions regarding what's coming next, adding new timelines and practices.

So, continue being gentle with yourself, and remember that being your own healer is a Grand Experiment you will conduct *for the rest of your life*. And that is as it should be. After all, you're worth the investment of time and energy, love and compassion. Wouldn't you rather it be you, then, and not some stranger, who's in charge?

TOOL—YOUR WITCHY HERBAL CABINET

We've discussed a bit about herbal medicines and herb lore in this lesson, dear Initiate, so it's appropriate that you take the time to make some decisions about what herbs you would like to keep on hand for your magical uses. There are many herbs that are common favorites among experienced Witches, so those are a good place to start. Adding to those would be the herbs you use for any medical *issues*, and finally, there are herbs and herbal products you will likely wish to keep on hand for one-time use, such as those you would keep for cuts and burns, headaches, etc.

Where you store these herbs can vary greatly, depending on how many you wish to keep on hand, and how much space you're able to devote to their storage. For the individual storage of each herb, I like to use recycled jam jars, quart- and pint-sized canning jars, but my favorite are the little milk-bottle-shaped containers our favorite little cold cappuccino drinks come in. My beloved is very fond of those drinks, so I've collected scads of them over the years, and I like them because they're just the right size for most of the herbs I use, except for the ones I use a lot of, such as calendula or mugwort (for those, I use the quart jars). They're also easy-pour, and they're something I can reuse over and over again.

As far as which herbs you might need, only you can really say what *you* need; however, I can tell you what I seem to use a lot of in both my home and my classrooms, as follows:

For magical use, I try to keep a good supply of angelica, balm of Gilead, dandelion, heather, jasmine, lavender, lemon (peel), lemon balm, mugwort, patchouli, pine, red clover, rose, sandalwood, sweetgrass, white sage, and wormwood; and the resins amber, copal, frankincense, myrrh, and dragon's blood, among a wide assortment of many others. Ready-made mixes I try to keep on hand are money-drawing powder (page 321); meditation, invocation, and grounding teas; and Ebony Rose incense (simply a mix of the resins Ebony Nights and Damascus Rose).

For medicinal purposes, besides the herbs for my current conditions, I like to keep a good supply of astragalus, calendula, comfrey, echinacea, lavender (and lavender oil), oatmeal, oatstraw, tea tree oil, turmeric, and valerian, among a wide assortment of many others. Besides my regular medicines for my family's personal health issues, I like to keep these ready mixes on hand: ginger extract; calendula and lavender tinctures; comfrey, calendula, and yarrow creams; echinacea and valerian caps; and a mix of astragalus, echinacea, and turmeric for capping (the turmeric will eat caps in long-term storage, so this mix must be kept in glass and capped as needed), for helping fend off cold and flu bugs if the people I work with are sick. I also like to make sure I always have olive and almond oils, beeswax, a good supply of gelcaps, and some rum, glycerin, and wine vinegar on hand for making tinctures. Your Witchy herb cabinet will of course be unique to your own needs.

PATHWORK FOCUS: THE CALLING TO THE HEALER'S PATH

Witches can be healers of many varieties and flavors, including but not limited to: healers who work primarily with Western herbs; healers who work with Eastern herbs and acupuncture; Witches who are involved in the more "conventional" healing arts, such as allopathic ("Western") doctors, nurses, and support staff; chiropractors; midwives; and more. There are also holistic healers; crystal healers; nutritionists; massage therapists; and healers who work only with subtle energies, such as Witches who do Reiki and other forms of therapeutic touch.

Whatever form you choose for helping others as a healer, if that is how you would like to serve your community, you are definitely needed—there just aren't enough true healers in our little subculture. Whatever type of practitioner we choose to help guide us on our path of health, if we are to be treated effectively, it is best to be honest and forthcoming about our bodies with those who are there to help us. I believe it would be much easier to tell a Witchy or Wiccan healer that we think we inhaled too much sage smoke at the ritual, or that we need stitches because a covenmate was sloppy when casting the circle and dropped his athame on our foot, or that we burned our hoo-hoos when we leapt over a fire naked, than it would be to tell someone who won't have the slightest idea what we're about. I mean, these things *do* happen! To not have to explain our religion over and over again to those who are treating us is refreshing and a huge relief as well.

In light of that, it is my considered opinion, having had some really amazing healers in my life, that a good healer, first and foremost, is *present*! This includes not only keeping appointments, but also being available to a client in need even if it's "after hours"; sometimes emergencies *happen*! A healer should of course be compassionate; gentle, yet unafraid to do the work needed; patient; and effective. A sense of respectful humor considering the above would be ideal too. A healer of whatever persuasion should keep up on the trends in her field, so that she may be most effective. She should be good at listening to what her client *isn't* saying as well, picking up on the clues he gives her in between the words he says about his pain. She should charge a reasonable rate, so that she may of course make a living, while still allowing her client to afford her care. She should also be respectful of his requests (perhaps he would like to light a candle or cast a circle before she treats his burned scrotum), in order to put him at ease as well as further the healing process. She should of course exhibit good personal hygiene, and her office should be clean and orderly as well. She should always support her client's right to choose, and she should also be able to recognize when she can't help him, and be willing and able to send him to another healer without hesitation.

If the Healer's Path calls you, welcome! You are most assuredly needed. In time, you will need to decide what kind of healer you would like to be. Now is the time to be looking at getting some basic information on your topic. Perhaps talking with someone in your community who does the kind of healing you are interested in would help you to make more solid decisions about the Healer's Path prior to initiation. Good luck, and again, welcome! Your clients are already lining up!

The Herbalist's Path. This is presented here, as healing and herbs, for the typical Pagan, often go together. If herbs call to you as a Pathwork focus, a way to give back to your community, you are not alone. Many Witches feel the call of these sacred and life-giving plants.

You may want to focus your studies primarily on *magical* herbs, creating incenses, oils, ointments and creams, teas, and other goods that will help people with their magical intentions. Of course, you will be working closely with the earth and moon energies, harvesting and preparing, creating and charging your "Witches' brews" in accord, and at the right time. Many Wiccans, however, may question your claim as to having made something magically, and so you may want to consider this when you present your products for sale, if you choose to sell them. Folks generally do not trust that some stranger has made something magically, and honestly, they shouldn't, as they don't even know you. For some folks, "making something magically" consists of putting the brews together during a particular moon phase, and then letting the bottles and jars sit on his altar overnight. For some, this would be a magical act. For others, it may not be.

If you choose to make and sell herbal products, I wish you well, and I would hope that your definition of "magically made" is made clear to your customers. They have a right to know the technique if you are to make such claims. And it is perfectly respectable to say that you didn't make something magically *per se*, but you did make it on the ____ moon, in ____ astrological sign, on a sunny day last May or whatever.

If you choose to study and eventually serve your community with your knowledge and expertise with *medicinal* herbs, that would fall more into the Healer's Path category. Just be aware that the government and big pharmaceutical companies are still trying to figure out how to regulate and control herbs, so you would best serve your community by staying educated on the current governmental shenanigans. It's best if you plan to pursue herbal healing to take a course or go to school and get an herbalist's certificate. There are still limitations on what an expert herbalist can legally do and say, but the laws change constantly. So going to school for this Pathwork focus, if you feel the calling, is a great way to start.

INITIATE PATHWORKINGS

Go for a holiday walk! While enjoying the sunshine and energy of the season, see how many herbs, magical and medicinal (as well as culinary, though many are both or all three), you can identify.

If possible, do some wildcrafting. Remember to never take more than one-third (some say one-fifth) of what's there, and if there isn't that much, take none. Leave an offering to the plant of something personal (such as a strand of your hair), something precious to you (such as tobacco, ganja leaves, or a small crystal), or helpful to the plant (such as water or compost).

Ponder the nature of sacrifice. Acknowledge and give yourself a pat on the back for all you've given up to pursue this Path. Consider that there may be something else you would be willing to give up for a while, in order to honor the energies of the season.

Plan your Witchy herb cabinet. Think about all the herbs you would like to keep on hand, and why you think they're important. Then, as you can afford to, begin adding to your stock. Remember to store them in glass, preferably in a cool, dark place.

HOMEWORK

Write a Lughnasadh ritual, from grounding and centering to opening the circle. Be sure to include altar decorations, cakes and wine choices, and what you'll serve for the feast afterward, if applicable.

Write an essay on the nature of sacrifice, with a focus on the Divine Victim and your views as to the validity of Murray's and Kurtz's work on the subject.

Read **Lammas Night,** by Katherine Kurtz; and *chapters 5 through 7* in **God of the Witches** by Margaret Murray, as well as *chapter 8, "Lughnasadh, 31st July,"* in **A Witches' Bible** by the Farrars.

Lightworking: Dreaming your healing Path

Take some time this month and plan spellwork for your own personal healing. Consider the moon and sun energies and their possible effects on your health and your spellwork. Be sure to incorporate a deep meditation, divinatory reading, or sacred dreaming activity (or better, do all three!) to discover both your ailments and their possible causes, and the paths you may wish to take to heal them.

For your grimoire

Write a paragraph or two about the nature of sacrifice, then compile a list of sacrifices you feel you've made, as well as sacrifices you believe you will someday need to make in order to pursue your personal spiritual Path.

26: The August Lesson

> *...for all things are but one thing at the last analysis and there is no part of us that is not of the gods.*
> —Dion Fortune

THE ESBAT—THE STORY

Power. Purpose. The energy fills you as you finish making your preparations. Tonight, on this most auspicious moon, you are determined to take a stand, to open yourself to possibility; to truly own your power. You sprinkle white sage and mugwort on the censer, and the air begins to crackle with psychic energy as you slip into a light trance. You purify and charge, cast and call, opening yourself to the messages of your most powerful allies, your patron god, your matron goddess. Utterly still and silent inside, you receive their messages for you and your life in this cycle, and you make such notes as you feel are important so that you will remember. You ponder these messages, take some time to glean whatever remaining details they wish to give you, and then ring your chime for the next phase of your rite.

Drifting, you tell them you are ready to begin thinking about service, that you wish to give back some of the bright hope and promise they've given you on this sacred road. You open your arms, palms upward, to illustrate on the physical plane your utter reverence and willingness to serve. You begin a chant of

THE AUGUST LESSON CORRESPONDENCES

Focus: Esbats

Energy keywords: personal power; moon; magnetism; spellwork; mirroring the mirror

Tool: the Self as Vessel

Pathwork focus: the Astrologer's Path

Herbs and flowers: Artemisias (wormwood; moonwort; sagebrush), white yarrow, white roses

Incense: moon goddess; Artemis; goddess hymn

Stones and metals: moonstone; pearls (black and white, round and freshwater); silver; platinum

Overarching energies: nurturing and culling the harvest

Radiant energies: striving

Sun enters: Leo

love and devotion, which turns into a very personal song, a self-song describing something of yourself or your love for them, perhaps even simply chanting their names over and over... it matters not how the chant is structured, for it is your very own self-song, meant to be a Mystery, a vow, a pact between yourself and your beloved deities. As you sing, the energy starts swirling around you, and as power is raised, the energy swirls faster and faster, bringing you to a peak of power and purpose, just as you'd intuited when you planned this night of worship. You smile in recognition and approval at your efforts, deeply satisfied at how strongly and acutely you can feel the intense power you're raising, and in that very action, the moon "locks eyes" with you, holds you transfixed... you know you reflect her; that she and you are mirror images, so closely does your will run with hers. The energy you've just raised spins, like luminous threads around you, and suddenly begins to take form around and through you. An image comes to your mind, the image of a chalice, silvery bright, reflecting the light of the moon, which, in turn, reflects her light back to you, filling you to overflowing... Your gods gather around you then and they give you the most profound truth and love; they show you that you ARE that chalice! Your heart catches in your throat, bringing tears of joy to *your eyes. You speak then of your love, your devotion, your adoration, and how, through this, you wish to serve them in any way you can. You understand clearly now that you are their vessel, full with purpose and power and much sacred knowledge and wisdom.*

With that very thought, the chalice form around you begins to thin, and you can sense, feel, see with your psychic vision the energy of your chalice as it overflows, spilling out over your tools, your altar, throughout your entire home while much of that sweet flowing "chalice" energy still remains around you, translucent, yet complete, shining in form. You can see in your mind's eye how that energy is to be used to help others, to give unselfishly in the service of your gods, while never allowing your own energy to become depleted, for then you would have nothing to give anyone. Never have you been so aware of your purpose, never so certain that you are, indeed, a tool of the Old Ones; as vessel, as the primed pump, both blessed and humbled to be their priest/ess, honored to act, from this day forward, in their beloved service.

THE ENERGY OF THE ESBAT

Esbats, as we know, are most often when we Witches do our most serious spellwork. Whether we're working to heal our planet, ourselves, or others in one or many different ways, from physical to financial to emotional and more, most of us do indeed take these workings very seriously.

Last month, we discussed becoming our own healers. This month, we are called upon to look at reaching out with our energy and healing those around us, such as this great organism we call Mother Earth. What does "healing the earth" mean, exactly, and how can we go about it? For some of us, it means we literally put energy into earth healing, either through magic that is followed up with concrete actions (such as meditating on finding places that need our help, then perhaps gathering others of like mind to go plant trees, clear out trash, or even make decisions to let the land in certain areas rest from the constant strain we put on it with our festivals and requests for blessings from it), or through spending—or not spending—our dollars carefully, supporting only those we feel are acting in the earth's best interest, or in a myriad of other ways that resonate with our hearts, such as reducing our energy footprint, recycling, growing gardens, etc. For others, healing the earth means we help others to find their spiritual path, either through providing public works, teaching and writing (like yours truly!), or becoming healers, therapists, and more.

Even if we choose not to enter the public realm, we must understand that, as priests and priestesses of Wicca and Witchcraft, how we present ourselves through our dress, our words, and our actions speaks very much to the mundane world of what our faith is all about. In other words, *we set an example* for our brothers and sisters whether we intend to or not. The mundane community will look to us as the representative of all things Witchy, so it's a good idea to present yourself in a positive light, while still holding to the personal integrity of being yourself.

As far as our personal work, owning our power is indeed called for, as many of us are intimately involved in the mundane world. Indeed, most of us have to deal with it every day, either through our jobs and careers, our extended families, our own or our children's schools. Dealing with the mundane world can sometimes be so taxing that we forget we are people of power and magic, and the values of that world can inhibit our power—if we allow it to.

For example, some Witches feel they need to "pay" their gods with a certain quantity or quality of worship time before they feel it's acceptable to ask for something. Some folks feel that it's wrong to simply do spellwork to achieve an end without having paid enough time to some sort of spiritual "bank," but this is neither true nor in our best interest. For we are, again, priests and priestesses of the gods, and by virtue of this, we are often *their* tools, *their* "benders and shapers" of energy, and there's no taboo on using energy to also help ourselves or others by using energy ethically. Some Witches will not do spellwork of any kind without first doing a reading to gauge the energies and possible outcomes of any spell. This is a wise practice, though I personally don't feel it's always necessary. For many forms of general magical work, I simply get on with the spell, unless I'm having an intuition there's something wrong. However, before doing any kind of complicated, dark, or controversial spell, I usually do both a meditation and a reading (or two ... or three!) on the working before proceeding. You may have ideas of your own regarding this, and you should follow what feels right to you.

We must remember also, in our earth-healing work as well as in our interactions with others, that people usually do what they think is right, so it's not appropriate to judge or try to "help" those who may have no wish to be helped. This can be a tricky business, and the last thing we want to do is fall into the trap of self-righteousness that doesn't allow others their view. Yes, we can (and should!) keep the courage of our convictions, but we must always try to temper our words with diplomacy, or we could very well alienate the same folks we seek to help.

TOOL—THE SELF AS VESSEL

When we think of ourselves as working on our spiritual vessels, what does that mean? For someone on the Dedicant's Path, it means we are learning to find and build a connection with our personal gods and goddesses, opening up to their truth and love, striving to understand our place in the universe. For someone on a more advanced Path, such as yourself, dear Initiate, it means all this and quite a bit more. For as you advance in knowledge and experience, indeed, once you initiate into this religion, you hone (and *own*!) that vessel, becoming even more truly that direct connection to your deities, often serving to help those coming up behind you through offering assistance with divinatory readings, dream interpretation, herb lore, more advanced duties in ritual and much, much more. In my "real life" classrooms, the Initiates are very much the "graduate students" who are encouraged to assist in the teaching and loving care of the newer students who are following fast behind them. Not all students initiate, however, and of those, even fewer seek to become clergy, but are instead content with learning the basics and not much more, attending public Sabbats or practice their own celebrations when it's convenient, effectively treating their religion as little more than a hobby.

For the Initiate student, the spiritual journey changes, deepens, intensifies. For once a Witch begins to advance his study, he begins to take that vital step toward truly becoming clergy; he begins to act as *representative* of the Lord and the Lady, to reach out to others as a mentor and guide. As such, he must at once see himself in a much more serious light, as the example of the spiritual vessel that is being filled from within through his own power and energy practices, as well as the example of one who is beginning to prepare for the outpouring that is true priesthood. At this time, it is important to take a thought to how we present ourselves, but more importantly, how we *think of ourselves*. This, to a great degree, is what the shadow work is all about: to help the Witch grow in power through practice, prayer, devotion, and healing his shadows.

For many folks, having special ritual garb, jewelry, and various "touchstones" (items or actions one uses repeatedly to help enhance that between-the-worlds energy and feeling) helps us remember that we are magical beings; servants; tools of our personal gods. The region we live in can sometimes dictate or adversely affect some of these practices. However, we needn't let our communities limit us in any way. For example, I have lived in communities where even at the most casual of public rituals, everyone wore ritual garb and sacred jewelry as well as their Sacred Cords, and more recently, I've lived in a community where the local Pagans didn't seem to even know what ritual garb was, often referring to these sacred garments as "costumes." At one time, this caused me to re-examine my feelings and beliefs about the importance of ritual garb and sacred jewelry, which I was grateful for; for it's always beneficial to re-think long-held beliefs to make certain our traditions serve us, and not we, them.

These examinations brought me back to the beliefs I have long held to be true for myself personally: First, that circle is a special and sacred time; therefore, wearing special clothing and jewelry is appropriate by setting these times apart as such. Secondly, ritual garb is often made or embellished in circle, and at the very least, is most certainly *consecrated to magical use*, so wearing these items loans power and energy to our rites. Third, as our bodies often heat up a great deal physically during magical workings, ritual garb is practical, since traditionally we wear nothing underneath, so the body stays cooler. Fourth, I believe that our garb, like our tools—indeed, just like the magic circle itself—separates us from the mundane world, reminding us that we are in that special and sacred "place that is not a place, in a time which knows no time." And finally, as Dion Fortune so wisely states (and I must agree), regarding going before the Lady: it is "not fitting to appear in the presence of the Goddess in mundane garments."[91] Now this is not to say that we can't still pray, meditate, and connect with our gods spontaneously in ordinary clothes, but when we've *planned to act with intention*, such as in a ritual, in my opinion and in my experience, planning also to wear sacred garments is the most appropriate option. But, as always, your Path is your Path, so your mileage may vary.

PATHWORK FOCUS: THE CALLING TO THE ASTROLOGER'S PATH

The Path of the Astrologer is one that will take years and years of study. This art has been around for thousands of years, and there are many books about it on the market.

---

91. Dion Fortune, *Moon Magic* (Samuel Weiser, 1978), 128.

Astrologers must be good at math, or have access to a computer program for creating charts.

There are two basic types of astrology—sidereal, which gives a planet's position by constellation, and tropical, which gives the planet's position by sign. Most of the astrology we hear and read about is based on tropical, although there are many who believe that sidereal is the more accurate. Sidereal astrology takes into consideration the fact that over the thousands of years in which astrology has been studied, the constellations have actually moved—they are no longer in the place they were when this science came into existence. But that's for your personal study, should you choose this Pathwork focus.

If you *do* feel called to the Astrologer's Path, as stated, it is good to have excellent skills with math, or have a good computer program for the calculations, and to know how to read an astrological ephemeris. One must also be able to be completely neutral in one's interactions with individuals one has done a natal chart for, as any personal feelings can really sway the way one looks at a person's chart. It would follow, then, that the misinterpretation or exaggeration would affect the way that chart is interpreted to that person as well. So of course, the astrologer would need to possess the self-knowledge (and self-*discipline!*) required to back away from any chart interpretation he doesn't feel capable of being neutral about. In addition, he must exhibit impeccable diplomacy and tact. You can't just blurt out, for example, that someone has sexual abuse karma without tempering this information with kindness and care. This Pathwork focus requires good follow-through, as chart calculations take a great deal of time, but the interpretation can take even more. So the Witch that specializes in astrology would have to be willing to commit to a long course of study, and keep up with it. Becoming an astrologer, just like becoming a priest or priestess, is a lifetime commitment.

The first thing I would recommend to get you started, since you have to do this by the time you get your Adept (the traditional second degree) in this course, is to have your chart done. Then, take some time to read (and re-read, and re-read) the interpretation. Make many notes about what rings true to you, for good or for ill, as well as what doesn't. Then, look this information up. Find its source. Make sure you understand your chart really well, and know your strengths and weaknesses astrologically. Then, begin calculating a few charts (or even have the math part done by computer), and start doing some basic interpretations of these. Make sure you only do charts for classmates, covenmates, and close friends at first, and tell these people you need their brutal honesty as to your accuracy in order to learn. Best would be to do charts for folks who have already had them done. After several of these "practice" charts, you may even want to tackle doing your own yourself. I would recommend waiting on doing your own chart until several months have passed since you *had* it done, so your interpretation will be fresh. Then, do the chart and compare it to the one you had done. If possible, compare the charts you created and interpreted for your covenmates or friends with the ones they had done previously, too. Remember you must be completely honest (and not ego-driven!) with yourself as to your accuracy. Then, you will easily see where you need more study. Correct your mistakes, learn from them, and then continue doing charts, and stay in practice. And keep studying. There is always new information. You will want to keep up on it.

INITIATE PATHWORKINGS

Take a moonlight walk! If possible, out in a place away from city noises or lights. Try to feel the presence of your patron god(s) and matron goddess(es) around you. Tune in to what the energies of the area are saying. How do they feel? How do you feel?

Give your tools a bath under the full moon in a bowl filled with a mugwort infusion. Notice what subtle differences there are when you use the tool again afterward. What's changed? Note it in your grimoire.

Make a point of saying goodnight to the moon every night this cycle; pay special attention to her cycles and phases. Pay attention to how she makes you feel.

Mirror the mirror. Ancient knowledge says that if you look into the full moon in a mirror, you can see forever. Try it this month, and record what you see and feel.

Bless a chalice of water under the full (or dark) moon. Drink in the energies and note any changes in your body, emotions, or other areas.

Bless (or gather) some water under the full moon, and add it to a full moon bath. Cleanse yourself deeply; start a new path.

HOMEWORK

Contemplate presenting a public ritual or ROP you would like to someday do for someone, such as a Wiccanning, handfasting, etc. **Write that public ritual (or ROP),** and consider *actually presenting* your awesome contribution to your community or friends.

    Read part I in **Dreaming the Divine** *by Scott Cunningham,* and **the last section in Part I of** **A Witches' Bible,** by the Farrars (which starts on page 153, and is titled "Birth, Marriage, and Death").

Lightworking: Journey to the moon

Take some time this month and ponder taking an astral journey to the moon, in order to hunt (and claim!) power! Imagine what energies you might find there, how you will find your power, and win it. Then, plan a meditation or sacred dreaming rite to make it happen!

For your grimoire

Continue (or begin) working on your table of correspondence for moon energies. Consider phases, rising and setting times, signs the moon is in, Mercury retrogrades' effects on the moon, void-of-course moons, and any other planetary energies you feel would have an effect.

27: The September Lesson

*Sacred sleep is one manifestation of the process
of removing spirituality from the hands of the experts
and placing it where it belongs: in the hearts, minds,
and dreams of the worshipers themselves.*
—Scott Cunningham

MABON—THE STORY

You finish the last of the preparations for your Sacred Dreaming ritual as you stifle a huge yawn. Evening has fallen beautifully, and with it, a gentle rain shower came to wash the world. Your window is open just the right amount, to let in fresh air, which you pause a moment to breathe deeply. The scents of rich earth, grass, a tiny hint of flowers mingle with the scent of incense burning in your sacred space. The room, just cleaned, sparkles with candlelight, and the bedclothes, pulled back, reveal freshly washed sheets. Another deep breath near the window sets your breathing rhythm as you finish preparing yourself for sacred sleep.

You purify and charge, cast and call, and make your sacred entreaty. There are questions you need answered, puzzles to be understood, and tonight's dreamwork seems the best means for obtaining clarity and purpose. You remember the dream temples of old, and have tried to re-create something of those energies in your room. Your dream books and tables of correspondence are

THE SEPTEMBER LESSON CORRESPONDENCES

Focus: Mabon

Energy keywords: main harvest; the Lady mourns for her loved one; sacred dreaming; thanksgiving

Tool: crystal ball/water bowl and coin

Pathwork focus: Dreamweaver

Herbs and flowers: chamomile; ganja; hops; valerian; lavender

Incense: magic temple; ebony nights

Stones and metals: lapis; aquamarine; sodalite

Overarching energies: main harvest

Radiant energies: harvest

Sun enters: Libra

all here, ready for morning's interpretations, as are other methods of divination, in case you need clarification. Pens and markers and beautiful papers await your morning work as well, some of them in beautiful colors so that you may decorate the pages as you desire. You pause a moment near these sacred tools and write out an affirmation that the answers you seek will come to you tonight. Finally, you begin to speak to your gods of your needs, your desires, and your many questions regarding your life during this cycle. Your entreaty then turns to words of gratitude for having come as far as you have on this Path, of your hard work and study that wasn't like "work" at all to you, but rather a true joy to learn. As you remember and speak to your chosen gods and goddesses, your words gradually turn to songs of praise and happiness. There is so much to be thankful for at this turn of the Wheel, so much you intend to express at your Sabbat feast tomorrow. For tonight, however, you have only your devotion and your questions. Your song ends on a high and joyful note with your arms open in heartfelt openness. Yes, you are open, ready, and grateful for any sacred messages they wish to send you. You smile contentedly, pull the bedcovers back the rest of the way, and climb in.

You lie on the cool, soft, lightly scented sheets, snuggling in and arranging yourself into your favorite, most comfortable position. Your final words of praise and thanks fall to mere mutterings, then whispers, and finally, sighs of contentment as your body is suitably tired, ripe for the dreaming, and you drift away from the realities of waking life easily, joyously embracing the solitude and serenity of the dreamer's Path and the Dream Realm.

THANKSGIVING—THE ENERGY OF THE HARVEST

I've spoken many times of gratitude and what an important role it plays in our spiritual lives. I also understand that it can be difficult when our lives aren't going well, to remember to count our blessings. It can be hard to remember those simple words, but once you do, more gratitude comes, and if you can get outside at that moment, look at the beauty around you and breathe the sweet fresh air, it can help you remember your blessings more easily.

In our Mabon rituals, as well as the feasting afterward, it is highly appropriate to speak of our thanks and our gifts. I remember many years ago, my sister and I came up with this idea of stating what we were grateful for as we sat down to our family of origin's (FO's) traditional Thanksgiving dinner. It didn't go over too well, so my sister and I ended up simply speaking of our gratitude to each other. Subsequent years found us both trying to encourage our tablemates along these lines, but I didn't have much luck with it until I began celebrating my spiritual Thanksgiving, Mabon, with those of like mind. Pagans, for some reason, seem to jump right into the idea.

I have come to believe that gratitude is a great key to much that ails us in our daily lives, indeed in our entire culture. We humans are always so regretful of what happened *yesterday*, agonizing over our wrongs and the words and actions of those who have wronged us, in addition to being filled with fear over our imagined *futures* and which predictions of disaster we need to subscribe to. The truth of the matter is that all we ever have is the *moment*. We've heard this before, haven't we, dear Initiate? "Yesterday is ashes; tomorrow is wood. Only today does the fire burn brightly," goes the Inuit saying, and as travelers on this Sacred Road, we can hold this to be true. Of course we mustn't forget those who have hurt us to the point that we let them do it again and again, but we can let the hurt go, allow ourselves to heal, and find joy in today, for "tomorrow" never truly arrives. Yes, we can plan for the future, as this is wise and practical, but we cannot live that future until it becomes *today*.

Mabon, as we know, is the main harvest, and as such it is especially appropriate that we look at our inner harvests at this time. What have we sown into our lives this cycle? What are we harvesting? These questions are important to ask, to help ourselves see and understand the weavings and ways of our own nature along with the will of our chosen deities. For even in choosing them, we must acknowledge that they, too, have chosen us. They will give us answers, warnings, gifts, sometimes at the least expected moments, but if we stay open, we can indeed use the information to help us heal.

THE ENERGY OF DREAMING

For some folks, dreamwork is their primary divination method. One of the complications of dream interpretation is that there are probably as many interpretations to one's dreams as there are people on this planet. There have been dozens and dozens of books published on dreamwork in the occult field alone, and, as the study of dreams is as old as humankind, there are hundreds (possibly *thousands*!) of dream interpretation books encompassing all walks of life, all cultures, all spiritual belief systems. To study this field can be very confusing, what with all the contradictions and twists and turns. Chinese medicine, for example, puts forth that not having dreams of any kind indicates the subject is in the best possible health. Japan, according to Scott Cunningham, is the only culture left in the world that still has dream temples. Jung's *Man and His Symbols*, a very popular book with Pagans, can seem off-putting to some folks, with his assertion that any connection the dreamer has with the Divine indicates the dreamer has delusions of his own grandeur, and is therefore an arrogant beast that must be knocked down a peg. Other authors hold that such connections surely mean that the dreamer is special and beloved of the gods. So if helping others with their dreaming speaks to you as one of your spiritual gifts, I encourage you, dear Initiate, to read many authors on the subject and make your own assessments as far as whose work sings to you, and to also keep a very open mind as to your clients' dream symbols and beliefs; those will weigh more heavily on their dream interpretation than your system will.

There can be such vast differences in thought—for example, if a dog lover dreamed of a big black dog, that animal would symbolize to him great loyalty, affection, unconditional love. Another person however, may have been bitten by a big black dog when she was a kid, and so to her, a big black dog would be a symbol of pain and terror. Several years ago, I saw a dream expert on a popular talk show who said that one of the best ways to come up with a personal system of symbols for dream interpretation was to think in terms of someone asking her, "Okay, I'm from Mars. What exactly *is* a big black dog?" which of course would make the dreamer have to think pretty hard about what that symbol actually means to her in order to explain it to someone who has never heard of or experienced such a thing, thereby coming to understand her own personal system of dream symbols that much better.

Whatever system of symbols you decide to follow (and again, I strongly encourage you to create your own), it's a good idea at this time to start tracking your dreams. Our dreams can tell us so much about our lives and our spiritual Path, that to miss out on using this incredible personal resource, regardless of whether you wish to serve your community by becoming a dreamweaver, would be to throw away a true gift. To get yourself used to being aware of and tracking your dreams, I recommend that you first moderate any prescription medication or recreational substance use you can, as these things can "fog up" or even completely block your dreams, but what is even more important to this study is getting *enough* and *uninterrupted* sleep. If your sleep is short, you may not achieve the deeper levels that open you up to the starlight vision, and if it's constantly interrupted, you may not be able to achieve the REM cycles that are crucial to dreaming.

Once you feel ready, you can start tracking your dreams by simply suggesting to yourself before sleeping that you will remember your dreams and wake up enough to write them down. Then, of course, follow through by doing just that. As you continue to give yourself that suggestion and track your dreams, it will get easier to remember them, and easier to wake up, make a few notes, and go back to sleep. Some folks report that when they are in this habit, they often will barely remember waking in the night, but in the morning, they have notes written about their dreams, although they don't remember making the notes themselves. And then as you continue with dreamweaving, you can actually get to a place where you can control your dreams, and many schools of thought dictate that if you are control of your dreams, you're in control of your life.

A few ideas for getting you there: Once you have been in the habit of tracking your dreams for a while, and have become a stronger dreamer, you will start noticing that you remember more and more of them. Once you get to this place, start seeing how aware you can make yourself within your dreaming. Try to wake up within the dream by looking at your hands (your purpose), or your feet (your Path). Once this happens, tell yourself that you're dreaming, and if you can stay in the dream state at this point, it becomes what is called a *lucid dream*—a clear dream in which the dreamer is *aware*. It is from this point that the dreamer can begin to control his dreams. Astral projection then becomes an adventure in flying, rather than a simple fragment of memory or dreamstuff to be interpreted, although that certainly has value too. With practice and continued tracking, becoming conscious and propelling oneself into a lucid dream state can render astral projection as an avenue to achieve higher learning on the astral plane.

TOOL—THE CRYSTAL BALL

Not every Witch will be drawn to these amazing and powerful tools. I personally was never even remotely interested in owning one, as they always seemed to be so expensive, and, however beautiful they were, they didn't really call to me. Plus, I'd never thought I was very good at scrying. At the same time, I've always acknowledged that I cloud-scry (I see things in the clouds) and fire-scry, as well as spontaneously just ... *see* things, especially runes, in nature. I've since come to understand that these methods and mediums are quite valid and are still, indeed, forms of scrying. The point I'm trying to make is that I believe most folks have this ability, and any medium that can hold your attention enough to help you trance, or which forms a symbol that "pops out" at you, can absolutely be considered a tool for scrying. To this end, we can choose to be open to what our chosen deities send us.

My crystal ball came to me quite unexpectedly, given the above, to say the least. I was at a gem and mineral show with my partner and a student in the fall of 2010, less than a year ago as I write this. I was looking at some beautiful crystals and crystal balls one vendor was presenting, when I picked up *mine*. Suddenly, the sound and light around me seemed to darken and go still, the energies of the ball seemed to pulsate as the inner planes fired color and sparkle, drawing me immediately into its depths, compelling me forward just like the gateway to my Lord's realm—a power place I'd discovered years prior—had done. I was utterly fascinated, and could barely wrench my eyes away long enough to put it down. But I had to put it down, as I was stone broke, and couldn't even afford it at the deep discount the seller so generously offered. I was obsessed with it, of course, and went back to it again and again throughout the show.

Needless to say, my beloved partner was very sneaky that day, and a few weeks later on my birthday, delightedly plunked it into my open and very willing hands to my squeals of delight and excitement. We were united at last! I connected with the stone's deva that very night. Since then, I've worked with this amazing tool every full and dark moon, as well as several times in between. It has spoken to me in profound ways, as only a crystal ball can, and I've learned a few things I wish to share here with you.

The first thing I advise, if you decide to purchase a crystal ball, is to let it bond with you and get to know your energies *really* well at first. As Mercury was heading into a retrograde period within a week, I knew I couldn't trust any communications for a while, which was just as well, as I really wanted the bonding period to happen first anyway. The new moon occurred just two days after my birthday, so after a thorough cleansing and brief "get acquainted" moment on that new moon, I decided I'd follow what the old custom folk traditions suggest for a new tarot deck: I slept with it for a while. My idea was to sleep with it until the full moon, which led to the decision to carry it around with me as much as possible during my waking hours as well, so it could get to know all of my energy patterns. My beautiful crystal ball then became my little symbiant; upon arrival home from work each night, I would don an athletic bra and nestle it in between my breasts, carefully tucking in my shirt in case it popped out, and carrying it with me in everything I did: cooking meals; taking evening walks; having long, heartfelt talks with my partner; writing. Weekends found me following the same routine throughout the entire day.

Then, on the full moon, I bathed my crystal ball in a mugwort infusion, and set it out on my balcony where the moonlight could hit it, to boost up its psychic power. You may recall from your own magical journaling, dear Initiate—the moon was full on Yule, and there was also a lunar eclipse that year, just after midnight here in the Pacific Northwest. My beloved, a decidedly nocturnal beast, woke me at the time of the eclipse. I carried my crystal ball downstairs into the darkened courtyard of my apartment complex just as the moon emerged from shadow. As if in concert with my wishes, a light rain began to fall, so I lifted the crystal up to the sky to receive this timely blessing. I then returned the crystal to the mugwort bath on my balcony, where it remained for the next day and a half, for a total of three days during the full moon period. Afterward, I wrapped it in silk, where I keep it now. As Mercury was still in retrograde, I waited until it had gone direct for my first attempt at *actual* scrying.

At that point, I simply opened myself to its energies, and wrote down its instructions. I was eager to take it to class and share it with my students, but was told an unequivocal "no" to this action. Humbled, I remembered that this has long been the way with some of our most powerful tools, as they are not toys to take to "show and tell" but rather allies to be respected and treated with care. I continue to learn from this wonderful and unexpected ally, and should you be called to one such as this, I hope you will learn much, too, for a crystal ball will enhance your other divinations, your connections to the earth and your personal deities, and deepen your dreaming in amazing ways, both subtle and profound.

PATHWORK FOCUS:
THE CALLING TO THE DREAMWEAVER'S PATH

As we get closer to the Dark Time, it is appropriate to go within, and dreamwork is a good way to do this. In ancient times in the vast majority of cultures, there were dream temples, where the querent could go, perform a dreaming rite just before bed, and sleep in the temple to receive sacred dreams. There were priestesses and priests on staff to help the dreamer understand and interpret her dreams, and it was considered very unwise to not follow the instructions the gods gave in the dream.

If you choose to become a dreamweaver—that is, to help others with the intention, rituals, and interpretation of their dreams—it would be a good idea to become a strong dreamer first, which you likely already are, dear Initiate, if this Pathwork focus is calling to you. From here, you may wish to explore how to create or help others create their own dream temples and sacred dreaming rituals. I would also suggest studying several different dream symbol systems as well as your own, which you have undoubtedly been adding to for a while (if not, the time to start this vital table of correspondence is now!), and then, keeping those symbol systems in mind, when helping others to interpret their dreams, ask first, "What does ____ mean to you?" Or even, as mentioned above, say, "Okay, pretend I'm from Mars. What exactly is a ____?"

You will best serve to help others understand their dreams, in my opinion, by learning a little about the person's background and their own symbols and beliefs, as well as their personality type and temperament. Go gently. Ask lots of questions and trust your own intuition before delivering your interpretation. Remember that this is a lost art in most world cultures, but that it can (and should!) be brought back, for the highest good of all. Keep your humility, and especially when starting out, remember to ask for honest feedback. Best of luck with this, and blessed be! Dreamweavers are surely needed in our little subculture, as well as the greater culture, though of course Pagans will be more receptive to the idea in today's times.

INITIATE PATHWORKINGS

Go for a holiday walk! You'll likely need it after that big ol' feast you just ate. Take the time to tune in to the earth tides, and see which way they pull you across the Wheel.

Take a cleansing bath before your ritual. Add a little salt, or if you're close to an ocean or large lake, add a jar full of pre-collected water to the bath, to add the energies of that living body of water. While bathing, ponder all that you wish to be cleansed of, and let your worries and cares be washed away.

Do a water meditation. Fill a glass, vase, cauldron, or other water vessel, and drop a silver coin into it (or use a crystal ball). Allow yourself all the time you need to ponder and listen.

Take some time to focus on gratitude. What are you thankful for today? Even hard lessons can help to spur tremendous growth. What difficulties have ultimately led to your higher learning? What would you change if you could do it again? What would be the same?

Allow yourself to enjoy your inner harvest. What have you accomplished this cycle? If it doesn't seem like much, try to think of how your life would be if you had done the opposite. Strive to be grateful to yourself for how much you've grown, learned, and harvested at this time.

Tell someone you love how much you love them. Write it in a letter, so they'll have something to treasure in years to come. Speak from your heart, and make this giving a priority. Be blessed.

HOMEWORK

Write a Mabon ritual, if you've never written one before (such as if you took my Dedicant-level course), from grounding and centering to opening the circle. Be sure to include altar decorations, cakes and wine choices, and what you'll serve for the feast afterward, if applicable.

Make a list of everything you have harvested thus far in this cycle, or on your spiritual Path. What are you grateful for? What would you have done differently, if you could? What were the harder lessons? Make a complete inventory of your inner qualities, with total honesty, yet without judgment or blame; simply take a deep look at what you've brought to pass, both the "good" and the "bad."

Read **Dreaming the Divine***, part II* by Scott Cunningham and *chapter 9, "Autumn Equinox, 21st September"* in **A Witches' Bible** by the Farrars.

Lightworking: dream temple or shrine

Take some time this month and ponder sacred dreaming. Plan spellwork, either in conjunction with your moon work or as a separate ritual, and then use the talents and skills you've learned thus far on your Path, dear Initiate, to create a dream temple of your bed and bedroom, or perhaps a small shrine to the activities of dreaming and dream analysis. Then, plan a sacred dreaming ritual. Ponder the questions you would like to have answered, and proceed from there, planning all the actions and elements, from casting and calling to cakes and wine (this would likely be your breakfast the following day, which I recommend be as grounding as possible).

For your grimoire

Begin (or continue) a table of correspondence for dream symbols.

28: The October Lesson

We can't know the day unless we know the night; we can't perceive the glory of light until we examine the darkness; we can't go outside of ourselves until we go within.
—Raven Digitalis

SAMHAIN—THE STORY

Darkness. The Gleaning. Hecate's Realm; Hecate's Time. You cast your circle warily, and somewhat wearily. You've been working on so many issues, healing so much that's been broken lately that it's been a bit draining. Still, you want to do this deep personal cleansing as you enter the Dark Time, for you've come full circle from the bright wishes you had nearly a year ago, the manifestation of some dreams, as well as the breaking of others, and you know this is the right time of year for assessing, discarding, coming to terms, measuring up.

As you refresh the herbs in your censer, you settle down into a dark meditation. In your mind's eye, you are humbled by all that there still is to do, to understand. You drift. At once, you are at Hecate's Crossroads, a place you recognize, having been here before. This time, you know she won't be as gentle; this time, you know she has things to say to you about your own darkness, your Mysteries and fears, your masks. When she reaches out to you, encouraging you to rise, you don't hesitate.

THE OCTOBER LESSON CORRESPONDENCES

Focus: Samhain

Energy keywords: the gleaning; the Dark Time;
　　honoring our beloved dead; the darker deities

Tool: the mask of the Unified Self

Pathwork focus: the Intuitive Reader's Path

Herbs and flowers: mugwort; sweetgrass

Incense: past lives; apparition

Stones and metals: obsidian; pewter; sodalite

Overarching energies: meat and herb harvest

Radiant energies: assessment

Sun enters: Scorpio

She offers you the choice of which Path to take and you begin your journey with her at your side.

*She takes you to a small cave near a stream, and you cleanse yourself before entering. She tells you that this is the place of your darkest shadows, your hopes and fears for yourself and your life. She helps you settle in on the warm sand, then she sits before you and bids you look into her eyes. They are black and deep, and you find your consciousness swirling, swimming in pain and fear ... in Mystery and magic ... in the full power of your passions, your sexuality and anger. She tells you that only those energies that feed you are going to help you survive and succeed, that the energies that diminish you in your daily life will eventually bring you to illness and failure, rendering you unable to help those who mean the most to you. She tells you that **you** must be your first priority, as you cannot hope to give anything to others if you have little to no energy yourself. She then asks you to honestly tell yourself (and her) what your life's next priority is.*

You start to tell her what you think she wants to hear, what you've convinced yourself all along that your next priority is ... or the next one ... or the next. You speak long with her, arguing your points, as she tells you that your words do not match your intentions or your actions. She asks you to reassess, not to judge yourself, but to look honestly, fearlessly within; that only through love and truth will you find your highest ideal, your best self to put forward into the world. She tells you that you've been living in illusion, behind a mask; the mask of your culture, perhaps, or your upbringing, your domestication, your fears. She says that this is the place of reassessment, and that in order to leave this cave you must discard all of your masks. She hands you a dark crystal, telling you that when you've done so, it will clear.

She leaves and you sit in meditation for a long time, pondering her cryptic words about masks and illusions. You decide to be as brave as you can possibly be with yourself, and look, open-eyed and open-hearted, at your life, your actions, your behaviors and intentions. You see that there have been many times in your life when, although your intentions were good, your actions fell short of the mark. You see the lies, the deceptions, the false pride and avoidance. You also see the virtuous actions, and you slip into justifications with these, telling yourself that it's okay that you hurt people and neglected them, as you were acting with what you knew to be true at the time. Then, you realize the truth of the energy; that often, it simply doesn't matter what we thought or what our intentions were, but rather what manifested as a result of the actions we set into motion. You remember what your teacher's always saying, that the wise priestess thinks all the way through to the consequences of her actions.

You start to become agitated, upset over your mistakes, and Great Hecate tells you to detach, that this is not a place of judgment, but of change and of healing. You then find yourself looking dispassionately at these energies, neither beating yourself up over them nor making excuses. You see what it is to **stand**. And you do, indeed, stand up, take responsibility in your own mind and heart, telling yourself you will make your apologies where needed, heal the past and move toward the future reassured, cleansed of the mistakes of your past, ready to begin again to build that bright future you so deserve. You remind yourself of the last lines of the Wiccan Rede, as well as the saying "Give thy word sparingly and adhere to it like iron," and vow to yourself that you will do better by yourself, your gods, and the people you love, even as you straighten your posture.

The twilight recedes to a colorful dawn. Sunlight streams into the cave, filling it with light, and you stand and move toward the entrance hopefully. You look down at the crystal in your hand, finding the clarity you so crave, and step forward into the fresh bright air of the morning.

THE ENERGY OF THE DARK TIME

You've been around the Wheel more than once now, dear Initiate, and you're likely tuning in to the energies of the season more readily than ever before. Samhain is coming, heralding time for family and friends, spiritual connections and deep introspection. Now is a really good time to work on your divination and meditation skills, as well as dreamwork and general mental health issues. Also included in this energy pattern is the energy of our *masks*.

I hope you've begun the process of getting your natal chart done by now, as this is a vital and required step in your Initiate's Journey. It's good to examine our rising sign at this time, for it says so much to us about our masks—the face we show the world. Of course we all wear many masks; no one of us is 100 percent transparent to the world. During the Dark Time, then, it's good to assess and re-assess who we are, where we're going in our spiritual journeys, as well as where we'd like to end up as spiritual beings. There's even a naming technique, based on the Qabalah, that requires the practitioner to use part of this information (the querent's vision of the Godhead) as part of the magical name.[92] I think this is a great idea, as it gives one something to aspire to; to aim for, in one's journey toward spiritual wholeness. Hearing or saying that name (or segment of a name) can remind one constantly of these higher spiritual aspirations.

So the rising sign, then, can be examined as yet another tool for discovery, another way to understand not only ourselves, but even more, how others see us, as the rising sign is so significantly in front of us, since this is the constellation that was coming up on the horizon (hence the term *rising sign* or *ascendant*) at the time of our births. We can look at both the positive and the negative energies of this sign to help us see ways in which we can heal our communications with others to create stronger, healthier relationships.

THE DARK TIME TOOL—THE MASK OF THE UNIFIED SELF

For years now, I've done a divinatory method using sacred masking, which I call a "soul mask," as a way to symbolically and artistically express the depths of soul I read in myself or another person. Soul masks can reveal a lot about the subject, and

---

92. William G. Gray, *Attainment Through Magic* (Llewellyn, 1979).

although it can be challenging to do so, they *can* be made for oneself. My suggestion would be to work with materials such as leather, heavy fabric, or even a mask *base* of some kind to get the mask started if you're doing one for yourself. Another option is to use a plaster and gauze material on a mannequin or pre-fabricated mask base, or have a friend do the initial part for you directly onto your own face. The material is available in any craft store, with instructions on the package.

Once the mask base is made, you can take some sacred alone time, slip into trance, and read those energies you are presenting to the world. When I'm doing a mask for a client, I make a sketch while the mask is drying so I'll know where all the colors and symbols will go, and then while I'm painting, the interpretation is revealed to me. During this process, more symbols and colors suggest themselves, and the soul mask, as well as the reading/interpretation, is fine-tuned. This is not as easy to do for the self, but, just as with any reading for yourself, if you can be totally honest with what you see, it can be a rewarding and insightful way to learn much about yourself.

PATHWORK FOCUS:
THE CALLING TO THE INTUITIVE READER'S PATH

There are many, many divination methods available to the Witch (and non-Witch!) today, and most of us have a favorite or two. In the Circles system, it is recommended that you be proficient in two methods by your Adept initiation. However, if you feel called to the path of divination in general, it's best to have a working knowledge of several to *many* systems, with well more than two proficiencies by the time you reach Adept level. Here is a (very) partial listing:

- Tarot cards
- Runes
- I Ching
- Animal cards
- Phoenix cards
- Hand reading and/or palmistry
- Scrying (reading signs and symbols in crystal balls, bowls of water, wax drippings, clouds, tea leaves, etc.)

- Pendulum reading
- Ogham

Divination energies

Any method involving the reading and interpreting of symbols or signs to read the energies of our past and our present circumstances, as well as possible futures, is considered divination, although there are many schools of thought that separate "fortune telling" from "true" divination, often in an "us vs. them" mentality. The thing to remember whenever reading signs or symbols for yourself or others is that the symbols will reveal the energies in the air at the time of the reading, nothing is set in stone, and it is ill advised to take the reading so literally that there is only one possible interpretation. Absolute statements such as "You will meet a tall, dark stranger" or "You will die if you do _____" are sensationalist and ungrounded thinking. A good reader will see and interpret the energies as simply possibilities, and rarely offer any type of absolute, opinion or otherwise.

As far as divination methods, there are so many kinds of cards, stones, and symbols on the market now that the earnest student has more to choose from than ever before. People are coming up with new ways and tools every day. Again, the important thing to remember about any divinatory reading is that nothing is set in stone, irreversible, or permanent. The energies present at the time of the reading are what are being read, and (even by virtue of receiving this information) those energies can and often do change, sometimes quickly, sometimes quite profoundly. Many people who get "bad" readings become upset and think it's the end of the world, but what's important to remember about any divinatory reading is the old adage: Forewarned is forearmed. If we have a pretty good idea of what *may* happen, we undoubtedly have a pretty good idea about how to prevent it. And really, more often than not, a good reading will cause the querent to ask *even more pertinent questions*, leading him to his own understandings and interpretations of his life and energy patterns.

Remember too that the interpretation is a vital part of any type of divinatory reading. If all you do is tell someone what you see and then give no interpretation of that symbolism, all you are doing is observing, not giving a reading!

Tarot cards have been around for thousands of years, but were most recently revived in the early nineteenth century by the appearance of the Rider-Waite deck.

It was the only deck available for years, but the recent resurgence of interest in the occult from the 1960s to today has spurred many artists and occultists to create new and unusual decks. There are seventy-eight cards in the average deck, twenty-two of the major arcana and fifty-six of the minor. Readings done by those with extensive knowledge of, or deep intuition into, the tarot can be very powerful and illuminating.

The *runes*, according to Norse mythology, were brought to mankind by the All-Father God Odin, after he hung by one foot, upside down from the Yggdrasil (the Tree of Life) for nine days and nights. A rune is an *energy pattern*; the runestaves (the strokes of the runic pattern) we draw are both an evocation and a symbol of that energy pattern. There is some speculation, though little actual evidence, of a practice of reading runestaves from slender sticks that, when tossed onto the ground, revealed the pattern of significant runes. Most commonly, people use runestones: small pieces of various materials with the runic symbols already drawn on them. These can be pulled from a bag and read in a pattern, or the entire bag can be tossed on the ground and read (this is the most extensive type of reading). Runes can be drawn or painted on many things, for many reasons. Besides divination, runes can be used for spells (often using bind runes), the actual writing of secret or sacred information, and evocations or invocations of energy patterns (which are actually spells of another flavor entirely).

The *I Ching* (ee-**cheeng** or ee-**jing**) is a method of reading markers such as yarrow stalks (traditional), I-Ching coins or pennies. The markers are cast and noted, creating a series of six lines called a hexagram, and then the results are read according to the Chinese *Book of Changes* (the I Ching itself).

Animal or medicine cards teach us much about our power animals, or totem spirits, and the medicine they offer as we travel through the sacred journey that is life. These valuable cards can help us understand animals who watch over us for a short period or a lifetime.

Phoenix cards speak to our interest in and possible revelation of past lives or past-life energies. These cards are chosen face up, according to which pictures move you the most, and then the past life energies are read, both in the card's description and its meaning.

Palmistry is the study of the lines on the palm as well as other aspects of the hand, and is both an excellent and highly personalized form of studying our future and our past. We can see a lot in our heart line, our head line, our life line, and our love line. *Hand reading,* according to some folks, as opposed to "just" reading the palm, is the study of the whole hand, from the shape of the hand itself, to the shape of the nails, the texture of the skin, the lines and the mounts. It is quite comprehensive, and many hand readers denounce palmistry as being incomplete.

I am not sure I would call this art *only* a divination method, as it, like astrology, is so much more: It is a method of deeper self-knowledge, of exploring one's Path, of one's fate, and one's karma. It all shows up in the hand, or in the natal chart.

Scrying is any method of reading signs, symbols, or outright scenes in everything from the common yet mystical crystal ball to the more economical tea leaves or bowl of water. A common Witches' tool for scrying is a cauldron of any size, filled with water, with a silver coin (such as a dime) resting on the bottom. The coin gives the reader a focal point, and symbolizes the moon. Really, anything one can lose themselves in, can become unfocused and dreamy and slip into trance, will work for scrying.

Scrying can be pretty powerful, but I submit that it takes a little patience for some of us to get to the point of seeing things fairly readily. It also takes a great deal of self-honesty, as do all divination methods.

The *pendulum* is really good for a yes or no answer, but can also have its foggy areas (there is a swing for "maybe" or "no answer" also). It seems the gods like to have their options. What is done, usually, is that the querent braces the hand holding the pendulum on a table or a knee, asks first what will indicate a "yes," a "no," and a "maybe" type of answer, and then proceeds with the questions at hand. Sometimes the answers are clearer, but without the details and insights the other systems offer.

The *ogham,* like the runes, is an ancient method of writing (Celtic), and the symbols can also be used for divination, meditation, and spellwork. According to Bill Whitcomb, the oghams were not so much alphabets as we think of them, but rather analogs of alphabets. These "tree alphabets" were passed along by oral tradition only, until the "decline" of Druidism.[93]

As stated, this is but a partial list. There are many, many methods of divination, and I believe all divination should be done both with seriousness and with a light heart. Again, nothing is set in stone. It can be confusing at times, to say the least. It has been said that it is best to have one's cards, runes, or palm read by another, rather

---

93. Bill Whitcomb, *The Magician's Companion* (Llewellyn, 2004), 189.

than trying to do it for oneself. I agree, although practicality dictates the opposite in many cases. It is easy to delude ourselves, to pretend not to see what is truly there, so total honesty is *essential* in your interpretations, whether for yourself or someone else. I recommend writing down readings as much as possible, just as I recommend writing down spells and rituals, so that we can look back later for troubleshooting purposes. It's also a good way to check ourselves on our techniques as well as our honesty.

Most Wiccans have one or two methods that resonate with them, and use primarily those methods for a few to several years, or even longer, before becoming interested in other techniques. Again, it depends on what sings to the individual, but for the student, I recommend trying several before settling on any one method. I recommend this because it is good to have a back-up in case the reading is unclear. One can then use another method, see if the answers from both systems resonate with each other, thereby helping the seeker get more clarity.

Remember that proficiency is important when you start doing readings for people—you don't want to be looking stuff up constantly, especially if you're charging folks. I recommend working with a few methods, doing readings for yourself (watch that honesty!), graduating to your close friends and family first. Then, as you get better and better, start doing readings for more "outer circle" folks, all the while asking for honest, prompt feedback to help you learn. Then, when you feel comfortable, you could go ahead and do "public" readings for a fee, if you choose. One way to measure when you're ready to do readings for a fee is when you start to rely more and more on what you intuit, or pull psychically from the symbols before you, and rely less and less on books for your answers. Ellen Cannon Reed, in *The Witches' Tarot*,[94] in discussing the importance of both study and practice, says it best: "And the minute you look at a card and it begins to tell you something that differs from the book, throw out the book." This then, would be the point at which one becomes an *intuitive* or *psychic reader* in my opinion, someone who uses the various divinatory tools as a means to an end, and is no longer simply a "reader of" the runes, the cards, etc. But we're a long way from that stage here. Please remember, too, that true proficiency, unless you have a natural intuition for divination that borders on the psychic, will take years to achieve, so don't be too hard on yourself. Just keep practicing, and your skill and intuition will grow in their own time.

---

94. Ellen Cannon Reed, *The Witches' Tarot: The Witches' Qabala Book 2* (Llewellyn, 1993), 146.

INITIATE PATHWORKINGS

Go for a holiday walk. Feel the energy of the earth winding down, and the veil thinning out. If possible, walk near dusk on Samhain. Open yourself to your ancestors and your beloved dead. See if you can hear or see any messages they may have for you.

Try a different type of divination than one (or ones) you've done before, or try stretching yourself with the techniques you already use. Still using the book for your tarot interpretations? Try doing a reading without it (you can look it up later, if you're nervous). Never tried scrying? Might be a good idea to try—you never know what's going to sing to you.

Open to the energies of the Mystery and the darkness in meditation. Try to come to the heart of matters that disturb you or keep you from your true purpose. Ask the help of your darker matron goddesses and patron gods.

Create a sacred mask for yourself, tuning in to the energies of what makes you, you. Render those energies on the mask in paint or some other medium; whatever's comfortable and fulfilling for you.

Ponder what is coming to be in your life and what is fading away, as well as that which abides. What would you change, if you could? How would you change it? Take some time and consider actually making such changes.

HOMEWORK

Write a Samhain ritual, from grounding and centering to opening the circle. Be sure to include altar decorations, cakes and wine choices, and what you'll serve for the feast afterward, if applicable.

Read **The Inner Guide Meditation** by Edwin Steinbrecher, and *chapter 10 "Samhain, 31st October" in* **A Witches' Bible** by the Farrars.

Lightworking: Hecate's tapestry

Take some time this month and ponder the tapestry of your life. Plan spellwork, either in conjunction with your moon work or as a separate ritual, and then use the talents and skills you've learned thus far on your Path, dear Initiate, to create a weaving of sorts, either actual or astral, symbolizing all that you have woven into your life, including those threads that are now spent and need to be re-woven, finished, or eliminated. Be blessed.

For your grimoire

Begin (or continue) a table of correspondence for *Darkside issues*, as well as a table for some of the *darker gods and goddesses* you have worked with (or wish to work with).

29: The November Lesson

The Goddess does not rule the world; She is the world.
—Starhawk

THE GODDESS—THE STORY

Late in the evening, on a dark moon in the heart of the Dark Time, you cast your circle, breathing deeply of the cool night air. Everything is calm and still in your inner landscape, even the city noises seem to have diminished, as you ground and center. Your focus and intention are utterly clear: you wish to know the Divine Feminine on a deeper level. You call the quarters, call the God, and even before you call her to you, you know she is here: your most cherished matron goddess, the Lady, the One.

You let the dark energy of the night fill you, let your questions swirl around your consciousness, knowing that the most important issues will always surface first in your meditation. You allow yourself to relax into the moment, letting the energies of the night, the Mystery, and your beloved goddess to come as they will.

*Immediately you see pictures of situations that have served to complicate your life. Just as immediately, you understand on a deep level that it was **you** who created those situations. How not to? It's your life, after all. You start to berate yourself for some of your more glaring mistakes when suddenly you feel a*

THE NOVEMBER LESSON CORRESPONDENCES

Focus: the Goddess

Energy keywords: receiving; beckoning; female energy

Tool: scythe or crescent blade

Pathwork focus: the Spiritual Counselor's Path

Herbs and flowers: roses; lilies; wild roses

Incense: myrrh; ebony nights; individual goddess incenses

Stones and metals: jet; silver; pearls (both black and white); lapis

Overarching energies: divine gleaning

Radiant energies: personal gleaning

Sun enters: Sagittarius

soft hand on your shoulder. In your mind's eye, you see your goddess lift your chin so you have to look into her eyes. At first you simply notice how beautiful her eyes are, but then, you see the same scenes you were just ripping yourself over, but in her eyes, you can see the underlying patterns. "Ooohhh…" you sigh, as understanding and clarity come. You see the situations so differently now; some of them were completely out of your control, and you see that no matter what you could have done in those situations, it wouldn't have made a difference, as those energies were karmic, predetermined. You see other patterns, causal energies that weren't your doing, either, as they came about as a result of life lessons others needed to learn. Finally, you see the patterns you had a conscious choice in, which, either by accident or design, you most certainly are responsible for creating.

"But a mistake is not a sentence," she says in your ear when you start berating yourself again. You look deeper, with more compassion and clarity, and understand now that you did the best you could in most of those situations, and in the ones where you didn't, you finally allow yourself forgiveness.

With that very act, you realize that this quality of forgiveness you have long admired and respected in your matron goddess is a quality you also possess. "Forgiving ourselves is simple, but never easy," she says, and you open yourself even further to the Mysteries you so crave. At once, you see yourself in situations where you acted in ways that made you proud and satisfied with yourself, and then, one by one, your goddess shows you that she would have handled those energy patterns in much the same way. You realize, more and more, how very much like her you really are, and you breathe deeply of the energy of that simple truth. The lines between you and your beloved goddess blur, become wide bands of connection, and you no longer know where you leave off and she begins.

"We are one," she whispers in your ear, "the same Mystery, the same love, the same energy. That which you most admire and respect in Me is who you already are, deep within." Even as she says these words, you can feel the truth of them, and this truth pervades your entire being.

*"We are one," you repeat, and you know it's true. You bask in the moment, and feel yourself filling with love and strength and power. Later, as she leaves your space, you can feel those aspects of her that are most like you solidify and settle into your being. "We are one," you say again as you open your circle, knowing that she has, indeed, been with you from the beginning, just as she tells us in The Charge. With this knowledge, you also realize she will **always** be with you, for you are more like her than you ever imagined you could be, and you will spend a lifetime both holding and ever striving for this aspiration. A humble journey, yes, but one filled with honor and pride. You say it again, to seal the spell and fix it in your mind before going about your day: "We are one." Holding that energy of power and purpose, you move forward into your day, newly confident, and filled with love.*

LOVE—THE ENERGY OF THE GODDESS

As our spirit's intuitive and receptive side, Goddess energy is the dark and mysterious force that helps us to truly listen, to receive, and to give love—first to ourselves, and then to others. Just like the moon's glow between the shadows at night, Goddess energy finds the harmony between beings and things, showing us our sameness, which enables us to relate and feel compassion. In our dreams and meditations, she appears as the stern and protective yet kind and compassionate figures of grandmother and matron, as well as the innocent maiden and sexually self-actualized whole woman.

"You cannot get to Her but through Me," the God says, and taken in the light of our natural energy patterns, this is profoundly true. For if we just sit on our butts waiting for her to come around, it's not likely to happen. To come to the Goddess, for all of us on this Sacred Road, requires action, and action is defined and labeled on this Path as male energy. It's also true that we cannot get to the God but through the Goddess, for to be able to understand his truth, we must first be receptive to that truth, and, again, receptivity is defined and labeled female. Balance. The Lord and the Lady watch over each other just as surely as they watch over us.

We in our culture put the label "female" energy on the energies of receiving: indrawing, pulling, enfolding, encircling, listening, and receptivity. We also know that men are just as capable of using these energies; it's just that these energy patterns, whether through nature or nurture, are more prominent in women and, of course, the Goddess. As we walk our spiritual paths, and especially as we become stronger and more powerful as Witches, it is our responsibility to make sure we aren't inadvertently using these energies to manipulate others.

Imagine a scene at a party. A woman and a man see each other for the first time from across a crowded room, and a spark of attraction occurs. What will the man most likely do? He'll at some point head toward the woman, but at the very least he'll try to make (or maintain) eye contact. Without even realizing it perhaps, he is sending his intention toward her; he projects. What does the woman do? She might smile, perhaps become shy and look away, then look back up to see if he's still watching her. She then thinks about how much she would like for him to come talk to her, so she opens herself up by smiling and presenting a receptive and receiving energy; she beckons.

For a man who is not interested, if the woman is very focused on her beckoning, he could possibly feel that energy as though it was his own. For a man on this magical Path, it's important not only to learn to shield against inadvertently projecting his own energy out, but also to become aware of and shield against allowing any unwanted energy to pull him in.

The energy pattern of receiving can work very much to a woman's benefit, but it can also work to her detriment. Imagine a woman who is so tuned in to her receptive energy, with little to no awareness or ability to use her projecting/active energy. She'd likely not get a lot done, and probably expect the world to come to her (because, if she has strong beckoning powers, it often does), rather than going out and making a way for herself. Other ways this can manifest negatively is with the person who expects her loved ones to automatically know what she wants and to give that to her.

Attitudes of entitlement are often just extreme manifestations of this type of energy pattern. And again, this energy pattern is not at all limited to females; but with our culture's domestication, this naturally occurring receiving energy just manifests more often in women.

TOOL—THE CRESCENT KNIFE

The *crescent knife,* also sometimes called the *boline,*[95] is a rare find in magical communities today. Reminiscent of the Druids' golden crescent, reputed to be the blades with which they cut their sacred mistletoe from the mighty oak trees,[96] that they let fall only onto cloths of pure white linen, the crescent knife is a rare find indeed. If you choose to purchase one of these blades, you will find they are wonderful tools for harvesting herbs and other sacred garden items, such as flowers for the altar, fruits and vegetables for Sabbat feasts, etc. Some crescent knife blades currently on the market are of stainless steel, some are copper, and some are brass, reflecting the color of the ancient golden blades.

PATHWORK FOCUS: THE CALLING TO SPIRITUAL COUNSELING

Spiritual (or pastoral) counseling is a wonderful calling—good counselors are sorely needed in our community, as everyone needs someone to help them sort things out from time to time. In a healthy coven, this role is often filled by the High Priestess or High Priest, but what of the lone Witch in need of help? For the solitary traveler, times of despair can be especially lonely and uncertain. We turn to psychologists, psychiatrists, and other types of counselors, and if we're lucky they will accept our beliefs, but it is only rarely that they even partially understand, much less share them. If the issue we're trying to heal is spiritual in nature, perhaps touching on a past life, we can feel rather lost when the help they offer is not realistic to the devoted Witch.

The Wiccan spiritual counselor should be someone who has a great deal of compassion, nurturing, and strength. He should have a good listening ear—to hear the

---

95. The white-handled knife is also sometimes called a "boline" or "bolline," which can be confusing.

96. Robert Graves, *The White Goddess* (Noonday Press, 1948), 230 and 284.

words that *aren't* being said, as well as the ones that are. He should be warm, non-judgmental, and well read in both the helping fields and the earth-based paths. He should be unafraid to tell his clients the truth—but he should absolutely be able to do so with gentleness and honor. In essence, he should be very connected with the Goddess within, and hold those qualities close to his heart.

In addition, he should know the local laws regarding counseling, and have his patients sign waivers if need be, stating that he is acting in the capacity of spiritual counselor, and not a mental health professional with a degree, unless he also holds such a degree. Above all, he should never advertise himself as something he is not.

Personal responsibility then, is even more important here, and a good spiritual counselor will never, ever leave his clients hanging. If there are problems in a person's karma, such as baggage from a past life, then client and counselor should ideally work together through journeying, ritual, and/or practical (mundane) avenues to facilitate healing. This can take several to many sessions, but this process is imperative to the quality of the client's life. Just discovering the problem is not enough. Follow-through is core and key to healing of any kind, and the responsible thing to do is to finish what is started before sending the client on her way. If the pastoral counselor's Path sings to you, that is wonderful! You are sorely needed in your community! Now is the perfect time to begin exploring and reading along these avenues.

INITIATE PATHWORKINGS

Get outside! Take a long walk at sunset and notice the subtle changes in energy as we go from the God's time to the Goddess's time. Breathe deeply of the night air and notice the activity around you slowing down, from the most obvious levels of traffic and human hustle-bustle to the sounds of birds and insects. Notice which sounds increase and which ones decrease. Note the feel of the energy flow.

Plan a special goddess dinner for yourself. What foods are "goddess" foods? Depending on the energies of your matron goddess, you could be preparing and eating seafood, salad, or something deeply earthy like a hearty stew. Ponder what would be a good goddess dinner, and then make that! And enjoy! Don't forget to leave her an offering.

Take some time to explore and play with the Goddess energy inside of you. If your matron goddess is a rough-and-tumble sort, you could be practicing archery, running, riding horses, or fencing. If she's a more romantic type, you could find yourself playing with makeup and clothes, either on yourself or a friend, or exploring your sexuality in ways you only dreamed of, either alone or with one or more partners.

Have a conversation about different goddesses with a friend. See how much you can remember about archetypes and specific goddesses from various cultures. Push yourself to find the information locked inside your brain, heart, and spirit. Listen to your friend's opinions, too, and apply whatever bits of wisdom you learn into your life. Never stop learning!

Spend a day in silence. Open yourself to your matron goddess(es) of the depths of your love, and ask her to help you listen. Do a deep meditation during the day sometime, and take a long walk as well. Listen to the sounds, and then listen to the spaces "between" the sounds. Honor and respect your receptive, enfolding "female" side; your intuitions and creativity, your nurturing and compassion, your "motherly self" who supports and understands.

Remember that spending this special silent time does not mean using sign language, writing notes on paper, or making other attempts to make yourself "heard." This is about *not needing* to be heard, but simply (and actively) listening and being receptive.

Sing goddess songs. Take some time to learn some new ones, as well as singing the older ones you know. Sing your heart out for her.

HOMEWORK

Write a goddess devotional/adoration for a specific goddess or a favorite archetype.

Read (or continue reading) **The Inner Guide Meditation** by Edwin Steinbrecher, and *chapters 7, 9, and 10 of Part II of* A Witches' Bible by the Farrars.

Lightworking: honoring our female side

Take some time this month and ponder your own female side (as we on this Path think of female energies). Plan spellwork, either in conjunction with your moon work or as a separate ritual, and then use the talents and skills you've learned thus far on your Path, dear Initiate, to honor those energies. Allow yourself to feel the energies of receptivity, beckoning, and the emotions to inspire you to a greater vision and version of yourself.

For your grimoire

Begin (or continue) a table of correspondence for goddess energies. Include several archetypes, exploring at least one you haven't worked with before.

PART
FOUR

FLOODING THE VESSEL:
ADEPT INITIATION

30: Benevolence: The Call to Service

*Being a priestess isn't something you **do**; it's something you **are**.*
—Artemis (as spoken to Thuri in meditation)

In this book, we've covered the emotions around our relationship with ourselves in the first triplet of moon chapters (Core/Ground, Pride, Power); our relationships with other incarnate beings in the second triplet of moons (Compassion, Connection, Understanding); our relationships with our gods and guardians through the third triplet of moons (Devotion, Purpose, The Path), and our relationships with the magical/Pagan/Witchy community as a whole through the Solar Wheel section in general. The last triplet of moons covered spiritual Pathwork (Expansion, Fruition, Overcoming) in particular, bringing us to a place of peace, fullness, balance, and hopefully a readiness to serve completed in the last moon chapter, "Wholeness."

Throughout the Solar Wheel chapters we've covered many different callings: spiritual gifts we may feel we've been given that we can then turn around and use to glorify our gods through service work, though my list for this book is not finished yet. There is one more Pathwork focus to present—teaching. I've left being a Craft teacher until the last, as I feel it's not only the most complicated calling to explore, but also because it contains within it a little bit of everything presented, plus a whole lot more. Yet even when this last calling is fully explored, please understand that this list of possible spiritual callings is by no means "complete"—not by any stretch of the imagination! Indeed, we can serve our gods in any way we and our gods wish for us to.

BENEVOLENCE: THE ENERGY OF SERVICE

Benevolence: (1) Desire for the well-being or comfort of others; love for mankind; charitableness. (2) Any act of kindness or well-doing; charity; humanity.[97]

In searching for a title for this chapter, I was a bit pressed to come up with something that accurately described the feelings we have that compel us to the service of our gods. For the traveler who wishes to continue this journey—which you clearly do, dear Initiate, or you wouldn't be considering the approaching Adept initiation—there is a strong pull to serve, to act as that conduit, that channel for your gods and goddesses, to be that essential aide to help new seekers to find their way. Chances are you're feeling a strong desire to uplift or facilitate the betterment of others; you feel a great love, compassion, empathy for other human beings—or at least for other Pagans, an urge toward charitableness; kindness that compels you to serve—*benevolence*! As we've explored, that calling can manifest in many ways. That being said, I wish to welcome you to this unit, to the Path of Service that is most certainly singing to you, and to congratulate you on having come this far.

One's spiritual calling is that still, small voice that rings ever more loudly and truly as time goes on, and we're never quite right unless and until we find a way to answer that call. In *The Soul's Code: In Search of Character and Calling*,[98] James Hillman speaks at length about this search. He speaks of fate, destiny, what Plato called our "daimon"; an image or pattern; a soul-companion who travels with us, compelling us to our destinies. He calls this daimon or patterned image our *acorn,* and he speaks from the beginning about this calling we all have, something that compels us to follow a certain path: "You may remember this 'something' as a signal moment in childhood," he states, "when an urge out of nowhere, a fascination, a peculiar turn

---

97. *Funk & Wagnalls Standard Dictionary* (J. G. Ferguson Publishing, 1978), 130.

98. James Hillman, *The Soul's Code: In Search of Character and Calling* (Random House, 1996).

of events struck like an annunciation: This is what I must do, this is what I've got to have. This is who I am."

This is who I am. Yes, this is what his book, and the Pathwork Focus segments of this book, are all about. I've spoken of my early years on this Path many times; how I passionately pursued learning all I could about Greek mythology after reading that first blue-cloth-covered book, looking out my window to the moon or going across the street to the empty field to do devotionals to Artemis. I can still vividly remember that pivotal moment Hillman so eloquently points out; the moment my *acorn* first appeared. I was only nine years old and had just learned what the word *myth* meant: Falsehoods. Lies. I was stomping across my front yard, holding tightly to that precious blue book, shaking it and furiously (and loudly) proclaiming to no one in particular, "How can they say that this is a *lie*? How can anyone possibly *know*?" For I knew the stories and legends of the ancient Greek gods were true! Tears stung my eyes; my heart was racing! I went immediately to her, my beloved Artemis, and spoke of my devotion to her, how I'd always, *always*, believe, no matter what anyone said, and moreover, I promised her my *loyalty*! And somehow, in that moment, *I just knew* I'd grow up to spread the word about the Old Gods. Hillman's work hit me so profoundly because I could see so clearly the very day I found my own *acorn*. You may remember a pivotal moment like this one, too. Whether you do or don't, however, I highly recommend his work, for, as he says, "You are born with a character; it is given; a gift, as the old stories say, from the guardians upon your birth."

WHAT IT MEANS TO BE AN ADEPT

In most magical traditions, being an Adept means you're really, really good at what you do, and you're comfortable *owning that truth*. To know that you are skilled and powerful is not ego, but rather a healthy balance of honor and humility. Neither self-effacing nor false pride have a place on your Path, dear Initiate, for you have bravely battled your shadows, and know that they will ever pursue you, yet you are confident you can keep them at bay, so long as you remain mindful. You have honed your skills and your power, and have found peace in trusting your intuition and your chosen deities. You've opened up to your spiritual calling, and have perhaps even identified your *acorn*. You are comfortable with writing and presenting rituals, whether solitary or for others, and your working tools by now are no longer new and shiny. You likely refrain from anger when you hear ignorant people spewing hatred about Witches (*and* Wiccans, which, sadly, some who identify as Witches actually do), but rather you calmly express what needs to be expressed, choosing your battles carefully while remaining true to who you are. You remember and try to heed the great words of that guy Anonymous: "Discretion is being able to raise your eyebrow instead of your voice."

Most of all, you feel that bright call to service, singing to you every step of the way. This then, is exactly how you know you are ready to traverse the Adept Gate. How to know if you're prepared is another beast entirely.

HOW TO KNOW IF YOU ARE PREPARED

Circle duties by now should be second nature. You will have written (and possibly presented) a complete set of Sabbats (the lesser ones as a Dedicant, the greater ones as an Initiate); thirteen Esbats; and any spellwork needed. You have acted in a leadership capacity in rituals at least a couple of times, and you are confident in your awareness of when to release the cone of power. You have written at least one Rite of Passage (ROP)—your initiation—and by the time you're finished with this course, you will have written your Adept initiation, totaling at least two ROPs. In light of this, you are more than qualified to lead a coven or working group, should you choose to do so.

Divination skills are improving; you should be really good at one method, with explorations into another becoming much better. You should be confident doing divinatory readings for others in at least one method.

Dreamwork should be clearer now, and you should have a good working table of symbols, able to interpret most of your dreams, and feel ready to help others to understand theirs.

Energy work should be good to proficient in the areas of chakra spinning, sensing the cone of power, and evoking, aspecting, and invoking elements. You should be becoming more skilled in aspecting your closest matron goddess or patron god, and feel ready to try invoking her/him.

Psychic skills/intuition should be relied upon more now, as well as the confidence that goes with them. You should be *meditating* regularly, and learning more about yourself and your gods and goddesses through this.

You have had your *natal chart* done, or have done it yourself, and understand the basics of its interpretation.

Shadow work is ongoing, and you understand that it always will be, in order to keep yourself healthy and vibrant.

Knowledge of your Craft is well rounded, and you know where to look up information when you don't know something. You have accepted that no Witchy teacher or author has all the answers, and when new information is presented that uproots previous beliefs, you have the ability to assimilate that information and move forward with it.

Your reading list is complete for this course. If some of the books were unavailable, you found an acceptable substitute, with the counsel of your in-real-life teacher, matron goddess, or patron god.

Daily worship, daily energy work, and living as a Witch is, of course, a big part of *who you are.*

You know what it is to have a Sacred Charge (see page 109 in chapter 8, "Compassion") and are fully prepared to serve such a person should your gods put him or her in your Path. You understand that the list given is a guideline that you and your personal deities may change completely to reflect your truth, your Path, and the Path of your future charges.

Your Pathwork focus options should be narrowed to no more than two. Remember that these can be changed later—the point here is that there is a direction; some idea of where your spiritual gifts lie. Some beginning study in these areas is a bonus, but not required. The calling to serve, however, the *benevolence* required must be in your heart and on your mind; there must be an attitude of helpfulness befitting clergy, a willingness to help when needed, and enthusiasm for such service.

PATHWORK FOCUS:
THE CALLING TO THE WITCHCRAFT TEACHER'S PATH

I present this most complicated and complex Pathwork focus for last, as teaching Witchcraft encompasses so many facets of the other callings presented. Like the guardian, the teacher has someone else's best interests to look out for. Like the dreamweaver and the intuitive/psychic reader, she must be able to help others interpret symbols and signs, in order to best serve and help them. Like the pastoral counselor, the healer, and the herbalist, she will be called upon to help people find the best ways to heal themselves. Like the sacred clothier, she will be required to know the ins and outs of creating ritual garb, that she may help her students find sacred garments that are truly magical, personal, and comfortable. Like the stone whisperer and the craftsperson, she will be required to know something of stones and ritual adornments in order to help her students make the best choices for themselves. That is, if they'll listen to her!

I have often said that I love my students, and this is most assuredly true. I have also been fortunate enough to have never had a single student who didn't teach me *something*. However, the ratio of *serious* students to those who are just playing at being Witches is relatively small, and this is a "hazard of the job" most Witchcraft teachers have to deal with. So no, teaching is not always bliss. Sometimes, the student comes to class with the attitude that they know it all already and wish to start "at the top" so to speak, or thinks that because they've read one book by one author, so they're now qualified to be called "Witch," or worse, call themselves "natural" Witches, without knowing even the basics of energy work, ethics, or their own religion, for that matter. These are usually the students who become furious to the point of quitting classes and refusing to communicate with the teacher because he won't take them through initiation because *they are not ready*.

Prior to initiating any student, I ask myself many questions about his readiness, his attitude, his ethics, and his personal responsibility. I question him about his daily practice, and I test him and watch him more than he knows, both in mundane life as well as the magic circle. Charm takes a person only so far, as does the study, however extensive, of personal Pathwork. A healer without much Witchy training is still only a healer with *some* Witchy training. Likewise for an herbalist, a dreamweaver, etc. Our spiritual callings are how we will eventually serve our gods and our community, yes, but these are *not* what makes us Adepts. So to be ready for this Gate means one is trained and educated *as an Adept*, and that is the one and only thing that traversing that Gate is about in damn near any coven or tradition out there. The Witchcraft Teacher must know this at once, because, for any priest/ess to take a candidate through any ROP is to take them through a life-changing and spiritually charged Gate, which means *we are vouching for that person* in the eyes of our gods, our guardians, and all the spirit world. This naturally assumes a great deal of responsibility for both that candidate's education and his future practices. Whether or not he knows his stuff, the teacher will be held accountable, again, to all the spirit realms mentioned above, as well as the entire magical community. So teaching Witchcraft is a serious responsibility, and the further along the Path the student is, the more seriously the teaching (and learning!) must be taken.

To be a Witchcraft teacher requires tremendous patience, diplomacy, and emotional and spiritual strength, for never will your inner worth be more tested and/or your boundaries pushed harder! Being a spiritual teacher is one of the most rewarding, thankless, honorable, frustrating, exhilarating, exhausting, purely joyful, and devastatingly heartbreaking things a person can do on this Path. Again, I truly do love my students, even the less-than-stellar ones, and I wouldn't trade my teaching work for anything in the world, for to me, there simply is no greater reward. As stated above, being a spiritual teacher is my *acorn*.

If you are called to be a Witchcraft teacher, that's great! Our community needs more teachers who love what they do. My suggestion in the Basics chapter about symbolizing the calling of Witchcraft teacher by putting a rainbow of some sort (or simply rainbow colors) on your ritual garb is to remind you that this calling does indeed include a little bit of everything, and that there's always color and beauty after a storm. And speaking of storms ...

A caveat: your students are not your friends!

I speak from decades of personal experience when I tell you this, dear Initiate, so I can tell you that trying to have a personal relationship with a student *never* works out, and frequently ends in heartbreak (yours, not theirs; they're typically oblivious to your pain). James Hillman warns against this as well: "The failure to distinguish sufficiently between the rather ruthless limits of mentoring and the rather broadly mundane responsibilities of parenting—as when parents try to be guiding instructors, and mentors make a family of their following—leads to bitter breakups between apprentices and mentors."[99] He goes on to say that the "younger person's" (in our case the student's) desire to be cared for (by the mentor) in a more personal way is the main reason these relationships fail. I would have to say that's true on both sides. The reasons to avoid such personal relationships with your students are many, including:

One: First and foremost—they aren't looking for friends! They're looking for Witchy instruction! Simple enough, right? Sometimes, however, we teachers see such great

---

99. James Hillman, *The Soul's Code: In Search of Character and Calling* (Random House, 1996), 164.

potential for a real connection with a student that it's hard not to have that desire for friendship. It's difficult enough to be that "ruthless" mentor Hillman points out, which we *must* be, in order to train a Witch properly so that he doesn't hurt himself or others. In addition, his complete training is of utmost importance when we are vouching for him in the spiritual planes. If this person is also your friend, it can be very difficult to maintain the proper detachment required to keep him (and yourself, as teacher) on track. And there is nothing, *no thing* more important than giving him the spiritual growth and training he requested in the first place. It is your sacred duty, and *it is your job!*

Two: This isn't about you! As the Witchcraft teacher, you are a *mentor*. It is your job to make sure your student is lifted up, sure of herself, secure and happy in her spiritual journeying; keeping her feet on the Path. Especially as our teaching here is of a spiritual nature, which cuts to the very core of our existence, your students are relying on you to be a calm, rational presence—a person they can look up to, and sometimes that means they will have you on a pedestal. As their training progresses, it will become your job to jump down off of that pedestal as often as possible, to lift them up enough to see you as their equal and eventually become strong enough *to go on without you*. But that's a "someday" thing that they simply won't allow you to do for a while, so try not to get a nosebleed way up there, and remember, always, that these dear people are your *Sacred Charges*; they are in your care, and your spiritual responsibility is to watch over them, not to have expectations of any kind.

Three: Of lesser importance, they will treat you like an acquaintance but you must treat them like a friend. That is to say, they will *not* be there for you! And that's not their fault. It's not their job. This can result in resentful and bitter feelings on your part, which you *cannot* express to them, as your job is, as stated, *to keep their feet on the Path*. To be *as a friend* to them, whereas they will most often treat you like *an acquaintance*, which means you might sometimes be overlooked, ignored, and made invisible. But that is, so to speak, one of the hazards of the job, and you must know this going in; a good teacher helps her student form his own opinions, form his own ideas, and forge his own way by *getting out of his way*, and illustrating her point through a "show me," not a "tell me," construct. So he breaks your heart; oh well! Lest you think that's even *slightly* important, see reason number one.

The thing is, a Craft teacher has to practice a certain level of detachment in order to best serve his students. The detachment of mentorship is much more appropriate for a spiritual teacher and his student than the attendant attachment involved in a healthy, fulfilling, and mutually beneficial friendship. Truthfully, even former students are often not good candidates for those mutual friendships, as the dependency on "teacher" to continue being the spiritual counselor, the intuitive, the helpmate, and guide never really ever goes away, which means the "teacher-friend" *still* needs to remain in that detached, mentor capacity in order to best serve the "former-student-friend," because it's *still* his sacred duty—his *job*.

But being your friend is not, nor has it ever been, *their* job. And that's exactly as it should be. This was illustrated to me quite clearly when I met recently with a former student I'd been very fond of. Her life wasn't going all that well; she had many struggles, so she contacted me with a need to "unload." I hadn't heard from her in over six months (she'd dropped out of class without a word and didn't respond to any of my or her former classmates' attempts at contact), and I'd been concerned about her—turns out with good reason. Still, I was excited about meeting with her, and, ever hopeful, I deluded myself into thinking, "Perhaps now, a friendship might work." After a very long conversation that included the revelation of many eye-popping truths about herself and her life, I realized another, vitally important truth, for *myself*: that a mutual and healthy friendship with her was *not* going to happen, as it was clear that she needed me as a mentor far more than I needed her as a friend. And at the end of the day, dear Initiate, when our sacred duties (and Sacred Charges) call, well, that's where we must go. The discovery of this truth was bittersweet, however; just as I was getting myself into a blue funk over my misperceived "loss," my beloved Lady Artemis confirmed my realization for me in a way that snapped me to attention immediately and humbled me greatly: as the conversation was drawing to a close, the young woman held out her hand to me, and said, "Here. I was told to give you this."

Into my open hand, she dropped a beautiful, perfect, and shiny new acorn.

HOMEWORK

Write your own list of guidelines or rules regarding having a Sacred Charge. What do you feel is important in this area? You may wish to check mine, and then make additions and subtractions you feel are appropriate.

Write an essay on service. What does it mean to you to serve your personal patron god(s) and matron goddess(es)? Be sure to include both the challenges and the joys of this connection.

Spend a day in contemplation. Similarly to the day of silence you spent in the November chapter, try spending an entire day, from rising to sleeping, in a space of quiet and openness—both focusing on the natural sounds around you, and in hearing your own inner voice. Invoke your central stillness. Breathe in the silence of solitude. Let those you live and interact with know what to expect ahead of time, so you won't have to try to field questions during this time.

Take your own space and time on this day, and allow yourself to contemplate the energies around you, to hear the sounds between the sounds, as well as the silences, and the patterns they form. In addition, allow yourself to contemplate the step you're about to take. What will life be like for you once you traverse the Adept Gate? How will it be different for those you love and share your life with?

Make your first attempt at invocation (*if you feel ready!*), or plan to do so as your *ordeal* for your Adept initiation, or for the rite itself.

Begin your final preparations for your Adept initiation rite. It's decision time! Now is the time to choose what ritual garb (if any) you will wear for your Adept initiation, as well as whether you will gift yourself with any new adornments, such as a new power ring, a special necklace, or even a circlet. In traditional systems, the Adept level (the traditional second degree) is only allowed to wear a plain band. You may or may not wish to follow this practice. Another idea is to add to your ritual garb or Sacred Cord some sort of symbol expressing your spiritual calling: a special piece of jewelry, a section of thread wrapped around your cord near the end, or a piece of ribbon or other decoration fastened to your garb in some special way. If you don't already have a Sacred Cord, you may wish to weave one (see *Dedicant* for instructions[100]), and a few of you may also wish to unweave and reweave your cord with the colors of the Adept, which are the colors of earth (green, brown, white, or black) to symbolize this Gate, either before or after your ritual. Those of you who wish simply to add an earth color to your cord without reweaving it will have to be a little creative in your work. It can be greatly satisfying to unweave and reweave it, however, as you are beginning a new part of your spiritual Path.

---

100. Thuri Calafia, *Dedicant: A Witch's Circle of Fire* (Llewellyn, 2008), 289.

Finally, as you read the next chapter and finish up any reading from your list, you'll probably want to *begin making notes* of any special actions, decorations, guests, or foods you would like present for your ritual and celebration.

31: The Wisdom of Silence

The Adept must not merely tread the Path, he must be the Path.
—Dion Fortune

CIRCLE OF EARTH—THE ADEPT STORY

You wipe the sweat from your brow as you crest the final rise before you and look down into a deep, vast bowl. The valley below you is completely surrounded by mountains, just as you'd seen in your vision. Squinting into the late afternoon sun, you look across the bowl to the mountain you believe houses the cave you need to get to—the cave that holds the Rainbow Pathway. Yes, there is a shadowed area there, near the summit, you muse . . . and it . . . might be a cave. You sigh contentedly. It's been a long journey, a journey of joy and heartache, of work and passion and illuminated truths, but mostly, it's been a journey of love. For love brought you here: your love of your gods and guardians, love of self, of your community, but mostly, the love of this sacred road—this, your spiritual Path. It was love that helped you map your way here, love that kept you hiking toward this sacred site all day, and it is love that has helped you to accept and find joy in your calling. Tonight, it will be love that will fuel your passion, and love that will drive you to make your vows of service to your gods. You just need to find that Rainbow Pathway.

You begin skirting a narrow track toward the peak you identified, and . . . yes, it is . . . it has to be a cave on the front of the summit. Right? You shake your head, laughing that anything on the journey to becoming an Adept could be that easy, and begin reviewing your ritual plans, your intentions, and your vows. Before you realize it, however, you find the track has branched off, and you've descended a hundred feet! You fight your way through the brush and relocate the narrow track going across the slope toward the mountain in question, and begin again to hike across.

Again, you find yourself lost in thought as your inner dialogue takes over your concentration. Still planning the rite you've already planned to the last detail, laughing at your blunder of not seeing when the track turned, and memorizing your vows. Concentrating, you run through them one more time ... then another ... and another. You then begin to ponder what life will be like after this Adept's Gate is won. After a quarter hour, you realize the track has subtly changed course again, and you look up to find that you have indeed descended again, this time even further! The shady dip in the mountain in question, which you're sure is your cave, is even further away now, and you're starting to wonder if you'll make it there at all today. You scramble up the mountainside through the brush again, locate the crosswise track again, and again laugh at yourself for not noticing your descent. Your laughter isn't quite so heartfelt this time, however, for evening isn't that far away, and you need to make it to the site by nightfall. In your visions of this rite, you stepped onto the path just as twilight faded and night descended on this, the night of the dark moon; you must be there on time!

Yet even with these few thoughts, you see you've distracted yourself from your purpose for a third time, descended yet again, and now, on top of that, there's a rocky stream before you, deep and wide and cascading down the mountain; you must go around the rocks to cross it, and the only way around it ... is down. You finally reach a shallow enough place to cross only to find you've now descended into the bowl an additional two hundred feet! You cross the water and begin scrambling upward again, muttering to yourself about time and the stresses of making this journey. Caught up in your inner discourse, you don't see the rocks you're walking on are unstable, and suddenly you find yourself slipping and sliding, barely staying upright until you've descended yet again for hundreds of feet, and the mountain that is your goal looms even higher, and the shadow you've been aiming toward, which may or may not be the cave you're looking for, is now about four hundred feet above you, feeling like a lifetime away.

You stop, suddenly acutely cognizant of what you've been doing. Chattering. Distracting yourself from your purpose. The symbolism coupled with the actuality of your actions hits you profoundly. Of course; the Adept level is about the ability to keep silent, even, and perhaps especially, keeping the silence within. You ground and center, allow yourself to experience this journey as the gods have given it to you, and suddenly you know exactly what to do. Instead of looking to the mountain as your only possible goal, you resign yourself to the fact that maybe you don't know the way that clearly, and that maybe, just maybe, after all these years you still don't have all the answers. "Of course not," you tell yourself. "No one does." Humbled, you simply breathe, still your mind, and say a humble prayer for guidance before allowing silence and intuition to take the lead.

In that very moment, you feel it: the sureness of your course, just as though you'd mapped it out yourself. Down and down into the bowl you go, down and down to the valley floor. The air is warmer and thicker here, the landscape more lush. The sunset is glorious; the sky is filled with color, and the mountain peaks all around you are rosy pink with the glow of the Sun God's fiery touch. Down still more you walk, and if you keep your mind quiet, trying not to panic about the time, you find that your feet know exactly where to go.

You walk easily and swiftly through the tall grasses, following no trail but just letting your inner stillness reign, letting your intuition guide you. Birds call softly across the hilly landscape, and you pass small meadows and gentle hills. You glance up at the mountain you'd been heading for as you get closer, and laugh to see the shadow you'd been bent on pursuing is not a cave, but rather a large outcropping of rock, creating a large, looming shadow that juts across the path you would have taken, which would have stopped you cold. Shaking your head at your own folly, you again fall to silence, opening yourself to whatever the gods choose to show you as the sunset fades to twilight. You breathe deeply of the earthy scents, calming yourself, refusing to panic. You pass a small meadow: white yarrow glowing brightly with the last of the fading light, seeming to float in midair. Finally, you round the wide corner of a small hill and stop dead in your tracks. There, before you in the swiftly growing darkness, is a large deep cave with a northern entrance, faintly glowing with rainbow colors on the sandy floor. Thanking your gods for the journey and for their infinite patience, you breathe a sigh of relief and rush forward, setting your foot firmly on the Rainbow Pathway just as darkness falls.

ADEPT LORE:
THE FOURTH POWER OF THE MAGUS—TO BE SILENT

Silence has been written about by many great and wise teachers, from every religious system in the world. The inner quiet that is silence has been long known to bring peace and understanding to the heart and the spirit. Silence has been spoken of as being the altar of God, the voice of God, the mother of truth, and the "perfectest herald of joy."[101] And, just as in the story above, silence is necessary as we learn and grow on the Path, for it is in meditation and stilling the inner voice that we receive our best guidance, for we cannot hear the gods if we are constantly chattering at them.

In terms of the Adept Path, silence is very much your ally. As you know already, dear Initiate, speaking too much or too loudly about our workings can dilute our enthusiasm for the work, so we don't blab too much about our upcoming spellwork or ritual activities (except with the people involved, of course). Keeping quiet about who our brothers and sisters of the Craft are to mundane folks who wouldn't understand is a given; we protect and defend them with our discretion. Silence about our Rites of Passage to our juniors on the Path is necessary if we wish for them to have as moving an experience as we've had, and silence about others' experiences in circle is about privacy and, again, discretion.

There's another aspect of silence to be aware of as well. As you begin your service work, even if you do not feel a calling to be a spiritual counselor, you will still quite often find yourself on the receiving end of sacred and deeply personal information. Certainly if the person is intending to put themselves or others in danger you must speak out, but by and large, spiritual leadership just doesn't present us with that many life-threatening situations. It is much more common that you will sometimes be the recipient of potentially emotional damaging information (such as a person planning to cheat on their lover, for example), and, out of a spirit of wishing to help, you might be tempted to share what they've told you, but then, your silence will be even more important. For it is one thing to go to your spiritual teacher or mentor for advice regarding how to help a student, for example, and another thing entirely to share that information with, say, that person's mate or family (again, unless it's life-threatening). The information you will be asked to hold is a sacred trust; it will be up to you to keep it in good faith. Remember the last lines of the Wiccan Rede, and harm none with your words and actions.

The Adept's Path—The energy of service

---

101. William Shakespeare, *Much Ado About Nothing*, as spoken by the character Claudio.

You've come a long way, dear Initiate! You've chased some pretty daunting shadows; honed your power, energy, and will; learned much about this Witch's Path; and built your astral temple. You've written a complete set of Sabbats, done countless spells and a full cycle of Esbats at the very least, and explored at least fifteen ways you can serve your community. You are skilled, learned, and powerful, and you are ready to traverse that earthy Gate that heralds and begins the Adept level.

Going forward, you likely will have many questions. Should I start a coven? Should I do public works? Should I teach classes, do healings, readings, spiritual counseling? How much should I charge for these actions? *Should* I charge? Is charging money for spiritual services *ethical*?

The answers are as varied, and indeed, as manifold as there are Witches. In the Pagan community, the issue of how, when, and what to charge is constantly being debated. Some teachers believe that it's morally wrong to charge for Craft classes, probably because of the old adage that one is "serving two masters" if one charges for spiritual teachings, implying that the teacher's own honesty and morals might be questionable, if, for example, a student's ethics are off but the teacher needs to pay his mortgage. I think that letting a student slide on ethics just to get their money may happen on *occasion*, yes, but for the most part, Witchy teachers (and counselors, readers, healers, etc.) are simply trying to survive, just like everyone else, and regardless of money, will not initiate a student whose ethics are questionable. We are answerable to our gods, after all, for anyone we take through any Initiatory Gate, and *we know that!*

In my personal experience, I charge a median rate with a sliding scale based on income and the honor system for classes because I have found that people *value* what *they give value to*. In other words, they seem to hold more respect and appreciation for that which they have to *earn*, and can be somewhat disrespectful for that which is simply given to them for "free." During my early years, when I felt it was wrong to charge a set fee and simply took donations (with turning in homework as the only requisite "fee" for class), students frequently blew off classes (no call, no show), came into my home and ate and drank the refreshments I offered, yet rarely donated *anything*, and regularly "forgot" their homework, promising to bring it "next time," which of course never happened. When I offered free class attendance to coven members, those very members began doing the exact same things as the students listed above and, in addition, frequently attended coven activities and Sabbat celebrations empty-handed, and sometimes also exhibited questionable ethics in their personal lives. And again, the same kinds of things happened when, as a book promotion for *Dedicant*, I offered "scholarships" to Circles School Dedicant classes at my book signings, based on a contest with a quiz and a drawing. Yet, far and away, my paying students have proven to be the most reliable, the most serious and studious—complete with stellar homework, as well as being the most proactive in healing their own lives. Yes, *people value what they give value to.* Very much so.

So, if you should choose to teach or provide readings, workshops, counseling, etc., to your community, the bottom line is that venue rent needs to be paid, supplies need to be purchased, and sometimes guest speakers need to be compensated. Most Witchy teachers devote a few to several hours before a class or workshop preparing, and of course, must purchase fuel or bus fare to get to the venue as well. Our time is *worth something*, dear Initiate, and the most common form of energy exchange in our culture at present is money. Now, some teachers will do other forms of energy exchanges, so you may wish to consider this time-honored option. I do so myself, but not all teachers will.

One night a few years ago, as I entered the temple where I was teaching at that time, a young woman was waiting to talk to me about possibly starting classes. I outlined a bit about how the classes work, and she got very excited and interested. When she asked how much I charged, however, her face fell. She said she was currently unemployed and couldn't afford the fee. I told her about the discounts I offer as well as the fact that I am open to energy exchanges, as I don't wish to turn away anyone who is earnestly seeking. I gave her the example of one young lady (we'll call her "Shimmer") who came to Circles School at the beginning of the summer one year. Shimmer wished to do an energy exchange. She said that even though she could afford the class fees, she wanted to save some money, as well as to honor sustainability and a barter system by offering to exchange something of value with me. Shimmer lived on a farm, so every class or two, she brought me the most beautiful produce! She brought me the freshest herbs and tomatoes, hot peppers, and countless other organic goods that were deliciously ripened on the vine and heavy with rich lushness, throughout the summer and fall. The produce was of such high quality and some of it so specialized that the value of it caused me to extend her energy exchange "payments" far into the future. When Shimmer left to go on a much-needed sabbatical after a death in her family, she left with me owing her several classes. Once she returns, her classes will resume with her owing me nothing for at least a season.

Another student, out of the goodness of her heart, brought my partner and me each over a dozen pairs of high-quality shoes (she worked for a major athletic shoe chain), and also gifted me with beautiful and useful items when she decided to move, so that when she found herself in a position of being short on cash and thought she'd need to quit classes, I would hear nothing of it, and continued with her, because she'd already given me so much of value.

Sometimes a teacher can even offer such energy exchanges. Back in my native state of Colorado several years ago, I once needed a fence put up. I couldn't do the work all by myself, so I offered my students an hour-for-an-hour exchange: labor for classes. Many of them jumped on it, and we had a great time, guzzling iced tea, laughing and sweating in the hot summer sunshine, and we got the fence up in one weekend. I didn't take payments from some of them for months afterward, but it was totally worth it!

So, my dear student, you will need to search your heart, consult with your personal deities, and look yourself in the eye regarding whatever fees you choose to charge. I wish you the best of luck with these decisions, as well as all good blessings on your chosen path of service. Once you do begin, remember to remain humble. As Christopher Penczak says, "Don't believe your own press."[102] You will likely help numerous people, in ways you can't begin to imagine, and they will come up to you at events, classes, and festivals and tell you how your public Sabbat or your workshop, etc., *changed their life*! Or wide-eyed beginners will tell you how they just learned _____, and wish to share that information with you, information that will oftentimes be so basic in nature that you'll be tempted to remark that you've known that one since the gods were born. Don't. These beautiful beginners are simply sharing, and they look up to you. Try to remember your own beginnings, treat them as you would have wished to be treated by a community elder, and don't allow yourself to become puffed up with your own importance.

---

102. Christopher Penczak, *Magick of Reiki* (Llewellyn, 2004), 109.

APPROACHING THE ADEPT GATE

When we are grounded, we are humble and close to the Earth.
We live simply, in a state of grace.
—Anodea Judith

The Ordeal

Just as with your Initiate's Gate, there should be an ordeal of sorts involved. The Adept ordeal (and ritual) should emphasize your ability to walk your talk, so just as with your initiation, the ordeal should be a challenge. Only you can decide what this challenge should look like. I suggest you assign yourself the task of facing a personal fear. If the Initiate's Gate is designed to poke you in the chest, so to speak, to see if you can keep your balance, then the Adept's Gate requires a harder thrust, to knock you *off balance*, and see if you can keep from falling down (whereas the Master's Gate is designed to knock you on your ass and see if you can get back up again!). So, to that end, I suggest at the very least challenging yourself to face some real fears, to stand up and perform a public service of some kind, in addition to attempting invocation for the first time. Other Mystery work is appropriate, too, if you've already become comfortable with Drawing Down (another option would be to Draw Down a different deity, perhaps one that is the opposite gender of the one you've already invoked).

The Ritual

In my experience and study, second degree rites differ very little from most initiatory rites, with the exceptions listed below added to the basic framework. In addition, you may wish to review some of the elements offered in some of the second degree rites you'll find in books both on and off your reading lists, adding your own unique touches, eliminating things that don't work for you, and adding new and different ideas that sing to you personally. As there are so few extra things added, I suggest reviewing initiation rituals in general, as well as the following:

The places of bodily anointing is changed. In the traditional second degree rites, an inverted pentagram pattern is used, to symbolize "As above, so below," or an inverted triangle (point down) can be used for the same symbolism, if the candidate is uncomfortable with the unfortunate adulterated use of this symbol by Satanists. These actions can easily be done by oneself, and are perfectly valid. Some traditions use such anointing, and some do not. In the initiatory ROPs I perform, I usually simply anoint the third eye area.

Power is willed into the candidate by the initiator. In some practices the wording "all of" is used, which, for myself, unfortunately conjures images from films such as *The 10th Kingdom*, in which the old Witch said in a deep voice, reminiscent of James Earl Jones as Darth Vader, that she was going to give Christine "all of" her power. Truthfully I can't help but question how the initiator manages to go on in life or in magic, as the words *all of* pretty much implies the initiator is thereafter completely devoid of power. Um, how does that work, please? The willing of power through a laying on of hands is a time-honored practice, used in many magical traditions, not just Wicca, but *all* of it? I don't think so. Of course, in solitary rites, there is no real equivalent, but one could conceivably open oneself to the Universal energies, to the will of one's personal deities, and simply allow yourself to receive whatever power they wish to bestow. In addition, Drawing Down can be used as a beautiful and profoundly appropriate way to open to such power. Certainly, invocation, especially the first time, leaves one changed in deep and meaningful ways.

The presentation of tools is done by the candidate, rather than the initiator. This is something I suggest in *Dedicant* for first-degree initiation, as one should have a firm knowledge of the Witch's tools by that point, and if they do not, in my opinion, they have no business attempting the Gate. In my personal practices, since this step has already been taken, when I give an Adept initiation, I usually request that the candidate *perform an act of magic* with the tools of a given direction, and see what they do with the task. More on that below.

The legend of the descent of Inanna is read or acted out. The reason for this is not given. My thought is that it emphasizes that all Rites of Passage have a death and rebirth aspect, as your life really does change a great deal after such rites. This aspect can be illustrated and symbolized in a myriad of ways at various points in the rite or the prep for the rite: meditating for an extended length of time in a dark closet; taking your ritual bath; or crawling through a tunnel of some kind, to name a few.

The candidate's spiritual calling is emphasized. The only place I found which speaks to a candidate's gifts is in the Dianic tradition. In your rite, dear Initiate, I believe you most certainly will wish to address your calling, and to mark it in some manner on your garb or cord, either before, after, or during some special segment of your rite.

A few more ideas, from my own practices

As stated, part of my Adept initiation rites includes the candidate *performing an act of magic* with tools placed at the elemental points. You can easily do this for yourself, and to create an element of surprise—and therefore, more of a challenge—you can draw sketches or write names of several tools and elementally obvious items (such as an egg or a rock) that you will also have present in your rite, toss the paper representations into a container, and at the right time in the ritual, pull out two or three at a time to tell you which you'll be working with. Then take those items and perform an act of magic with them.

Have a ritual bath. This isn't mentioned or used in a lot of ROPs I've witnessed or read about, but it is always a part of mine. I feel the rebirthing feel of the rite is very satisfyingly fulfilled with this act. I usually give my initiation candidates the task of bringing me a jar of water from the ocean, but if you're inland, you could use any body of water. This water is then added to the ritual bath, along with special herbs I feel will be helpful to the candidate, and the petals of two white roses (I always buy a half-dozen, using two for the bath and three for the altar, and I keep one to dry and hang on my wall in a fan shape, since I'm always saying I'm my students' "biggest fan"), as well as a little scented oil. A candle that elementally represents the Gate (in this case, green, black, brown, or white for earth) is decorated and placed near the bath.

A special dish of earth, obtained by the candidate for this rite, is placed in the north, to gather energy from the rite, and to help with grounding. The soil can be later sprinkled over gardens or houseplants in blessing.

Fill yourself with light. This is especially helpful if you've been feeling overwhelmed by all your shadow work, or if you feel there's still something looming or threatening to interfere with your moving forward on your path. What I did for a covener years ago who was struggling with his own darkness was to bring dozens of colored votives to the circle, and reminded him of all of his good qualities, one by one, while he lit the appropriate colored candle, breathing in the light and accepting the truth of what it symbolized. I then placed the candles all around the room behind him while he knelt at the altar, and when he turned around to see them, the effect was *dazzling*! You can do this for yourself easily, as well, and if you keep your eyes cast down, trying not to look at the others *too much* as you place each candle, the effect of all of them lit up around you can indeed be sweetly moving.

Gift yourself with a new power ring, circlet, torque, or other special jewelry that will remind you of your accomplishments and your station. Consecrate it in the ritual, and wear it for the first time during the rite.

HOMEWORK: YOUR SPECIAL ADEPT RITE

Time to start putting it all together. Just as with your initiation rites in *Dedicant*, dear Initiate, your challenge and your final homework for this course level is to create a satisfying and wonderful Adept initiation rite for yourself. Be sure to include any elements from other rites, even some of the elements from your initiation rite, as many of the pieces are the same, or similar, which sing to you personally. Be sure to choose an appropriate date, and moon. Tradition dictates Imbolc as *the* classic ROP date for Wiccan degrees, but I like to present these gates, if at all possible, during the season in which they're exalted, to emphasize the elemental energies, such as autumn for Initiations, and winter for this Adept Gate. It's also especially rewarding to hold the rites at or near the seasonal *transitions* in which they're exalted, such as Yule for the Adept Gate, as the season is going from water to earth. However, I realize this sometimes would require a great deal of waiting, so choosing a date when the moon is waxing or full in an earth sign works beautifully, too. Of course the timing is something only you can decide.

Then, do it up right! Make your ritual and celebration something special and wonderful! You've truly worked hard to gain this Gate, I know. I believe I mentioned at the beginning of the book that this Initiate level is tough. You should be damn proud of all that you've accomplished. Be sure to also gift yourself with a favorite meal, which includes good grounding foods, such as red meat (if you're an omnivore, steak is a great choice!), potatoes or other root vegetables, whole grains, legumes. Ditto your cakes and wine. These things should be absolutely delicious, fabulous, and special—as special as you are. You've come a long, long way in a mere year and a day, my darling, and you deserve the best, so please, do not skimp on dessert!

Be Blessed, dear Adept! And welcome to this side of the Gate!

Take some time and rest well, for your gods are calling, dear Adept, and will have you on your feet soon enough! Welcome, welcome, a thousand times, welcome—your community needs wise leaders like you! May your gods bless and keep you.

Appendix

A SIMPLE NOURISHING AND GROUNDING TEA

Mix equal parts, more or less to taste

chamomile

oatstraw

lavender

nutmeg

INVOCATION TEA

3 parts mugwort

1 part cinnamon (chips work best)

1 part allspice

1 part angelica (don't use if you are pregnant)

1 part chamomile

1 part dried cherry

1 part spearmint

3 parts dandelion root

THE CHARGE OF THE GODDESS[103]

Listen to the words of the Great Mother, who was of old called Artemis, Astarte, Dione, Melusine, Aphrodite, Cerridwen, Diana, Arionrhod, Brighid, and by many other names:

Whenever you have need of anything, once in the month, and better it be when the moon is full, you shall assemble in some secret place and adore the spirit of Me, who is Queen of all the Wise. There, in your circle of worship, I will reveal to you the secrets of the deepest Mysteries. You shall be free from slavery, and as a sign that you be truly free, you shall be naked in your rites. Sing, feast, dance, make music and love, all in My praise, for Mine is the ecstasy of the spirit and Mine also is joy on earth. My law is love unto all beings. Keep pure your highest ideal; strive ever toward it; let nothing stop you or turn you aside. For Mine is the secret that opens upon the door of youth, and Mine is the cup of wine of life which is the cauldron of Cerridwen which is the holy grail of immortality. I am the gracious Goddess Who gives the gift of joy to the human heart. Upon earth, I give the knowledge of the spirit eternal, and beyond death I give peace and freedom and reunion with those who have gone before. Nor do I demand ought in sacrifice, for behold, I am the Mother of all things, and My love is poured out upon the earth.

Now, hear the words of the Star Goddess, the dust of whose feet are the hosts of heaven, whose body encircles the universe:

I Who am the beauty of the green earth and the white moon among the stars and the mysteries of the waters, I call upon your soul to arise and come unto Me. For I am the soul of nature Who gives life to the universe. From Me all things proceed and unto Me they must return. Before My face, beloved of gods and humankind, reveal your innermost self and let your spirit soar! Let My worship be in the heart that rejoices, for behold, all acts of love and pleasure are My rituals. Therefore, let there be beauty and strength, power and compassion, honor and humility, mirth and reverence within you. And you who seek to know Me, know that your seeking and yearning will avail you not, unless you know the Mystery: For if that which you seek you

---

103. The original version of *The Charge of the Goddess* can be found in *A Witches' Bible* (page 297) by Janet and Stewart Farrar. This beloved piece of prose is credited to Doreen Valiente, although there is some speculation as to how much of it she wrote and how much Gerald Gardner wrote. Starhawk modernized the language and her version is probably the most common one used in the wider Pagan community. I found a few lines in the original that resonated deeply with me, so I modernized the language of those lines, and added them back in for the version you see here, which originally appeared on page 263 of my book *Dedicant: A Witch's Circle of Fire*.

find not within yourself, you will never find it without. For behold, I have been with you from the beginning, and I am that which is attained at the end of desire.

THE CHARGE OF THE GOD[104]

Listen to the counsel of the Great God of the Forest, Who was of old called Herne after the call of the hind, the Horned One, Gentle Savage, Green Man, Cernunnos, Pan, the Dark One who watches from the shadows, the Protector who stands between dark and light, the Bright One, Helios, Apollo, Ra, Lugh, and by many other names:

I am the Lord and the hunter, the hunted and the saved. I call to you from the shadows of the forest, from the darkness of your own Mysteries and the pure clean light of the sun. I am here, on the edge of the shadows, your Protector and Guardian, your intent and your secret dreams. I breathe life into promise, faith into the tired heart. If you choose to walk with Me, My silence will teach you all you need to know, for behold—I am the protective Guardian of your spirit, nudging you toward the edge of the forest where Mystery meets the truth that illuminates your soul. I am father, brother, husband, son, friend. I am the harmony of dark and light, the cycle of life, the seed of all that is great and strong within you.

Know that you must ever seek Me, ever searching, ever returning, for this is the cycle of Nature, of Divinity, of the Sacred Spiral. You come to Me as you leave Me, you leave Me as you arrive, and ever the cycle turns. It is this turning, this motion that restores balance to all things.

Know that in your turnings there is the promise of My seed. Just as winter is dormant, so the summer is abundant. As I die and become reborn, so you too will turn away, and then turn toward Me, for I am the King of birth and death, of silence and prophecy, and the Truth of the Mystery that the answers you seek lie within your own soul—in silence, in the sounds of nature, and in the faith that eternally sets you free.

---

104. Originally appearing on page 175 of my book *Dedicant*, this is a piece I channeled when I was first called by my patron god Cernunnos. My belief is that it was he, as well as my patron god Helios, who "dictated" the piece to me in meditation that summer day.

MOON WORKSHEET

Moon number _____ Begins new moon_____ Ends new moon _____
(date)   (date)

I'm going to do my Esbat on _____ the _____ moon in _____,
(date)   (phase)   (astrological sign)

which is also called the _____ moon.
(snow, hunters, mead, etc.)

At issue this moon cycle: _____

_____

_____

The intention for my working is: _____

_____

_____

_____

Astrological and astronomical considerations: _____

_____

_____

_____

Supplies needed: _____

_____

_____

_____

_____

_____

_____

Special considerations for this working (I will fast, I will do this in silence, I will go to a certain place, etc.): _____

_____

_____

_____

_____

My _____ reading for this rite (if applicable) showed these possible outcome:

_____

_____

_____

_____

Emotions, thoughts, perceptions prior to the rite: _____

_____

_____

_____

_____

Follow-through required: _____

_____

_____

_____

_____

_____

Final outcome as I perceive it: _____

_____

_____

_____

_____

_____

Glossary

Acorn—According to James Hillman (see page 394), one's acorn is the energy pattern or guide ("daimon") that determines his destiny, seen in a defining moment, usually in retrospect.

Adept—An Adept in the Circles is the same as a second degree in most traditions of Wicca.

Adept-at-hand—A term I use to describe an Adept, either male or female, who fills the role of Handmaiden and who prefers this term.

Adoration—The next step up from a devotional, the adoration usually elicits an emotional response in the worshiper.

Affirmation—An affirmation is a positive statement, usually said as a form of gentle magic, for the purpose of making desired changes in one's life.

Akasha (*uh-kah-shuh*)—The ethers, the collective energy-consciousness of all beings, all incarnations, all time. Some psychic readers state they are actually reading, as if from a script, when they access the akashic record.

Allopathic—Western medicine, or a Western doctor (MD).

Ally—A benevolent spirit or substance; a helper.

Archetype (**ark**-eh-tipe)—Usually used in describing a deity, an archetype is an energy pattern that encompasses many gods.

Aspecting—The next step up from evocation, where one is "a hair's breadth apart" from the entity they have evoked.

Astral projection—Leaving one's body to journey: sometimes in a dream state, sometimes not.

British Traditional Witchcraft (BTW)—What used to be referred to as "trad" Wicca, British Traditional Wicca refers to older (circa 1940s and forward) Wiccan traditions—usually Gardnerian or Alexandrian.

Chakra—Means "wheel," and is an energy vortex in the spiritual body. It is said that there are seven major chakras, and schools of thought vary greatly on how many minor chakras there are.

Circles system—This system of learning, invented by the author: *A course of study that follows the Wheel of the Year and emphasizes study at the times of year when the energies of the topic are exalted. Circles School of Witchcraft and Wicca follows the Circles system.*

Compersion—"Joy in another's joy in another," invented by the poly community to mean the opposite of jealousy.

Crescent knife—A blade shaped like a crescent moon, with a long tang going into the attached handle. Often used to harvest herbs and other sacred items.

Crone's Sickle—I came up with the idea and term "Crone's Sickle" to describe the last slender crescent of the waning moon, which occurs a few days before the new moon. The Crone's Sickle phase is very good for endings, cutting threads, for seeing the seeds of light in a Mystery or shadow pattern, etc.

Daimon—See *Acorn*

Dedicant—In the Circles system, and in most systems, a Dedicant is a first-year or beginning level student who often has made a pledge to study her Path for a specific period of time, usually for a year and a day.

Deepening—The feeling of an energy pattern or spiritual belief becoming much more strong in a person. A spiritual deepening is a feeling of being in a state of grace, and our beliefs and convictions seem to fill us with power and love.

Devotional—Prayers that are focused on how much you love your chosen deity. They are usually spoken directly to them, as in "I love you," rather than "I love her."

Diana's Bow—In many traditions, "Diana's Bow" is the term used for the slender crescent just a few days out from the new moon, as it looks a bit like a bow. This is very good energy for engaging in new projects.

Domestication—Ruiz's word for cultural programming. See *The Four Agreements* for more detail.

Drawing Down—See *Invocation*

Dreamwork—The work we do in recording, analyzing, and interpreting our dreams.

Earth tides—The pulling of the energies of the Wheel of the Year, which can often be felt by travelers of all kinds of earth-based paths. It is the overwhelming, yet somehow subtle feeling of being *presently* in a seasonal energy pattern that is a click or two (or more) ahead of where you are on the Wheel at the current time.

Empath—One who *literally* feels the emotions and passions of another.

Empathy—Being able to relate to someone's emotion or passion, typically from having experienced similar ones.

Ephemeris—Astrological tables showing where each planet is at any given time. An ephemeris will also show the phase of the moon, as well as retrograde planets.

Evoke, evocation—To draw an energy pattern or Godform into your circle.

Gate—See *Initiatory Gate*

Great Rite—A ritual using sex as the means of raising energy.

Great Wheel, The—Life. We go around the Wheel of the Year annually; around the Great Wheel once per lifetime. In the larger sense, the life of a person, or a planet.

Grimoire—Book of Shadows (BOS). One's diary, recipe book, magical journal.

Guardian—A term I made up to describe the second priestess in a coven (essentially the female version of a High Priest), as well as the person who feels the call to watch over rituals instead of running them (see page 310 for the Pathwork focus of Guardian).

Handfasting—A Wiccan wedding, typically lasting a year and a day.

High Priest/ess (HP/S)—A coven leader, or the leader of the present ritual. In some traditions, a HPS is someone who has achieved the third degree, whether s/he runs a coven or not. This is also sometimes used to refer to one's Wiccan teacher, though it's less common.

Immanence—The belief that all beings are sacred, have a spirit.

Incarnation—A lifetime, as in "my current incarnation" or "in a past incarnation."

Initiate—In the Circles system, and in most systems, a first degree. Someone who has gone through an initiation.

Initiatory Gate—An initiatory Rite of Passage. Also, a term referring to the moment, place, and energy within a Rite of Passage when the exact moment of initiation takes place; in some ROPs, there is an actual physical gate the candidate must traverse in order to be initiated.

Intentional community—People who choose to live together, pool resources, and work toward a common goal.

Invoke, invocation—To draw an energy pattern or Godform into your body.

Kundalini—The "serpent" that weaves in and out between our chakras as it rises on the liberating current or plunges downward on the manifesting current. Neither current is "better"—they both have their purposes.

Lucid dreaming—A type of dream in which the dreamer is aware she is dreaming; awake within the dream, so to speak.

Mandala—A drawing or written symbol that holds power. For example, a pentagram is a mandala.

Master—A Master in the Circles system is the same as a third degree in most traditions of Wicca.

Matron—From the Old French, meaning "mother." A reference to the Goddess (or goddesses) one feels closest to and is guided by, as in "my matron goddess." Lots of folks in the Pagan community refer to their guiding goddess as a "patron," a leftover from ancient times when patron came to mean "benefactor," or "protector," which was continued when the early Church relegated the Old Gods to the role of "saints." However, if you look closely, you'll usually find the word *patroness* farther down on your dictionary's page, described as the *female* "patron," thereby stripping it of power by rendering it a watered down version of "patron." When in doubt think of it this way: is the woman who carried you in her womb for nine months your *father*? Do you go up to her and say, "Hey, Dad-*ess*?" I believe it's high time we give our closest guiding goddesses their due respect and power by calling them by their proper title of "matron," which means "mother."

Mercury retrograde—When any planet is retrograde, it simply means that the planet is moving so slowly that it appears to be going backwards. When Mercury in particular is retrograde, communications tend to go wonky, so it's generally held that it's best to avoid doing magic, signing contracts, or trying to communicate about sensitive issues during this time. Mercury goes retro about every three months, for a period of about three weeks.

Mitote—(*mih-toe-tay*) From Ruiz, the *mitote* is the cacophony of voices we tend to hear in our heads, which tend to obscure the inner, still voice of wisdom.

Moon tides—The energies of the moon and her cycles, which we as Wiccans feel and use.

Mundane—The ordinary, the everyday (can be derogatory, but usually isn't meant that way).

Natal chart—An astrological chart; a mathematically calculated "picture" of the sky at the date and time of one's birth.

New Religion, The—A euphemism for Christianity, commonly used in the Pagan community.

Old Religion, The—A euphemism for Wicca/Paganism, commonly used in the Pagan community. While history has shown us there is no "one" Old Religion, many of us refer to our religion as such, for simplicity in referring to the nature-based religions of our ancestors. We can look at any eclectic Wicca/Witchcraft Path (indeed, Paganism itself) as a great tree, with roots in the ancient world, pulling up energy and ancestral wisdom from the depths of the earth throughout time, with branches that sweep the sky, gathering light and truth, sending out creativity, diversity, and newfound paths to our descendants in future worlds beyond our imagining. This book, as with all the Circles series books, reflects that philosophy, which is why it is described as a course of study in the Old Religion.

Oracle—Often, when one has invoked the God/dess, they "stand back" and allow the Divine to speak through them, or using their voice. This is known as "performing Oracle."

Pagan Standard Time—A humorous term used to try to excuse the late start of events or the late arrival of key people to those events, because they're either too disorganized or too inconsiderate to keep their promises. Many people laugh about it, but many more are rather annoyed with the whole concept.

Path, the—Refers to one's spiritual path.

Pathwork focus—The focus on what may (or may not) be our spiritual gifts.

Pathworking—Not to be confused with Qabalistic Pathworking, in Circles School and the Circles system books, Pathworkings are activities we can do to help us tune in to the energies of the time, season, and lessons at hand.

Patron—From the Old French, meaning "father." A reference to the god (or gods) one feels closest to and is guided by, as in "my patron god."

Perfect love, perfect trust—More than just a phrase, it is the only way we can enter a circle, in perfect love and perfect trust of our gods.

Polyamory—"Many loves." A term coined by Morning Glory Zell for people who feel they can love romantically more than one person at a time. Polyamory is not to be confused with swinging, which is focused more on recreational sex with good friends; polyamory on the other hand is more focused on loving relationships that may or may not be sexual.

Polytheism—The belief in/love for many gods.

Posture of power—A gesture or series of gestures that speak to the energy of the lesson.

Priest/ess—Someone who has studied for a year and a day, who has Initiated into Wicca, either in a solitary ritual with just her personal gods, or in a group rite.

Qabala, Qabalah—An ancient Hebrew system of mysticism and organization of energies.

Rainbow Pathway—In the Circles system, the Rainbow Pathway refers to the Spiritual Path, the Sacred Road we all travel in pursuit of our highest ideal.

Religion of clergy—Wicca is often referred to as a "religion of clergy" because after initiation, we have no "go between" standing in the way of our connection to our personal gods. We are *our own* priests and priestesses.

Retrograde—See *Mercury retrograde*

Right Action—The right thing to do; the action that will best serve us on our spiritual paths.

Rite of Passage (ROP)—Anytime a person undergoes a major life change that is ritualized, it is called a Rite of Passage. The typical Rites of Passage in a Wiccan's life are (not necessarily in this order): *Wiccanning* (a baby blessing), *Moon rites* (celebrates a young girl's first blood), *Young men's rites* (celebrates the passage to manhood), *Dedication*, *Initiation* (the first degree), *Handfasting* (marriage), *Adept Initiation* (the second degree), *Master Initiation* (the third degree), *Elderhood* or *Croning* (I see this as sort of like retirement, YMMV), and *Crossing* (death or memorial services).

Sacred Charge—Someone who one is responsible for spiritually; one who is inviolable and under our wing, so to speak. For more details, see page 109 in chapter 8, "The Fourth Moon—Compassion."

Sacred Cord, the—The Sacred Cord is like a knotwork spell of a Witch's lifetime spiritual Path, to date. It is sometimes worn doubled and knotted, sometimes "thrice round, with some to hang down," and sometimes a different way altogether. The cord typically also holds the Witch's sacred blade(s).

Skyclad—Naked, clad only in the sky.

Soul mask—A mask made while both the subject and the artist are in trance, which reveals symbols and colors significant to the subject's spiritual Path.

Soul mates—People who have incarnated once or many times before, who have a strong bond to each other. It is generally held we all have twenty or thirty of these people, sometimes referred to as our "tribe."

Spiritual warrior—One who pursues her spiritual Path with conviction and purpose.

Stand (as in "to stand up")—Mundane culture calls this "standing up": taking responsibility not only for one's actions but also being proactive about one's duties, both sacred and mundane.

Stone whisperer—A term the author made up for those folks who, like dog or horse whisperers, can feel and sense the essence of a stone's spirit, who feel a deep affinity for those energies and can use those energies as they choose.

Thirteen Harmonies—The author's spin on *the Eightfold Paths*; the eight ways to make magic as illustrated in Gardner's Book of Shadows, in Bill Whitcomb's *Magician's Companion*, and the work of Janet and Stewart Farrar.

Toltec—According to Ruiz, the Toltecs were an ancient society of scientists and artists, women and men of knowledge. Anthropologists refer to the Toltecs as a nation or a race of people who once dwelt in southern Mexico.

Trad Wicca—Also known as BTW, British Traditional Wicca refers to older (circa 1940s and forward) Wiccan traditions—usually Gardnerian or Alexandrian.

Tradition—A denomination of Paganism or Wicca, a way of doing things.

Transcript—In the Circles system, the transcript's function is much as a transcript's function in higher education. It is the summary of one's Witchy education, experience, gifts, and community service. An idea I came up with in order to keep a student's grimoire private, while still giving his teacher, coven leader(s), or peers an idea of where he's at on his personal Path.

Tree of Life—An exercise, originally found in *The Spiral Dance* by Starhawk, which is now probably the most commonly used action in the Pagan community for grounding and centering ourselves, both in private and public rites.

Twin souls—Said to be extremely rare, twin souls are two people who were once one light and got split apart somehow. Some say we only have three or four lifetimes with our twin soul.

Waning moon—A "dying" moon—the cycle from full moon to new.

Wards—Guardians who permanently, or semi-permanently watch over one's home, campsite, family, etc. We "set wards" when we ask these guardians to stay and watch over our spaces and people.

Waxing moon—A growing moon, the cycle from new moon to full.

Wiccan Rede—A long poem of obscure origins, the last line of which states "An it harm none, do as you will."

Widdershins—Counterclockwise.

Wildcrafting—Harvesting herbs or vegetables in nature. Ethics dictate we always ask permission of the landowner and the plants themselves, and never take more than a third of what's there.

Bibliography

Adler, Margot. *Drawing Down the Moon*. New York: Penguin, 1979.

Anand, Margo. *The Art of Sexual Ecstasy: The Path of Sacred Sexuality for Western Lovers*. New York: Tarcher, 1989.

Blum, Ralph. *The Book of Runes*. New York: St. Martin's Press, 1982.

———. *Rune Play*. New York: St. Martin's Press, 1985.

Buckland, Raymond. *Buckland's Complete Book of Witchcraft*. St. Paul, MN: Llewellyn, 1997.

Budapest, Zsusanna. *The Grandmother of Time: A Woman's Book of Celebrations, Spells, and Sacred Objects for Every Month of the Year*. New York: HarperCollins, 1989.

———. *The Holy Book of Women's Mysteries*. Oakland, CA: Wingbow Press, 1980.

Burt, Kathleen. *Archetypes of the Zodiac*. St. Paul, MN: Llewellyn, 1996.

Calafia, Thuri. *Dedicant: A Witch's Circle of Fire*. Woodbury, MN: Llewellyn, 2008.

Caldecott, Moyra. *Women in Celtic Myth*. Rochester, VT: Destiny Books, 1988.

Campanelli, Pauline. *Ancient Ways: Reclaiming Pagan Traditions*. St. Paul, MN: Llewellyn, 1991.

————.*Circles, Groves, and Sanctuaries*. St. Paul, MN: Llewellyn, 1993.

————. *Rites of Passage: The Pagan Wheel of Life*. St. Paul, MN: Llewellyn, 1994.

————. *Wheel of the Year*. St. Paul, MN: Llewellyn, 1989.

Campbell, Joseph, with Bill Moyers. *The Power of Myth*. New York: Doubleday, 1988.

Castaneda, Carlos. *The Eagle's Gift*. New York: Pocket Books, 1981.

————. *Journey to Ixtlan: The Lessons of Don Juan*. New York: Pocket Books, 1972.

————. *The Second Ring of Power*. New York: Pocket Books, 1977.

————. *A Separate Reality: Further Conversations with Don Juan*. New York: Pocket Books, 1971.

————. *Tales of Power*. New York: Pocket Books, 1974.

————. *The Teachings of Don Juan: A Yaqui Way of Knowledge*. New York: Washington Square Press, 1968.

Cunningham, Scott. *Cunningham's Encyclopedia of Crystal, Gem & Metal Magic*. St. Paul, MN: Llewellyn, 2002.

————. *Cunningham's Encyclopedia of Magical Herbs*. St. Paul, MN: Llewellyn, 2000.

————. *Dreaming the Divine: Techniques for Sacred Sleep*. St. Paul, MN: Llewellyn, 1999.

————. *Living Wicca: A Further Guide for the Solitary Practitioner*. St. Paul, MN: Llewellyn, 1993.

————. *Wicca: A Guide for the Solitary Practitioner*. St. Paul, MN: Llewellyn, 1988.

Cunningham, Scott, with David Harrington. *The Magical Household*. St. Paul, MN: Llewellyn, 1994.

D'Adamo, Peter J. *Eat Right for Your Type*. New York: G. P. Putnam's Sons, 1996.

Denning, Melita, and Osborne Phillips. *The Llewellyn Practical Guide to Creative Visualization for the Fulfillment of Your Desires*. St. Paul, MN: Llewellyn, 1980.

Digitalis, Raven. *Shadow Magick Compendium*. Woodbury, MN: Llewellyn, 2008.

Eisler, Riane. *Sacred Pleasure: Sex, Myth, and the Politics of the Body*. New York: HarperCollins, 1995.

Farrar, Janet, and Stewart Farrar. *A Witches' Bible*. Custer, WA: Phoenix Publishing, 1996.

————. *The Witches' God*. Custer, WA: Phoenix Publishing, 1989.

————. *The Witches' Goddess*. Custer, WA: Phoenix Publishing, 1987.

Fortune, Dion. *The Goat-Foot God*. York Beach, ME: Samuel Weiser, 1980. First published in the United Kingdom in 1936.

————. *Moon Magic*. York Beach, ME: Samuel Weiser, 1978. First published in the United Kingdom in 1956.

————. *The Sea Priestess*. York Beach, ME: Samuel Weiser, 1978. First published privately in the United Kingdom in 1938.

Gardner, Gerald. *High Magic's Aid*. Hinton, WV: Godolphin House, 1996. First edition published in 1949.

————. *The Meaning of Witchcraft*. Boston: Weiser, 2004. First published in 1959.

————. *Witchcraft Today*. New York: Citadel, 2004. First published in 1954.

Gawain, Shakti. *Creative Visualization*. New York: Bantam, 1978.

Goodman, W. Charisse. *The Invisible Woman: Confronting Weight Prejudice in America*. Carlsbad, CA: Gurze Books, 1995.

Graves, Robert. *The White Goddess*. New York: Noonday Press, 1948.

Gray, William G. *Attainment Through Magic*. St. Paul, MN: Llewellyn, 1979.

Greer, John Michael. *The Long Descent: A User's Guide to the End of the Industrial Age*. Gabriola Island, BC: New Society Publishers, 2008.

Hay, Louise. *The AIDS Book*. Santa Monica, CA: Hay House, 1988.

————. *You Can Heal Your Life*. Santa Monica, CA: Hay House, 1984.

Herer, Jack. *The Emperor Wears No Clothes: The Authoritative Historical Record of Cannabis and the Conspiracy Against Marijuana … and How Hemp Can Save the World!* Van Nuys, CA: AH HA Publishing, 1985.

Highwater, Jamake. *Myth and Sexuality*. New York: Meridian, 1990.

Hillman, James. *The Soul's Code: In Search of Character and Calling*. New York: Random House, 1996.

Hipskind, Judith. *The New Palmistry*. St. Paul, MN: Llewellyn, 1994.

————. *Palmistry: The Whole View*. St. Paul, MN: Llewellyn, 1977.

Ingerman, Sandra. *Soul Retrieval: Mending the Fragmented Self*. San Francisco: HarperSanFrancisco, 1991.

Jones, Evan John, and Chas Clifton. *Sacred Mask, Sacred Dance*. St. Paul, MN: Llewellyn, 1997.

Joudry, Patricia, and Maurie D. Pressman. *Twin Souls*. Center City, MN: Hazelden, 1993.

Judith, Anodea. *Wheels of Life: A User's Guide to the Chakra System*. St. Paul, MN: Llewellyn, 1999.

K, Amber. *Covencraft: Witchcraft for Three or More*. St. Paul, MN: Llewellyn, 1998.

Kloss, Jethro. *Back to Eden*. Twin Lakes, WI: Lotus Press, 2004. Originally published in 1939.

Kurtz, Katherine. *Lammas Night*. New York: Ballantine, 1983.

Leland, Charles G. *Aradia, or, the Gospel of the Witches. A New Translation by Mario Pazzaglini and Dina Pazzaglini*. Blaine, WA: Phoenix Publishing, 1998.

Levine, Roz. *Palmistry: How to Chart the Lines of Your Destiny*. New York: Fireside, 1992.

Mann, Nicholas. *The Dark God*. St. Paul, MN: Llewellyn, 1996.

Mariechild, Diane. *Mother Wit: A Guide to Healing & Psychic Development*. Freedom, CA: The Crossing Press, 1981.

McFarland, Phoenix. *The Complete Book of Magical Names*. St. Paul, MN: Llewellyn, 1997.

Melody. *Love Is in the Earth: A Kaleidoscope of Crystals*. Wheat Ridge, CO: Earth-Love Publishing, 1995.

Middleton, Julie Forest. *Songs for Earthlings*. Philadelphia: Emerald Earth Publishing, 1998.

Monaghan, Patricia. *The New Book of Goddesses & Heroines*. St. Paul, MN: Llewellyn, 2002.

Monroe, Robert. *Journeys Out of the Body*. Garden City, NY: Doubleday, 1971.

Moore, Thomas. *Soul Mates: Honoring the Mysteries of Love and Relationship*. New York: HarperCollins, 1998.

Murray, Margaret. *The God of the Witches*. London: Faber and Faber, 1952.

Norwood, Robin. *Why Me, Why This, Why Now*. New York: Carol Southern Books, 1994.

Orbach, Susie. *Fat Is a Feminist Issue*. New York: Berkley Books, 1980.

Paxson, Diana. *Brisingamen*. New York: Berkley Books, 1984.

———. *The White Raven*. New York: Avon Books, 1988.

———. *The Wolf and the Raven*. New York: Avon Books, 1994.

Penczak, Christopher. *Magick of Reiki*. St. Paul, MN: Llewellyn, 2004.

Pollan, Michael. *The Omnivore's Dilemma*. New York: Penguin, 2006.

Reed, Ellen Cannon. *The Goddess and the Tree: The Witches' Qabala Book I*. St. Paul, MN: Llewellyn, 1993.

———. *The Witches' Qabala: The Pagan Path and the Tree of Life*. York Beach, ME: Samuel Weiser, 1985.

———. *The Witches' Tarot: The Witches' Qabala Book 2*. St. Paul, MN: Llewellyn, 1993.

Reif, Jennifer. *Mysteries of Demeter*. York Beach, ME: Samuel Weiser, 1999.

Richardson, Alan. *20th Century Magic and the Old Religion: Dion Fortune, Christine Hartley, Charles Seymour*. St. Paul, MN: Llewellyn, 1991.

Ruiz, don Miguel. *The Four Agreements*. San Rafael, CA: Amber-Allen Publishing, 1997.

———. *The Mastery of Love*. San Rafael, CA: Amber-Allen Publishing, 1999.

Spretnak, Charlene. *Lost Goddesses of Early Greece*. Berkeley, CA: Moon Books, 1978.

Starhawk. *Dreaming the Dark: Magic, Sex, and Politics*. Boston: Beacon Press, 1982.

———. *The Fifth Sacred Thing*. New York: Bantam, 1993.

———. *The Spiral Dance: A Rebirth of the Ancient Religion of the Great Goddess*. New York: Harper and Row, 1979.

———. *Truth or Dare: Encounters with Power, Authority, and Mystery*. New York: Harper & Row, 1987.

———. *Walking to Mercury*. New York: Bantam, 1997.

Steinbrecher, Edwin. *The Inner Guide Meditation*. York Beach, ME: Samuel Weiser, 1988.

Stewart, R. J. *Celtic Gods, Celtic Goddesses*. London: Blandford, 1990.

———. *Celtic Myths, Celtic Legends*. London: Blandford, 1994.

Stone, Merlin. *Ancient Mirrors of Womanhood: A History of Goddess and Heroine Lore from Around the World*. Boston: Beacon Press, 1979.

———.*When God Was a Woman*. New York: Harvest/ HBJ Books, 1976.

Thorsson, Edred. *Runelore: A Handbook of Esoteric Runology*. York Beach, ME: Samuel Weiser, 1987.

Tolkien, J. R. R. *The Hobbit, or There and Back Again*. New York: Ballantine, 1937.

———. *The Lord of the Rings: The Return of the King*. New York: Houghton Mifflin, 1967. First published in 1955.

Turner, Patricia, and Charles Russell Coulter. *Dictionary of Ancient Deities*. Oxford: Oxford University Press, 2000.

Valiente, Doreen. *An ABC of Witchcraft Past and Present*. Custer, WA: Phoenix Publishing, 1973.

———. *Natural Magic*. Custer, WA: Phoenix Publishing, 1975.

Weed, Susun S. *New Menopausal Years: The Wise Woman Way*. Woodstock, NY: Ash Tree Publishing, 2002.

Whitcomb, Bill. *The Magician's Companion*. St. Paul, MN: Llewellyn, 2004.

Index

A

addiction, 41, 194, 198, 330, 343–344

Adept, 5–6, 10, 27, 34, 41, 48, 52, 156, 164, 178, 181, 191–192, 228, 231, 239, 245, 322, 357, 375, 391, 394–396, 398, 402, 405–409, 412–415, 423, 429

Adept Gate, 10, 41, 178, 231, 395–396, 398, 402, 406, 408–409, 412, 415

adoration, 26, 51, 150, 153–156, 230, 313, 353, 389, 418, 423

affirmation, 62, 66, 83, 93, 119, 129, 131, 175–176, 203, 218, 228, 256, 319, 329, 336, 338, 362, 423

agape, 110

alcohol, 125, 192–193, 207, 236, 335, 339–341, 344

alcoholism, 125, 344

allies, 12, 19, 25, 27, 131, 158, 169, 216, 341, 351, 368, 408, 423

allopathy, 6, 339–340, 342, 346, 423

altars, 27, 85, 87, 96–98, 149–150, 154, 158, 187, 213, 225–226, 256–257, 260, 266, 269–270, 291–292, 294, 304, 309–310, 324, 327, 347, 349, 353, 370, 380, 387, 408, 414

animals, 25, 36–37, 64, 75, 107–108, 126, 261, 264, 322, 364, 375, 377 antlers, 306, 322

Aphrodite, 78, 418

Apollo, 419

Aquarius, 260

Aradia, 46

archetypes, 95, 234–235, 313, 389–390, 424

Aries, 288

Artemis, 5, 26, 28, 94, 116, 152, 178, 231, 352, 393, 395,
  401, 418

aspecting, 4, 26, 33, 48, 51, 102, 109, 112–113, 132–133,
  145, 150, 153, 156, 168, 183, 197–198, 209, 223, 231,
  233, 240, 261, 290, 305, 396, 408, 413, 424

astral projection, 37, 48–49, 56, 67, 70, 83, 86, 104, 106,
  119, 122, 134, 136, 147, 150, 159, 162, 170, 172, 185,
  188, 199, 202, 211, 214, 224, 226, 242, 294, 359, 366,
  380, 409, 424

astral temple, 48–49, 56, 67, 70, 83, 86, 104, 106, 119,
  122, 134, 136, 147, 150, 159, 162, 170, 172, 185, 188,
  199, 202, 211, 214, 224, 226, 242, 409

astrological ephemeris, 9, 293, 357, 425

astrology, 8–9, 36, 43, 60, 166, 237, 293, 348, 352, 356–
  357, 378, 420, 425, 427

athame, 80, 99, 323, 346

B

banishing, 218, 300

bard, 35, 207, 270, 282–283

Beltane, 207, 266, 275, 295–296, 298–299, 303–304, 309,
  315

benevolence, 393–394, 397, 423

Bible, 32, 39, 48, 191, 252, 257, 267, 294, 304, 324, 349,
  359, 370, 380, 389, 418

binding, 238–239

blade, 35, 82, 86, 97, 99–100, 135, 139, 151–153, 178, 291, 322–323, 384, 387, 424, 429

boline, 387

Bonewits, Isaac, 264

Book of Shadows, 32–33, 38, 48, 88, 92–93, 191, 228, 252–253, 335–336, 395, 418, 425, 429

Brighid, 259, 261–262, 418

Burning Times, 279, 311

C

Campanelli, Pauline, 32

cauldron, 70, 80, 82, 202, 207–208, 259–260, 369, 378, 418

Celtic, 12, 39, 261, 282, 330, 378

censer, 2, 87, 207, 291, 351, 371

Cernunnos, 26–27, 94, 419

Cerridwen, 207, 418

chakras, 4, 28, 48, 55–57, 61–62, 64–67, 70, 74–75, 82–83, 86–87, 94, 96, 101, 103–104, 106, 114–115, 117–119, 122, 130, 132, 134, 136, 142, 145, 147, 150, 153, 156–157, 159, 162, 164–165, 167–168, 172–173, 180–181, 183, 188, 190, 193, 196–199, 202, 205–206, 209, 214, 217, 219–221, 223, 222, 226, 230–231, 234–235, 237, 240–241, 396, 424, 426

chalice, 1–2, 80, 82, 87, 207, 291, 329, 352–353, 358

chanting, 48, 63, 79, 97–99, 106, 122, 130, 142, 154, 191, 215, 233–234, 239, 260, 283–285, 288, 324, 351–352

Charge of the God, The, 109–110, 112, 146, 150, 234–235, 239, 241, 265, 299, 310, 329, 385, 418–419

Charge of the Goddess, The, 5–6, 41–42, 47–48, 64–65, 76, 87, 109–110, 112, 146, 149–150, 163–164, 189–190, 233–235, 239–241, 265, 281, 284, 298–299, 301, 310,

317, 328–329, 344, 346–347, 351, 361, 385, 396–397, 401, 408–411, 418–419, 428–429

Circles system, 5, 8, 11, 38–39, 375, 410, 423–424, 426–428, 430

Circles School, 410, 424, 427–428

community, 2, 5, 8, 15–17, 22, 34–37, 39, 41, 53, 59, 74, 76, 124, 126–127, 130, 143, 150, 162, 164, 172, 174, 176–180, 184, 232, 244, 252, 255, 269–278, 282–285, 291–293, 300, 302, 305–306, 311, 318, 322–323, 331, 346–348, 354, 356, 359, 365, 387–388, 393, 398–399, 405, 409–411, 415, 418, 424, 426–427, 430

compassion, 22, 37, 95, 105–109, 111, 113–119, 138, 146–147, 151, 158, 169, 174, 209, 214, 222, 228–229, 238–239, 252, 255, 272–273, 339, 344, 384–385, 387, 389, 393–394, 397, 418, 429

compersion, 277–278, 424

cone of power, 63, 262, 274, 288, 300, 310, 396

consciousness, 11, 29, 36, 40, 48, 58, 65–66, 82, 88, 93, 95, 101, 118, 130, 143–144, 153, 158, 169, 187–190, 203, 214, 247, 249, 252, 262, 372, 383

consecration, 110, 195, 205, 356, 415

covens, 4–5, 12, 27, 34–35, 41, 53, 99, 109, 112–113, 178–179, 184, 270–271, 278–281, 283–285, 310–311, 323, 331, 346, 387, 396, 398, 409, 425–426, 430

Craft, the, 1, 29–30, 76, 130–131, 263, 289–290, 293, 323, 374–375, 393, 396, 400–401, 407–409

crescent knife, 323, 387, 424

Crone, 50–51, 66, 135, 424

Crone's Sickle, 50–51, 66, 135, 424

crystals, 4, 59, 94–95, 97, 116, 154, 188, 195, 207, 227, 234, 255, 259, 261, 263–267, 269–270, 285, 296, 300–301, 304, 309–310, 346, 348, 362, 366–369, 373, 375, 378

D

Dark deities, 47, 50–51, 105, 149, 162, 201, 240, 256, 262, 297, 372

Dark God, 32, 67, 83, 103, 105, 119, 133, 147, 150, 159, 169, 185, 198, 210, 224, 240, 250, 289, 297, 306, 309, 312–313, 316, 322, 348, 383, 385, 419

Dark Goddess, 32, 47, 67, 76, 83, 103, 105, 119, 133, 147, 149–150, 159, 169, 185, 198, 210, 224, 240, 262, 297, 312, 322, 383, 385

dark moon, 32, 46–47, 50–52, 55, 66–67, 83, 94, 103, 105, 119, 133, 147, 149, 159, 162, 169, 184–185, 198, 201, 210, 215–216, 224–225, 256, 313, 322, 348, 358, 367, 383, 385, 406, 419

Dark Mother, 55, 95

Dark Time, 27, 32, 47, 66–67, 83, 94–95, 103, 105, 119, 133, 147, 150, 159, 169, 176, 184–185, 198, 201, 210, 215, 224, 238, 240, 247, 249–250, 252, 256–257, 259, 262, 289, 297, 306–307, 309, 312–313, 316, 341, 348, 358, 368, 371–374, 376, 383, 406, 413

Deepening, 3–4, 25, 74, 105, 173, 252, 424

deosil, 64

deprogramming, 52, 94–95

devotion, 22, 26, 28, 52, 86–88, 149, 151–153, 156–158, 166, 168, 170, 176–178, 229, 240–241, 352–353, 355, 362, 387, 393, 395

devotionals, 26–27, 33, 40, 42, 48, 51, 67, 83, 87, 104, 119, 126, 130, 132, 134, 147, 153–156, 159, 167, 169–170, 185, 198–199, 210, 217, 221, 224, 230, 234, 241–242, 313, 389, 395, 423, 425

Diana's Bow, 50, 69, 161, 425

Dianic, 12, 15, 413

discernment, 70, 99, 136, 138–140, 147, 254

discipline, 4, 48, 61, 92, 95, 106, 108, 115–116, 184, 203–206, 208

divination, 8, 37, 39, 42, 140, 256, 281, 362, 364, 374–380, 396

Divine Victim, 328, 330, 349

Drawing Down. *See* invocation

dreamweaver, 37, 362, 365, 368–369, 397–398

dreamwork, 39, 141, 294, 361, 364, 368, 374, 396, 425

drugs, 15, 191, 339–340

Druids, 35, 56, 306, 378, 387

E

earth tides, 11–13, 25, 28–29, 39–40, 240, 261, 265–266, 328–329, 369, 425

eclectic, 12, 99, 184, 310, 427

Eightfold Paths, 48, 429

empathy, 106–108, 118, 136, 146, 394, 425

empowerment, 89–90

energy, 4–6, 8–9, 11–13, 18, 21, 23, 26–31, 33, 36, 39–40, 43, 48–52, 55–67, 69–74, 77–83, 86–88, 90, 92–101, 105–110, 113–118, 120–122, 124–128, 130–133, 135–140, 142–145, 150–153, 156–158, 161–169, 172–173, 175–177, 179, 181–185, 188–190, 192–198, 201–203, 205–207, 209–210, 214–217, 221–223, 226–229, 232–242, 245, 248–251, 256, 259–267, 270–271, 274, 276, 279, 283, 287–290, 294–301, 305–306, 308–313, 315–318, 320, 323–325, 327–332, 334, 338, 340, 342, 344, 348, 351–356, 362–364, 367, 372–374, 376–377, 380, 383–388, 394, 396–398, 408–411, 414, 423–428

energy exchange, 215–216, 410–411

ephemeris. *See* astrological ephemeris

equinoxes, 39, 275, 293–294, 370

Esbats, 8–9, 33, 48, 50, 66–67, 72–73, 81, 83, 98, 102–103,
    113, 119, 133, 147, 158–159, 169, 185, 198, 210, 224,
    242, 351–353, 396, 409, 420
ethics, 19, 21, 23, 73, 76, 122, 128, 138, 217, 239, 257,
    298, 319, 354, 398, 409–410, 430
evocation, 4, 8, 18, 26, 48, 51, 132, 145, 183, 197, 209,
    223, 230, 263, 289, 377, 396, 424–425
excess, 4, 125, 188, 192–194, 206, 208
Expansion, 75, 187–189, 192, 393

F

faeries, 30, 221–222, 288
Family of Origin (FO), 363
festivals, 2, 30, 127, 130, 207, 220, 262, 265, 271, 275–
    276, 281, 284, 292, 299, 305, 331, 353, 411
Five Sacred Directions, 22
Fortune, Dion, 32, 135, 224, 254, 351, 356, 405
fruition, 201, 203, 205–206, 210, 318, 393

G

Gaia, 157, 168, 235, 271, 311–312, 338
ganja, 142, 188, 191–193, 236, 296, 335, 339, 348, 362
Gardner, Gerald, 15, 48, 191, 254, 418, 424, 429–430
Gate, 1, 10, 40–41, 48, 152, 179, 188, 191, 202, 206, 219,
    230–231, 242, 308, 311, 396, 398, 402, 406, 409, 412–
    415, 425–426. *See also* Initiatory Gate
Gemini, 306
Graves, Robert, 32–33, 254, 282, 387
Great Rite, 48, 70, 73, 76–80, 82, 94, 114–115, 206–207,
    232, 300, 303, 309, 396, 407, 413, 418, 425
Great Wheel, 82, 113, 164, 210, 247, 250, 289, 373, 425

guardians, 6, 25, 29, 36, 104, 130, 142, 191–192, 220, 227, 240, 288, 306, 308, 310–312, 316, 320, 328, 337–338, 393, 395, 397–398, 405, 419, 425, 430

H

handfasting, 91, 164, 358, 425, 429

healing, 6, 15, 22, 28, 33–34, 36–37, 51, 56–57, 60–62, 66, 72–73, 80–83, 88–89, 92–93, 95, 101–103, 106, 108–109, 111, 116, 118–119, 122, 127–129, 131, 133, 138, 140–142, 145–147, 158–159, 165–167, 169, 174, 176, 180–181, 184–185, 191, 193, 206, 210, 215, 223, 225–228, 230, 238, 251, 256, 261–262, 264–265, 267, 288, 293, 296, 299–303, 312, 319, 325, 328, 330, 332–339, 342–344, 346–349, 353, 355, 363–364, 371, 373–374, 387–388, 397–398, 410

Hecate, 122–123, 135, 137, 139, 146, 235, 371, 373, 380

hedonism, 59, 192, 204–205

herbalist, 36, 253, 328, 340, 342–343, 347–348, 397–398

herbs, 36, 56, 70, 78, 86, 105–106, 122, 136, 142, 150, 162, 172, 188, 191, 193, 202, 214, 226, 248, 253, 260, 263–264, 270, 288, 296, 303, 306, 316, 319–320, 327–330, 337–342, 345–348, 352, 355, 362, 371–372, 384, 387, 410, 414, 424, 430

historian, 33, 38, 248, 253–255

humility, 16, 42, 70, 124, 136, 144, 172–175, 177, 180, 182, 184, 195, 227, 229, 329, 369, 385, 395, 407, 411–412, 418

I

Imbolc, 207, 259–262, 266–267, 315, 415

Initiatory Gate, 230, 409, 425–426

intentional community, 276–277, 284, 426

intuition, 22, 36–37, 50, 59, 75, 78, 108, 111, 136, 138–139, 142, 147, 153, 229, 282, 303, 308, 337–338, 340, 354, 369, 372, 375, 377, 379, 385, 395–397, 401, 407

intuitive reader, 36–37, 372, 375, 379, 397

invocation, 4, 31–32, 43, 48, 51, 78, 93, 115, 153, 156–157, 183, 197, 205–206, 209, 223–224, 226, 229–236, 240–241, 257, 263, 267, 284–285, 289–290, 311, 345, 366, 396, 402, 412–413, 417, 425–427

J

jewelry, 35, 292, 317, 323, 355–356, 402, 415

K

karma, 21, 42, 60, 73, 126, 128, 137, 299, 357, 378, 384, 388

kundalini, 66, 190, 196–198, 205, 209, 221, 223, 226, 230, 426

L

Litha, 207, 266, 311, 315–316, 318, 323–324

love spells, 73, 99, 113, 166, 238, 300–301, 385

lucid dreaming, 37, 294, 366, 426

Lugh, 328, 419

Lughnasadh, 327–328, 349

M

Mabon, 207, 361–364, 370

magical name. *See* power name

Maiden, 331, 385

mandalas, 131, 426

matron goddess, 4–5, 8, 12, 18, 26, 28, 51, 67, 83, 86, 94, 103–104, 110, 119, 126, 134, 147, 151, 156, 158–159,

161, 170, 177–178, 185, 199, 210, 215, 224, 227, 231,
    240, 242, 281, 307, 317, 322, 351, 358, 380, 383–385,
    388–389, 396–397, 402, 426–427

Mercury retrograde, 9, 60, 67, 83, 104, 119, 121, 134, 147,
    159, 169, 185, 198, 210, 224, 242, 359, 367–368, 425,
    427–428

mirror, 32, 81, 103, 145, 151, 352, 358

mitote, 173, 185, 427

moon tides, 11–12, 25, 39–40, 47–48, 82, 239–240, 266,
    296, 329, 424–425, 427

Mother, 1, 22, 28–29, 40, 55, 64–65, 71, 91, 95, 126, 137,
    141–142, 167, 184, 192–193, 261, 264–265, 296, 299,
    312, 329, 331, 353, 408, 418, 426–427

mugwort, 78, 136, 231, 345, 351, 358, 367, 372, 417

mundane, 27, 30, 38, 112, 132, 205, 222, 279, 281, 291,
    311, 322, 354, 356, 388, 398–399, 408, 427, 429

Murray, Margaret, 32, 254, 324, 327, 330, 349

Mysteries, 8, 33, 36–37, 39, 42, 50, 55, 66, 78, 149, 173,
    202–203, 211, 215, 228, 230, 233, 247, 250, 256, 259,
    290, 295, 297, 299, 303, 306, 308–309, 316, 330, 352,
    371–372, 380, 383, 385, 412, 418–419, 424

mythology, 32, 35, 76, 89, 145, 282, 304, 377, 395

N

natal chart, 36, 41, 43, 60, 162, 166, 357, 374, 378, 396,
    427

nudity, 105, 150, 279–280, 346, 418, 429

♀

occult, 16, 131, 202, 207, 264–265, 292, 364, 377

Oracle, 232–233, 236–237, 427

Ostara, 207, 261, 266, 287–289, 291, 293–294, 315

Overcoming, 142, 166, 184, 194, 198, 213, 215–221, 223–224, 240, 283, 319, 393

P

Pan, 419

pastoral counseling, 37, 387–388, 397

Path, the, 5, 9, 52–53, 70, 89, 109, 112, 123–125, 146, 173, 176–178, 184, 187, 192, 206, 208, 220, 224, 229, 356, 375, 393–394, 397, 399–400, 405–408

Pathwork, 5, 27, 34–36, 38, 182, 245, 248, 253, 260, 264, 270, 282, 288, 291, 293, 296, 301, 306, 310–311, 316–317, 322–323, 328, 346–348, 352, 356–357, 362, 368, 372, 375, 384, 387, 393, 395, 397–398, 425, 428

Pathwork focus, 34–36, 38, 245, 248, 253, 260, 264, 270, 282, 288, 291, 293, 296, 301, 306, 310–311, 316–317, 322–323, 328, 346–348, 352, 356–357, 362, 368, 372, 375, 384, 387, 393, 395, 397, 425, 428

personal responsibility, 19, 21–22, 86–87, 113, 125–126, 140, 146, 195, 272, 284, 298, 333, 388, 398

Pisces, 270

polyamory, 73, 77, 277–278, 284, 428

posture of power, 48–49, 65, 82, 101, 117, 132, 144, 156, 167, 183, 196, 209, 217, 222, 233, 240, 428

power, 2–3, 6, 8, 12, 15, 17–18, 22–23, 25, 27, 33–34, 37, 48–53, 57–58, 64–65, 67, 72, 75–77, 82–83, 85–92, 94, 96–108, 111, 117, 119, 121, 123, 125, 130, 132–137, 139, 144, 146–147, 155–159, 161–162, 167–170, 175–177, 182–185, 187–188, 194, 196–197, 199, 205, 209–210, 214–217, 222, 224–229, 232, 234, 237–240, 242, 249, 259–260, 262–263, 266, 274, 280–282, 284, 288–290, 296–298, 300, 302, 308–311, 315, 317–318, 321–322, 324, 337, 342, 351–356, 359, 366–367, 372,

377, 385, 393, 395–396, 402, 407, 409, 413, 415, 418, 424, 426–428

power animal, 25, 37, 64, 107, 322, 377

power name, 22, 87, 96, 161–162, 219, 280–282, 284, 374, 413

Priapic wand, 261, 306, 309

pride, 16, 69–71, 74, 80, 82, 102, 111, 123, 151, 171, 180, 184, 222, 248, 271, 302, 373, 385, 393, 395, 415

prima donnas, 5, 124, 127, 144, 273

private inner power name, 281, 284

projecting (energy), 8, 48, 72, 100–101, 172, 181, 300, 308, 312, 386

protection, 11, 36, 86–87, 94, 100, 105, 113, 122, 152, 173, 240, 305, 307–308, 310–312, 316, 318, 385, 408, 419, 426

psychic, 4, 25, 37, 41, 95, 104, 107, 111, 140, 147, 174, 217, 221, 265, 310, 351, 353, 367, 379, 396–397, 423

purpose, 3, 22, 52, 70, 78, 88, 99, 106, 110, 119, 121, 130–131, 143, 156, 159, 161, 163–164, 166, 169, 176–178, 184, 206, 215, 217, 248, 261–262, 264–265, 267, 280, 287–288, 297, 317, 323, 345, 351–353, 361, 366, 379–380, 385, 393, 406, 423, 426, 429

R

Rainbow Pathway, 405, 407, 428

religion of clergy, 8–9, 331, 355, 427–428

reverence, 110, 150, 162–163, 166–167, 169, 179, 188, 191, 195, 279, 329, 351, 418

Right Action, 34, 62, 71, 125, 127, 133, 136, 188, 213–214, 288, 429

runes, 42, 78, 131, 134, 139, 220, 227–228, 318, 366, 375, 377–379

S

Sabbats, 1, 8, 10, 29, 40, 42, 113, 127, 178–179, 244, 247, 261, 321, 328, 330–331, 355, 362, 387, 396, 409–411

Sacred Charge, 107, 109–110, 112–113, 146, 150, 189, 238–239, 241, 301, 329, 361, 397, 400–401, 408, 428–429

Sacred Cord, 34, 188, 221, 238, 356, 402, 428–429

sacred clothier, 34–35, 288, 292, 397

sacred prostitution, 37, 302

sacred sexuality, 75, 77, 109, 114, 205, 209, 228, 296–299, 301–302, 309

sacrifice, 76, 278, 327–331, 348–349, 418

Sagittarius, 384

Samhain, 207, 221, 299, 328–329, 371–372, 374, 380

Scorpio, 372

scourge, 106, 116–117, 142

scrying, 207, 260, 366, 368, 375, 378, 380

service, 4–5, 9, 22, 27, 34–36, 39, 43, 52–53, 109–110, 113–114, 117, 150, 152, 162, 164, 172, 174, 176–177, 179, 184, 232, 236, 245, 274–275, 302, 305, 308, 323, 329, 351, 353, 393–394, 396–397, 402, 405, 408, 411–412, 430

sexual healer, 37, 296, 301–302

sexual orientation, 15–16, 110, 128, 278, 300

sexual surrogates, 37, 301

shadow, 11–12, 16, 22, 32–34, 46, 49–50, 52–53, 56, 66, 70, 72, 77, 82–83, 86, 88–89, 92–93, 95, 102–103, 106, 116, 118–119, 122, 136, 140, 142, 146, 150–151, 158, 162, 169, 172, 175–176, 178, 180, 182, 184–185, 188, 194, 198, 202, 210, 213–216, 219–220, 223, 226–227, 242, 256, 262, 306–307, 316–317, 321, 355, 367, 397, 406–407, 414, 424

shadow work, 12, 22, 32–33, 49–50, 52–53, 66, 72, 77,
    82–83, 88, 93, 95, 102–103, 106, 116, 118–119, 146,
    150–151, 158, 162, 169, 175–176, 180, 182, 184–185,
    188, 194, 198, 210, 213–215, 219, 223, 226–227, 242,
    262, 316, 321, 355, 397, 414, 424
sickle, 50–51, 66, 124, 135–137, 139, 424
silk, 117, 259, 261, 266–267, 368
skyclad. *See* nudity
solstices, 39, 244, 249–250, 315, 324
soul mask, 374–375, 429
soul mates, 137, 374, 429
spellwork, 8, 39, 71–72, 74, 96–97, 109, 127, 133, 206,
    238–239, 257, 264, 267, 285, 298, 300, 304, 313, 319–
    320, 324–325, 349, 352–354, 370, 378, 380, 389, 396,
    408
spiritual counseling, 37, 173, 387, 408–409
spiritual vessel, 4, 6, 27, 52, 102, 229, 242, 265, 355
spiritual warrior, 172–173, 175, 180, 184, 203, 215–216,
    229, 242, 244, 310, 313, 429
Starhawk, 383, 418, 430
stone whisperer, 38, 260, 264, 398, 429
Sun God, 3, 46, 69–70, 149, 167, 244, 249–250, 255, 266,
    287, 296, 306, 308, 312, 315–316, 322–324, 327–329,
    352, 384, 405, 407
surrender, 42, 150–152, 156–157, 162, 167–168, 177–178,
    197, 228–229, 259, 298

T
Tantra, 37, 76, 301
tarot, 139, 367, 375–377, 379–380
Taurus, 296
temple, 48–49, 56, 67, 70, 83, 86, 104, 106, 119, 122, 134,
    136, 147, 150, 159, 162, 170, 172, 185–186, 188, 199,

202, 211, 214, 224, 226, 242, 361–362, 364, 368, 370, 409–410

third eye, 27–28, 136, 142, 145, 413

thirteen harmonies, 47–48, 56, 62, 70, 77, 86, 96, 106, 115, 122, 130, 136, 142, 150, 154, 162, 165, 171–172, 181, 188, 191, 202, 206, 214, 221, 226, 230, 429

Toltec, 430

torque, 415

touchstones, 27, 217, 355

"trad-bashing," 272

trance, 37, 48, 63–64, 66, 117, 130, 136–137, 142–143, 150, 154, 171, 173, 191, 196, 206, 226, 231, 302, 305–307, 351, 366, 375, 378, 429

trance dancing, 63, 142–143

transcript, 38–39, 43, 430

Tree of Life, 8, 28, 55, 65, 82, 94, 96, 151, 171, 188, 217–218, 240, 345, 377, 430

twin soul, 110, 430

U

Understanding, 135–138, 144, 146, 153, 216, 222, 227–228, 238, 264, 384, 393

V

Valiente, Doreen, 97, 418

Veil, 159, 234, 299, 328, 380

W

wand, 194, 197, 261, 291, 306, 309

waning moon, 11, 47, 50, 121, 123–124, 327, 329, 334, 424, 430

wards, 29, 104, 134, 430

waxing moon, 11, 26, 47, 50, 69, 161, 171, 415, 430

wholeness, 48–49, 156, 216, 220, 223–225, 227–229, 239, 374, 393
Wiccan Rede, 132, 373, 408, 430
widdershins, 64, 430
wildcrafting, 337, 348, 430
Wise Grandmother. *See* Crone

Y
yarrow, 86, 306, 345, 352, 377, 407
year and a day, 4, 8–10, 29, 39, 41, 47, 57, 204, 210, 224, 255, 261, 279–280, 293, 327, 366, 415, 424–425, 428
Yule, 131, 247–250, 255–257, 261, 332, 367, 415